The Development and Structure of the English Educational System

GW00372922

The Development and Structure of the English Educational System

Keith Evans

 University of London Press Ltd

ISBN 0 340 17606 7 Boards
ISBN 0 340 17607 5 Unibook

University of London Press Ltd
St Paul's House, Warwick Lane, London EC4P 4AH

Printed and bound in Great Britain by
T. & A. Constable Ltd
Hopetoun Street
Edinburgh

Contents

Preface

This book has grown out of a series of handouts prepared for and distributed to hundreds of students who have attended (and perhaps suffered!) my 'main hall' lectures on the development of contemporary educational institutions at Elizabeth Gaskell College of Education. It covers the history of English education since 1800 and the contemporary structure and development of the educational system in England and Wales, both of which are areas of study undertaken in some form by the majority of Certificate, Bachelor of Education degree and Postgraduate students preparing to enter the teaching profession. In the main the book has been designed to meet the particular needs of these students, but it is also intended to provide a useful foundation for those pursuing relevant courses at the Advanced Diploma or Master of Education degree levels.

Given that the development and structure of the English educational system is often a compulsory subject in relation to which many students have only a limited background knowledge and academic facility, what seems to be most appreciated by them is a thorough attempt to organise the material so as to facilitate effective initial assimilation and later recapitulation. They are also interested in the submission of realistic guidelines for personal reading and further study, and in the provision of sound advice on how best to tackle their written work in the area concerned. Thus this book lays no claim to quality of literary style or original scholarship; its hallmarks are the systematic presentation of the relevant material and the definitive attempt to provide the kind of structured and directed help which most students need but do not find commonly available in other texts.

The book consists of a total of fifteen chapters, all of which deal with a largely self-contained topic. Each chapter commences with a formal declaration of its purpose. This establishes the critical themes from the very outset and focuses the student's attention upon them; it is hoped that the details will then fall more readily into their proper place and a clearer perspective will emerge as a result.

The actual substance of each chapter is clearly divided into a number of major parts, each part being designated by a main heading preceded by an arabic figure. A quick look at these main headings affords a ready appreciation of the basic aspects which compose the whole of the topic concerned. In like fashion each major part is further sub-divided into subsidiary sections and other constituent elements; this allows the chronological sequence of events and developments, the legislative provisions of various Acts, the recommendations and results of official reports, the analyses of underlying influences and determinant factors, the structural or institutional components of a given framework and other such matters to be presented in a systematic and pre-digested manner which can be easily understood. But considerable trouble has been taken to ensure that this form of presentation (with its peculiar advantages) does not exact too high a price in terms of sheer readability. I hope I have succeeded in this respect.

Each chapter concludes with a 'follow-up' section designed to help the student further to develop and reinforce the knowledge and understanding already acquired. This begins by providing a short list of specific reading references from a limited number of secondary sources; mindful of the need for both continuity and manageability in relation to essential reading, most of these references are drawn from some five or six basic texts which are quoted recurrently. To avoid needless duplication the 'follow-up' section simply gives the name of the author and the title of his book, together with the specific reference; the full details of each publication quoted may be found in the lengthy bibliography provided at the end of the book (page 340 *et seq.*). This bibliography also serves as the basis for extended reading and study in depth, almost one hundred different sources being listed. It has been organised in separate sections to clearly distinguish general texts from those related to a particular sector or sphere of educational development; this should enable the student to relate the bibliography that much more easily to the various chapters of the book. With the exception of 'Official Publications', each section of the bibliography is arranged alphabetically; thus it should be an easy task to locate full bibliographical details for any book quoted in a 'follow-up' section. As the use of documentary sources is both desirable and fashionable the 'follow-up' sections often quote the booklet by K. Dawson and P. Wall in the reading list and also invite the student to consult relevant items in J. S. Maclure's much more substantial work on *Educational Documents: England and Wales 1816-1968*. Finally the 'follow-up' section offers a means by which the student may judge whether his knowledge and understanding of the substance of a particular chapter is really satisfactory. To this end it sets out a wide range of important matters which the student is asked to clarify in his own mind; where this exercise presents any serious difficulties the indications are that some further study is necessary.

A special feature of the book is the additional and quite separate chapter on essay writing (pages 314-32). As most students who use this book will be required, at some time or other, to submit written answers to formal essay questions on the subject, it was deemed both expedient and desirable to provide real assistance in this direction and thereby help the student to meet this particular need with an adequate measure of success. Accordingly this final chapter identifies and elaborates the essential attributes of sound essay writing in this disciplinary area; it also lists some forty specimen essay questions for the student's consideration and, in summary form, presents 'model' answers for four of them.

In conclusion may I take this opportunity to express my gratitude to those who have helped me to produce this work. Miss Sheila Walsh, secretary to the Education Department of Elizabeth Gaskell College, made a major contribution to the typing and duplication of the original handouts on which this book is largely based. Mr G. F. Crump, then serving as Chief Education Officer for Preston, kindly gave me the benefit of his comments on the first draft of the chapter on 'The Post-War Structure of the English Educational System'. And throughout the long exercise leading to final publication the publishers have proved a real source of continuing support and sound advice. Whilst acknowledging the generous help of all these people, I must however emphasise that any shortcomings the book may have are my sole responsibility.

Bolton, Lancashire   KEITH EVANS
1974

ERRATUM

Chapter One on *The Context of English Educational Development* relates to the period 1800-*1970* (see pages v and 1), not 1800-1870 as printed.

Chapter One
The Context of English Educational Development 1800-1870

Purpose: to introduce the overall context in which educational development in England and Wales has taken place over the last two centuries, and to examine the vital relationship, past and present, between education and society at large. The end result should be an appreciation of the importance of reasonably wide background knowledge to the satisfactory study of educational development during any period of historical or contemporary time.

Educational development does not take place in a vacuum; it occurs within the context of the whole of society. Thus the nature of an educational system varies according to time and place. The aims, the extent, the organisation, the curricula and the methodology of education will reflect the existing institutions and the dominant attitudes, values and forces which characterise a particular society. In this sense the history of English education since 1800 is not simply the superficial story of expanding and changing provision in various fields and at different levels: it also involves an understanding of nineteenth and twentieth century English society, especially in terms of the forces working within it that help to explain the developments and problems which emerged in the field of education. In other words, the development of English education cannot properly be understood unless it is seen in sociological perspective and related to the overall context of the time. To facilitate clearer examination, this complex context may be somewhat arbitrarily divided into various dimensions.

1 Demographic

Variations in the growth and distribution of population have exerted a considerable influence upon the educational scene since the late eighteenth century.

(a) Nineteenth Century
This was a period of unprecedented population growth (from nine to thirty-three millions for England and Wales) and rapid urbanisation. The sheer size of the younger generation ultimately broke the monopoly of voluntary provision in elementary education and necessitated the direct

intervention of the State. Once the Factory Acts began to take real effect after 1840, the growing number of children on the streets produced an urban social problem which helps to explain the 1870 Elementary Education Act and the subsequent drive for compulsory attendance.

(b) Inter-War Years

This was a period during which the birth-rate fell to its lowest level in British history, with the possibility of a stagnant or declining population emerging. This was associated with a critical sex imbalance amongst those of marriageable age, resultant of the heavy loss of male lives on the Western front during the First World War. The new demographic context relieved the previous pressure on school places and made available the life-long services of a very large group of dedicated spinster teachers. Although the educational system encountered other serious difficulties during the inter-war period, it was never faced with a shortage of teachers. Indeed, in these years, for a female teacher to announce her forthcoming marriage was tantamount to handing in her resignation; at a time when there was often the threat of unemployment within the profession, this was a policy which it was felt could be afforded and justified.

(c) Post-War Era

Recent demographic trends have produced a difficult context for educational advance since 1945. Already required to raise the school leaving age and to provide secondary education for all, the authorities were suddenly faced with a significant rise in the birth-rate, punctuated by two 'bulges' in the late 1940s and mid 1950s. This situation was exacerbated by an acceleration in the geographical redistribution of population and by the growing influx of Commonwealth immigrants. Meanwhile the correction of the former sex imbalance, the move towards earlier marriage and the consequent high wastage rate among young female teachers, produced an acute shortage of teachers which has only very slowly been overcome. It was not until after 1964 that the birth-rate took a definite and continuing downward turn and the demographic pressure on the schools began to ease off.

2 Economic

Educational development and economic matters have come to have an increasingly close relationship because any modern system of education both provides for the needs of the economy and inflicts a heavy charge upon it.

(a) Needs of the Economy

One of the major functions of the educational system is to subserve the basic manpower needs of society. This function emerged with the Industrial Revolution and became increasingly important as the economy became more advanced and sophisticated. The present need is for a highly skilled and differentiated labour force, able to promote and capitalise upon scientific and technological advance for the economic benefit of the nation. Thus the demands made by the economy and its developing occupational structure upon the educational system have changed with time.

(i) *Mid-Nineteenth Century*

The need for a disciplined labour force for the factory system and a growing pool of skilled artisans and clerks partly explains the developing interest of employers in elementary education as a means of instilling obedience and minimal learning into the younger generation of the working class.

(ii) *1880-1939*

The increasing concern over the provision of technical and secondary education was partly attributable to economic influences. The challenge to Britain's industrial supremacy and the beginnings of her comparative decline in the last quarter of the nineteenth century provoked a new sense of urgency in the field of technical education. The rise of new scientifically-based industries, the growth of the welfare state and its attendant bureaucracy, and the increasing importance of tertiary (especially professional) occupations in the early twentieth century combined to encourage the expansion of secondary grammar and higher education.

(iii) *Post-War Era*

The need for a much more highly skilled and finely differentiated labour force (rather than an *élite* plus the 'mass') has supported the drive for comprehensive secondary education and the remarkable expansion of further and higher education. It became widely accepted that economic survival depended upon avoiding the previous wastage of talent associated with inadequacy and inequality of educational opportunity. The vastly increased expenditure upon education was justified in terms of it being a long-term investment in human resources which the country could not afford to neglect.

(b) Cost to the Economy

For educational development the price of growing dependence upon public funds has been increased vulnerability to economic vicissitudes and to the constraint of what the nation is able and prepared to afford. Thus the state of the economy and the priority enjoyed by education at any particular time have had a direct bearing on the nature and extent of educational development.

(i) *Late Nineteenth Century*

The official commitment to economic retrenchment following the Crimean War helps to explain the introduction of the stringent 'payment by results' for grant-aided elementary schools, whilst the dual system of voluntary and State provision introduced by the 1870 Elementary Education Act was partially justified by W. E. Forster in terms of 'sparing public money'. Not until 1891 was the principle of free elementary schooling finally accepted. Meanwhile the reluctance and failure to embark upon the development of a national system of secondary education is also partly explained by the widespread opposition to the cost of doing so; indeed, when the venture was at last undertaken after the turn of the century a substantial part of the cost was to be defrayed by parental fees, an arrangement which continued to operate until 1944.

(ii) *Inter-War Years*

This period provides a classic instance of educational development being at the mercy of changes in national economic fortunes. The unprecedented enthusiasm and high hopes for education which found expression in Fisher's 1918 Education Act foundered on the rocks of Britain's serious economic difficulties. The post-war slump and later the world economic depression constrained successive governments to curtail national expenditure and educational development was singled out on two occasions for particularly rough treatment. The Geddes Committee (1922) recommended that educational spending be cut by one-third and the May Committee (1931) was no less severe. The projected day-continuation schools, the free-place system for secondary grammar education, the new percentage grant arrangements devised by Fisher to encourage more generous provision, and teachers' salaries and superannuation were all, in one way or another, victims of the economic backlash. The Hadow reorganisation process, which pointed forward to secondary education for all and was launched upon in 1928, inevitably made very slow headway in the face of a serious lack of funds.

(iii) *Post-War Era*

The remarkable increase in public expenditure upon education since 1945 is a reflection of the much higher priority accorded to it by governments and the community at large. For the first time educational development has become a really major burden on the economy, ultimately surpassing defence as the largest single item of public expenditure. Gradually the point has been reached where further significant educational advance, if not based on an improvement in our economic rate of growth, can only be made at the expense of the other social services or the already overburdened taxpayer. The clear determination of educational priorities and the effective deployment of limited funds have become absolutely critical. More than ever before the various sectors of education are in sharp competition with one another (e.g. 'priority for primaries' policy) and there is the growing danger that cost-effectiveness rather than educational considerations will influence the future direction of development (e.g. decisions for or against open-plan schools).

3 Scientific and Technological

The industrialisation and urbanisation of Britain involved an ever-increasing dependence upon scientific and technological developments, to the extent that they came to underpin and impinge upon our very way of life. Yet traditionally English education had neglected these fields of study and consequently pressures were brought to bear upon it.

(*a*) Late Nineteenth Century

The 'scientific movement', pioneered and led by Prince Albert, Lyon Playfair, Bernard Samuelson, Herbert Spencer and Thomas Huxley, challenged the prevailing neglect of scientific and technical studies and helped to produce the higher-grade elementary schools, the organised science schools, the early technical colleges and the new civic universities. The foundation and development of the Department of Science and Art for the official encouragement of scientific and technical instruction of utility to industry and commerce was a foremost expression of the movement's influence. The gradual widening of the elementary curriculum and the limited concessions made to the study of the natural sciences in the grammar schools and the ancient universities may also be ascribed to its existence.

(*b*) Post-War Era

The 'technological movement', punctuated by the Percy (1945) and Robbins (1963) Reports, has emphasised the need for the educational system to produce more scientists, technologists and technicians if the country's future in an increasingly competitive world is to be safeguarded. By the mid 1950s the veracity of this argument was finally recognised, with the result that technical and technological education at the further and higher levels became the most impressive single growth area in English education. A particularly important side effect has been the Industrial Training Act (1964) providing a framework within which individual industries, in co-operation with local education authorities, have developed schemes for the training of industrial manpower at all levels.

The ripples of these movements, given critical strength by economic considerations, will extend down the rest of the century, perhaps with even greater influence upon the educational system.

4 Social

The technological and economic transformation of the country during this period had important social connotations which bore upon educational development.

(a) Class Stratification

The triumph of industrial capitalism resulted in the crystallisation of deep-rooted class divisions and the pyramid-like stratification of Victorian society:

(i) the working class or proletariat (with its own 'elite' of skilled artisans);

(ii) the middle class or bourgeosie (with its various sub-divisions);

(iii) the upper class of landowners and gentry (a declining minority slowly fusing with the wealthier middle class).

The development of education in nineteenth-century England was very closely tied to this class structure. Elementary schooling, narrowly conceived and self-contained, was all that working class children could hope to receive. Secondary and higher education was the preserve of the well-to-do, with the very wealthy looking to the public schools and the universities and the comfortably off to the endowed grammar schools and private secondary institutions. Thus there developed two parallel and mutually exclusive systems of education to mirror the class-conscious nature of Victorian society. But the need to open 'other than elementary' education to outstanding talent irrespective of social class background gradually changed this situation. During the twentieth century the basis of social class stratification has become less plutocratic and more merito-cratic, with the educational system becoming a major vehicle for upward social mobility. This process has been closely associated with the develop-ment of the educational ladder linking the elementary schools and the State grammar schools and with the establishment of secondary education for all. However, whilst the old social divisions have been eroded, class differences have continued to wield a most significant influence upon the distribution of real educational opportunity within the system.

(*b*) Working Class Movements

The unenviable plight of the proletariat within Victorian society naturally gave rise to such developments as the co-operative movement, the trade union movement and the Labour movement, all dedicated to improving the lot of the workers. These movements took a growing interest in education as one of the essential means of securing a better deal for the working class, pressing for State intervention and provision on a broadening and increasingly generous front. At the close of the nineteenth century the influence of the Trades Union Congress was exemplified in the introduction of free elementary education and the first demands for secondary education for all. Thereafter, and especially following the Second World War, the organised working class movement exercised a steadily growing influence upon educational policy and development at both the central and local levels. This whole process was facilitated by political and religious changes and by a transformation of public attitudes which combined to produce a context increasingly favourable to socialist designs.

5 Political

The field of education was markedly affected by the radical changes taking place in this critical context during the period concerned.

(*a*) Rise of Democracy

Within a century the parliamentary system was gradually transformed so that by 1930 true political democracy had been achieved in terms of 'one adult, one vote' and the supremacy of the elected House of Commons. Before the first Reform Act (1832) the landed oligarchy monopolised political power, whilst in the mid-nineteenth century they shared it with the rising manufacturing and commercial middle class. Not until after the second Reform Act (1867) did the working class begin to receive the vote and a share of political power, although it was to take many years before this class could properly organise and capitalise upon its superiority of numbers. But the gradual change, completed after the First World War by the enfranchisement of women, was in the long-term full of consequences for education, especially as it provided the seed-bed for the emergence of the modern Labour party.

(*b*) Influence of Political Parties

Here one must distinguish between the three major political parties and their attitudes towards and influence upon educational development.

(i) *Tory or Conservative Party*

In the nineteenth century this party tended to display less interest in education and more opposition to State intervention than its Liberal counterpart. It supported voluntary provision and denominational schools, being tied to the Anglican cause in elementary education and to the independence of the public and endowed grammar schools in secondary education. Nevertheless, the Conservatives were responsible for the epoch-making Balfour Act (1902), which laid the foundations of a national system of State education. During the twentieth century the party has tended to maintain a fairly 'conservative' position in relation to changes in secondary schooling and the widening of higher educational opportunity. Its support of the selective against the comprehensive approach to secondary education, of the maintenance of the private sector of education and of the university as the 'model' higher educational institution are all symptoms of an *élitist* outlook on education. The greatest concern over the erosion of traditional objectives and standards in education has emanated from this political quarter. Yet the 1944 Education Act was the work of a war-time coalition government led and dominated by the Conservative party.

(ii) *Whig or Liberal Party*

In the nineteenth century it was this party which showed most interest in education (e.g. 1833 parliamentary grant, 1870 Elementary Education Act), with its Radical left leading the way in terms of pressing for State intervention and provision. In the actual field the party tended to be tied to the Nonconformist and secularist causes in elementary education, being the main support for the School Boards and undenominational religious instruction. Conversely the Liberal party was unsympathetically disposed towards the Anglican and Roman Catholic denominational schools, especially in respect of giving them increased financial support from public funds. This party was the major progressive influence in the Edwardian era, laying the foundations of the welfare state (e.g. 1908 Old Age Pensions Act, 1911 National Insurance Act) and broadening the approach to education (e.g. school meals, school medical service, free-place system) in the years before the First World War. The Liberals were also mainly responsible for the 1918 Fisher Act, which, although ill-fated, was not without significance in the process of educational advance. The party's rapid decline in the inter-war period robbed it of further major influence on educational development, although in recent years Liberal support for comprehensive secondary reorganisation and the widening of higher educational opportunities has helped the Labour party.

(iii) *Labour Party*

Arising out of the trade union movement and various socialist intellectual groups (e.g. the Fabians), this party was not established until 1900. In its early days the growing Labour party was content to wield influence through Liberal governments, but after 1918 it emerged as an independent force in British politics. Disillusioned by the Fisher Education Act, it officially embraced secondary education for all as part of its political programme (1922), briefed the Hadow Committee to investigate provision for senior elementary pupils, attempted to raise the school leaving age (1930), supported multilateral schools as an alternative to tripartite secondary organisation and campaigned for the abolition of the private sector. After 1944 the Labour party clearly emerged as the main source of support for the populist conception of education, condemning the eleven-plus examination and the associated selective pattern of secondary schooling and promoting the rapid expansion of further and higher education in the public sector. The independent schools, the direct grant schools, the grammar schools, the universities and external examinations, traditionally linked with quality in English education, have all had their position questioned from this quarter.

6 Religious

The nature and strength of this influence on English education changed greatly during this period. In the nineteenth century education was dominated by church interests, for the churches did so much to provide, maintain and control the schools. Only slowly and reluctantly did they accept the developing role of the State in the field of elementary education. Yet it is clear that nineteenth-century religion in England was a middle and upper class concern; the 1851 census reveals a very low church attendance on the part of the urban proletariat which was religiously apathetic. Thus the religious struggle in English elementary education was fought over the heads of working class parents, though it was a struggle to determine the atmosphere of the schools which their children might attend. The nineteenth-century 'religious difficulty' was an obstacle to educational advance and inevitably produced a secular reaction demanding a State take-over in the elementary field, but this was never strong enough to defeat religious influence (cf. France). During the twentieth century apathy and irreligion spread far beyond the urban working class and the organised churches have had increasing difficulty in maintaining their position and power in the educational field. The proportion of denominational 'places' in the State system declined from

53% in 1900 to only 23% in 1970, the development of secondary education for all gravely weakening the churches' position in the total framework. Yet paradoxically this comparative decline in importance was accompanied by an improvement in the financial arrangements for denominational schools to maintain the dual system in being. At the beginning of this century all voluntary schools had to meet their own capital costs: today the voluntary controlled schools are completely State-financed whilst the voluntary-aided schools are committed to only 25% of their capital costs.

However, in considering the religious context one must always distinguish between the attitudes and influence of the various groups within it.

(a) Church of England

Claiming prior rights in education inherited from the mediaeval church, the Anglican community was the most important single religious pressure group in English education. The neglect of its educational responsibilities by the established Church in the eighteenth century was followed by a sudden rejuvenation of interest in the early nineteenth century. Since then the Anglican influence has exemplified itself in the National Society's work, the Anglican training colleges, the opposition to the School Boards, the demand for increased financial aid for denominational schools at both the elementary and secondary levels, and the acceptance in 1944 of compulsory Christian religious worship and instruction in all State schools.

(b) Roman Catholic

Following the Catholic Emancipation Act (1829) and the large Irish influx of the 1840s the Roman Catholic community grew in strength and was accepted back into the main stream of English life. In 1847 the Catholic Poor School Committee received its first instalment of State financial aid for elementary education purposes. Thereafter, the Roman Catholic interest continually strove to increase the number of its own denominational schools and to obtain the maximum possible public financial aid for their support. In this respect the Roman Catholics were the allies of the Anglicans and supported the latter in their hostility to the School Boards and the rate-aided public elementary schools. During the twentieth century, whilst accepting the integration of its schools into the State system (1902 Act), the Roman Catholic Church has successfully defended the maintenance of the dual system and the denominational atmosphere of its schools, without having to pay a high price for this (see the 1944 Act and its detailed arrangements for voluntary-aided and special agreement schools).

(c) Nonconformist

The considerable influence of the Free Churches upon education in the eighteenth century crystallised itself at the elementary level in the establishment of the British and Foreign School Society in 1814. Supported by the various Nonconformist sects, this body strove to expand elementary educational provision for the children of Dissenters. Though it received State assistance from the central government after 1833 on the same terms as the Anglican National Society, it was outstripped by the latter in the actual provision of places. Worried by the dominant position of the established Church in elementary education, the Nonconformists switched from the ideal of providing their own schools to the support of the case for undenominational public elementary schools provided and controlled by the State. Between 1870 and 1914 the Nonconformists (linked politically with the Liberal party) were a major pressure group in the field of English elementary education; they welcomed the 1870 Act, they supported the School Boards and they opposed rate-aid or increased central grants to help the denominational schools. By the inter-war years, however, the Nonconformists had ceased to be of major importance in English politics and no longer enjoyed their former influence on the educational scene. Since 1870 the great majority of their schools had been handed over to the State.

(d) Secularist

This group emerged in the nineteenth century as a result of the growth of irreligion and of irritation with religious obstructionism in the field of education. The secularist ideal was the establishment of a State system of secular elementary schools devoid of all religious influences and connections. The Birmingham Education League, formed in 1869 to press for universal, compulsory, free and unsectarian elementary education, drew upon much secularist support; although unsuccessful the pressure at least resulted in the 1870 Act's allowing the School Boards to opt for the abandonment of religious worship and instruction in their schools, even if only very few did so in practice. The secularist cause was later taken up by the trade union movement and the Labour party (1895–1911), but was quietly dropped by them because of the opposition of their own Roman Catholic members. However, the cause has recently revived somewhat in the shape of the secular humanist movement which is currently pressing for the abolition of compulsory religious worship and instruction introduced by the 1944 Act.

7 Philosophic

There has been a significant change in the basic philosophy underpinning social attitudes and practices. In particular there was the move from the 'individualism' of the nineteenth century to the 'collectivism' of the twentieth century.

(a) *Laissez Faire* Philosophy

With its emphasis on individual freedom and the strict limitation of State activity to the defence of the realm, the maintenance of law and order and the saving of public money, the influence of this philosophy proved double-edged. Whilst it challenged the continuance of antiquated and unreasonable laws and worked in favour of legal, religious and political reform, it produced a backlash effect in the socio-economic field, setting the stage for the 'jungle' capitalism of the early and mid-nineteenth century in which the stronger could tread upon the weaker on a class basis. The *laissez faire* philosophy was conveniently embraced by the upper and middle class ruling oligarchy; it justified governmental indifference to the condition of the proletariat at the close of the Industrial Revolution on both economic (Adam Smith's ideas) and demographic (theories of Thomas Malthus) grounds. According to this philosophy the improvement of social conditions was to be left to humanitarian and philanthropic activity and to individual exertion and 'self-help'. In relation to education the *laissez faire* philosophy favoured little being done rather than very much, blessed voluntary efforts whilst condemning State provision, and supported the independence of the public and endowed grammar schools from State interference.

(b) 'Collectivist' Philosophy

With its emphasis on the needs of society and the rights (socio-economic as well as political and religious) of the majority of its members, and especially of the younger generation, the influence of this philosophy was broadly socialist. Given the initial artificial inequalities of Victorian society, individual freedom was rejected as a solution; the emphasis shifted to the equalisation of advantages through collective action, justifying State intervention and the curtailment of individual rights in the interests of the welfare of the mass of the community. Locked in a dire struggle with *laissez faire* throughout the later nineteenth century, this philosophy won its first clear victory in the field of factory and mines reform and went on finally to win the day. It became the very basis of the Labour party's political programme, and greatly influenced the changing attitudes of the other two major parties (the Liberals more so, the Conservatives less so). The turning point was the Edwardian era, when inspired by this philosophy the Liberals laid the foundations of the welfare state. Since then the philosophy has found its most forthright expression in the work of the post-war Labour governments, although their Conservative counterparts have found it increasingly necessary to embrace the spirit of the same philosophy. Obviously the rise of the 'collectivist' philosophy has proved extremely favourable to the development of education in terms of both objectives and actual provision. Collectivist influence in the late nineteenth century was already strong enough to bring about State intervention, compulsory attendance and free provision in elementary education. During the present century it has served to sanctify the developing State system of education as such, to secure the development of the educational welfare services, to broaden the conception of the educational process, to bring about secondary education for all and to expand opportunities in higher education. Its progressive influence has been at its most intense since the 1944 Act which was itself a clear expression of this philosophy.

In the nineteenth and early twentieth centuries the role of education was basically conservative and passive: the system of education grew out of the contemporary society, at best mirroring the established social and culture pattern and at worst slowly and painfully responding to any shifts in that pattern. The mechanics of change were as follows:

> Various forces (demographic, economic, scientific, technological, political, religious and philosophic) → changes in the nature of society → delayed effects on the system of education.

In more recent times education has emerged as a progenitor as well as a derivative, as a progressive influence as well as a conservative force. The educational system is no longer simply shaped by society, but is helping to shape that society by exercising a growing influence upon it. The extent to which the educational system can and should be used as a means of social engineering and change is a controversial issue, but clearly the relationship between society and education has become increasingly two-way. The rise of meritocracy over the last half century has been largely facilitated by the widening of secondary and higher educational opportunities. For many the quest for an egalitarian society begins with the educational system, hence the interest in and the support for comprehensive schooling, compensatory education and nursery provision. That a 'brave new world' can be built on educational foundations was a wide-spread conviction after the Second World War, and this belief has still not been abandoned or seriously eroded. The struggle forward continues with education as one of the acknowledged centrepieces.

Follow-up: Ideally this involves the widest possible reading so that you become familiar with the broad historical and contemporary background to educational development in England and Wales. In particular, it is important to become conversant with the major forces and movements which have operated in English society since 1800 and which have a bearing on educational development. The two books listed below adopt a pronounced sociological approach to the subject and can be recommended. For full bibliographical information: see pages 340-4.
Read Musgrave, P. W., *Society and Education in England since 1800*
    Wardle, D., *English Popular Education 1780-1970*

Chapter Two
Developments in Elementary Education 1800-1870

Purpose: to convey some impression of the inadequate and unsatisfactory nature of elementary educational provision for the mass of the population in early nineteenth-century England, and to consider those influences and developments which gradually brought about an improvement in the situation prior to the 1870 Elementary Education Act.

The development of elementary education in England and Wales during the period 1800-1870 may be considered in three major parts.

1 The Situation at the Turn of the Century

The evidence of an official investigation (the report of the parliamentary Select Committee on the Education of the Lower Orders of Society, 1818) led Lord Brougham to describe England at this time as the worst educated country in Europe. It showed that only one quarter of the child population was receiving any education at all, and for the great majority of these its duration was very short. Moreover, many of those privileged to receive some elementary education were attending the ineffectual dame and common day schools or merely going to Sunday school one day per week. A very large number of poor children, estimated at over one and a half million, were wholly without any means of elementary instruction, with the rapid growth of population and demand for child labour both calculated to make the situation worse. The traditional means available for bringing about an expansion of provision were extremely meagre; private individuals and voluntary bodies working in the field were dependent on the limited and unreliable funds obtained from endowments, donations and parents' pence. Nor was such expansion generally agreed to be necessary or desirable. Against the backcloth of the French Revolution most of the propertied governing class feared the possible consequences of educating the poor more than the possible dangers and disadvantages of not doing so. In particular they were concerned lest the provision of elementary education for the poor should produce a growing dissatisfaction with their lot in life at the close of the Industrial Revolution. Better to let sleeping dogs lie.

But within early nineteenth-century English society various influences and considerations were combining to help the cause of elementary education for the lower classes.

(*a*) Humanitarian

As the Industrial Revolution concentrated and sharpened the misery of the poor there was a remarkable development of private benevolence throughout the country in the early decades of the new century. This growth of philanthropy found a focus in the Society for the Bettering of the Condition of the Poor which gave a place to elementary education in its overall design. Humanitarian opposition to the employment of child labour and support for factory reform legislation was also of long-term significance for the development of elementary education.

(*b*) Religious

Stimulated by the Methodist example, the Church of England underwent a serious revival in the early nineteenth century and through the Evangelical movement found a new Christian purpose which had important educational results. The establishment of the National Society in 1811 heralded the start of a new Anglican drive in the field of elementary education, which drew its inevitable response from the Nonconformists who founded the British and Foreign School Society in 1814 for the same purpose. In this way the religious revival and the denominational rivalry of the early nineteenth century pumped additional interest and resources into the provision of elementary education.

(*c*) Social

The brutish ignorance and behaviour which characterised the back-streets of the growing industrial towns and the riots and disorders which sprang out of contemporary social conditions could not be ignored or repressed indefinitely. Gradually an increasing number of the governing class became apprehensive and turned to elementary education as a possible civilising and steadying influence on the turbulent mass of the urban proletariat. Their interest was in an elementary schooling deliberately aimed at the religious and social conditioning of lower class children.

Thus the cause of expanding elementary education obtained increasing support: the great problem was how to bring this expansion about.

2 Efforts to Expand Elementary Education 1800-1833

Although the practical results were limited, these years saw considerable efforts being made to increase the provision of elementary educational facilities. Such efforts took three main forms.

(a) Projection of the Sunday School Movement

The pioneer work of Robert Raikes to meet the needs of pin-factory children in the town of Gloucester was quickly followed by the founding of the Society for the Establishment and Support of Sunday Schools in 1785. As a result of support received from most denominations and from factory-owners interested in insuring themselves against any loss of child labour during the working week, the Society achieved a national impact. By the turn of the century there were over three-quarters of a million children attending Sunday schools up and down the country; thirty years later the figure had reached about one and half million. Although in terms of numbers the achievement of the Sunday school movement was impressive, its practical effects were much more limited. Many of the volunteer teachers were inexperienced and poorly educated and secular education (in the three Rs) was gradually drowned by sectarian religious instruction. The real significance of the Sunday school movement was threefold:

(i) it raised the ideal of universal elementary education and pointed the way towards it;

(ii) it kindled the denominational rivalry between Anglicans and Nonconformists which was to provide in double-edged fashion so much of the drive and difficulty in the field of nineteenth-century English elementary education;

(iii) it pioneered the monitorial system; Raikes met Joseph Lancaster and some believe that the latter developed his system from the beginnings made by the Sunday schools.

(b) Development of the Monitorial System

Shortage of money and shortage of teachers were the two fundamental problems facing any attempt to expand elementary education in the early nineteenth century. The solution provided was the monitorial system, elaborated and popularised by Andrew Bell, an Anglican clergyman, and Joseph Lancaster, a Quaker schoolmaster. Although their respective systems differed in detail they rested on the same basic principles, the foremost of which was that of mass-production in elementary education by applying the division of labour to the process of simple instruction. The central idea was to enable a single schoolmaster to cope with a very large number of children by the employment of monitors, i.e. making use of the older and abler pupils to teach the others. The monitorial system depended on the schoolmaster taking responsibility for the organisation and discipline of the school and for the clear instruction of the monitors in particular elements of the three Rs, so that they could duplicate the exercise with their different monitorial groups.

[handwritten margin notes at top: "industrial structure analogous to school org." "Societies broad influence/provision" "Macro / Micro Educal. Model. individual from / school org."]

Membership of such groups was determined by attainment rather than age and promotion from one group to another took place as proficiency increased. Lancaster boasted that the system made it possible for one master to teach a thousand pupils. The major attraction was its cheapness; the annual cost of instructing a child in a typical Lancasterian school was 7s 6d, whilst the more austere arrangements of Bell's system reduced the sum even further.

The churches were quick to take advantage of the opportunity offered by the monitorial system, the charity schools of the eighteenth century being adapted to its use as well as new schools established for its introduction. The National Society for Promoting the Education of the Poor in the Principles of the Established Church (1811) adopted Bell's system to extend rapidly the provision made for elementary education by the Anglicans; simultaneously the British and Foreign School Society (1814) adopted Lancaster's system to expand the opportunities available for Nonconformist children and others. The resultant denominational rivalry drove both sides to strenuous efforts and helped to attract considerable funds to the task. Both societies set up 'model' schools for the swift training of schoolteachers who would operate the monitorial system. By 1830 the system was enabling the National Society to provide elementary education for about one-third of a million children.

In spite of its shortcomings the monitorial school was a considerable improvement on the dame, the common day and charity schools inherited from the eighteenth century; the children did obtain a superficial smattering of the three Rs and were conditioned to a sense of good order and discipline. The subject of much contemporary interest and enthusiasm, the monitorial schools did much to popularise elementary education and encouraged those who thought in terms of making such provision universal. *But* in certain respects the influence of the monitorial system was far from beneficial:

[handwritten margin note: "More from pupteur than nobleur desire"]

   (i) little worthwhile education resulted from the mechanical instruction of younger by older pupils;

   (ii) denominational rivalry became very bitter, thus crystallising the 'religious difficulty' in elementary education which was to prove such an obstacle to future progress;

   (iii) the mould was set for the elementary school of the later nineteenth century with its mechanical methods, low standards, large classes, cheapness and narrow educational ideals.

(c) Demands for State Involvement

The spread of the Sunday schools and the monitorial system was accomplished by the efforts of voluntary bodies without a single penny of

plastic pencil lead ?

public money being subscribed thereto by the State. But a minority of progressives, unkindly described as the 'education mad' party, recognised that voluntary resources were too limited and pressed for State involvement in one form or another. Gradually the government policy of non-intervention in relation to child labour and elementary education was undermined by the work of various pioneers both inside and outside Parliament. There are a number of landmarks in this erosive process.

1807 *Whitbread's Parochial Schools Bill* suggested the establishment of a national system of rate-aided parish schools to be run by elected parish committees and providing two years' free elementary schooling for poor children. But the Bill was cut to ribbons in the Commons and thrown out of the Lords.

1816 *Parliamentary Select Committee* was established to inquire into 'the Education of the Lower Orders of Society'. Two years later, inspired by Lord Brougham, this body submitted the first official report on elementary education and in its findings provided much ammunition for those who favoured State involvement.

1820 *Brougham's Parish Schools Bill* envisaged a national system of elementary education based on the provision of buildings by the manufacturing class, with running costs being met by local rate-aid, redistributed endowments and small fees. A religious compromise was attempted by placing the control of staffing and curricula under the established Church, whilst suggesting that religious teaching should be undenominational. The Bill inevitably foundered on the combined opposition of the employers and the churches.

1833 *Roebuck's Education Bill:* in the more favourable setting resulting from the first Reform Act (1832), and inspired by the examples of Prussia and France, John Roebuck, a Radical member of Parliament, submitted a plan for 'the universal and national education of the whole people'. The Bill provided for a Minister of Public Instruction (with Cabinet status), elected School District Committees to operate as local authorities, central and local rate-aid to supplement parents' pence, compulsory attendance from six to twelve years of age and normal schools for teacher training. The solution to the 'religious difficulty' was sensible and practicable. Where a particular sect was numerically strong it was to be allowed its own denominational schools; otherwise, schools were to provide undenominational religious instruction whilst also providing limited 'rights of entry' to the various sectarian ministers concerned.

Even for a reformed Parliament Roebuck's Bill was too ambitious and expensive to have any hope of being accepted. But the Bill stimulated Parliament's interest sufficiently for that body to follow its rejection by the grant of £20,000 for 'the erection of elementary schools': as this offer was not an isolated but a continuing one with no fixed ceiling, it was of the utmost significance. Indeed the 1833 parliamentary grant was the beginning of State assistance for and involvement in the provision of elementary schooling. Moreover, the failure of Roebuck's Bill had also been balanced by the passage of the 1833 Factory Act which resulted in the first effective regulation and limitation of child labour, a development of acute significance for the future of elementary education. The very first inroads upon the established philosophy and policy of *laissez faire* had now been made.

3 The Era of Voluntary Initiative and State Assistance 1833-70 Dual system,

The annual parliamentary grant for elementary education rose from £20,000 in 1833 to £30,000 in 1839. The exact nature of and means of dispensing the grant at this time is noteworthy. It was essentially in 'aid of private subscriptions', thus being available only to those voluntary bodies which could first raise 50% of the total cost of the projected school building and guarantee to meet the running costs thereafter. Thus in practice State assistance was limited to those localities possessing the requisite interest and resources to muster half the cost, which discriminated against the poorest urban areas where the need was greatest. Initially all the public funds made available were channelled through the National Society (about 80%) and the British and Foreign School Society (about 20%) which vetted applications for assistance on behalf of the Treasury. There was no attempt to inspect the schools receiving grant money or to control the appointment of staff or the curriculum. Because the Treasury wielded so little real control over the sums expended, the central government determined in 1839 to set up a special body to exercise its responsibilities in the field of elementary education: the establishment of the Committee of the Privy Council for Education set the stage for the work of Dr Kay, later Sir James Kay-Shuttleworth, who did so much to improve the situation in the middle years of the century before the report of the Newcastle Commission (1861) and the introduction of the Revised Code (1862).

(a) Sir James Kay-Shuttleworth

Doctor, poor law commissioner, social reformer and educationist, he was appointed first Secretary of the new Committee and for ten years he worked twelve hours a day to improve the state of elementary education and to impair the state of his own health. During the 1840s and

1850s his energy and influence brought about a major advance, though he was always acutely aware of how much more needed to be done.

His *achievements* were varied and considerable:

(i) the initial development of a central administrative agency for dispensing State financial assistance to elementary education, through the religious organisations, and for maintaining contact with the growing number of grant-aided schools. This agency, located at Whitehall and responsible to the Committee of the Council, grew into the Education Department of the later nineteenth century and was the original forefather of the present Department of Education and Science;

(ii) the establishment of Her Majesty's Inspectorate (1840), which, with the agreement of the religious organisations, was to serve as the link between Shuttleworth's central agency and the grant-aided schools. Kay-Shuttleworth's influence, as expressed in the first instructions to H.M. Inspectors, worked in favour of a wide-ranging and diplomatic role, rather than a narrow, inquisitorial one, for this new body. Whilst ensuring that grants were put to proper use, the inspectors were to be more concerned with affording 'assistance' and 'encouragement' than with 'exercising control': they were, on request, to offer advice to the promoters of elementary schools not aided by public grants and were to collect any information calculated to shed light on the general state of elementary education in England and Wales;

(iii) the impressive increase in the annual parliamentary grant to elementary education, which rose from £30,000 to over £800,000 during the period 1839-61, and the development of a system of specific grants for a widening range of items and purposes. Following the Committee's Minutes of 1846 State assistance was extended well beyond the original 50% building grant; public monies became available to help defray current costs, especially after the introduction of capitation grants (tied to minimal attendance requirements) in the mid 1850s;

(iv) the dilution of the key problem of teacher training and supply, which was at the root of limited provision and poor standards in elementary education. Through the 1846 Minutes Kay-Shuttleworth launched the pupil-teacher system which was to serve English elementary education down to the end of the century. The new arrangements were based on a five years' apprenticeship for interested and able thirteen-year-old pupils who engaged in 'on the job' training in approved grant-aided schools; the best pupil-teachers were then offered Queen's scholarships to undertake a further two year course at a denominational training college. With the State providing financial assistance for the support of training colleges, the religious organisations responded well and by 1859 there were some thirty-odd such institutions offering places. By this time the new system had produced over 7,000 trained certificated teachers, whilst twice as many pupil-teachers were in the schools. Significant inroads were made into the shortage of teachers and monitorial methods began to retreat before the advance of class teaching.

His *disappointments*, resultant of the contemporary 'religious difficulty', are also noteworthy in certain respects:

(i) the failure to bring about the establishment of a State Training College, as a forerunner of others, free of denominational influence and control. This idea had been canvassed in the late 1830s, Parliament had voted the sum of £10,000 for the project and the new Committee was commissioned to make it a reality. But when Kay-Shuttleworth drafted a detailed scheme for a 'purely civil' Training College it quickly foundered on the religious issue. He then turned to the establishment of Battersea Training College as a private venture in 1840, to show the possibility of developing teacher training in a broad Anglican setting which would not offend tender consciences. However, personal and financial difficulties, combined with the narrow sectarian influence of the Oxford Movement within the established Church, led him to surrender the college to the National Society in 1843. Thus for the rest of the century the field of teacher training was monopolised by the denominational colleges which were never able to provide enough places to meet the real needs of the elementary schools: even the 1870 Act failed to change the situation and it was not until after 1902 that State training colleges began to develop;

(ii) the failure to provide special help for those poor urban areas unable to muster 50% of the cost of a new school building. In 1843 Kay-Shuttleworth helped to devise a Factory Bill which not only extended the regulation of child employment but provided for a developing system of elementary schools in factory areas. Government loans were to be made available for the establishment of such schools, but the real cost was to be largely defrayed by the employers through the parish rates. Control of the schools was vested in the Church of England, and Anglican religious worship and instruction were provided for, albeit with a 'conscience clause' to make the arrangements more generally acceptable. However, such was the violent outcry from the Nonconformist ranks that a political crisis arose and the government withdrew the Bill. The Nonconformist reaction was so strong that it resulted in the 'Voluntaryist' movement: intensely suspicious of government intentions in elementary education the Congregationalists and others refused State grants and campaigned for a reversion to the purely voluntary principle. Had this ploy succeeded the Anglican schools would also have lost their State financial assistance, but in practice the result of this masochistic exercise was to put the Nonconformists at a serious disadvantage in the denominational school race and later to incline them to the support of direct State provision. Meanwhile the failure of the 1843 Factory Bill postponed a further major government initiative in the field of elementary education for over a quarter of a century.

Obviously these were difficult times. The faith and fortitude of Kay-Shuttleworth was nothing less than heroic; in spite of the disappointments his contribution was absolutely critical to the progress of elementary education in the nineteenth century.

(b) Newcastle Commission 1858-61

The Report and the significance of this body may be considered in the following terms:

(i) *Context*

The need for financial stringency after the expense of the Crimean War and the serious shortcomings of elementary education in State assisted schools as revealed in inspectors' reports, combined to bring the parliamentary grant under close scrutiny in the late 1850s. As the new Education Department created in 1856 was directly responsible to Parliament it was now essential to justify the monies annually expended on elementary education and to ensure their proper and effective use.

(ii) *Terms of Reference*

'To inquire into the present state of popular education in England, and to consider and report what measures, if any, are required for the extension of sound and cheap elementary instruction to all classes of the people.' In spite of the unfavourable context the commissioners adopted a more liberal approach than is generally appreciated or acknowledged; in their work they showed much more interest in the extension and improvement of existing provision than in cheapening the cost of it.

(iii) *Findings*

These gave qualified approval to the existing situation. On the credit side the report pointed to the considerable improvement which had taken place since 1818 as a result of voluntary efforts and State assistance. The significant rise in the proportion of children receiving some sort of elementary education and the beneficial influence of the pupil-teacher system were particularly noted. But on the debit side the report spotlighted the sheer inadequacy of provision in the poorer areas, the unsatisfactory nature of the unassisted schools, the short duration and irregularity of attendance and the early leaving age of the great majority of pupils. The report further emphasised the widespread incidence, even in grant-aided schools, of inefficient teaching simply for the want of sufficient concentration on the task of giving the children a thorough grounding in the three Rs; too much attention was being focused on the older children and on non-essential subject matter.

(iv) *Recommendations*

That the commissioners were the prisoners of their age found expression in their conservative response to a number of critical issues. They rejected the idea of State provision and control in favour of the continuance of voluntary initiative and self-help; whilst State assistance was acceptable, any attempt to introduce compulsory attendance or free elementary schooling was condemned. Beyond this the Commission based its positive recommendations on two essential requirements. Firstly, it underlined the need for more financial assistance for the voluntary bodies, and even for the extension of such aid to previously unassisted schools, especially in the poorer areas. To this end State aid in the simple form of block capitation grants was to be supplemented by local rate aid channelled through a new framework of County and Municipal Education Boards. Secondly, it insisted on the need to ensure that the public funds so provided were put to proper use and accordingly suggested that grant assistance should be tied to minimal attendance requirements for the capitation allowance and to annual examination requirements for the receipt of rate aid. The total result of adopting the recommendations would be to increase the resources available to the elementary schools, to raise their standards of attainment and to simplify and partly decentralise the administration of grant aid.

(c) Robert Lowe and the Revised Code (1862)

The report of the Newcastle Commission was duly considered by Robert Lowe, Vice-President of the Council and head of the Education Department 1859-64, who was an efficient administrator with an aristocratic outlook rather than a visionary educationist with a real sympathy for popular education. Inevitably he was impressed by the report's emphasis upon the need to ensure value for money rather by its insistence upon the need for more to be made available. The result was the Revised Code of 1862, which stressed the former and ignored the latter. In any case the introduction of rate aid for the support of elementary education was a religiously explosive issue which neither Lowe nor his Whig masters were prepared to face. The Revised Code, which was to survive in a progressively modified form for some thirty years, introduced a new set of regulations which subjected the grant-aided elementary schools and training colleges to a strict 'payment by results' system.

Its *features:* the detailed regulations of Lowe's Code ensured that the new system had a number of distinctive features:

(i) the abolition of the specific grants for furniture, books and apparatus, of pupil-teacher stipends and of teachers' merit grants and pension rights introduced by Kay-Shuttleworth;

(ii) the sharp reduction of State grants to the training colleges partly through the curtailment of the number of Queen's scholarships;

(iii) the strict relation of State grants for elementary education to attendance and attainment. H.M. Inspectorate was henceforth committed to the task of annually examining the registers and the proficiency in the three Rs of all children of six years and over in State assisted elementary schools which now had to earn their grant. Each child could earn the school the sum of twelve shillings; according to the average number in attendance throughout the year four shillings per pupil was paid, whilst successful examination performance earned a further eight shillings (i.e. 2s 8d per child for each of the three Rs). The examinations were conducted at six graded levels (Standards I-VI) and no pupil could be entered at more than one level or repeat a grade already successfully undertaken.

Lowe boasted of the new system: 'If it is not cheap, it shall be efficient; if it is not efficient, it shall be cheap.' In fact the annual parliamentary grant for elementary education fell by 23% during the first five years of the Code's operation.

Its *advantages* (these cannot be, but often are, ignored):

(i) a considerable rise in the school population and greater regularity of attendance;

(ii) an improvement in school organisation and in competence in the three Rs, especially amongst those grant-aided schools which had been the weakest;

(iii) a dilution of the previous stress on religious teaching in favour of secular instruction as the former was not eligible for grant;

(iv) a much-needed reduction in the administrative burden of the Education Department now that it ceased to deal directly with teachers, pupil-teachers and the earlier wide range of specific grants.

Its *disadvantages:* the system came under increasing criticism and challenge because of the retrogressive influence it wielded in various directions:

 (i) the over-pressurisation of the children and the comparative neglect of the fast and slow learners in favour of the 'bread and butter' middle section;

 (ii) the narrowing of the elementary curriculum as a result of the inevitable concentration on the three Rs, with its corresponding and derivative effect upon the character of training college courses;

(iii) the demoralisation of teachers who lost their semi-Civil Service status and were reduced to the role of hired drill instructors, attendance officers and register falsifiers whose income came to depend on the results they achieved in circumstances often beyond their control;

(iv) the rapid growth of distrust and hatred for the H.M. Inspectorate by the majority of elementary teachers as the latter were subjected to the former's new inquisitorial role;

 (v) the fall in the recruitment of pupil-teachers and the output of trained certificated teachers, associated with a rise in average class size and a decline in the standards of entry into elementary teaching.

In the final analysis both the Newcastle Commission and Robert Lowe were content to rely on the voluntary bodies to bear the main burden of providing for the expansion of elementary education. The Revised Code was not calculated to increase the number of elementary schools or to improve their geographical distribution; it merely tended to make the existing grant-aided schools more efficient. But by the late 1860s the changing context was making it increasingly clear that the voluntary organisations could not manage and that there was a need for much more direct involvement by the State. The stage was being set for the 1870 Elementary Education Act, by which at long last the poorer districts would receive the attention hitherto denied them.

Follow-up: Attempt to cover as much of the following ground as possible.

1 *Read* Bagley, J. J. and A. J. *The State and Education in England and Wales, 1833-1968*, Chapter 1

Dawson, K. and Wall, P. *Society and Industry in the 19th Century: Education*, pp. 1-27

Curtis, S. J. and Boultwood, M. E. *An Introductory History of English Education since 1800*, Chapter 1, pp. 1-12, and Chapter 4, pp. 54-74

Barnard, H. C. *A History of English Education from 1760*, Chapters I, VI, VII, XI and XII

2 *Consult* Maclure, J. S. *Educational Documents: England and Wales 1816-1968;* items 1, 3, 4, 5, 6, 9, 10 and 11 are relevant.

3 *Clarify the following: the exact nature of the dame, common day and charity schools inherited from the eighteenth century; the findings of the parliamentary Select Committee on the Education of the Lower Orders of Society, 1818; the influences favourable to elementary education in the early nineteenth century; the differences between the monitorial systems operated by Bell and Lancaster; the attempts of the 'education mad' party to secure early State involvement; the contribution of Sir James Kay-Shuttleworth to the advance of elementary education; the details of the pupil-teacher system; the precise recommendations of the Newcastle Commission; the effects of the Revised Code (1862) and the nature of its subsequent progressive modification.*

Chapter Three
Elementary Education in the School Board Era 1870-1902

Purpose: to provide the background to and an appreciation of the vital importance of the passage of the 1870 Elementary Education Act and the subsequent influence of the School Boards to the emergence of a national system of elementary education in England and Wales.

The study of the very considerable subject matter involved in this topic may well be divided into two major parts.

1 1870 Elementary Education Act

This critical landmark in our educational history formed the watershed between mere State assistance for and direct State provision of elementary education. As such it represented the first bold and effective legislative initiative undertaken by government in English education, involving the creation of the earliest local authorities for education and opening the way to the development of a more positive and widening role for the State in this field.

(a) Underlying Causes

By the late 1860s various influences had combined to make elementary education a national issue and to convince many important people that a radical extension of State involvement was now vitally necessary. It was the work of such influences which prepared the way for the introduction and acceptance of the 1870 Act.

(i) *Demographic*

The continued population explosion, especially in the major towns and cities was swamping the efforts of the voluntary organisations to provide adequate elementary educational facilities under existing arrangements. Even Edward Baines, the Congregational protagonist of pure 'Voluntaryism', was forced to admit defeat and accept the idea of State provision.

(ii) *Social*

As the Factory Acts progressively raised the minimum age of child employment in a growing range of occupations, centres of dense population were faced with the problem of thousands of children on the streets, with nothing better to do than turn to petty crime or otherwise misapply their energies. It has been estimated that the 1867 Factory Act alone debarred an additional one-fifth of a million children from paid employment. Having demonstrated the connection between idleness and ignorance on the one hand and vice and crime on the other, W. E. Forster asked Parliament, 'Dare we then take the responsibility of allowing this to continue one year longer than we can help?' (*Hansard*, cxcix, 17 February 1870). The answer was to get the urchins into school.

(iii) *Political*
The 1867 Reform Act extended the franchise to the industrial working class and convinced even the aristocratic Robert Lowe that it would now 'be absolutely necessary (to) prevail on our future masters to learn their letters' (*Hansard*, clxxxviii, 15 July 1867). Thus the dangers of an illiterate electorate helped to marshal opinion favourable to the cause of universal elementary education.

(iv) *Economic*
The Paris Exhibition of 1867 gave grounds for foreboding in relation to Britain's long-established industrial lead and commercial supremacy. The rapid advance of some of Britain's continental competitors was explained by the greater priority they gave to educational development. Introducing his Bill to the Commons, W. E. Forster insisted, 'We must not delay. Upon the speedy provision of elementary education depends our industrial prosperity' (*Hansard*, cxcix, 17 February 1870). Industrialisation had reached a more complex stage and the need for literate and skilled workers was growing both absolutely and comparatively.

(v) *Military*
During the 1860s contemporary observers were much impressed by the results of the American Civil and Austro-Prussian Wars and by the emergence of modern Germany. Military strength and national power clearly seemed to benefit from the provision of universal elementary education; it was even declared that the dramatic victory in the Seven Weeks' War was forged in the elementary schools of Prussia. Given Britain's recent mediocre performance in the Crimean War, these were considerations which could not be lightly ignored.

(*b*) Contemporary Ferment
Whilst the Manchester Education Aid Society (established 1864) and similar urban organisations elsewhere campaigned nationally for more public funds and more vigorous State action, and supported the ill-fated attempts of certain private members (e.g. H. A. Bruce) to institute new

legislation, W. E. Forster, the new Vice-President of the Council and head of the Education Department in Gladstone's first Liberal ministry 1868-74, mounted a parliamentary investigation into the state of elementary education in four large cities. The report submitted on the situation in Liverpool, Manchester, Leeds and Birmingham confirmed the government's worst fears: the total extent of provision was quite inadequate, the available schools unevenly distributed, the unaided schools virtually worthless and the benefits of instruction seriously undermined by irregular attendance and very early leaving. The inquiry's statistical returns showed that of the six to twelve years age-group in the cities concerned, nearly one-half received no elementary schooling at all whilst a mere one-third attended inspected schools. It was assumed that this depressing sample picture was typical of the condition of elementary education in the growing urban industrial areas.

The Gladstone government determined to 'grasp the nettle' and W. E. Forster was elevated to Cabinet position to prepare and present the necessary legislation. Meanwhile the different interests organised themselves to bring pressure to bear on the government in the hope of securing a legislative solution in accordance with their particular viewpoint.

(i) *Birmingham Education League* (*1869*)

Representing the Nonconformist, secularist and radical cause, the League campaigned energetically for 'universal, compulsory, free and unsectarian' elementary education in the months before and during the passage of the Act. The success of this nationally-organised body would have meant the displacement of the existing denominational schools, the great majority of which were Anglican, by direct State provision throughout the country; thus the tradition of religious initiative and control in English elementary education would have been overthrown. However, the League was weakened somewhat by its own internal divisions; whilst the secularist minority pressed for the complete abandonment of religious worship and instruction in the State elementary schools, the majority of supporters favoured its retention in unsectarian form. Moreover, the public at large were unlikely to accept the sheer expense of the Birmingham programme or its extremely rough treatment of the established Church.

(ii) *National Education Union* (*1870*)

Representing the Anglican interest mainly, but supported by the Roman Catholics and the Methodists, this body campaigned for the continuance of the denominational monopoly in elementary education, with the churches simply receiving more generous financial help to do the job. In the latter respect the Union pressed for the introduction of local rate-aid for the denominational schools to supplement the central grants already available. The majority of elementary teachers lent their support to the Union against the League at this time. But the Union also suffered from internal dissension especially in relation to the conscience clause issue; the moderates felt that the acceptance of a conscience clause, giving parents the right to withdraw their children from sectarian religious worship and instruction, was a reasonable price to pay for the public financing of denominational schools, but the more extreme elements denounced such a course of action as inimical to the denominational identity and atmosphere of the Anglican and Roman Catholic schools.

Gladstone and Forster were unprepared to give way to either pressure group. Instead they embraced a compromise solution suggested by Robert Lowe which would allow the churches a 'period of grace' to meet the country's elementary educational deficiencies and would provide for direct State provision where such deficiencies were not completely eliminated. Thus the government opted for a dual system inevitably calculated to draw an unfavourable reaction from both the League and the Union; nevertheless it proved to be a way forward basically acceptable to most moderate opinion both inside and outside Parliament.

(c) Main Aims and Provisions

The declared purpose of the 1870 Act was to 'cover the country with good schools' and so enable all parents to secure elementary education for their children. This was to be done, not by dismantling the existing system, but by the State simply 'filling the gaps' left by voluntary effort, thus 'sparing the public money where it can be done without' and retaining the 'co-operation and aid of those benevolent men who desire to assist their neighbours' (*Hansard*, cxcix, 17 February 1870). The main provisions of the Act followed naturally from this over-all strategy.

 (i) The country was divided into several thousand school districts, pending an investigation into existing facilities in each one and a possible declaration of deficiency by the Education Department.

 (ii) Where the existing facilities were not 'sufficient, efficient and suitable' the churches were given a six months' 'period of grace' to rectify the situation, with 50% State building grants made available during this time but not beyond.

(iii) School Boards, elected by local ratepayers, were to be established in all districts where a deficiency remained once the six months' period had elapsed. These Boards were given the responsibility of covering the residual deficiencies and were presented with a wide range of associated permissive powers. They could accept the transfer of voluntary schools into their hands, establish their own new elementary schools, levy local rate-aid for their work, compulsorily acquire building land, decide for or against religious instruction in their schools, remit the fees of poor children, enforce compulsory attendance through the bye-laws and appoint their own permanent officials.

(iv) The Board schools were to be financially supported by central grants, parental fees (maximum 9d per week) and rate-aid, whilst the voluntary schools were expected to defray their costs from central grants, parental fees (no maximum prescribed) and church subscriptions, with rate-aid being deliberately denied them. For both types of school the amount which could be earned in central grants under the 'payment by results' system was increased.

(v) The 'religious difficulty' was met by two important and distinct clauses of the Act. The Cowper-Temple clause related to the School Boards only, giving them the choice between undenominational religious instruction and none at all; the former option was defined as worship and instruction devoid of any 'catechisms or religious formularies distinctive of any particular denomination'. This was intended to secure the rate-aided Board schools from the threat of denominational religious teaching. The timetable conscience clause affected both the Board and the voluntary schools; it laid down the parents' right to withdraw their child from religious worship or instruction, and to facilitate this the schools were required to time-table religious teaching at the beginning or end of the day. This was designed primarily to meet the difficulty of single-school areas where the only elementary school available was a denominational (usually Anglican) one, but it also met the needs of atheist and agnostic parents sending their children to Board schools giving undenominational religious instruction.

(*d*) Reaction to the Act

The original Bill as first presented to Parliament included the provision of rate-aid for denominational schools and gave the churches a period of twelve months to cover deficiencies. Accused of a sell-out to the Anglican interest by its own Nonconformist and Radical supporters, Gladstone's government was forced to make amendments unfavourable to the churches. Nevertheless, some Liberal members felt unable to support the Bill in its amended form and the Act, which received the royal assent in August 1870, was viewed with dissatisfaction from both ends of the politico-educational spectrum.

(i) *The National Education League* saw the Act as nothing more than a short step in the right direction, with free, compulsory and unsectarian elementary education in a purely State system of schools having eluded its grasp. In spite of the amendments which its influence had helped successfully to press upon the government, the League still considered the measure was far too soft on the denominational interests and had lumbered the country with a dual system which would be hard to get rid of. For the next quarter-century the Nonconformist, secularist and radical supporters of the National Education League agitated for the acceptance of the original Birmingham programme.

(ii) *The National Education Union* could only find consolation in the fact that the Liberal government had dealt less severely with the church interests than many of its supporters had demanded. At least they had obtained a six months' 'period of grace' during which, with the aid of State building grants, they would be given the first opportunity to make up the deficiencies. Thereafter a significant increase in the central grants which the denominational schools could earn would become available. The denominational atmosphere of the Anglican and Roman Catholic schools would remain unimpaired; it was recognised that the practical significance of the right of withdrawal would prove minimal anyway. In a word, Gladstone's solution was a dual system which retained a very important place for the denominational schools, not a purely statutory system which absorbed or ostracised them. *But* the churches also had strong grounds for dissatisfaction with the new settlement. The cessation of building grants after the 'period of grace', the prospective competition of the rate-aided and potentially 'godless' Board schools and the prior right of established School Boards to meet ensuing deficiencies were all very ominous. They seemed to portend a gradual erosion of the churches' influence in the field of elementary education. Naturally the Anglicans and Roman Catholics were anxious to stimulate more generous subscriptions from church members for the support of their own schools, to capture control of School Boards established in deficiency areas and to persuade some future Conservative government to change the arrangements in a way much more favourable to them.

But to the nation at large the objections from these sources were of secondary importance: the 1870 Act was to make available to all parents an elementary education for their children and that was what really mattered.

(e) Significance and Limitations of the Act

Forster's measure established a new framework for the provision of elementary education which ensured that deficiencies were gradually overcome and a school place made available to all children in the country. In the context of that time it was a major triumph to devise and implement legislation which established the first local authorities and infringed the former monopoly of provision held by the churches; to overcome the hostility of the established Church and the employers of child labour, and to persuade a traditionally reluctant Parliament to accept the introduction of rate-aid for elementary education, was no mean feat. The 1870 Act put new life into the efforts of the voluntary organisations and produced educational pace-setters at the local level in the shape of the larger, progressive School Boards.

But the 1870 Act did not provide for compulsory or free elementary education. Nor did it make any fundamental difference to the 'payment by results' system which was accepted in principle and thus perpetuated in practice for a further quarter-century. From the outset the denominational schools were at a disadvantage because of their lack of rate-aid. Worst of all, whilst setting the stage for the provision of many more elementary places, the Act did nothing to ensure a parallel expansion in the supply of suitably-trained elementary teachers. Thus, although Forster's measure amounted to a critical breakthrough, there were many loose ends to be tied up in the years that followed its passage through Parliament.

2 Subsequent Developments in Elementary Education

The passage of Forster's Act gave rise to the School Board era 1870-1902, a period during which the elementary educational scene was characterised by much change and many problems.

(a) Expansion of Provision

The inevitable competition between the School Boards and the church interests within the new framework ensured a rapid increase in available elementary school places. In 1870 the voluntary system had afforded less than one and a quarter million places; by 1900 the dual system was providing over four and a half million and the ideal of universal elementary education had been realised. The Anglicans and Roman Catholics made a supreme effort during the 'period of grace' and tenaciously clung to their schools in succeeding years. As a result of more than doubling their provision the churches were still providing (without rate-aid) 53% of the total elementary places available in 1900. Meanwhile, by filling the gaps not covered by the increased effort of the churches the School Boards had gradually come to provide well over two million places. Starting as they did from nothing this was an impressive achievement for these new local authorities and one not really envisaged by the denominational interests in the early 1870s.

(*b*) Compulsory Attendance

The 1870 Act simply authorised, but did not require, the School Boards to frame local bye-laws for the enforcement of attendance between five and thirteen years. The London School Board took full and immediate advantage of this power and its example encouraged other Boards to follow suit; but the majority proved extremely laggard and as more places became available the government took further action.

1876 *Sandon's Act:* this provided for the establishment of School Attendance Committees, with power to frame and enforce bye-laws for compulsory attendance, in those districts still without a School Board and made it the parents' legal obligation to ensure that their children received 'efficient elementary instruction'. Employers were forbidden to employ children under ten years and were only to hire those over ten years on the production of a labour certificate issued by one of H.M. Inspectors authorising release from school. But even this measure proved unsatisfactory in practice because the passage and enforcement of suitable bye-laws was not made a statutory requirement; the rural areas in particular did not respond adequately to Sandon's measure.

1880 *Mundella's Act:* this measure adopted a more direct approach by requiring all School Boards and School Attendance Committees to pass bye-laws for compulsory attendance and to enforce them. They were to require unconditional attendance from five to ten years, whilst providing exemption arrangements for the ten to thirteen year olds on grounds of proficiency (i.e. reaching a given Standard under the 'payment by results' system) or satisfactory attendance during each of five consecutive years (the so-called 'Dunce's Certificate'). No child could be held at school beyond his fourteenth birthday.

Thus from 1880 compulsory elementary education was a legal reality throughout the country, though it was only gradually that the magistracy and parents were conditioned to accept the new situation. Attendance officers continued to fight an uphill struggle in many areas until the turn of the century and the 'half-time' system (under which the older pupils were allowed special exemption to divide each day between work and school) lingered on in the textile areas until 1918. Meanwhile, the context was thought sufficiently improved to raise the minimum school leaving age permitted under the bye-laws to eleven years (1893) and then to twelve years (1899). But beyond this minimum the age of actual school leaving varied considerably according to the exemption conditions laid down for the district concerned.

(c) Free Tuition

The 1870 Act expected parents to contribute towards the cost of providing their children with elementary education, although in the case of the Board schools an inflated upper limit of 9d per week per child was imposed. However, Section 25 did provide for the remission of fees for necessitous children in both Board and denominational schools, but this became a source of controversy when certain School Boards refused to remit such fees for children in church schools, whilst those Boards dominated by the Anglican interest remitted to these same children on a generous scale. In 1876 the anomalous situation and the bitter controversy surrounding it was resolved by transferring the responsibility for remitting the fees of necessitous children in church schools from the School Boards to the Poor Law Guardians; the price of this move was to attach a social stigma to those parents unable to pay for their children's elementary education at a church school. Meanwhile the payment of school fees bore hard upon many working class parents, especially those with large families suffering from the economic vicissitudes of the Great Depression. By the mid-1880s with compulsory attendance now taking effect, elementary school fees had become a burning issue and the Trades Union Congress demanded their abolition. The London School Board, faced with much truancy and absenteeism, identified the continuance of fees as an obstacle to educational progress. In 1891 the government responded to the growing pressure with an Act which required all school districts to provide within twelve months free places for the children of all parents requiring these. The loss of income sustained by the schools was compensated from central sources by an extra capitation grant of 10s per child per annum; on balance this proved of most advantage to the Board schools where the fees had tended to be lower. Not all working class parents took advantage of the new situation, some preferring to pay fees for the privilege of sending their children to the more respectable or exclusive (e.g. Methodist) elementary schools. By the end of the century one-sixth of the elementary school places were still fee-paying, but no parent was paying such fees without desiring to do so. This residue of elementary school fees was not finally abolished until 1918.

(d) 'Payment by Results'

The 1870 Act accepted the basic principles underlying the Revised Code and even sanctified the system by giving it statutory authority. At the same time, however, Forster's measure made the actual grants payable more generous and thus began the slow and irregular process of liberalising Lowe's creation. The trend was for the Education Department to dilute the former stress on the three Rs and to widen the elementary school curriculum by offering grants for the teaching of other examinable subjects. The 'New Code' of 1871 offered a range of 'specific' subjects to be undertaken by individual children who had reached at least Standard IV in the three Rs; in 1875 various 'class' subjects were made available for the examination of all pupils in Standards II-VI. Thus elementary school children came to be taught English grammar, history, geography, simple science and practical subjects as successive codes widened the range of grant-earning possibilities. Gradually there was a significant shift in the curricula pattern and in the philosophy underlying elementary education which pointed forward to the enlightened Code of 1904. During the 1880s the annual examinations in the three Rs were placed on a sample (one-third minimum) basis, whilst the schools were given the opportunity to earn an additional 'merit' grant for organisation, discipline and general quality. In the mid-1890s Sir George Kekewich, appointed Permanent Secretary to the Education Department in 1889, finally abandoned the 'payment by results' system in favour of a single grant based on attendance and a satisfactory 'general inspection' report. At last the teachers had room for some manoeuvre in terms of curricula and method, whilst the children were delivered from the worst aspects of the mental drudgery promoted by the Revised Code. Meanwhile, the process of liberalisation had been accompanied by a remarkable rise in the Education Department's annual expenditure on elementary education, from less than £1 million in 1870 to over £5 million by the end of the century.

(e) Pioneering Influence of the School Boards

Some of the larger School Boards emerged as pace-setters in the development of elementary education, their claim upon the rates in highly developed urban areas facilitating such a role. In the last quarter of the nineteenth century this progressive minority of public authorities was responsible for various forms of educational advance.

(i) the introduction and expansion of higher-grade elementary education which afforded a secondary-type schooling (with a scientific, technical or commercial bias) for abler working class children who were prepared to stay on beyond the age of twelve. The Sheffield School Board pioneered this development in 1880 and the example was followed by Bradford, Nottingham, Halifax, Manchester, Leeds, Birmingham and London; by the late 1890s there were some seventy higher-grade schools with over 25,000 pupils and many more 'higher tops' in ordinary elementary schools, a development encouraged by the introduction of a new Standard VII in 1882. A trickle of students was even able to reach university by this new avenue of advance;

(ii) the establishment of pupil-teacher centres for the more effective preparation of pupil-teachers for the Queen's Scholarship examinations and training college entry. These centres, the first one of which was established by the Liverpool School Board in 1874, began to afford something approaching a secondary education for teacher trainees undergoing apprenticeship between thirteen and eighteen years of age. This approach for raising the level of the trainee's personal education was adopted by other large School Boards in densely populated urban centres;

(iii) the improvement of teachers' salaries and conditions of service. The larger, progressive School Boards paid certificated teachers more generously, did not tie their salaries to annual examination results and laid down conditions of employment safeguarding them against capricious dismissal or unauthorised extraneous duties (cf. denominational school managers and small rural School Boards);

(iv) the recognition of health, nourishment and disability as matters directly related to the success or failure of elementary schooling. It was the larger, progressive School Boards which pioneered the provision of school meals, school baths and school medical inspection and the development of rate-aided special education for the handicapped, initially for the benefit of blind, deaf and mentally defective children. This pointed the way towards the legislation of the Edwardian era and the general acceptance of a concern for physical welfare as part of the State's responsibility to the younger generation;

(v) the raising of standards in respect of school buildings, the supply of books and equipment and the teacher-pupil ratio, resulting in a much higher *per capita* expenditure than was acceptable to the denominational managers or the small School Boards. Over the years the latter bodies came under increasing pressure from the Education Department to match their standards of provision more closely to those of the pace-setters.

(*f*) Difficulties of the Church Schools

Throughout the School Board era the denominational schools laboured under the disadvantage of having no rate-aid available to them. Once the challenge of the 'period of grace' was passed the Anglican and Roman Catholic communities did not take too kindly to the long-term need for generous subscriptions as the only alternative to rate support. For many denominational schools a vicious circle developed; being short of money, they could not afford to employ the best teachers or provide satisfactory facilities, and this resulted in second rate examination results and reduced central grants, which in turn came full circle to affect adversely the schools' ability to escape this situation. As already shown, the displacement of fees by an extra capitation grant in 1891 was a mixed blessing to the Anglican schools; too many of them lost more in fees than they gained from the new 'fee grant'. Meanwhile, the pace-setting School Boards and the rising demands of the Education Department combined to increase progressively the annual *per capita* cost of elementary education. In the face of this growing financial pressure a considerable number of Anglican schools gave up the struggle and transferred their buildings to the local School Board. Thoroughly alarmed, the churches turned to the Conservative government of Lord Salisbury (elected to office in 1895) and pressed for the extension of rate-aid to their schools. In fact, this long cherished hope was not met until 1902 and the denominational schools had to face another seven years of financial difficulty and deteriorating provision. At the close of the century the Board schools were spending 25% more than their denominational counterparts on the elementary education of each child.

(*g*) Report of the Cross Commission 1888

Sixteen years after the passage of the 1870 Act and amidst the subsequent developments just considered, a Conservative government appointed a Royal Commission under the chairmanship of Lord Cross to investigate the operation of the elementary education acts and to make recommendations for any improvements. Most of the commissioners were past supporters of the voluntary system, with Cardinal Manning, Roman Catholic Archbishop of Westminster, and Dr Temple, Anglican Bishop of London, predictably determined to push the ecclesiastical viewpoint very hard. But some of the commissioners were equally strongly committed to the further development of the School Boards' role and to the limitation of church influence and control in elementary education. Thus the division of opinion in Parliament and the country was sharply reflected in the composition of the Commission; unable to agree upon certain vital matters the commissioners were forced to draw up separate Majority and Minority reports duly signed by two-thirds and one-third of the members respectively. There were three areas of serious disagreement.

(i) *The Religious Issue*

The Majority report stressed the importance of positive religious and moral training for all children and the conviction that parents desired this. Whilst conceding the conscience clause, it recommended the repeal of the Cowper-Temple clause to enable denominational religious teaching to be introduced into the Board schools. The church interest was to be further secured by extending rate-aid to the denominational schools, freeing them from the payment of rates on their premises and giving them an equal right with the School Boards to fill any emergent gaps in provision in their school districts. But these demands were rejected by the Minority report which defended the Cowper-Temple clause and suggested that church schools in financial difficulty should simply surrender themselves to the local School Board. Moreover it also recommended that undenominational schools under public control should be available for every child whose parents desired them; this demand resulted from anti-denominational dissatisfaction with the continuance of many single-school areas in which parents were obliged to send their children to an Anglican school.

(ii) *The Higher-Grade Elementary Schools*

Sympathetic to the complaints of the endowed grammar schools and not well disposed towards the School Boards, the Majority report questioned the legality of the development of rate-supported secondary-type schooling in higher-grade elementary schools. It recommended that the term 'elementary education' as used in recent legislation should be more stringently defined so as to protect the grammar schools and other bona fide secondary institutions from unfair competition. But the Minority report championed the cause of higher-grade elementary education and encouraged the School Boards to expand such provision; it admitted the need to clarify the meaning of elementary education, but only in a way which would recognise and regularise this progressive and worthwhile development.

(iii) *The Pupil-Teacher System*

The Majority report backed its maintenance as the only 'available (and) trustworthy' source of teacher supply, although insisting that pupil-teacher centres and half-time attendance at them should became a standard part of it. The Minority report condemned outright the continuance of 'on the job' training and advised the complete abandonment of the system in favour of extended full-time education for would-be teachers. But such a radical suggestion could only be considered as part of the much larger question of the future of secondary education in England and Wales.

Because of the highly controversial nature of these issues it is not sur-prising that, apart from the development of more pupil-teacher centres, no immediate action was taken in relation to them. The line of least political resistance was to leave things be. But the longer term significance of the Cross Commission can be discerned from the ultimate solutions once these particular nettles were really grasped after the turn of the century. In 1902 the Majority report's recommendations materialised in respect of rate-aid for the church schools and the abolition of the higher-grade elementary schools, whereas in the case of the pupil-teacher system the Board of Education finally applied the solution recommended by the Minority report.

However, the Cross Commissioners did share some common ground as well and recommendations were made which had a greater and more immediate effect than is usually appreciated:

 (i) the 'payment by results' system was sharply criticised and its further relaxation called for in order, amongst other things, to give room for greater curricula attention to science, technical and manual instruction of an elementary sort and for an improvement in the relationship between teachers and H.M. Inspectorate. The Education Department responded with the liberal Code of 1890 and within a decade the wishes of the Commission had been met;

 (ii) the duration of compulsory schooling caused dissatisfaction and the Commission recommended that it should be extended by raising the minimum age at which exemption arrangements could apply. The Acts of 1893 and 1899, already mentioned earlier in this chapter (page 35), were in line with the Commission's desire;

 (iii) the Commission underlined the need for more generous elementary provision in terms of accommodation, playgrounds, books and equipment; this demand was written into the annual Codes of the 1890s although often to the discomfiture of the denominational schools;

 (iv) the need to increase the supply of trained certificated elementary teachers and to raise the standard of training college courses was recognised by the Commission and various means of achieving this were suggested. To supplement the efforts of the forty-odd rather small voluntary colleges already in existence, the Commission recommended the establishment of undenominational day training colleges in association with the universities and university colleges. The latter institutions would provide the academic training whilst special lecturers would be responsible for the principles and practice of education; this would enable prospective elementary teachers to study for a degree whilst undergoing their professional training. In accordance with the latter possibility it was further suggested that some student teachers would benefit from a three-year course of training. By the end of the century there were some sixteen such institutions which pointed the way to the University Education Departments of the future. Indeed, the new day training colleges quickly came to supply a quarter of the trained certificated entrants to elementary teaching (1900). If the Minority commissioners had had their way, day training colleges would have been established under the auspices of the larger School Boards as well as the universities. This was not to be, but the idea later found expression in the municipal training colleges established by the new local education authorities under the 1902 Act.

Thus the report of the Cross Commission, as well as throwing much light on the divisive issues of the School Board era, wielded a quite significant influence upon later developments in elementary education.

Follow-up: Attempt to cover as much of the following ground as possible.

1 Read Bagley, J. J. and A. J. *The State and Education in England and Wales, 1833-1968*, Chapter 2

Dawson, K. and Wall, P. *Society and Industry in the 19th Century: Education*, pp. 28-35

Curtis, S. J. and Boultwood, M. E. *An Introductory History of English Education since 1800*, Chapter 4, pp. 73-79

Barnard, H. C. *A History of English Education from 1760*, Chapters XIII and XIX

2 Consult Maclure, J. S. *Educational Documents: England and Wales 1816-1968;* items 14 and 18 are relevant.

3 Clarify the following: the significance of the 1867 Factory Act, the 1867 Reform Act, the Paris Industrial Exhibition (1867) and the Austro-Prussian war (1866) to the introduction of the 1870 Elementary Education Act; the programme and influence of the Birmingham Education League; the viewpoint and work of W. E. Forster as head of the Education Department 1868-74; the compromise features of the 1870 Act; the precise terms and significance of the Cowper-Temple and timetable conscience clauses; the benefits and limitations of the 1870 Act; the nature of the part-time system of elementary education; the main steps in the progressive relaxation of the 'payment by results' system; the development of the higher-grade elementary schools and pupil-teacher centres; the contribution of the larger, progressive School Boards to elementary educational advance; the nature and extent of the difficulties faced by the denominational schools in the School Board era; the positive results of the work of the Cross Commission.

Chapter Four
Developments in Secondary Education during the Nineteenth Century

Purpose: to describe the extremely unsatisfactory condition of secondary education in the early nineteenth century and to illuminate the painful process by which this field was gradually reformed, reorganised and expanded to meet more adequately the demands of Victorian society and, in particular, the needs of the upper and wealthier middle classes.

Any attempt at a clinical treatment of the present topic is beset by certain difficulties which should be recognised at the outset. Firstly, the term secondary education did not come into general and official use in England and Wales until the close of the century; and secondly, throughout the period concerned there was no clear dividing line, especially in respect of non-classical instruction, between secondary education on the one hand and elementary and technical education on the other. Nevertheless it is convenient and helpful for the historian of nineteenth-century English education to use the term secondary, looking upon such education as that traditionally associated with classical studies and possible entrance to university and increasingly provided on a fee-paying basis for the almost exclusive benefit of the upper and middle classes. This said, the study of the development of secondary education in nineteenth-century England may be divided into two major aspects.

1 The Condition of Secondary Education in the Early Nineteenth Century

Contemporary sources of evidence show that secondary-type educational provision at this time was both inadequate in its extent and generally most unsatisfactory in its substance. However, any further analysis must distinguish between the various and distinct sources of secondary education then available.

(a) Endowed Grammar Schools

There were some six hundred or more of these schools, originally endowed by pious founders for the free education of local inhabitants in the learned languages and still maintaining their traditional connection with the established Church. Whilst the great majority were still only small local

grammar schools, a tiny minority of them, led by the mediaeval foundations of Winchester and Eton, had emerged as national institutions
depending largely on fee-paying boarders drawn from the ranks of the
aristrocracy and gentry; by the beginning of the nineteenth century the
latter were already being referred to as the 'great public schools'.
Authoritative contemporary sources of evidence, both official and
otherwise, are most severe in their strictures of the endowed grammar
schools at this time. The personal investigations of Nicholas Carlisle,
covering almost five hundred of these institutions and leading to the
publication of his *A Concise Description of the Endowed Grammar Schools
in England and Wales* (1818), proved highly unfavourable and his impression was later confirmed by the official inquiries of the Charity
Commission 1818-37. As late as the 1860s the Clarendon and Taunton
Commissions found much ground for serious criticism when they were
called to report upon the schools concerned. Such evidence has been the
basis of the orthodox historical viewpoint that by the early nineteenth
century a hundred years or more of growing neglect and malpractice
had reduced these schools to their lowest ebb in terms of educational
efficiency and public esteem. Only recently has further research provided
reason to question whether the picture was quite as bad as it has been
painted and particularly whether the condition of the schools was the
result of the negligence and cupidity of those entrusted with their functioning rather than the result of overwhelming educational, social and
economic pressures. Whilst space will not permit an elaboration of the
intricacies of this argument, it is possible to affirm the fact that the
endowed grammar schools had suffered a decline during the eighteenth
century and to attempt a balanced analysis of the main *symptoms* and
causes of this decline.

(i) *Inadequate Provision*

Even if the condition of the endowed grammar schools had been sound,
the extent and distribution of provision would have been a weakness.
The rapid growth and shift of population in the age of the Industrial
Revolution aggravated the shortage of such schools and crystallised
their maldistribution. In Tudor times there had been one endowed
grammar school for every six thousand inhabitants; by the early nineteenth century the ratio had deteriorated to one school to every twenty-
four thousand people. Not only had the country's population risen greatly
but the rate at which new endowed grammar schools were founded had
fallen very markedly. The charity school movement which attracted
philanthropic support towards purely elementary education and the
rising demand for non-classical instruction combined to make the

eighteenth century an inauspicious period in the growth of the endowed grammar school system. Meanwhile, most of these schools, founded usually in Tudor or Stuart times, were located in southern market towns, but the growing need for secondary education was in the developing industrial and commercial centres of the north.

(ii) *Unsatisfactory Government*

Falling standards in the social and official life of Hanoverian England, finding particular expression in political corruption and ecclesiastical indifference, reached their height in the later eighteenth century. Since the Restoration the endowed grammar schools had become subject to narrow Anglican control and increasingly reflected the laxity and abuses of the Church. Many trustees, drawn largely from the landed gentry, the established Church and the unreformed municipal corporations, became negligent and irresponsible in the performance of their duties. Some of the schoolmasters, most of whom were Anglican clergymen, were similarly affected. Official investigations into the administration of all charitable endowments as a prelude to Gilbert's Poor Law Act (1786) pointed to considerable irregularity in the management of trust property. The inquiries of Brougham's parliamentary Select Committee (1816-18), following the widening of its terms of reference to include endowed grammar schools, and subsequently of the Charity Commission (1818-37), revealed many flagrant abuses, including the misappropriation of endowment income and the existence of numerous sinecures and pluralist arrangements whereby schoolmasters drew salaries without performing any teaching duties. At the close of the eighteenth century Lord Chief Justice Kenyon, pronouncing upon a legal case concerning one of the endowed grammar schools, thought it fit to comment upon their 'lamentable condition' and to deplore the neglect of everything except the receipt of incomes. In 1812 Parliament finally registered its concern by accepting in principle the need for the inspection and stricter control of charitable endowments.

(iii) *Financial Difficulties*

Inflationary conditions in the later eighteenth century and during the period of the French wars subjected the endowed schools to pressure in two ways. Firstly, many schools on small fixed endowments faced a heavy and continuing fall in the real value of their annual income. At the turn of the century only a dozen schools enjoyed an endowment income of over £1,000; some 60% of them were endowed to the extent of only £100 or less which was hardly sufficient to pay a satisfactory stipend to the master. Secondly, given the rise in the age of university entry since Tudor times (i.e. from 15-16 years to 18-19 years), inflation gnawed at the ability and willingness of the parents of potential foundationers (i.e. those receiving free education) to afford their sons a full grammar education. Thus many schools were faced with a choice between the continuance of their classical tradition and the maintenance of their charitable function. Various results flowed from this unhappy conflict. To continue as a classical school usually involved the introduction of entry fees and extra charges for 'free' foundationers and increasing resort to the attraction of fee-payers (often boarders from further afield) to the neglect of free scholars. To maintain the charitable function often meant the acceptance of dilapidated buildings, inadequate books and equipment and serious understaffing. Sometimes for the sheer lack of local classical scholars a free grammar school would be degraded to the position of an endowed elementary school in which new capacity it would carry on its charitable role.

(iv) *Outdated Curricula*

As late as the early nineteenth century the bulk of the endowed grammar schools had failed to widen and modernise their curriculum which had originated in the Renaissance and which was based on the teaching of Latin and Greek supported by religious worship and instruction acceptable to the Anglican Church. Even the study of the learned languages had been reduced to an arid exercise in grammar and syntax, with far too little concern for the much greater educational benefits to be derived from an exploration and understanding of the life, thought and times of ancient Greece and Rome. Although many of the small number of new eighteenth-century foundations provided for English as well as classical studies and a minority of the older schools did introduce such subjects as mathematics, French, history and geography, well over two-thirds of the existing endowed grammar schools had undergone no curricula change. And at the beginning of the nineteenth century, in spite of the growing demand for a more modern and useful curriculum, any attempts to alter the situation still faced serious obstacles. Few of the schoolmasters serving the endowed grammar schools were either qualified or prepared to make the necessary adjustments. Secured in many cases by a freehold tenure of office which protected them from dismissal, and able to make a satisfactory living from the endowment salary and receipts from fee-payers, they had no interest in pioneering or accepting change. The majority were content to ignore the demands of both trustees and local parents in the knowledge that the foundation deeds usually justified such a stand and that they would be upheld in the Court of Chancery. Indeed the progressive trustees of Leeds Grammar School, who were interested in pushing curricula reform against the opposition of the schoolmaster, had their efforts stymied by the Eldon judgement of 1805 which pronounced it illegal to switch an endowment to the support of purposes other than those laid down in the founder's trust deeds. As the grammar school was defined as an institution 'for teaching grammatically the learned languages', this decision did much to bolster the position of the classics and their defenders. Even the Grammar School Act (1840), ostensibly designed to encourage and facilitate curricula change by the trustees, was so riddled with provisos that its impact was very limited. Thus the law served to support the conservative stand adopted by the schoolmasters. What curricula reform was achieved in the endowed grammar schools at this time took place on a very narrow front as a result of introducing other subjects as extras requiring additional fees, which usually denied them to the free scholars. Where such change occurred the additions were more likely to be elementary than modern subjects. The main business of the endowed grammar schools remained the teaching of the classics.

(v) Low Moral Tone

The ethos of many of these institutions was very unsatisfactory, being at its worst in the public schools and those few local grammar schools with a significant number of boarders. The boarding arrangements were characterised by scanty food and rough living. The system of fagging and the universal bullying ensured that all pupils in the public schools began as slaves and ended up as tyrants. A contemporary critic described these schools as a 'system of premature debauchery' which provided an early initiation into aristocratic insensitivity and vice. Shortage of staff left dormitory life virtually unsupervised and senior pupils took to drinking, gambling, cruel amusements, homosexuality and even association with prostitutes. There was little or no provision made for the boys' free time, organised games still being a thing of the future; outside classroom and dormitory fighting and blood sports were the main physical outlets. The headmaster's authority was maintained by means of terror and certain heads became renowned floggers. Most memorable was Dr Keate, headmaster of Eton 1809-34, around whom many legends grew. It was said that on one occasion he flogged a batch of Confirmation candidates because the list of names was submitted on a sheet of paper very similar to the usual punishment slips! In his sixtieth year Keate still found the energy to flog eighty boys in one day. The serious understaffing is the main explanation of this resort to such punitive discipline; at Eton there were only nine masters to almost six hundred pupils and sometimes Keate himself took control of one-third of these in the upper schoolroom. Of course the boys did not take kindly to such régimes and mounted several serious rebellions against authority in the late eighteenth and early nineteenth centuries. In 1797 Dr Inglis, then headmaster of Rugby and endearingly called the 'Black Tiger' by his pupils, had his study door blown off with gunpowder and only the reading of the Riot Act and the appearance of the military cowed the young insurgents. An outburst at Eton in 1818 persuaded even Keate to vacate the premises whilst his charges took a sledgehammer to his fine oaken desk! Winchester was recurrently affected by serious disturbances, a rising there in the same year requiring the intervention of soldiers armed with fixed bayonets before order was restored. Both pupils and masters regarded each other as natural enemies and acted accordingly; Keate expected all his pupils to lie to him and they rarely disappointed him in this respect. Clearly these institutions had their own corporate character and were described by Gladstone, one of their contemporary products, as 'the greatest pagan schools in Christendom'. Yet ironically many of the great statesmen of the age passed through these public schools and survived all their educational deficiencies; surely they emerged as national figures in spite of their schooling rather than because of it. Happily the majority of the endowed grammar schools, not being boarding institutions, did not have this problem to exacerbate their other shortcomings.

(b) Private Institutions and Means

The characteristic features of the endowed grammar and public schools were hardly calculated to recommend them to the rising middle class with its strong Nonconformist element or to the more discriminating families of the upper class. The result was an increasing resort to other means of obtaining a satisfactory secondary education.

(i) Private Tutors

A growing number of the aristocracy and wealthier gentry hired private residential tutors to teach their sons, whose education was sometimes rounded off by a grand tour of Europe. Middle class parents took to sharing the services of a private visiting tutor. In both cases these private tutors tended to give their charges a more modern and broader education than was available in the old grammar schools and the ancient universities.

(ii) Private Classical Schools

Usually run by Anglican clergymen for fee-paying pupils and sometimes including boarders, these small schools still placed the classical languages at the centre of the curriculum, but attracted the support of the gentry and professional people because of their respectable atmosphere, satisfactory boarding arrangements, somewhat wider curricula and greater teaching efficiency. Some two hundred such schools were in existence at the turn of the century.

(iii) *Private Academies and Schools*

By the early nineteenth century there were thousands of non-classical institutions of every size, kind and quality aspiring to provide secondary-type education for the emerging middle classes. Anglican domination of the endowed grammar and private classical schools as well as the ancient universities had produced the Dissenting academies of the eighteenth century; pioneering the widening and modernising of the traditional curricula, they provided the best secondary and higher education then available, but were in sharp decline by the early nineteenth century. Their progressive spirit had been passed on to the private academies offering an encyclopaedic range of subjects to the older student and the ubiquitous private schools providing a more practical education for the sons of merchants, manufacturers and superior tradesmen. Both types of institution were run by private individuals for profit although some of the private schools were founded and supported by particular religious sects. The Quakers, Methodists and Presbyterians, particularly active and prosperous in the field of business and industry, developed a small number of exclusive private schools, sometimes with boarding arrangements, which educated men like John Bright and others destined to play a significant role in the future public and economic life of the country. It was the private schools which supported the few educational experiments of the time: particularly noteworthy in this respect was the Hazelwood School in Birmingham run by the Hill family, with its wide curricula, main and optional subjects, progressive teaching methods based on the spirit of emulation and pupil self-government in matters of discipline and control. The common elements which distinguished the majority of private schools from their endowed grammar counterparts were the close supervision of pupils and the teaching of non-classical subjects. These were the features which attracted the middle classes to the financial support of such schools. But the private schools of the early nineteenth century had serious shortcomings. Depending on individual enterprise they were ephemeral in nature and strongly subject to profit motives rather than educational considerations in their development. Too many were conducted on a small scale in poor accommodation and with inadequate equipment. Those trying to attract the support of the lower ranks of the middle class gave a very limited education which was hardly superior to an elementary schooling. Even in the better schools there was no clear conception of how to develop non-classical secondary education. It was all very well to condemn classical studies and exalt useful and practical subjects, but it was a much more difficult matter to develop the teaching of the latter in a way that was educationally beneficial. At this time the approach was usually a barren catechetical one based on rote-learning and teacher questioning. In defending their own position the supporters of classical studies made the most of this palpable weakness.

(c) Secondary Education for Girls

This was provided on a limited but expanding scale for the daughters of upper and middle class parents by means of private governesses or private academies and schools of variable exclusiveness. Girls were debarred from the endowed grammar and public schools and there was no attempt to develop their intellect through the classics for their intelligence was considered inferior anyway. For the more socially distinguished there were very expensive boarding establishments in such places as Brighton; here young ladies would remain until about the age of eighteen preparing themselves for entry into Regency society. The main concern was for those female accomplishments considered important for the marriage market—dancing, singing, instrumental music, deportment, embroidery, painting, French, Italian and German. This was combined with a smattering of general knowledge obtained from catechisms of historical and geographical facts and some English and arithmetic. Time was allocated in inverse proportion to the educational importance of the subject and everything was pursued at a shallow level. In the towns there were cheaper day schools to serve the needs of the lower middle class whose daughters would leave at fourteen or thereabouts. Here the emphasis was on teaching the girls reading and writing, plain needlework and some arithmetic; beyond this they might use various catechisms to acquire a superficial knowledge of English grammar, history, geography and even science. Many such establishments were inferior to the better elementary schools. Of course, no real improvement was likely until the restrictive attitude towards female education was changed. But early feminists like the author Mary Wollstonecroft, who demanded a new approach to female education, were simply dismissed as eccentrics.

2 Reform, Reorganisation and Expansion

The middle years of the nineteenth century saw the endowed grammar and public schools facing growing criticism from various quarters. The utilitarians, hostile to the maintenance of outmoded practices and traditional institutions which no longer served the needs of contemporary society, condemned their useless curriculum. Supporters of the 'scientific movement' were particularly disgruntled at their almost total neglect of the natural sciences. The Evangelicals deplored the low moral tone and lack of Christian ethos displayed by some of them. The rising middle classes with their business interests and background demanded value for money in terms of educational relevance and efficiency. As the wealthy manufacturers sank their differences with the landed interest to form a composite upper-middle class, the rehabilitation of the public schools as a bulwark to their social supremacy became a matter of urgency. Meanwhile, the less wealthy elements of the middle class looked to the rejuvenation and transformation of the endowed grammar schools as a means of securing their social position in relation to that of the lower orders of society. The resultant developments were inevitably calculated to remove free scholars from the schools concerned and to make secondary education the exclusive preserve of the well-to-do, leaving the working classes with only elementary education available to them.

(a) Reform of the Public Schools

By the close of the century the upper-middle class had a considerable number of reputable and expensive public boarding schools available to them. Brought into close association by the Headmasters' Conference (established in 1869), these independent schools enjoyed a strong connection with Oxford and Cambridge with which they combined to educate and character-train the social *élite* of late Victorian times. The rehabilitation and expansion of the public school system hinged upon several developments.

(i) *Reforming Headmasters*

Internal changes in the public schools were largely the result of the efforts and example of a growing number of reforming headmasters. The beginnings of such influence can be seen in the work of Samuel Butler at Shrewsbury (1793-1836) and Charles Butler at Harrow (1805-29). It was critically advanced by the headmastership of Thomas Arnold at Rugby (1828-42) who made his school the generally accepted model for reform. In the middle years of the century it blossomed in the work of Hawtrey at Eton (1834-52), Kennedy at Shrewsbury (1836-66), Vaughan at Harrow (1845-59) and Cotton at Marlborough (1851-8). Later on, the cause of internal reform centred upon the outstanding contribution and influence of Edward Thring of Uppingham (1853-87). Gradually the material standards of provision were raised to afford a more favourable physical environment for the life of the schools. Helped by the reform of the old universities during the 1850s it was possible to improve staffing quality and ratios so as to secure more efficient teaching and supervision. A less arid approach to the teaching of the classics and some widening of the curriculum developed, although advance in these respects was rather limited before the report of the Clarendon Commission (1864). Most important, however, was the marked improvement in the moral tone of the public schools; the reforming headmasters effectively used the school chapel and the prefect system as a means of diffusing Christian values and responsible attitudes amongst the pupils.

Although the Arnold 'myth' (the idea that the reform of the public schools in the nineteenth century was the work of one outstanding man) is no longer tenable, his personal influence was very great and in some respects even critical to the future of the public schools. It is true that one of his predecessors at Rugby had done much to improve the buildings and accommodation of the school, but its atmosphere remained tyrannic and amoral and it was left to Arnold to transform Rugby into the ideal to be followed by countless numbers of future public school headmasters and teachers. His process of reformation, conducted in a highly impressionist fashion, was characterised by several noteworthy features. Firstly, he placed his trust in the Christian faith and a liberal culture as the foundation stones of a satisfactory education: the school chapel services and his own sermons, the study of the classics and the humanities were all central to life and work at Rugby where the aim was to produce Christian gentlemen. Secondly, he brought about a radical improvement of the school's internal organisation with particular emphasis upon ensuring more effective supervision of pupils; to this end he raised the staffing ratio on the basis of full-time residential appointments, arranged for smaller dormitories and a more civilised fagging system and developed a strong sense of mutual trust and respect between himself and the senior pupils to support the operation of a proselytising prefect system. Finally, he developed a wider curriculum with history, choir singing and organised games achieving a prominent place; the study of classics was revitalised by using them as a vehicle for the teaching of ancient history, literature, philosophy, politics and geography as well as the Latin and Greek languages. The impact of the Arnold tradition was initially strongest in the new public schools and only later began seriously to affect the older ones. From the public schools his reforming influence finally spread to the endowed grammar schools once they received a new lease of life from the work of the Taunton Commission (1864-8). His influence did much to restore public confidence in the traditional secondary institutions and his broad Christianity encouraged a growing number of wealthy Nonconformists to support them.

(ii) *Clarendon Commission 1861-4*

The rehabilitation of the public schools was also helped by the work and influence of the Clarendon Commission 1861-4, appointed to investigate the condition of the nine 'great' public schools. In spite of the positive lead given by Arnold, the situation was recognised as still unsatisfactory with Westminster and Charterhouse suffering continued decline. Although the criticisms and recommendations made by Lord Clarendon and his colleagues were rather muted, the Commission's report did result in certain limited improvements. Firstly, it led to the reform of the governing bodies to ensure a broader membership and more professional responsibility; hitherto their pursuance of pecuniary and clerical interests had been a serious source of weakness in the running of these schools. The need for such reform received the statutory backing of the Public Schools Act (1868) which established a small commission to undertake the task. But once reformed the governing bodies were to be trusted to proceed with other reforms without any further State interference. Secondly, the report led to a gradual broadening, though not a transformation, of the traditional curriculum. The classics remained the core, consuming over half of the teaching time, but their treatment was revitalised in 'Arnold fashion'. Beyond this, increasing importance was attached to the study of subsidiary subjects such as English, modern languages, mathematics and science. This was in line with the Prussian gymnasium programme recommended by the report and did something to dilute the traditional dominance of Latin and Greek in these schools. Thirdly, the report resulted in the reform of the foundation statutes so as to remove anachronistic restrictions upon the use of endowment funds; but the most important single result of this was to abolish the right of children of local inhabitants to enjoy a free education at these institutions in favour of open competition for fee-paying places. As very few scholarships were offered in lieu of the foundation places lost, this development was in line with the Clarendon Commission's expressed desire to rehabilitate these schools for the exclusive benefit of the upper-middle class.

(iii) *Rise of New Public Schools*

These schools, based on the reformed model, made a major contribution to the process of rehabilitating and expanding the system. These new public schools emerged during the middle and later years of the nineteenth century in one of two ways. In the 1830s the wealthier and more discriminating elements of the middle class had supported the development of proprietary day schools characterised by an absence of religious teaching, a wide and modern curricula, optional subjects and a respectable ethos. The prototypes, such as Liverpool Institute (1825) and University

College School, London (1828), were very successful and the movement spread. With the coming of the railways the next stage was to use joint-stock enterprise to develop proprietary boarding schools to meet the growing demands of the same clientele. The result was the establishment of Cheltenham (1841), Marlborough (1843), Rossall (1844), Wellington (1853), Epsom (1855), Clifton (1860), Malvern (1862), Haileybury (1864) and Bath (1867). Contemporaneously the Woodard Foundation, associated with the Anglican church, set up middle class boarding schools at Lancing, Hurstpierpoint and Ardingly. Whilst modelling themselves in many respects upon Arnold's Rugby, these new schools were more progressive in their approach to the curriculum. They aimed at providing an efficient education for professional and business careers at a time when more exacting entry requirements were being demanded for careers in the civil service, the army, medicine and the law. At Rossall non-classical courses were organised from an early date with particular professional destinations in mind. In most of these schools, whilst Latin was retained, Greek was usually omitted from the curriculum. Such was the movement which by the end of the century had added considerably, both quantitatively and qualitatively, to the public school system. The other source of expansion was the aspiring endowed grammar schools some of which, assisted by the aftermath of the Taunton Commission report (1868), gradually broke their links with their own locality and emerged as boarding schools enjoying a national reputation. Once they obtained membership of the Headmasters' Conference these endowed grammar schools became part of the public school system. Edward Thring transformed Uppingham in this way and Repton, Sherborne and Tonbridge are other good examples of such translation.

The continued growth of the upper-middle class with its social sensitivity, the coming of the railways giving easy access to the countryside and the growth of the Empire resulting in many well-to-do parents living abroad combined to ensure that the reform and expansion of the public school system could and would be taken full advantage of.

(b) Reform of the Endowed Grammar Schools

It was not until the last quarter of the century that the provision of secondary education for the lesser-middle class and more prosperous skilled artisans took a distinct turn for the better. Aware of continuing failure to meet the needs of this important section of the population, the government appointed the *Taunton Commission 1864-8* to investigate the situation fully. Nearly eight hundred endowed schools and over one hundred private and proprietary schools were visited, resulting in an extremely thorough report and many far-sighted *recommendations:*

(i) the establishment of a national system of secondary education based on a proper administrative framework which would include a central agency and a number of provincial authorities. Within this co-ordinative framework individual schools would retain their own governors with responsibility for appointing the headmaster, managing the finances and determining the curricula;

(ii) the differentiation of the schools into three categories (first, second and third grades) according to the existing socio-economic divisions within the middle class. The school fees, the school leaving age (eighteen, sixteen and fourteen respectively) and the curricula would vary according to category. It was emphasised that the greatest need was for third grade secondary schools to serve the lower-middle class and skilled artisans;

(iii) the need to rationalise the use of educational endowments to improve provision, to change trust deeds where they inhibited reform and to reform governing bodies as a means of infusing new life into the schools. Within this context the report recognised the particular need to extend and transform the provision of secondary education for girls;

(iv) the introduction of a 'scholastic register' for competent secondary teachers and of a national system of examinations for secondary pupils. Both these recommendations were designed to improve the efficiency of teaching and to check the dilution of the profession and the proliferation of local examinations.

If the Taunton recommendations had been implemented in their entirety, England would have obtained a national system of secondary education some thirty odd years before it was actually launched. Perhaps unhappily the stiff opposition of the headmasters (led by Thring) to any form of State interference in the secondary field received political support from the ranks of the Tory party. Given the Gladstone government's pre-occupation with elementary education, this ensured that the immediate results of the Taunton Report were meagre and disappointing. But, in an unspectacular way, it wielded a slow reformative influence right down to the end of the century and thus in the longer term produced a number of significant *results*.

(i) The Endowed Schools Act (1869) authorised the long and painful process by which the Endowed Schools Commission (1869-74) and later the Charity Commission (1874-99) reformed and redistributed the educational endowments and reconstituted the governing bodies of the endowed grammar schools. The result was to strengthen the financial base of the schools and to exert some indirect influence in favour of a wider curricula and more efficient teaching.

C

(ii) the redrafting of trust deeds facilitated the alienation of the grammar schools from their original purpose (i.e. the free education of children of local inhabitants). Whilst the Commissioners' schemes made provision for a small number of scholarships, the existing foundation places were scrapped and even endowments for elementary education were transferred to the local grammar school. This whole process was extremely unfavourable to the working class but was slowly driven to its conclusion in spite of protests. It secured the endowed grammar schools as a source of subsidised secondary education for the middle class and enabled a minority of them to pass into the public school system.

(iii) The Taunton emphasis on the need for third grade secondary schools and the possibility of granting some form of public financial aid to them helps to explain two important developments in the later nineteenth century. Firstly, the rise of higher-grade elementary education by which the larger, more progressive School Boards provided a secondary-type schooling at low cost was in tune with the Taunton idea. Secondly, an increasing amount of financial help from public sources was made available to the endowed grammar schools. At the price of widening their curriculum they were able to earn grants from the Department of Science and Art for the teaching of science, technical and modern subjects and to obtain funds from the new Technical Instruction Committees empowered after 1889 to dispense rate-aid for the support of local technical and secondary education.

(iv) The influence of the Taunton Commission made a major contribution to the improvement and extension of secondary provision for girls. Miss Frances Mary Buss at North London Collegiate School (1850) and Miss Dorothea Beale at Cheltenham Ladies' College (1853) had already emerged as pioneers in the field and both were able to impress the Commission with their evidence. Thus the needs of middle class female secondary education received considerable attention in the Report and in the years that followed real advance took place. In redistributing endowments the Endowed Schools Commissioners and the Charity Commissioners were authorised and encouraged to use any surplus funds for the establishment of new endowed grammar schools for girls. Bradford Girls' Grammar School and Leeds Girls' High School were two of the earliest such foundations and by the close of the century over eighty were in existence. But this process was a slow one, leaving much room for supplementation by private enterprise. In 1872 another pioneer, Mrs Maria Grey, enthused by the concern shown by the Taunton

Commission, founded the Girls' Public Day School Trust on a joint-stock basis. Over the succeeding quarter-century this body was responsible for the establishment of nearly forty reputable girls' secondary schools in London and the main provincial towns. After 1883 similar efforts to promote secondary education for girls were made by the Church Schools Company, although the number of new schools resulting was much smaller. In all these new foundations the old emphasis on female accomplishments gave way to the more 'solid instruction' recommended by the Taunton Commission; although the curriculum was modelled on that of the boys' grammar schools, the tendency was for the new girls' schools to adopt a more markedly modern approach. Indeed by the close of the century the girls' schools were setting the example in the development of new teaching methods and the recognition of the importance of professional training as a complement to academic knowledge.

By 1900 the condition of the public and endowed grammar schools had certainly improved, even though the lower classes (the sons of skilled artisans excepted perhaps) were now virtually denied entry to them. Girls' secondary education had benefited from a remarkable improvement during the last quarter of the century. But, failing the full implementation of the Taunton Commission recommendations, Britain still did not have a national system of secondary education resting on a proper administrative framework, nor, in an increasingly competitive world, was the extent of the provision adequate to meet the socio-economic needs of the time. Any decisive intervention by the State had been successfully resisted by those interested in protecting the public and endowed grammar schools from any real measure of public control. Matthew Arnold's repeated exhortation, 'Organise your secondary education', had not been met and this contributed very greatly to the administrative muddle in English education as a whole which had become intolerable by the 1890s. Meanwhile the Welsh Intermediate Act (1889), which did so much to organise and support a State system of secondary education in the principality, served to underline the need for further radical measures in England. All this led to the report of the Bryce Commission on *Secondary Education* (1895) which set the stage for the 1902 Education Act and the subsequent development of State secondary schools in England.

Follow-up: Attempt to cover as much of the following ground as possible.
1 Read   Bagley, J. J. and A. J. *The State and Education in England and Wales: 1833-1968*, Chapter 3

Dawson, K. and Wall, P. *Society and Industry in the 19th Century: Education*, pp. 35-41

Curtis, S. J. and Boultwood, M. E. *An Introductory History of English Education since 1800*, Chapter 1, pp. 13-20, and Chapter 5, pp. 80-103

Barnard, H. C. *A History of English Education from 1760*, Chapters II, VIII and XV

2 *Consult* Maclure, J. S. *Educational Documents: England and Wales 1816-1968;* items 12 and 13 are relevant.

3 *Clarify the following: the distinctions and differences between the various institutions offering a secondary education at the opening of the nineteenth century; the major shortcomings of the public and endowed grammar schools in the early nineteenth century; the contribution of Thomas Arnold's influence and the work of the Clarendon Commission to the reform of the public schools; the recommendations and actual results of the Taunton Commission; the nature and extent of the improvement in secondary education for girls during the nineteenth century; the condition and pattern of secondary educational provision at the close of the nineteenth century.*

Chapter Five
The Forging of a National System of Education: the 1902 Act

Purpose: to identify the influences and developments underlying the foundation of a really national system of education for England and Wales at the turn of the century and to underline the critical importance of the 1902 Education Act in the changes that took place.

Any attempt at a thorough understanding of why and how a national system of education was at last forged for England and Wales must rest on a satisfactory knowledge of the quarter-century which preceded the outbreak of the First World War (1914-18). Within this context the origins, the provisions and the results of the 1902 Education Act must be subjected to particular examination. The relevant subject matter may be considered in four main parts.

1 The Need for a National System

The need for a national system and hence for decisive legislative action had become a very pressing one by the close of the nineteenth century. That this need was increasingly recognised and supported by a growing consensus of influential opinion has various explanations.

(a) Administrative Muddle

The piecemeal development of State interest and involvement in education had produced a multiplicity of largely separate and unco-ordinated agencies working in the field. Central administrative responsibilities were wielded by the Education Department, the Department of Science and Art and the Charity Commission. Local administrative responsibilities were in the hands of the School Boards, the School Attendance Committees, the Technical Instruction Committees of the new County and County Borough Councils, the governors of the public and endowed grammar schools, and the managers of the voluntary elementary schools. As their respective spheres of responsibility had not been clearly defined the result was overlap, confusion and conflict. The need was for rationalisation aimed at the establishment of a single central department and a single type of local authority which could ensure co-ordination and efficient provision throughout the whole educational field and provide a satis-factory administrative foundation for the development of a national system of education.

(b) Position of the Voluntary Schools

This gave rise to increasing concern as the financial and administrative implications of the 1870 Act for these schools became clear. Denied the advantage of rate-aid the voluntary schools were hard-pressed to maintain the minimal rising standards of elementary provision: by the mid 1890s the Anglican Church claimed that for want of money the very survival of its schools was at stake. As the denominational schools were right outside the jurisdiction of the School Boards, the central government had continued to maintain direct administrative contact with their voluntary managers; by the end of the century there were over fourteen thousand such managing bodies for the over-worked Education Department to deal with and it had become an intolerable burden only margin-ally eased by the end of the 'payment by results' system. The need was to end or mend the dual system, the choice depending on one's attitude to the denominational schools as such. Whilst the Tory party and the Anglican and Roman Catholic Churches pressed for a new deal for the voluntary schools, the Liberals supported by the working class movement and the Nonconformists were unsympathetic and disposed to resist any attempt by the State to rescue them from their financial difficulties.

(c) Inadequacy of Secondary and Technical Educational Provision

The first sure signs of a threat to Britain's industrial supremacy had appeared at the Paris Industrial Exhibition of 1867, since when the growth of foreign competition and the comparative decline of British economic strength had given cause for growing alarm. Slowly but surely it was recognised that Britain's main commercial rivals, such as modern Germany, were equipped with superior systems of secondary and technical education. Various official investigating bodies and widely travelled individuals like Matthew Arnold insisted that our industrial and commercial future would remain increasingly vulnerable until such time as higher education was organised and expanded. Meanwhile the pupil-teacher system was being subjected to growing criticism because of its failure to provide prospective elementary teachers with a satisfactory level of personal education; Robert Morant and many others were con-vinced that the only proper solution was for the State to abandon the old system and provide a secondary education for those concerned. Another recognised weakness was the insufficiency of training college places resulting from the long-established reliance upon voluntary initiative in this field; the argument in favour of developing a system of State training colleges had become too strong to be denied any longer. Thus for one reason and another there was a need for much more vigorous and systematic State involvement in the 'other than elementary' field of education.

(d) Mounting Opposition to the School Boards

Whilst many of the small rural School Boards had proved inefficient and a source of embarrassment to the Education Department, the larger, progressive School Boards had aroused the growing hostility of the denominational interests, the endowed grammar schools and the new Technical Instruction Committees. To the sharp mind of Robert Morant, a rising professional administrator at Whitehall, the *ad hoc* School Boards were a serious obstacle to administrative efficiency and the creation of a national system of education. They did not cover the whole country and were not designed to undertake responsibility for the whole field of education. Worse still perhaps, they had become the objects of bitter political and religious conflict and as such were no longer calculated to serve the best interests of education. The new County and County Borough Councils seemed to offer a much sounder basis for the development of effective educational administration and provision on a broadening front at the local level.

2 Towards the 1902 Education Act

At the close of the nineteenth century a number of significant and successive developments combined to set the stage for the Balfour Act of 1902.

(a) 1888 Local Government Act

This established the multi-purpose County and County Borough Councils which were destined to become the vital base of a national system of education in England and Wales. In the following year the Technical Instruction Act took advantage of the new local government framework to project local rate-aid into the provision and support of technical education. By the late 1890s many of the resultant Technical Instruction Committees were widening their role to develop a growing interest in secondary education as well.

(b) 1889 Welsh Intermediate Act

This was the delayed result of the Aberdare report on *Intermediate and Higher Education in Wales* (1881) which had revealed the lamentable state of Welsh secondary education. Much worse off than England for endowed grammar schools, the strong Nonconformist community in Wales was disinclined to use them anyway because of their established Church connection; nor were there many reputable proprietary secondary schools available to fill the gap. The Act created joint education committees in each county and county borough of the Principality for the development of secondary and technical education. Rate-aid support was to be matched by treasury grants (subject to inspection) and supplemented by existing endowments. Within six months the Act was being effectively applied and at a later stage the Central Welsh Board (1896) emerged to co-ordinate the work and to undertake responsibility for inspection. The success of these measures pointed the way towards a similar rationalisation of English secondary education.

(c) 1893 Annual Code

This new code radically altered the existing regulations for evening class work undertaken by the School Boards. By removing the previous limitations on age and subject content, A. H. Acland, then Vice-President at the Education Department, allowed the School Boards to provide post-elementary evening instruction; this development was not welcomed by the endowed grammar schools or the new Technical Instruction Committees as it was seen as a threat to their preserve. Thus another source of administrative conflict and of hostility to the School Boards emerged.

(d) 1895 Report of the Bryce Commission

Although its terms of reference were limited to the field of secondary education, this Report inevitably concerned itself with the total administrative context and its recommendations and results accordingly assumed a wider significance. Whilst acknowledging the improvements which had taken place since 1868, the Report regretted the failure to implement fully the suggestions of the Taunton Commission. In order to establish 'a well-organised system of secondary education in England' the Bryce Commission made a number of far-reaching *recommendations:*

(i) the merging of the three separate central agencies into a single Ministry of Education to overlook the whole field of State education. To cushion national educational development from the vicissitudes and effects of party politics, it was further suggested that the Minister should be advised and assisted by a strong Educational Council of professional and independent members. The Minister himself would be responsible to Parliament for general policy and administrative control;

(ii) the nomination of the County and County Borough Councils as local authorities responsible for the development of secondary education. Although the majority assumed that the School Boards would remain responsible for elementary education, some of the commissioners favoured their abolition so as to allow the new multipurpose authorities to assume local responsibility for all types of education;

(iii) the expansion of secondary education by granting wide powers to the new local authorities to 'supply, maintain and aid' appropriate schools. Backed by rate-aid (2d in the £) and treasury grants, they were to develop and supervise an adequate system of secondary education for the needs of their respective areas. Although fees were certainly to be retained to help defray the considerable cost, it was recommended that there should be an 'adequate supply of scholarships' to provide an educational ladder for exceptionally able elementary schoolchildren;

(iv) the improvement of secondary education through the extension and rationalisation of external examinations for secondary pupils, the encouragement of professional training for secondary teachers and the introduction of a register of teachers to control the quality of staffing. It was further suggested that all secondary schools, including those remaining independent of public financial aid, should be subject to local recognition and central inspection.

Although its immediate implementation did not occur, the Bryce Commission Report was well-received and its recommendations proved a major influence upon the legislative action taken at the turn of the century.

(e) 1895 Return of the Tories to Power

With the Liberal party seriously weakened by Gladstone's retirement and its internal dissensions over Irish Home Rule and imperialism, Lord Salisbury's decisive electoral victory in 1895 was the prelude to a decade of uninterrupted Conservative rule at Westminster, a context which proved favourable for the Church interests and threatening for the School Boards. The Tories were committed to saving the denominational schools but were highly conscious of the explosive situation which would result from any attempt to rescue them from their difficulties or to cut the School Boards down to size. Thus there was much to be said for trying to cloud the critical issues by combining changes in the operation of the dual system with wider administrative reforms and provision for the expansion of secondary education. If the latter two issues could be used to engineer the abolition of the School Boards and the extension of rate-aid to the voluntary schools so much the better. But the tactical execution of this strategy was to prove a complex and difficult matter.

(f) 1896 Gorst's Education Bill

Sir John Gorst, the new Vice-President of the Council and Head of the Education Department, introduced a measure calculated to truncate and erode the influence of the School Boards in favour of the multi-purpose County and County Borough authorities and to strengthen the financial and denominational position of the Anglican interest in elementary education. Although he did not dare to provide for the outright abolition of the School Boards or for the extension of rate-aid to the voluntary schools, the Bill nevertheless foundered on the opposition of Tory members from municipal boroughs which did not welcome any increase in the power of the county authorities and on the horrified reaction of the Nonconformists to the repeal of the Cowper-Temple clause to facilitate denominational teaching in the Board schools. The controversial Bill was finally withdrawn and the Salisbury government forced to think again: in the following year it was content to increase central grants to the voluntary schools and to any 'necessitous' Board schools. But this was recognised as a temporary expedient and the future of the church schools remained uncertain.

(g) 1899 Board of Education Act

As educational reform at the local level and the modification of the dual system posed so many thorny problems, the line of least resistance was to deal with the administrative muddle at the central level. Based on the Bryce recommendations, the Board of Education Act (1899) provided for two significant developments:
  (i) the displacement of the Education Department, the Department of Science and Art and the Charity Commission by a single Board of Education commissioned with 'the superintendence of educational development in England and Wales';
  (ii) the establishment of an associated Consultative Committee to advise the new Board upon any educational matter referred to it.
Although the Act was criticised for not giving exact expression to the Bryce recommendations for an orthodox Ministry and a strong Educational Council, the measure did rationalise the situation at the central level and resulted in the pressures for reform at the local level becoming even more insistent.

(h) 1900 The Cockerton Judgement

Having identified the continued existence of the School Boards as the most serious obstacle to thorough-going administrative reform, Robert

Morant shrewdly judged that these bodies were more vulnerable to legal attack than to direct political assault. Established under the 1870 Act the School Boards had been empowered to use rate-aid for elementary education purposes; it followed that their support of secondary-type instruction in the higher-grade schools and more advanced evening classes was questionable in law. The Cross Commission (1888) had already alluded to this possibility and Morant determined to capitalise upon it. Assured of Gorst's unofficial support, he surreptitiously encouraged the London Technical Education Board to challenge the legal rights of the London School Board in respect of its rate-aided post-elementary provision. The result was the Cockerton judgement, in which the local government auditor so-named surcharged the London School Board with the amount spent from the rates on higher-grade schooling. Two subsequent appeals against this decision were turned down in the courts; worse still, the court decisions declared against the use of rate-aid for evening continuation classes as well as higher-grade schools. Although the presiding judges recognised the blurred limits of elementary education, their final pronouncements were tantamount to a legal condemnation of the position taken up by the larger, progressive School Boards. Given the illegality of the existing situation an emergency Act was quickly passed in 1901, authorising such Boards to continue their work under the auspices of the County and County Borough Councils until such time as the anomalous position had been thoroughly reviewed and dealt with. Whilst Gorst further reduced his declining political stature by hastily drafting an inadequate Bill, his private secretary, Morant, cultivated the friendship of the future prime minister Arthur Balfour and prepared the ground in detail. With the close of the Boer War in March 1902 the time was finally opportune for major legislative action by the Conservative government. For the church interest it had been a long, hard wait.

3 The 1902 Education Act

Although the new prime minister Balfour took responsibility for the drafting and the passage of this highly controversial measure, its real architect was Robert Morant who later served as Permanent Secretary to the Board of Education 1903-11. Thus the form and implementation of this critical enactment owed much to the vision and influence of one ambitious and clear-sighted professional. The provisions of the Balfour Act were designed to generate the necessary Conservative support through the religious issue whilst attracting more general support through their reform of local administration and secondary education. Thus the Act may be divided into three major aspects.

(*a*) Local Administrative Reorganisation

The existing School Boards, School Attendance Committees and Technical Instruction Committees were swept away and replaced by some three hundred local education authorities which covered the whole country. These new authorities were of two types.

(i) *Part II Local Education Authorities*

The second part of the Act designated the County and County Borough Councils as local education authorities to assume overall responsibility for elementary and 'other than elementary' education (i.e. secondary, teacher training, technical and adult education) in their respective areas.

(ii) *Part III Local Education Authorities*

The third part of the Act authorised any municipal borough with over ten thousand people or any urban district with more than twice that number to undertake responsibility for elementary education *only* in their own areas. About one hundred and eighty such authorities emerged from the Act as a result of this provision.

The resultant division of administrative responsibility in county areas where Part III enclaves arose was not to Morant's liking and he would have much preferred the County and County Borough authorities to have enjoyed a monopoly of control; but this was the political price which had to be paid by Balfour to obtain the support of Conservative members from many municipal boroughs and urban districts about to lose their School Boards.

(*b*) The Modification of the Dual System

The 1870 settlement was revised, ostensibly in the interests of educational efficiency, along certain lines:

(i) rate-aid was extended to the voluntary schools so as to cover their running costs completely; henceforth the churches were simply faced with the capital expenditure involved in the establishment of new schools and the extension or repair of old buildings. Costs arising from 'fair wear and tear' were to be charged to the local education authority. Thus the financial difficulties of the denominational schools were greatly eased and their survival ensured; it was anticipated that the new arrangements would enable them rapidly and significantly to raise their standards of elementary provision;

(ii) the voluntary schools were now to be administered as well as financed by the new local education authorities. Renamed 'non-provided schools' they were placed under the jurisdiction of the local education authority in relation to the secular aspects of the elementary education they provided. Their trust deeds were to be altered to allow for one-third of their managers to be nominated by the parent authority and the latter was given the power of veto upon the appointment of unsuitable teachers. Thus the denominational schools were to be much more closely incorporated within the State system. But they maintained a foundation majority on their managing bodies with the right to appoint the head and assistant teachers and continued to enjoy their denominational atmosphere and identity. The appointment and dismissal of staff for religious teaching purposes was placed outside the jurisdiction of the authority.

A significant omission from this aspect of the Act was any provision designed to override the Cowper-Temple clause. The High Church party had pressed very hard for access facilities to allow denominational teaching to be given to Anglican children attending the schools provided by the local authorities. But Balfour and Morant rightly judged this to be an extreme demand and the 'provided schools' (as the old Board schools were now renamed) were left to continue with the Cowper-Temple tradition of undenominational religious worship and instruction.

(c) Expansion of Secondary and Further Education

The Part II local education authorities were required to investigate existing facilities in the field of 'other than elementary' education and were empowered as far as 'seemed desirable' to use rate-aid for its support and development. In particular, the County and County Borough authorities were allowed to take action in a number of important directions:

(i) to support existing endowed grammar schools in return for representation on their governing bodies, to buy out private and proprietary secondary schools, to convert higher-grade schools and pupil-teacher centres and to establish their own County grammar schools. All these were means by which the Part II authorities could contribute to the launching and development of a State system of secondary education;

(ii) to provide scholarships for able elementary schoolchildren to transfer to secondary grammar schools where the majority of places would still be fee-paying. This would develop an educational ladder between the elementary system and the new State secondary schools which would be especially helpful to working class pupils intent upon a career in teaching;

(iii) to establish and maintain municipal training colleges for elementary teachers. The denominational monopoly in this field had already been broken into by the establishment of day training colleges under university auspices during the 1890s; the Part II authorities could now make their contribution to the further expansion of this non-denominational sector;

(iv) to expand technical education provision and support the efforts of recognised organisations (e.g. the Workers' Educational Association) active in the field of adult education. In this way the Part II authorities not only inherited the responsibilities of the previous Technical Instruction Committees but were commissioned to develop a wider field later categorised as 'further' education.

Thus the Part II local education authorities were to cover the whole field of State educational provision and were expected, in particular, to expand and improve that provision in the 'other than elementary' sector. Nevertheless the latter responsibility was permissive rather than mandatory, the means and extent of expansion and improvement being left to the discretion of individual Part II authorities.

The *passage* and *implementation* of the 1902 Act inevitably proved stormy and difficult. It took fifty-nine days of bitter debates to force the measure through Parliament, the great bulk of this time being consumed by argument over those sections of the Act concerned with the religious issue. The clear design to rehabilitate the denominational schools by placing them on the rates excited the combined wrath of the Nonconformists and secularists who had been relying on their slow financial strangulation to destroy the dual system. In the House of Commons Lloyd George led the Liberal opposition to the measure almost clause by clause, whilst in the country at large the Baptist preacher Dr Clifford marshalled huge Nonconformist demonstrations and warned the Balfour government of the dire consequences of 'putting Rome on the rates'. Once the Act became law its opponents refused to pay the education rate and a number of Welsh local education authorities simply refused to advance public monies to Anglican and Roman Catholic elementary schools in their areas. Some seventy thousand individual passive resisters were met by prosecution and even the distraint of their belongings, whilst the recalcitrant authorities were outflanked by the special Education (Local Authorities Default) Act of 1904. The latter measure allowed the Board of Education to finance any denominational school directly at the expense of central grants due to the offending authority in respect of all its schools. Gradually the opposition began to subside and the position was regularised. But the Liberal landslide electoral victory early in 1906 suddenly threatened to undo Balfour's work before it had had a chance to prove itself. During the period 1906-8 no fewer than three major Education Bills were introduced to withdraw rate-aid for church schools or to simply abolish the dual system. The day was saved for the denominational interests by the Tory majority in the House of Lords. Because of the resistance of the Upper House the church schools continued to enjoy the favourable terms extended to them by the Balfour Act, in spite of the new Liberal government's hostility to such arrangements. By the time the power of the House of Lords had been curbed by the Parliament Act of 1911, the context had changed again in a way favourable to the maintenance of the 1902 settlement. The Balfour-Morant system was working well and the more moderate elements on both sides increasingly recognised this fact. The secularist stance of the working class movement, which had lent more strength to the Liberal and Nonconformist position in the early years of the century, had now weakened and was on the threshold of official abandonment. The earlier religious bitterness had died down somewhat and, pressed by the emergence of a number of other serious problems, the pre-war Liberal government was much less inclined to risk another political storm by meddling yet again with the Balfour arrangements. When Morant left the Board of Education in 1911 he must have had the satisfaction of feeling that the Balfour Act and the framework it had set up and which he had done so much to develop was now reasonably safe from successful attack.

4 Retrospective Assessment

Whatever the contemporary opposition to and the possible criticisms of the 1902 Act, it must be regarded as one of the really major landmarks in the history of English education. Any balanced assessment of its significance must take into account a number of considerations.

(*a*) New Administrative Framework

In conjunction with the Board of Education Act (1899), it established a new administrative framework incomparably more cohesive and effective than its predecessor. On this sound basis Morant forged the crucial partnership between central and local government which has since remained fundamental to the English educational system. Through the new framework the State projected itself much more decisively into the field of 'other than elementary' education.

(*b*) State System of Secondary Education

It launched a State system of secondary education (albeit on traditional grammar lines) which enjoyed considerable expansion in the Edwardian era and during the First World War. Although the system was developed on a fee-paying basis, the Act's provision for scholarship awards to enable elementary schoolchildren to transfer to secondary grammar schools pointed the way towards the 'free-place' system (1907) and the ultimate rejection of the nineteenth-century concept of secondary education as the prerogative of the middle and upper classes. In its concern for the establishment of an educational ladder, however narrow initially, the Balfour Act reflected the beginnings of a contemporary shift from the plutocratic to the meritocratic rationale of secondary education.

(c) Elementary Education

It benefited elementary education by strengthening the financial resources of the voluntary or non-provided schools and subjecting them to a greater degree of public control, thereby setting the stage for an overdue improvement in their standards of provision. Further benefit accrued from the opportunity provided by the Act for the Part II authorities to develop teacher training facilities through the establishment of municipal colleges, twenty-two of which were founded in the years before the outbreak of the First World War.

(d) Administrative Dichotomy

It gave rise to the administrative dichotomy between Part II and Part III local education authorities which was to prove such a weakness in many County areas. Once the 1902 Act met the demands of the municipal boroughs and larger urban districts for a major say in local educational development, it was difficult thereafter to deprive them of the privilege even in the interests of educational efficiency. Thus the disappearance of the Part III authorities under the 1944 Education Act was accompanied by the emergence of divisional executives and excepted districts which continued to confuse and dilute the power of the County local education authorities. The fact that the 1902 Act sanctified the right of the urban locality to influence directly its own educational development has more recently made for difficulties in the formulation of a policy for major local government reform as it affects education. Morant favoured functional efficiency to local democratic influence; political considerations resulted in his being overruled and some would say that the educational price has had to be paid ever since.

(e) Progressive School Boards

It abolished the larger, more progressive School Boards which had championed the cause of educational advance in the closing decades of the nineteenth century. With these Boards went the higher-grade schools and the widening opportunity for secondary-type education on the cheap provided by them. As a result of the 1902 Act these schools were absorbed into the fee-paying system of State grammar schools or reverted to the strictly elementary role. The impetus given to technical and scientific education by the higher-grade and evening continuation schools of the progressive Boards was largely lost in the subsequent preoccupation with the development of State secondary education along traditional grammar lines. Finally, the local education committees, through which the new local education authorities were to exercise their responsibilities, were not directly elected like the School Boards and were seen by the Labour movement as less democratic institutions. Brian Simon, in his fine book *Education and the Labour Movement 1870-1920* has condemned the 1902 Act as a reactionary measure because of the fate of the progressive School Boards and their higher-grade schools. This is an interesting viewpoint that deserves consideration; it deplores the way in which Morant's administrative measures capitalised upon the Act to define rigidly the distinctions between elementary and secondary education which the higher-grade schools had done so much to blur, and it implies that the 1902 Act was a development calculated to injure the immediate educational interests of the working class. Such an interpretation explains the fact that of the many elements composing the contemporary Labour movement only the Fabian Society gave its support to the Balfour Act.

(f) Dual System

It entrenched the dual system and so perpetuated the problem of balancing the claims of the State and the interests of the churches in a changing social and educational context: the survival of the voluntary schools with their 'special position' caused serious difficulties for the Hadow reorganisation process after 1928, for the drafting of the 1944 Education Act, for the process of comprehensive reorganisation and for post-war educational finance. By the close of the inter-war period the problems associated with the dual system were present in secondary education as well as in the elementary and teacher training fields. In 1944 the church interests were still strong enough to negotiate the introduction of compulsory religious worship and instruction into all State maintained schools. The secularist would argue that the 1902 Act would have served posterity better if the denominational schools and colleges had been forced to contract into or out of a purely State system.

If the 1902 Education Act did not immediately create a national system of education in England and Wales, it certainly laid the foundations of one, especially in the administrative sense and in relation to secondary provision. Although it may be argued that the Balfour Act had some short-term reactionary effects, in the long run it provided a sound and elastic framework within which progressive educational development could and did take place.

Follow-up: Attempt to cover as much of the following ground as possible.

1 Read   Bagley, J. J. and A. J. *The State and Education in England and Wales, 1833-1968*, Chapter 4

Dawson, K. and Wall, P. *Society and Industry in the 19th Century: Education*, pp. 41-44

Curtis, S. J. and Boultwood, M. E. *An Introductory History of English Education since 1800*, Chapter VIII, pp. 162-72

Barnard, H. C. *A History of English Education from 1760*, Chapters XXIII and XXIV

Simon, B. *Education and the Labour Movement 1870-1920*, Chapter VII

2 Consult Maclure, J. S. *Educational Documents: England and Wales 1816-1968;* items 19 and 20 are relevant.

3 Clarify the following: the complex and confused administrative pattern at the central and local levels associated with educational provision at the close of the nineteenth century; the reformed structure of local government established in 1888 and its utilisation in the Technical Instruction Act and the Welsh Intermediate Act (1889); the precise recommendations of the Bryce Commission Report (1895) compared with the actual provisions of the 1899 and 1902 Acts; the significance of the Tory electoral victory in 1895 and of the Cockerton judgement of 1900; the broad outline of Morant's career and work 1895-1911; the major areas of educational concern affected by the provisions of the Balfour Act; the factors which secured the 1902 settlement from successful attack during the period of Liberal government before the First World War; the strengths and weaknesses of the 1902 Education Act as a contribution to the development of English education.

Chapter Six
The Broadening Conception of State Education

Purpose: to show how and explain why the conception of a national system of education in England and Wales was progressively broadened in the twentieth century, and to illustrate this key theme by reference to developments in elementary and secondary education, special provision and welfare services and educational thought and practice.

The basis of any satisfactory study of the present topic must surely be an appreciation of the fact that the over-all context in which educational development takes place was now changing more rapidly and markedly than ever before. By the turn of the century the age of *laissez faire* and rampant individualism was finally giving way to the inexorable encroachments of the socialist outlook and the collectivist approach to human needs and problems; in the years that followed the State assumed an increasingly wide and decisive role in the development and ordering of various major aspects of national life, the hope and belief being that such intervention would serve the best interests of the majority of the population. The Liberal party was able to lay the foundations of the welfare state in the short Edwardian era before the First World War and the new Labour party, committed to a socialist programme designed to raise the quality of life of the working class, was able to achieve political power on four separate occasions during the period 1923-70. Once the Liberals went into headlong decline and the Labour party emerged as the new source of alternative government, political considerations ensured that the Conservatives were not unaffected by the growth of collectivist influence and practice. The traumatic experience of two World Wars, in which the British nation had to pull together as never before in order to survive, produced a strong egalitarian tide to challenge traditional assumptions and practices: the final extension of the franchise to all adults, the increasing emancipation of women, the growing concern and pressure for real equality of opportunity irrespective of sex or social class and the quest for a 'brave new world' were all symptomatic of the changing outlook which emerged. The rise of educational psychology to maturity and respectability provided an increasingly firm basis for the paedocentric (i.e. child-centred) approach to education, with its emphasis on pupil needs, individual differences and the nature of the child learning process. Meanwhile, the philosophy of education, subjected to the influence of Dewey from across the Atlantic, became much more interested in and concerned about the social aims of education than had previously been the case; in this country the transition was exemplified in the move from Sir Percy Nunn's education for individuality thesis during the inter-wars years to Sir Fred Clarke's education for society argument after the Second World War. The growth of new industries and the rising importance of tertiary occupations were producing a more sophisticated economy and thereby changing the nature of its demands on the educational system; before the Second World War the main effect of this was upon the growth and improvement of secondary education and to a lesser extent technical education, but thereafter the impact was increasingly felt across the whole range of further and higher education as well. But, contemporaneously, stiffening foreign competition in overseas markets and the associated decline of Britain's staple industries produced serious economic difficulties which ensured that the resources available for educational development were usually very limited or subject to sudden cuts. The post-war slump following the First World War savaged many of the hopes which had found legislative expression in the Fisher Act (1918), whilst the world economic depression produced a period of acute financial stringency for education in the early 1930s. The cost of yet another World War then gave rise to the austerity period after 1945 and Britain's subsequent failure to achieve a satisfactory post-war rate of economic growth acted as a serious brake upon educational development. As the inter-relationship between the industrial and educational systems continued to be a very loose one until quite recently, with industry tending to prefer early leaving and on-the-job training whilst the schools neglected technical subjects and applied science, the economy found it that much more difficult to adjust to rapidly changing technological and market conditions after the First and Second World Wars.

Given the over-all context just described, the broadening conception of State education during the twentieth century may be considered in terms of four broad avenues along which it developed.

1 The Emancipation of the Elementary School

The nineteenth-century conception of elementary education, crystallised in the Revised Code of 1862, was a narrow utilitarian one and rigidly class-based. But the abandonment of the 'payment by results' system at the close of the century opened the way to a more liberal approach to elementary schooling. The twentieth century witnessed considerable change for the better, consequent upon and punctuated by a variety of influences and developments.

(*a*) Educational Psychology

The broad progressive influence of educational psychology came to enjoy a place of increasing importance in the teacher training colleges. The result was the gradual rise of the paedocentric or child-centred approach to education which had its initial and greatest impact upon the teaching of younger children. Educational psychologists stressed the importance of individual differences and pupil motivation in relation to learning at school. They felt that what was taught and how should be reconsidered in the light of pupil needs and interests and the nature of child development. Their influence certainly undermined the largely repressionist and rote-learning tradition inherited from the nineteenth century. Thus the inter-war period was characterised by a fair amount of experimentation and re-examination of curricula and teaching methods, although the widespread practical fruits were postponed until after the Second World War. The greater attention given to the physical and socio-emotional development of younger children and certain organisational changes which affected their education may also be attributed in part to the influence of educational psychology.

(*b*) Progressive Practitioners   mainly nursery + infant

The particular contributions of certain progressive practitioners who were themselves well versed in educational psychology and even helped to develop it, began to be felt. Margaret McMillan, who had served the Bradford School Board in the 1890s and later ran an open-air nursery school in Deptford, underlined the importance of physical well-being and creative activity to the satisfactory development of young children and even won Robert Morant and H. A. L. Fisher to her viewpoint. In her book *Education through the Imagination* (1905) the need to sustain the child's emotional development is stressed and expressive work in art, music, movement, handicrafts, poetry and imaginative story-telling are suggested as the best means to this end. Underlying her whole outlook was the conviction that the child's intellectual development depended on a sound emotional base. Maria Montessori, an Italian doctor who became interested and involved in the infant schooling of deprived children in Rome, emphasised practical and individual activity as the vital basis for learning. Her approach was more clinical and scientific than Margaret McMillan's but lacked its aesthetic dimensions. The teacher's function according to the 'Montessori method' was to organise the classroom environment by providing all sorts of purposeful materials to attract the young child's interest and to facilitate its mastery of basic concepts. She favoured the vertical grouping of infants and juniors as a socially beneficial arrangement and was opposed to the use of rewards and punishments. By 1914 she already had numerous disciples in Britain and her influence spread further afield after the First World War. The ideas of Margaret McMillan and Maria Montessori in many ways looked back to those of Froebel, the nineteenth-century pioneer of the kindergarten; their work helped to revitalise the efforts of the Froebel Society (established 1874) in Britain in the early decades of the new century. The main • impact of all this was upon nursery and infant education, but in the long run the effects were destined to assume wider significance.

(c) Official Change of Attitude Towards the Elementary Schools

An official change of attitude towards the elementary schools was announced by the Board of Education and inspired by Robert Morant shortly after the 1902 Act. The publication of the 1904 Elementary Code and the 1905 *Handbook of Suggestions for the Consideration of Teachers engaged in the Work of Public Elementary Schools* heralded the dawn of a new era for the elementary schools and their teachers. The new Code was responsible for a complete and wholesome restatement of the purpose of the elementary school which was certainly calculated to improve its public image. The *Handbook*, by its very title (suggestions *not* instructions, consideration *not* direction), symbolised the burial of the traditions and official attitudes associated with elementary education in the late nineteenth century. Taken together they introduced a new spirit and in various ways pointed towards a new ideal:

(i) by projecting elementary education as a vital public service to the nation and abandoning the old concept of its being a charity service for working class children;

(ii) by stressing the importance of developing individual abilities and interests and the building of character and moral training, thereby identifying a much broader purpose for elementary education;

(iii) by exalting the freedom and responsibility of the individual elementary teacher in the field of curricula and method and by revising the role of H.M. Inspectorate accordingly.

Of course it was easier to state new policy than to change the old ways of teachers and inspectors who had been conditioned over many years; but the Board of Education had given a clear lead and slowly but surely it received a growing response.

(*d*) Education Act 1918

The 1918 Education Act accepted the extension of State responsibility into the field of nursery education, although the post-war financial climate ensured that the response of the local education authorities to this new opportunity was disappointingly limited. The objective was restated in the 1944 Education Act but again without really significant effect upon the situation until over a quarter of a century later. Fisher's measure (1918), which raised the minimum school leaving age to fourteen, also required the local education authorities to provide special arrangements for the education of senior elementary pupils which pointed forward to a separate primary stage for the younger children.

(*e*) Hadow Report on *The Education of the Adolescent* (1926)

The Hadow Report on *The Education of the Adolescent* (1926) recommended the abandonment of the elementary/secondary dichotomy in English education, in favour of a continuous educative process divided into primary and secondary stages. This gave rise to the modern concept of primary education as a self-contained stage for children aged five to eleven years. The Hadow reorganisation, begun in 1928, presaged the death-knell of the term 'elementary' and its unhappy connotations in English education.

(*f*) Hadow Report on *The Primary School* (1931)

The Hadow report on *The Primary School* (1931) gave official expression and encouragement to many of the new ideas being put forward for the education of young children. It suggested that primary education should be seen, not in terms of subjects to be taught and facts to be learned, but in terms of experiences to be undergone and activities to be engaged in. Learning by listening and mechanical exercises was condemned in favour of learning by doing through the medium of purposeful practical and expressive activity. Whilst the report supported the streaming of older junior children in order to cope with widening ability differences, it hopefully recommended that the demands of the eleven-plus examination should be resisted in the interests of a pupil-centred approach to primary education. Of course, this was easier said than done, but many teachers did their best to respond because of their commitment to the principles involved. The report also had significance for the future organisation of primary education in that it recommended the separation of infant and junior children. Indeed, in one way or another, the ripples of this important Consultative Committee report have continued to influence development right down to the present day.

(g) Hadow Report on *Infant and Nursery Schools* (1933)

The Hadow Report on *Infant and Nursery Schools* (1933) reiterated the need for separate infant schools and backed the progressive influences already at work in infant education. Whilst not ignoring the need of the six- and seven-year-olds for formal instruction in the three Rs, the report condemned rigid timetables for infants and underlined the importance of natural activities and expression training. The Froebelian and Montessorian approaches were woven into an official rationale for the infant school. The report also pressed the desirability of a State system of nursery education and emphasised the particular need for such provision in deprived areas; in this respect it anticipated the recommendations of the Plowden report (1967) by over thirty years, but unhappily it failed to make any real impact upon the existing situation.

(h) Education Act 1944

The 1944 Education Act gave statutory recognition to the new primary stage and its associated schools and reflected the widening conception of primary education in particular by declaring the object of the educational process to be the development of the spiritual, moral, mental and physical capacities of each and every child. This is indicative of a broad and enlightened approach to education, which contrasts starkly with the much narrower conception holding sway at the beginning of the century.

(i) Changes of the Post-War Era

The post-war era has witnessed a steady advance of progressive attitudes and methods in primary schools. The formal approach and the eleven-plus examination have retreated together, allowing increasing scope for destreaming, the integrated day, vertical grouping, open-plan arrangements, group project activities, junior school French, individualised learning approaches and other manifestations of the progressive outlook and method. Such changes were welcomed and further encouraged by the Plowden report on *Children and their Primary Schools* (1967). But the extent of the ground gained by new approaches and methods can be easily exaggerated; their advance continues to face the combined resistance of large primary classes, teacher conservatism and public scepticism, and the mounting suspicion in certain quarters that the progressive tide has resulted in a deterioration in the teaching of vital basic skills may stiffen this opposition. Yet over the past quarter century its inexorable progress and broadening effect are hardly matters of dispute.

2 Secondary Education for All

As long as the nineteenth-century conception of elementary education survived, secondary schooling would remain the preserve of upper and middle class children. Significantly, and perhaps inevitably, the first State secondary schools developed under auspices of the 1902 Act were in fact 'grammar' schools in which the great majority of places were fee-paying. Terminologically the words 'secondary' and 'grammar' remained officially synonymous during the lifetime of the Board of Education 1900-44, and the purchase of places in State secondary schools was not abolished until the passage of the 1944 Education Act. Obviously this was a situation increasingly out of tune with the changing social context and it was gradually overcome by a process of erosion during the first half of the century. This process can be most easily considered and understood in terms of a number of major influences and developments underlying and composing it.

(a) Growth of the Scholarship System

First mentioned by the Taunton Commission, reiterated by the Bryce report and embodied in the provision of the 1902 Act which permitted the Part II authorities to grant scholarships, this idea was crystallised in the 1907 free-place regulations requiring State secondary schools (i.e. all those in receipt of grant) to make at least 25% of their intake available to elementary pupils of proven ability. The free-place system was to be operated on the basis of a qualifying examination to establish suitability for grammar schooling, but growing demand and limited supply was soon to ensure that this became an increasingly competitive affair. Between 1906 and 1914 the new departure was responsible for trebling the number of scholarships provided for elementary pupils to transfer to secondary education. Thus, whilst the traditional distinction between elementary and secondary schooling continued, the gulf between the separate and parallel systems was now narrowly bridged by a minority of very able elementary pupils passing into the largely fee-paying secondary schools. On the eve of the First World War only $2\frac{1}{2}\%$ of the appropriate age group actually in the elementary schools obtained free places; but by 1939, as a result of the growth in the number and size of the State grammar schools and the tendency to raise the proportion of scholarship places provided, there were some 10% of such pupils being transferred. Thus the position improved, but not remarkably so during the inter-war years. Even H. A. L. Fisher, the liberal-minded President of the Board 1916-22, though eager to widen the educational ladder and thus increase the proportion of beneficiaries, was content to accept an arrangement which inevitably limited the majority of children to an elementary education. The 1918 Education Act did not provide for any real change in the concept of secondary education and prosperous middle class parentage remained the best hope of obtaining it.

(b) Attitude of the Organised Labour Movement

The earliest demands for 'secondary education for all' were voiced by the Trades Union and Labour party conferences in the years before the First World War. On behalf of the working class they condemned elementary schooling as inadequate, demanded the raising of the school leaving age to sixteen years and the provision of a secondary education for each and every child. The educational ladder arrangements were likened to a 'greasy pole', calculated to benefit the lower-middle rather than the working class. Reassured by the changing image of the elementary schools, and attracted by the scholarship possibilities, a growing number of lower-middle class parents began to send their children to them, whilst the poverty barrier militated against many able working class children taking advantage of secondary school free places without associated maintenance allowances. Nor was the Labour movement content to accept compulsory part-time continuative education 14-18 years for ex-elementary pupils (as provided for by the Fisher Act, 1918) as a satisfactory alternative to secondary education for all. The latter objective became official party policy in 1922 when the Labour spokesman R. H. Tawney issued the publication *Secondary Education for All*. The first short-lived Labour government 1923-24 commissioned the Hadow report on *The Education of the Adolescent* (1926) which examined the condition of post-primary education and pointed the way towards the realisation of Tawney's hopes. In the succeeding years the Labour party not only supported the Hadow reorganisation process and attempted to raise the school leaving age to fifteen, but also used its power and influence at local government level to reduce the proportion of fee-paying places in State secondary grammar schools and to explore the idea of multilateral secondary schools to which all children could go.

(c) Reassertion of Post-Primary Growth

Following the Cockerton judgement and the abolition of the School Boards, Morant used his decisive influence as Permanent Secretary to the Board of Education 1903-11 in favour of enforcing a clear and rigid distinction between elementary and secondary education. The existing higher-grade schools and pupil-teacher centres were forcibly reconstituted as secondary grammar or ordinary elementary schools. The only permissible variant was the new higher elementary school provided for by special regulations which not only placed it very firmly in the non-secondary sector but also ensured, because of the onerous conditions and limitations to be observed, that local education authorities showed very little interest in its development. In 1906 Morant's policy received the backing of the Consultative Committee in its Report on *Higher Elementary Schools;* the need to prevent any post-primary outgrowth which might threaten to compete, however marginally, with the grammar schools and once again blur the distinction between elementary and secondary education was stoutly reaffirmed. But in face of the developing needs of industry and commerce and the changing social context such a simplistic and class-ridden approach by the Board of Education could not last for long. The mounting opposition of the National Union of Teachers and the organised Labour movement to the influence and policy of Morant, leading to his final downfall in 1911, prepared the ground for new developments. In 1911-12 the London and Manchester local education authorities launched their selective central schools for abler elementary pupils not transferring to secondary grammar schools; these central schools were to provide post-primary instruction with some industrial or commercial bias for the 11-15 years age group. By the outbreak of the First World War the Board of Education had not only recognised but had approved this development. Impressed by the problem of 'marking time' (i.e. occupying the senior pupils by repetitive exercises rather than by the breaking of new ground) in ordinary elementary schools, the Lewis Report on *Juvenile Education in Relation to Employment after the War* (1917) insisted on the need to reconsider the organisation and curricula of the upper forms of elementary schools. The Lewis Committee felt that such action was essential if its recommendation for the raising of the school leaving age nationally to fourteen years was to produce real educational benefits. H. A. L. Fisher clinched the issue when he told Parliament that one of the vital post-war tasks facing the Board of Education would be 'to develop upon sound lines what may be called higher-grade elementary education' (*Hansard*, vol. 108, 16 July 1918). To this end the 1918 Education Act required the local education authorities to make adequate provision for both advanced and practical instruction for senior elementary pupils 'by means of central schools, central or special classes, or otherwise'. The Act raised the school leaving age to fourteen years, provided for its further extension to fifteen years on the basis of local option and allowed individual elementary pupils to continue in school to the age of sixteen. The result was that a growing number of authorities joined London and Manchester in the development of both selective and non-selective central schools for elementary pupils over eleven. The seeds of the future secondary modern schools were already being sown. Meanwhile the emergence of full-time day junior trade and technical schools had introduced another dimension to post-primary growth. The trade schools were pioneered by the London local education authority and received recognition for grant purposes in 1905; they aimed at giving ex-elementary pupils specialised training in the manual skills and scientific principles associated with a particular skilled trade. The junior technical schools developed in the north of England somewhat later and became eligible for grant in 1913; they combined a continued general education with preparation for apprenticeship in such group industries as engineering, building and construction, or shipbuilding. Both types of school provided two- or three-year-courses for abler senior elementary pupils who would transfer into them at thirteen or fourteen. A much smaller number of junior commercial and art schools also emerged as part of this new development. By the mid 1920s these schools, operated under the Board's separate regulations for technical institutions, were forming an intermediate sector distinct from both the elementary and secondary grammar systems. In any move towards secondary education for all their existence would now have to be taken into account.

(d) Hadow Report on *The Education of the Adolescent* (1926)

Once it had become official policy to consider the particular needs of senior elementary pupils, the logical extension of this was to end the separation of elementary and secondary education and to think in terms of one continuous process of schooling composed of a primary and a secondary stage through which all children would pass. Such was the main thesis of the report submitted by the Consultative Committee to the government in 1926. Under the chairmanship of Sir W. H. Hadow the Committee had been commissioned by the first Labour government two years earlier to investigate the existing provision of non-secondary post-primary education and to make suggestions for its improvement. Its subsequent consideration of the organisation and substance of the education received by the ninety-odd per cent of adolescents not attending secondary grammar schools resulted in a report full of far-reaching *recommendations:*

  (i) the provision of secondary education for all through the abandonment of the old parallel and separate systems of elementary and secondary schooling in favour of a single and continuous educative process divided into primary and secondary stages at the age of eleven plus;

(ii) the raising of the school leaving age to fifteen years nationally (with effect from September 1932) so as to allow every child a minimum of four years of secondary schooling and to make such provision a viable curricula proposition;

(iii) the organisation of secondary education on a selective basis in order to relate it to the different abilities and interests of the children and their prospective age of school leaving and career possibilities. Accordingly the report suggested two main types of post-primary education, each to be associated with a particular type of institution. Firstly, there would be the secondary grammar schools to serve the needs of the ablest ex-primary pupils aiming at professional employment or university entrance; such schools would maintain their strong academic orientation and all pupils would continue in attendance until at least sixteen years of age. Secondly, there should be secondary modern schools developed from the existing central schools and senior elementary classes; although a secondary modern education would initially often have to be provided within the existing framework of senior elementary classes, the ultimate objective was to be its provision in 'another institution, with a distinctive staff, and organised definitely for post-primary education' (page 80). The modern school would serve the needs of the great majority of adolescents between eleven and fifteen years; in common with the grammar school the curriculum during the first two years was to concentrate on providing a sound general education, but thereafter it was to be differentiated by a more practical and realistic bias without ever becoming strictly vocational. The Report also acknowledged the valuable contribution being made to post-primary education by the junior technical schools and recommended that the development of this third element should be encouraged. But it was insisted that because of their vocational orientation the normal age of entry should continue to be thirteen years rather than eleven. The junior technical schools were not visualised as an integral part of the new secondary arrangements; rather they were seen as appendages of the technical colleges to which a small number of suitable pupils could make late transfers from the modern or grammar schools. Thus the Hadow strategy was really bipartite rather than tripartite in basis;

(iv) the acceptance of responsibility by the local education authorities for the mounting of suitable selection examinations for channelling pupils to the appropriate type of school; such arrangements were to include provision for the transfer of late developers from the modern to the grammar and junior technical schools. It was further suggested that the local education authorities and other interested parties should combine to frame a new leaving examination and certificate for the benefit of the modern schools and their pupils;

(v) the accordance of parity of support and esteem to the different types of post-primary school. The Committee was particularly insistent upon the need to ensure that the modern schools were seen as different from rather than inferior to the grammar schools, and underlined the importance of accommodation, equipment and staffing in this respect;

(vi) the promotion of administrative efficiency by devolving the responsibility for both primary and secondary education upon a single type of local authority. Quite rightly the Committee saw the continued existence of Part II and Part III authorities with their different roles as a serious obstacle to the satisfactory implementation of its other proposals.

After long consideration the Board of Education accepted the report in principle and the Hadow reorganisation process was officially launched by the issue of *The New Prospect in Education* (1928) and officially encouraged by an additional grant for the purpose. But the progress of reorganisation was slowed down by the financial stringencies of the world economic depression and by the particular difficulties associated with the decapitation of denominational elementary schools and the problem of sparsely populated rural areas.

(e) Education Act 1936

This measure attempted to facilitate and expedite the Hadow reorganisation process by raising the school leaving age to fifteen years (with effect from September 1939) and by authorising the local education authorities to pay specially favourable grants for the establishment of denominational secondary modern schools. Although the outbreak of war postponed the raising of the school leaving age, the latter provision enabled the Anglican and Roman Catholic Churches to enter into special agreements with particular authorities for the furtherance of reorganisation. By 1939 almost two-thirds of pupils over eleven were in reorganised schools although the proportion for the denominational and the rural school children was much lower than this.

(f) Spens Report on *Secondary Education* (1938)

Although the terms of reference related to this report did not include the new modern schools, the Consultative Committee, whilst concentrating its attention on the grammar and technical schools, found it impossible to ignore the wider context of post-primary education as a whole. Will Spens and his colleagues began by confirming the basic Hadow strategy and thereby encouraged the emergence of secondary education for all along selective lines; very impressed by the recent work of educational psychologists on the nature and importance of mental differences they felt it 'evident that different children from the age of eleven, if justice is to be done to their varying capacities, require types of education varying in certain important respects' (page 358), and that this was best provided in separate post-primary schools. However, the report also proposed a number of significant *refinements* to the existing policy:

(i) the abolition of all fee-paying places in State secondary education; this would mean that all grammar school places would be tied to eleven-plus examination success;

(ii) the conversion of a number of the existing junior technical schools into technical high schools which were to be accorded equality of status with the selective grammar schools. This newly conceived institution was to provide a liberal education with science and its applications as the curriculum core for abler children. The age range was to be 11-16 years and the schools were to be developed under the auspices of local technical colleges. Thus the technical school was to be drawn into the main stream of secondary education beginning at eleven plus; the basically bipartite strategy of Hadow was superseded by the clearly tripartite approach of Spens;

(iii) the improvement of the inter-relations of the post-primary schools by selection at eleven plus for all three types of secondary education supplemented by open-ended thirteen plus transfer arrangements. It was stressed that the satisfactory handling of the latter concern depended on the pursuance of a comparable curricula in all secondary schools during the first two years;

(iv) the realisation of parity of esteem for the different types of secondary school through administrative action. The report suggested a new code of regulations to cover the new and wider secondary field with the different schools being treated alike in relation to staffing, salary scales, buildings and facilities except where special considerations justified otherwise.

It is also noteworthy that the Spens Committee considered the possibilities of multilateral and bilateral secondary schools, only to reject them on grounds of size and other problems. However, it was admitted that some benefits (e.g. ease of internal transfer) accrued from all secondary pupils being taught together in the same school and the Committee was happy to see such experiments in areas of new or sparse population.

(g) Norwood Report on *Curriculum and Examinations in Secondary Schools* (1941)

The criticisms of secondary curricula and examinations by the Spens Report led to a wider and more intensive investigation of this particular field by the Secondary School Examinations Council under its chairman Sir Cyril Norwood. But the Council went well beyond its terms of reference to consider the organisation of post-primary education as a whole and the resultant report acquired enhanced significance because it crystallised the case for secondary education for all and its provision along tripartite lines. Its basic thesis was that all secondary pupils fall into one of three psychological categories, namely the academically-minded, the technically-minded and the practically-minded, and that each group is best served by a distinctive curriculum developed in an appropriate type of school. The Norwood analysis, though naïvely ill-founded in its basis, was welcomed in official circles for it equated most conveniently with the three types of secondary school thrown up by the Hadow reorganisation. In common with Spens, the Norwood Report did not favour the multilateral alternative but emphasised the importance of the different types of school pursuing a comparable curricula during the first two years of secondary education to facilitate a satisfactory system of late transfers. Having thus recived further confirmation of the efficacy of the Hadow strategy, the Board of Education and many local education authorities could rest happy that recent developments in post-primary education were along the right lines.

(h) Education Act (1944)

This was certainly a landmark in that it provided a statutory basis for secondary education for all, raised the school leaving age to fifteen years and abolished fee-paying places in State grammar schools. But significantly, whilst the local education authorities were required to provide secondary education for all appropriate to 'their different ages, abilities and aptitudes', the Act did not make any mention of selective or tripartite organisation. Thus, although the 1944 Act finally secured secondary education for all between eleven and fifteen years, it also left the way open for a reconsideration of the organisational pattern and set the stage for the long and bitter struggle between the selective and comprehensive approaches. In recent years the comprehensive tide, favouring the provision of a common form of secondary schooling for all ex-primary pupils, has been running strong, and since Circular 10/65 on *The Organisation of Secondary Education* (issued by the Wilson Labour government in July 1965) has been threatening to engulf the grammar schools and their tripartite context. Because of the inferior educational provision and status accorded to so many secondary modern schools under the selective arrangements, many see the comprehensive tide as yet another powerful and inexorable force calculated to wield a broadening and egalitarian effect upon the conception of what State education is and should be. Further details on this controversial matter are given in the next chapter (pages 108-14).

3 Educational Welfare and Special Services

The critical bearing of physical health and normality upon the capacity of children to take full advantage of the developing educational system was only gradually recognised. By the turn of the century, however, pioneers like the McMillan sisters were able to play on the public conscience with increasing effect and thereby stimulate measures designed to reduce the serious educational handicap faced by children suffering from poor health, under-nourishment and other disorders. The long-term result was greatly to widen the responsibilities of the State in the educational field through the introduction and expansion of special services and other associated developments.

(a) School Medical Service

Military recruitment during the Boer War (1899-1902) and the Departmental Committee report on *Physical Deterioration* (1904) having revealed the parlous state of health of the younger generation, the Education (Administrative Provisions) Act of 1907 founded the School Medical Service for the benefit of elementary school pupils. Initially the local education authorities were simply required to provide medical inspection, but many took it upon themselves to provide facilities for treatment as well; the latter function was therefore made mandatory by the Education Act of 1921 and before long every local education authority was equipped with at least one school clinic. The successful establishment of the service owed much to the initial enthusiasm of Sir Robert Morant who immediately established a new Medical Branch of the Board of Education, and to the sterling work of Sir George Newman who served as its head from its inception until his retirement in 1935. In 1918 the Fisher Act provided for the mandatory extension of medical inspection to State secondary pupils and also empowered the local education authorities to provide such pupils with treatment. Throughout the inter-war years treatment, where provided, for elementary or for secondary pupils, was to be charged to the parents if they could possibly afford to pay; but given the economic climate and social distress of that time many children received their treatment free of charge. In receipt of central grant-aid from 1913, the service was gradually expanded and strengthened until the 1944 Education Act gave it responsibility for both the free inspection and treatment of all pupils encompassed by the State system of education. Winston Churchill described the service as the greatest piece of preventive medicine undertaken in our history; certainly within Newman's period of office the health of the nation's younger generation had improved out of all recognition. Such was the reputation built up by the School Medical Service in the first forty years of its existence that the establishment of the National Health Service (1947) did not occasion its disappearance. Instead, the service has continued to operate down to the present day, merely adjusting its role to a changing context; in spite of the free family health service its existence would still appear to be critical to the well-being of many children.

(*b*) School Meals and Milk Service

The efforts of voluntary charity organisations to meet the needs of under-nourished children attending elementary schools had become clearly inadequate by the beginning of the century. Accordingly the Labour-inspired 1906 Education (Provision of Meals) Act authorised any local education authority to spend up to a ½d rate on the support of a school meals service, although it was stipulated that only necessitous children should benefit from such provision and that even then their parents should be required to contribute to the cost if at all possible. Thus the Act was merely permissive and hedged with limitations. Consequently the schools meal service developed very slowly and prior to the Second World War, except in times of massive unemployment, the proportion of elementary schoolchildren benefiting from it never rose above 3% of the total. It was the exigencies of war after 1939 which brought about a rapid expansion of the service and within five years no less than one-third of the children were staying for school dinners. The 1944 Act made it compulsory for all local education authorities to provide school meals for all pupils in State schools desiring them: thus the provision of school dinners became a social service and an integral part of the educational system, affecting both the primary and secondary stages. By the 1960s an average of two-thirds of the school population were taking advantage of the much expanded service and there is little doubt that such provision has made a significant contribution to the health and vigour of the post-war generation. The original hope that the service would ultimately become free for all children rather than merely for those in straitened circumstances has not been realised; indeed the cost of a school meal has increased six-fold over the past quarter-century in sympathy with the general inflation of prices and the stiffening competition for resources within the education service itself. Initially the teachers were required to undertake the super-vision of pupils having school meals but in the late 1960s successful union negotiations made it a voluntary matter. The result has been the recent recruitment and employment of special meal supervisors to ease the burden on those teachers prepared to volunteer their services in this respect.

Meanwhile subsidised school milk had been introduced into State schools in 1934, with provision for making it free to necessitous children. The 1944 Act then required the local education authorities to provide free milk for all pupils wanting it and twenty years later 84% were receiving it. Perhaps unhappily the privilege was withdrawn for secondary pupils in 1968, a victim of the Labour government's economic squeeze at the time. This served as a precedent a few years later for the Conser-vative government's termination of the school milk service for healthy junior school children. Such action has left the infants as the only recipients of school milk and this has been justified in terms of the lesser need of older pupils, the much improved standards of home consumption, the arrangements for special individual cases and the prior claims of other aspects of the educational service.

(c) Provision for Handicapped Pupils

The State first assumed responsibility for making provision for handi-capped children in 1893 when the Elementary Education (Blind and Deaf Children) Act empowered the School Boards to support schools for blind and deaf children under sixteen years of age. This was followed in 1899 by the Elementary Education (Defective and Epileptic Children) Act which permitted them to make similar provision for mentally defective and epileptic children. The 1902 Education Act transferred these powers to the new local education authorities and by the outbreak of the First World War they had been translated into positive duties. Thus this new type of concern developed gradually and in piecemeal fashion until the Education Act of 1921 consolidated and strengthened previous legislation by making the authorities responsible for providing suitable education in special schools for blind, deaf, physically handicapped, mentally deficient and epileptic children. During the inter-war period the provision was consequently limited to children with overt disabilities and it was related to composite groupings (e.g. the totally blind and the partially blind were not distinguished). Before 1944 provision for the handicapped was still looked upon as an 'extra' or a sideline; indeed during the 1930s the responsibility for the education of mental defectives was removed to the Ministry of Health, only to be returned quite recently. But the 1944 Act made provision for handicapped pupils an integral part of the educational system by underlining and elaborating by subsequent regulations the responsibilities of the local education authorities in this field. Like other children the handicapped were simply to receive an education appropriate to 'their different ages, abilities and aptitudes', but the authorities were to give particular regard to their special needs. The new approach also involved a much more refined categorisation and wider conception of handicaps (eleven separate groups replaced the previous five) to ensure more effective and fuller provision, and a recognition of the fact that the isolation of such children is justified only when their needs really preclude attendance at an ordinary school. Although these children have received more help and attention from the State educational system than was the case before 1944, provision continues to be far from adequate in relation to the number of children in need of such special support. It certainly seems that they have not over the past quarter-century been given the top priority they deserve in the competition for resources within the total educational system.

These developments were certainly the foremost expressions of the growing recognition of the importance of physical health and well-being to a child's progress at school. But they were supplemented by the enhanced position of physical education and organised games in the school curriculum, by the growing interest in nursery education and open-air schools, by progressive changes in school architecture and facilities, and by the spread of school camping and recreational activity.

4 Helping the Early School Leaver

The tendency for pupils to stay on at school beyond the minimum school leaving age is a recent development. Before the Second World War the great majority left school at thirteen or fourteen years, and with only a tiny minority of these attending evening classes the result was that they ceased to come under any sort of educational influence once they began work. This situation caused growing concern amongst those who recognised the educational needs of the adolescent and the failure of many employers to look on young persons as anything but cheap labour. Once again the concept of State educational responsibility was broadened to meet the situation, though some would consider the practical effects of this development to be rather limited and disappointing.

(a) Abolition of the Half-time System

The pernicious arrangement dating from the late nineteenth century by which senior elementary pupils could work half-time for millowners and farmers while still at school was finally outlawed by the 1918 Education

Act following a quarter-century of campaigning against it by the Half-Time Council and the National Union of Teachers.

(*b*) Projection of Day Continuation Schooling

The prospect of early school leavers receiving compulsory part-time education in continuation schools for one day per week was discussed before the First World War, recommended by the Lewis Report (1917), and subsequently provided for in Fisher's Act. Under the latter measure young persons who had left school were to attend day continuation schools for 320 hours per annum between the ages of fourteen and eighteen; the intention was that the first two years should be concerned exclusively with general education, with the possibility of introducing a substantial technical or vocational element thereafter. Alas, the post-war economic difficulties and the opposition of employers combined to ensure that the scheme did not materialise; the only beneficial result was the beginning of day release arrangements on a voluntary basis, but as late as 1939 this privilege was enjoyed by a very small minority only. Hence the 1944 Act included the provision for county colleges to support the compulsory part-time education of the 15-18 years age group of early school leavers. Yet again, the scheme has not been effected in spite of the exhortations of the Crowther (1959) and Newsom (1963) Reports in its favour. Initially its execution was blocked by shortage of resources and the claims of what were considered more critical sectors of the educational system. Thereafter its low educational priority was the result of the tendency for a growing proportion of pupils to stay on voluntarily and the decision to raise the school leaving age to sixteen years. Meanwhile the impressive expansion in the numbers on day release courses gave further reason for ignoring this provision of the 1944 Act. By 1963 the number of employees under eighteen who were released was seven times greater than the pre-war figure and had passed beyond the quarter of a million mark. Under the stimulus of the Industrial Training Act (1964) this progress was accelerated and by the close of the decade one-quarter of young employees were being released for part-time day courses. On the other hand, those employed in unskilled occupations had been ignored and the arrangements proved much more favourable to boys than girls. Thus there were still many young people leaving school at the first opportunity and thereupon completely severing their connection with the educational system.

(*c*) Raising of the School Leaving Age

For those who felt that the young adolescent was usually too intellectually and socially immature and vulnerable to face the responsibilities and pressures of adult life, the solution was the progressive raising of the school leaving age to postpone the experience and better equip the pupil for it. At the beginning of the century the confused system of local exemptions for the 12-14 years age group produced an average leaving age of about thirteen. This was condemned outright by the Lewis Report (1917) and the Fisher Act raised the school leaving age nationally to fourteen years whilst also permitting individual authorities to extend it to fifteen. Little or no advantage was taken of the latter power and it was at last accepted that the duration of compulsory schooling had to be decided centrally. In 1931 the second Labour government made an abortive attempt to raise the leaving age to fifteen throughout the country and because of the outbreak of war the 1936 Education Act also came unstuck in this respect. However, the 1944 Act raised the school leaving age to fifteen as from September 1947 and also provided for its further extension to sixteen years when opportune. The implementation of the latter intention was strongly recommended by both the Crowther and Newsom Reports and by the mid 1960s its inevitability was generally accepted; though postponed more than once because of temporary difficulties the raising of the leaving age to sixteen was finally instrumented by Order in Council in 1973. An undoubted benefit of this long delay was that it gave the authorities and the schools time to prepare for the extra year and it is to be hoped that this will go a long way to ensure that the enforced extension of their education will prove both acceptable and beneficial to those who would normally have left at fifteen. Certainly the prospect of having many less able and poorly motivated pupils reluctantly staying on has stimulated the Schools Council, teachers' centres and individual schools to give that much more thought to the needs and potential interests of this type of secondary pupil.

(*d*) Development of the Youth Service

This also arose out of concern for the education of the adolescent, especially those leaving school at the minimum age. The field was pioneered by voluntary effort (e.g. Y.M.C.A., N.A.B.C., Scouts, Girl Guides and Church youth organisations) during the late nineteenth and very early twentieth century. The State showed its first serious interest in such provision during the First World War when the Juvenile Organisations Committee was set up under the auspices of the Home Office; the Fisher Act recognised the case for granting financial aid to the voluntary agencies involved and in 1920 the Juvenile Organisations Committee was transferred to the Board of Education. But the post-war economic difficulties exercised a serious check upon development and it was not until 1939 that the local education authorities were urged to establish a properly constituted Youth Committee in their respective areas. The Board of Education set an example by setting up the National Youth Committee which took advantage of wartime needs and spirit greatly to expand the Youth Service. The 1944 Act gave it statutory recognition and required all local education authorities to provide for it as part of their responsibility in the field of further education. Unhappily this branch of educational endeavour did not enjoy a high priority in the post-war years and by the late 1950s the Youth Service was in a state of 'acute depression' as a result of continuing neglect. It was rescued from this situation by the Albemarle Report on *The Youth Service in England and Wales* (1960), the main recommendations of which were implemented almost immediately and in full to give renewed vigour to the 'Cinderella' of further education. Current thought upon the future of the Youth Service seems to be in favour of ending its isolation by incorporating it in a community approach to further education and social recreation. As this would bring early school leavers into earlier and closer contact with adult members of their local community such a development might prove extremely beneficial.

(e) Growth of Vocational Guidance and Training

The strong liberal tradition in English education has unfortunately militated against much response to the vocational interests and needs of the early school leaver. A special Education Act (1910) enabled local education authorities to provide vocational guidance for school leavers as part of their service, but the majority were content to leave the work to the local Labour Exchange. Meanwhile, however, the junior technical and commercial schools and to a lesser extent the central schools gave some real emphasis to vocational needs and subjects in their curricula approach. Although the development of the technical high schools was a reaction against this, the influence was to some small degree carried over into the secondary modern schools. The Employment and Training Act (1948) gave the local education authorities a second opportunity to take responsibility for their own Youth Employment Service and over 90% of them did so. In subsequent years a growing number of secondary schools appointed careers masters or mistresses to help the youth employment officers carry out their work. The importance of educational and vocational guidance as well as pastoral care is now sufficiently recognised for some large comprehensive schools to appoint full-time school counsellors. But in curricula terms the vocational cause continues to make slow and limited headway, although the raising of the school leaving age is wielding a favourable influence in this respect. Whilst commercial subjects and geometrical and engineering drawing are well established within the secondary curriculum, the developing interest in linked courses (i.e. with local technical colleges) and work experience for less able fifth formers is helping to broaden and strengthen the vocational element in the interests of better motivation.

Although it may be argued that the early school leaver still suffers a raw deal, it must be acknowledged that, short of implementing the county college scheme, the State and its educational system show much more concern for him than was the case before the Second World War.

Follow-up: Attempt to cover as much of the following ground as possible.

1 *Read*   Bagley, J. J. and A. J. *The State and Education in England and Wales, 1833-1968*, Chapter 5

Dawson, K. and Wall, P. *Society and Industry in the 19th Century: Education*, pp. 44-47

Curtis, S. J. and Boultwood, M. E. *An Introductory History of English Education since 1800*, Chapter VIII, pp. 172-92, and Chapter X, pp. 221-5; 232-5

Barnard, H. C. *A History of English Education from 1760*, Chapters XXV, XXVI, XXIX and XXXI

Armfelt, R. *The Structure of English Education*, Chapter VII

2 *Consult* Maclure, J. S. *Educational Documents: England and Wales 1816-1968;* items 21, 23, 24, 26, 27, 28, 30, 31, 32 and 33 are relevant.

3 *Clarify the following: the educational influence of Margaret McMillan and Maria Montessori; the significance of the new Elementary Code and the associated Handbook issued by the Board of Education in 1904-5; the importance of the Hadow Report on* The Primary School *(1931); the development of an educational ladder to link elementary and secondary grammar schools; the major provisions and actual results of the 1918 Fisher Education Act; the outstanding landmarks in the progress towards secondary education for all 1902-44; the main recommendations of the Hadow Report on* The Education of the Adolescent *(1926); the refinements to the Hadow strategy suggested by the Spens Report on* Secondary Education *(1938); the major and minor expressions of growing concern for the physical welfare of schoolchildren; the twentieth century developments designed to help the early school leaver.*

Chapter Seven
The 1944 Education Act and its Aftermath

Purpose: to underline and explain the outstanding importance of the 1944 Education Act and, in the light of its provisions, to consider certain post-war educational difficulties and developments.

The legislative foundations of the present system of education in England and Wales are still basically dependent upon the 1944 Education Act passed towards the close of the Second World War. The nature and implementation of this critical measure and a consideration of some of the associated benefits and problems may well be dealt with in five major parts.

1 Preliminaries

Basically the origins of the 1944 Act lie in the educational developments and problems of the inter-war period which have already been considered. But it was only when Britain became locked in another life and death struggle with Germany that the public desire for better educational facilities and opportunities became irresistible. Significantly perhaps, it was in early 1941, when Britain stood alone, that concern for post-war educational reform first emerged; within three years the official view upon what should be done had not only crystallised but had found expression in a major legislative enactment before the coming of peace. Two main landmarks may be distinguished in the process by which the wartime Coalition government of Winston Churchill prepared the ground for the 1944 Act.

(a) 1941 The Green Book
This supposedly confidential document was issued by the Board of Education to all interested parties in order to provide a basis for discussion on the subject of educational change. It provoked a flood of memoranda in the opposite direction from local authorities, the churches, teachers' organisations, professional associations, political groups and many other bodies. The Board then spent many months considering the response and searching for a consensus that would support an actual programme of reform.

(*b*) 1943 The White Paper on Educational Reconstruction

This was a declaration of government intent submitted to Parliament and formed the basis of the subsequent Act and for much of future policy. It covered the whole educational spectrum and recommended that far-reaching changes should be implemented by two means.

(i) *Legislative Reform*

The White Paper insisted on the need to alter and extend the existing legislative framework in a number of vital ways. Hence a new Act would provide for the expansion of nursery education, for the raising of the school leaving age and for the completion of the Hadow reorganisation process to ensure secondary education for all. In the latter respect it spoke in terms of 'three main types of secondary schools to be known as grammar, modern and technical schools' (page 10) and was thus clearly disposed towards a tripartite approach to the organisation of secondary education. However, this was associated with an insistence on the need for a common set of regulations to cover all secondary schools so as to ensure real parity in respect of premises, staffing and other resources. The powers of the local authorities in respect of further education were to be extended and translated into duties. Henceforth they would be committed to the support of county colleges for the provision of compulsory part-time education for the 15-18 years age group; in addition they would have to make adequate provision for the development of technical and adult education and the Youth Service. The existing power of authorities to provide school meals and milk was to become a statutory duty. The School Medical Service was henceforth to furnish free inspection and treatment to all those attending primary and secondary schools and the new county colleges. The existing law was to be amended to emphasise the importance of religious education and to enable the voluntary schools to play an effective part in future development. The latter question, which was the most thorny one dealt with by the Board in drawing up the White Paper, was considered at some length. That nearly three-quarters of the Board's official 'Black List' of schools with defective premises were under voluntary managers and that a mere 16% of denominational schoolchildren over eleven were in reorganised schools or departments was used as evidence to show that under the existing law the churches could not be expected to respond to the need for change and improvement. The recommended solution was not the abolition of the voluntary schools but detailed legislative measures that would at one and the same time considerably raise the level of public financial aid and significantly increase the degree of public control in relation to them. Finally, the system of local educational administration established by the

1902 Act was to be reformed in the interests of general efficiency and the provision of education in three successive and interrelated stages.

(ii) *Administrative Action*

The White Paper also expressed the view that in certain spheres legislation was unnecessary and progress could be achieved by administrative means. The improvement of the premises and facilities of primary schools and the reduction of the size of primary classes deserved priority for such action. The abolition of the free-place examination in its existing form and the remodelling of the curriculum for secondary schools could also be achieved without legislation. And finally, advances in the field of teacher recruitment and training and in the widening of opportunities for university education could be similarly effected.

The short-term financial implications of the proposed reforms were worked out in some detail and the estimates presented in an appendix; given the inevitable and substantial rise in cost, the proportion of the total annual expenditure on education to be met from taxes as distinct from the rates was to be raised significantly. Indeed, the only matter of consequence not covered by the White Paper was whether, in the light of past experience and future designs, there was a need for change in the nature and power of the central authority for education.

The architects of the Bill, duly presented to Parliament in December 1943, were Mr R. A. Butler (Conservative President of the Board) and Mr Chuter Ede (Labour Parliamentary Secretary to the Board) who worked with rare energy and dedication to produce a measure acceptable to all the interested parties. The greatest difficulty was the negotiation of the details of a new religious settlement necessary for the reform of the dual system; by the autumn of 1943 the astute diplomacy of Butler had even managed to resolve this serious problem. Meanwhile party differences over the organisation of secondary education for all resulted in an agreement not to mention tripartite arrangements as such in the provision concerned, thus avoiding any legislative attempt to bind the local authorities and prejudge the issue.

2 Provisions of the Act

Butler's measure received the royal assent in August 1944 after a slow but smooth passage through Parliament. It consisted of five main parts.

(a) Part I: Central Administration

This provided for:
  (i) the replacement of the Board of Education, with its mere superintendence role, by a new Ministry of Education responsible for

promoting national educational policy and development and for securing their effective execution by local authorities placed under its 'control and direction';

(ii) the replacement of the Consultative Committee by two Central Advisory Councils (for England and for Wales) authorised to investigate and report upon any educational matter they thought fit or upon any question referred to them. Subject to the inclusion of members of suitable professional experience, the constitution and composition of the Councils was left to the discretion of the Minister;

(iii) the requirement that the Minister present to Parliament an annual report upon the work of the Ministry and the Central Advisory Councils.

(b) Part II : The Statutory System of Education

This provided for:

(i) the reorganisation of local educational administration. The Part III authorities were abolished, leaving the County and County Borough Councils (146 of them) as the only local education authorities and as such they were to undertake responsibility in respect of all stages of education in their areas. Provision was made, however, for divisional administration (via divisional executives and excepted districts) in the larger county areas; by this means county local education authorities could delegate their functions (the borrowing of money and the raising of rates excepted) to subordinate bodies better acquainted with the local circumstances affecting different parts of their areas;

(ii) the extension and stricter definition of the responsibilities of the local education authorities. They were required to make sufficient and satisfactory provision for primary and secondary education and to secure adequate facilities for further education in respect of persons over compulsory school age. The latter requirement included the duty to establish and maintain county colleges for the provision of compulsory part-time continuative education to the equivalent of 330 hours instruction per annum for the 15-18 years age group. It now became a duty for the authorities to provide medical inspection and treatment and meals and milk for pupils in maintained schools and for county college students. Furthermore, in carrying out their duties they were to show particular regard for the needs of nursery education and the education of handicapped children. To ensure that all these responsibilities were being satisfactorily met the Act required the local education authorities to submit development plans, which would be subject to amendment, to the Ministry;

(iii) the organisation of the statutory system of education as a continuum made up of primary, secondary and further stages. Primary and secondary schooling was to be provided separately with transfer between schools at eleven plus. The education given was to be appropriate to the children's different ages, abilities and aptitudes and to the different ages at which they might be expected to leave school. Some may regard this stipulation (see section 8 of the Act) as favourable to the provision of distinct types of secondary education in separate schools, but there was no mention of tripartite or selective arrangements and the provision was open to interpretation by the local authorities;

(iv) the raising of the school leaving age to fifteen years and its extension to sixteen years once the Ministry was satisfied that it had become a practical proposition. Provision was made for effecting the extension by Order in Council so as to avoid the need for later legislation;

(v) the abolition of all fees for admission to State maintained schools. This meant that places in selective schools (grammar and technical) maintained by the local education authorities would henceforth have to be obtained on scholastic merit;

(vi) the introduction of standard requirements for school management and governance. Henceforth all schools within the statutory system were to have a body of managers (primary) or governors (secondary). Such bodies were to be appointed by the local education authorities in the case of County schools; voluntary schools were to include representatives of the local education authority on their managing or governing bodies, but the arrangements in all respects were subject in their case to Ministry approval;

(vii) the modification of the dual system. Whilst it was retained and even extended to the secondary field, the detailed provisions forced the denominational schools to choose between their desire for more independence and their desire for greater financial support. Those schools established and maintained by the State (named 'provided' schools since 1902) were now to be called County schools. The schools founded by the churches (called 'non-provided' schools since 1902) were renamed voluntary schools and were to be divided into three categories according to the particular balance of privileges received and obligations accepted. The first category was the voluntary special agreement school which emanated from the 1936 Education Act. Under this measure the churches entered into over five hundred special agreements with local education authorities for the establishment of denominational secondary modern schools on the basis of 50-75% of the capital cost being borne by public funds. Because of the war only thirty-seven of these projects had materialised; the Act provided for the revival and implementation of any of the unfulfilled agreements on the original terms offered. The voluntary special agreement schools which emerged were allowed to provide denominational religious worship and instruction and their governing bodies were to enjoy a two-thirds majority of foundation trustees. But the appointment and dismissal of staff ('reserved' teachers for denominational religious teaching purposes excepted) was in the hands of the local education authority and the governors were committed to meeting one half of the capital cost of alterations and repairs to the school's exterior. Current costs were met by the local authority, as they had been since 1902 for voluntary schools. The second category was that of the voluntary controlled school and involved the surrender of their denominational independence and character in exchange for complete financial support from public funds. Two-thirds of the managers or governors of these schools were to be representatives of the local education authority. They were committed to undenominational religious worship and instruction (the latter according to an agreed syllabus), although special arrangements could be made for individual pupils in response to parental application for the provision of religious teaching according to the school's trust deed. Thus this category was not far removed from the ordinary County schools. The third category consisted of voluntary aided schools which retained the most favourable denominational position, though at a considerable price. Having provided the premises of these schools the churches undertook to meet half the cost of external alterations and repairs to the premises and in return received certain privileges. The denominational atmosphere remained completely intact and the church nominated two-thirds of the managers or governors. Indeed the school managing or governing body was given the responsibility for the appointment and dismissal of all (not just religious) teachers, though subject to the approval of the local authority.

The Act allowed the churches a period of six months to determine the category into which each of their voluntary schools should fall. Whilst more than half of the Anglican schools chose 'controlled' status, the Roman Catholic schools strongly preferred but reluctantly accepted the other more expensive possibilities;

(viii) the introduction of compulsory religious worship and instruction into all schools within the statutory system. In County and voluntary controlled schools (subject in the latter case to the special arrangements already mentioned) the religious education was to be undenominational and in accordance with an agreed syllabus drawn up by the Anglican and Free Churches in association with the teachers' organisations and the local authorities. In both County and voluntary schools religious worship and instruction would continue to be subject to the right of parents to withdraw their children from it. Moreover, the Act provided that, except in the case of voluntary aided schools or 'reserved' teachers, no teacher could be required to give religious instruction or should be penalised for not doing so. The provision for compulsory religious teaching in the schools was justified in terms of Christian heritage and the wishes of the majority of parents, but it was also expedient as a sop to the churches which had given ground over the reform of the dual system;

(ix) the execution of responsibility for the training and supply of teachers by the central authority. To fulfil this vital duty the Ministry was empowered to direct local education authorities to contribute in various ways to the support of the system of teacher training. One calculated result of this was the proper and equitable financing of teacher training. Hitherto all local authorities had employed teachers, whilst a minority were left with the burden of training them. New arrangements now emerged which divided the cost between central and local government on a 60:40 basis and required all local authorities to contribute to a pool according to the number of teachers they employed;

(x) the redefinition of parental duty in respect of the child's education. Previously parents had been required to ensure 'efficient elementary instruction in reading, writing and arithmetic'; now they were made responsible for ensuring their child received 'efficient full-time education suitable to (his) age, ability and aptitude, either by regular attendance at school or otherwise' (section 36). This requirement could be met by satisfactory home tuition or attendance at a registered independent school as well as through the statutory system.

(c) Part III: Independent Schools

This provided for:

(i) the registration of all independent schools with the Ministry as a statutory requirement for their continued operation or initiation;

(ii) the inspection of all independent schools by the Ministry, involving the possibility of removal from the register where standards of provision were judged inadequate. In this respect the nature of the premises, accommodation, instruction and proprietor were specified to be of particular importance. The Act provided for appeal to an

Independent Schools Tribunal where the proprietor was aggrieved by an unfavourable decision of the Ministry;

(iii) the introduction of Part III of the Act on 'an appointed day'. Thereafter, anyone conducting an unregistered independent school would be criminally liable.

In 1944 the private sector consisted of some ten thousand schools of various sorts and sizes, encompassing about one-twentieth of school pupils. The need was to protect the public from fee-paying schools providing an unsatisfactory education and thus the Act provided for a closer oversight of the private sector by the State. It was not, however, until 1957 that the Ministry found enough breathing space to apply this part of the Act.

(*d*) Part IV: General

This provided for:

(i) the reorganisation of central grants for education by means of Ministry regulations to place them on a more generous and equitable basis. Although the specific and percentage grant system introduced by the Fisher Act (1918) was retained, the actual grant formula was revised to raise the proportion of total expenditure met by the Treasury from the pre-war figure of 48% to a new level of 55%. The amount of aid received by any individual authority would vary according to its rateable wealth and size of school population and special additional assistance was made available for the poorest authorities. Thus a real attempt was made to shift more of the financial burden on to the shoulders of the central government as a necessary pre-condition of effecting the progress envisaged by the Act;

(ii) the grant of scholarships, exhibitions, bursaries and other allowances for further and advanced educational study by both the local education authorities and the Ministry. This was calculated to widen opportunities for undertaking full-time courses in teacher training and higher education;

(iii) the statutory recognition of the Burnham Committees and the salary scales for teachers agreed by them. This meant that henceforth all local education authorities were legally committed to paying Burnham scales (primary/secondary or further) once they had been agreed and approved by the Minister;

(iv) the consideration of parental wishes in relation to the education of their children within the context of the statutory system. But this general principle enunciated in section 76 of the Act was subject to serious qualifications; parental wishes were to be met only 'so far as is compatible with the provision of efficient instruction and training and the avoidance of unreasonable public expenditure', and in practice this put the local education authorities in a pretty strong position.

(e) Part V: Supplemental

This provided for:
   (i) safeguards against the danger of government by regulation. All regulations made under the Act or thereafter modified by the Ministry were to be laid before Parliament for forty days (with the possibility of being annulled) to acquire the force of law;
  (ii) a proper interpretation of the Act by giving definitions of various terms used (e.g. agreed syllabus, independent school, young person) and by clarifying the limits of the Act (e.g. inapplicable to Scotland and Northern Ireland).

3 An Assessment

The 1944 Act was probably the greatest single advance in English educational history, its provisions showing real breadth of outlook and considerable educational vision. Borne on the tide of wartime hopes and goodwill it even instrumented, in the interests of educational progress, a major revision of the dual system without engendering the usual acrimony. It has, in fact provided a fairly satisfactory legislative framework for the unprecedented expansion and development of the statutory system of education over the last thirty years. But, like many other measures, time has shown the 1944 Act to be a mixture of strengths and weaknesses.

In the 1943 White Paper Mr Butler readily admitted that 'legislation can do little more than prepare the way for reform' (page 26). Nevertheless, in various ways his measure made a really significant contribution to educational progress after the war.

(a) It wisely retained and purposefully refined the developing partnership in English education between the central and local authorities. The national interest in education received greater emphasis than hitherto, the new Ministry assuming clear responsibility for the control and direction of educational policy and development. The local education authorities were faced with many statutory duties which the Ministry was responsible for ensuring they fulfilled: the Minister was equipped with the necessary powers of enforcement and was authorised to administer and interpret the Act through the issue of statutory regulations and orders. Thus the balance of power changed to the disadvantage of the local authorities, but the central authority remained subject to the influence of Parliament and public opinion and was not authorised to initiate any new departures which contravened the letter or spirit of the Act. In a word, the increased power of the Ministry was strictly dependent upon and limited by the Act itself. The result was that Butler's measure allowed the central authority to give much more unity and direction to educational development, without being able to ride rough-shod at the expense of other interested parties.

(b) It rationalised the system of local educational administration by removing the distinction between Part II and Part III authorities and by giving statutory recognition to a single continuous educative process to be organised in three successive stages (primary, secondary and further) under one type of local education authority. Accordingly the County and County Borough Councils were given exclusive ultimate responsibility for the local administration of education, and the resultant diminution in the number and increase in the effective size of local education authorities made for improved provision and administration. The situation was further helped by the revision of the dual system in such a way that the voluntary schools were drawn much more firmly under the jurisdiction of the local authorities and received the financial wherewithal to meet the demands of the new Act.

(c) It provided free secondary education for all, finally burying the elementary tradition with all its shortcomings and class connotations. The raising of the school leaving age ensured a minimum of four years' secondary education for each child and the abolition of fee-paying places at State secondary schools met the demand for formal equality of educational opportunity for all. This was considered to be the most outstanding single contribution made by the Act to the future of education in England and Wales.

(d) It set the stage for the expansion and improvement of further and higher education. The establishment of secondary education for all obviously had implications for the stages that lay beyond it; once the secondary schools produced an enlarged number of appropriately qualified students, the demand for places in further and higher education would inevitably increase. Moreover, the local education authorities were now equally committed to making adequate provision in further education as in the primary and secondary fields. Thus both colleges of further education and teacher training colleges could hope to escape the comparative neglect they had suffered in the inter-war years. Finally, the provision for Ministry and local authority grants for students undertaking further or advanced studies was also calculated to wield a critical and beneficial influence in this field and in the growth of university education.

(*e*) It reformed the system of educational finance, thereby distributing the cost burden more equitably whilst at the same time encouraging and facilitating more generous provision. From 1944 to 1958 the main grant formula ensured that each local education authority received a specific central grant for education expressed as a percentage of its total net expenditure. This meant that the central government was committed to matching an authority's expenditure, thus encouraging the more progressive authorities to press ahead fast. It is no accident that public expenditure on education grew at an unprecedented rate 1944–58, or that the government changed the grant system to a general and fixed one by the special Act of 1958. Since then the local authorities have received a general 'rate support grant' to cover all their locally administered services (including education), and the annual sum is negotiated in advance. However, the new system, although objected to by the educational interest, has been manipulated to ensure a continuing high-level flow of resources into education.

Nonetheless, given the benefit of hindsight, there are various criticisms that may be levelled at the 1944 Act and it is significant that certain sections of informed educational opinion believe that a new legislative enactment is long overdue.

(*a*) It was over-ambitious, its provisions ranging over the whole educational field without any clear indication of priorities. Given the limited resources available for education, especially in the immediate post-war decade, the Act was unable to achieve many of its intended purposes within a reasonable time of its passage and meanwhile the relevant context was changing. Part III of the Act did not come into operation until 1957 and the county college scheme was quietly and it seems irretrievably shelved. The intended raising of the school leaving age to sixteen was progressively postponed and the provision of State nursery education on a widening scale virtually ignored until the early 1970s. It was not until after 1956 that technical education (within the further and higher stages) began to receive serious attention and the revitalisation of the Youth Service had to wait upon the Albemarle Report (1960). The junior schools for the 7-11 years age group, in respect of premises and accommodation had been represented in the White Paper as the 'Cinderellas' of the statutory system, yet it was not until 1970 that a clear policy of 'priority for primaries' emerged. The vigorous expansion and reform of teacher training was delayed until the 1960s, whereupon too much was attempted too quickly. The Act attempted so much that it can be argued that in the post-war setting an improvised and piecemeal response to its many demands was inevitable as well as unfortunate.

(b) It tolerated certain weaknesses in the reorganisation of local educational administration. Some of the 146 Counties (e.g. Rutland) and County Boroughs (e.g. Hastings) were really too small to operate as viable authorities, but they undertook the role on grounds of status rather than size. To placate certain municipal boroughs and large urban districts which ceased to be Part III authorities, the Act made provision for divisional administration in the county areas. As divisional executives were not democratically elected (apart from in excepted districts) and made for more expense and less efficiency in the administration of county education, there was a strong case against their existence. These particular weaknesses were given considerable attention in the Maud Report (1969) on the reform of local government which recommended the elimination of the smaller and minor authorities.

(c) It retained the dual system in a modified form in spite of its having proved such an obstacle to educational progress since 1902, and it introduced compulsory religious worship and instruction for all schools within the statutory system. The new arrangements and their later development have been subject to sharp criticism from secular and humanist sources. The considerable independence accorded to voluntary aided and special agreement schools by the Act was justified in terms of their meeting half of their capital and repair costs. Yet, faced with increasing financial pressure after the war, the churches successfully negotiated a further improvement in the financial arrangements for these schools. As the result of amending acts in 1959 and 1967 the church contribution was lowered to 20% and for the first time since 1870 building grants (of 80% of total cost) were made available for the establishment of new voluntary aided schools. Thus such schools are now able to maintain a denominational atmosphere and a favoured position, whilst the State meets all their running costs and 80% of their other costs. The result would seem to be an anomalous situation in relation to the principles governing the religious settlement of 1944. Indeed, the critics insist that experience has shown that the 1944 Act began an erosive process, the logical extension of which is the final acceptance of a Scottish solution by which denominational schools, whilst retaining their particular identity, will be completely financed from public funds. To some people this would be a betrayal of one of the fundamental principles which has governed educational development in

England and Wales since 1870. The provision for compulsory religious worship and instruction has produced more widespread and growing criticism, leading to the recent pressures (especially from the Humanist Association) for the repeal of this particular requirement. Thus the Act has thrown up a new area of sharp controversy where there was not one before.

(*d*) It left the organisation of secondary education for all to local discretion, provision according to 'age, ability and aptitude' being consistent with either selective or comprehensive arrangements. The lack of clear central direction produced a patchwork of local solutions which varied very greatly in the extent to which they afforded the sort of opportunities envisaged by the Act; this in turn left the way open for the organisation of secondary education to become a bitter party political issue. One unfortunate side-effect of the prolonged and continuing controversy over this matter has been the waste of so much time and energy upon the secondary sector to the comparative neglect of other educational problems (e.g. the state of primary education).

(*e*) It failed to achieve the egalitarian ideal which inspired its passage because of the continued existence of the independent schools, the anomalous position of the direct grant schools (with their large proportion of fee-paying places) and the favoured treatment accorded by most local authorities to their grammar schools. Given this loaded context the secondary modern schools were unable to realise that parity of status and esteem to which so much official lip-service had been paid, and equality of educational opportunity through secondary education for all became a pious hope rather than the reality intended. Nor could comprehensive reorganisation within the existing framework completely solve this problem, for the Act had left the private sector largely unaffected.

4 Post-War Difficulties

The 1944 Act had to be implemented in the face of two critical problems:

(*a*) Shortage of Accommodation

Enemy action had destroyed about 200,000 school places during the war years when school building was temporarily suspended, and the raising of the school leaving age necessitated the provision of an extra 400,000 places virtually overnight. As the schools were competing for short resources with other deserving sectors of national life (e.g. housing and industry) in the period of post-war austerity, improvisation and post-ponement were the inevitable results. Rising costs and the post-war rise in the birth rate further embarrassed the Ministry and the local education authorities as they strained to make Butler's dream a reality. The county college scheme, the need for nursery schools and the hopes of the Youth Service were soon all being ignored. Additional places were provided by an emergency operation which depended on the use of wooden huts and utility furniture. Meanwhile hundreds of dilapidated primary schools originally built in the nineteenth century, had to continue serving the needs of the post-war educational system. Far too many secondary modern schools were also housed in unsatisfactory premises and lacked proper facilities for their adolescent pupils. As late as 1963 the National Union of Teachers' report on *The State of our Schools* clearly showed that the problem was still a really major one. *and still is, in Norfolk.*

(*b*) Shortage of Teachers

The loss of teachers killed on active service, the strict curtailment of teacher training during the Second World War, the raising of the school leaving age and the unexpectedly sharp rise in the birth-rate all combined to produce a serious and continuing shortage of teachers. Again the situation had to be met by various expedients, some of which ran counter to the spirit, if not the letter, of the 1944 Act. An Emergency One-Year Training Scheme for ex-servicemen produced an extra 35,000 teachers during its period of operation. Over-size classes (i.e. 40+ primary and 30+ secondary) were accepted as a matter of course. The Ministry instituted a strict quota system to ration the distribution of qualified teachers and could not afford to eliminate the unqualified from service. The three year course for teacher training could not be introduced until 1960. Not until the late 1950s did the government find the resources to mount the real solution: from 1958 a crash programme was launched to expand the training colleges and this expansion continued under the impetus of the Robbins Report (1963). But it was not until the early 1970s that the situation was finally brought under reasonable control.

5 Selection versus Comprehension

In 1942 both the Labour Party Conference and the Trades Union Congress gave their official support to the idea of a common school as the basis for secondary education for all. Three years later the Labour government of Clement Attlee was swept into power as a result of the post-war election. Yet in the immediate post-war years the great majority of local education authorities organised secondary education selectively along tripartite or bipartite lines (only half of them bothered to develop secondary technical schools). Some authorities established bilateral schools, but only a tiny minority established or planned multilateral or comprehensive schools; the Isle of Man, Anglesey, and certain parts of rural Wales embraced the common school for reasons of practicality and economy, but only London and Coventry chose and effected this alternative on grounds of principle. The Ministry, though desisting from any open and bold attempt to push the tripartite approach, refused to recommend multilateral or comprehensive organisation and insisted that such experiments should involve the development of very large schools of about 1,600 pupils to ensure the emergence of an economic sixth form. It was not until they were on the verge of electoral defeat in 1951 that the Labour leadership produced *A Policy for Secondary Education* and came out strongly in favour of comprehensive education. Meanwhile innumerable Labour-controlled authorities had done little or nothing to advance the cause of the common school in spite of the room for manoeuvre allowed under the 1944 Act. When Churchill's Conservative government took office, six years of Labour rule had resulted in the actual establishment of some thirteen comprehensive schools which accounted for less than 0·5% of the secondary school population. This curious fact has a number of explanations:

(a) a lack of real enthusiasm for the comprehensive school on the part of the Labour leadership, which saw the State grammar school (now at last opened completely to talent) as the best answer to the competition of the independent public schools. Many Labour leaders, both central and local, were grammar school products themselves and their loyalty to the traditional institution inevitably died hard; throughout the inter-war years they fought to secure open competition for all State grammar school places and this had limited their horizons;

(b) a deep distrust of multilateral and comprehensive schools on the part of the professional civil servants at the Ministry and professional administrators serving the local education authorities. The majority of these professionals had received a grammar school and university education and their sympathies lay with an elitist approach to educational opportunity. The Labour party, long starved of office, did not find it easy to challenge their advice;

(c) the process of conditioning and associated developments related to the organisation of secondary education going back to the early 1920s. Convinced of the overriding importance of individual ability differences and secure in their belief in the efficacy of intelligence testing, the Hadow, Spens and Norwood Committees had sanctified the selective approach to secondary education. Given the pre-war development of grammar, technical and modern schools the line of least resistance after 1944 was the tripartite solution, and the many other problems faced by the local authorities at this time ensured that the temptation to take it was very great;

(d) the serious doubts about comprehensives, and even outright hostility toward them, amongst the teaching profession. Secondary modern teachers quickly became jealous of the independence of their own growing empire with its particular character and opportunities for non-graduates, whilst selective school teachers remained fearful of academic traditions being lost in a common school and of having to cope with the whole ability range. Even the National Union of Teachers, which had resolved to support comprehensive experiments at its 1943 Conference, became distinctly luke-warm in its attitude.

Thus by 1951 comprehensives had made only insignificant headway at the expense of the selective system. For the next thirteen years of Conservative rule Ministry policy was to use its influence (especially financial) to limit comprehensive advance to new purpose-built schools which did not injure the fortunes of existing grammar schools. The Conservative government was happy that the tripartite or bipartite approach should continue, although Sir Edward Boyle ultimately began to educate some of his party colleagues to see properly developed comprehensives as an acceptable alternative. But meanwhile the selective system and the associated eleven-plus examination were having to face growing criticism and mounting challenge; this was the result of a number of influences and developments:

(a) the gradual recognition that the tripartite approach rested on palpably false premises and highly questionable procedures. Norwood's three psychological categories with their different qualitative minds was naïve and unacceptable as a basic proposition. Professional educationists such as Brian Simon, John Daniels and Philip Vernon went on to undermine the long-standing reputation of intelligence tests as a reliable predictor and means of eleven-plus selection. In 1957 a high-powered investigation on behalf of the National Foundation of Educational Research revealed a 12% margin of error in the existing selection procedures; translated into national terms this meant that some 70,000 children were being mis-selected at eleven-plus every year. It was also shown that, in a context which cried out for the later reassessment of the initial selection, less than 1·5% of eleven-plus failures were subsequently transferred from modern to selective schools. Finally, the psychological ill-effects of eleven-plus failure on pupil motivation and progress, especially in the case of borderline candidates, were also investigated and to some extent substantiated. If eleven-plus selection was already unpopular with a growing number of parents and teachers, it was now shown to be unreliable and unfair as well;

(b) the organisational and geographical anomalies which emerged and could not be defended. The selective system conformed to no generally accepted pattern; indeed many authorities chose to ignore the technical school and organised along simple bipartite lines. The result was a hotch-potch of arrangements which differed in detail and were the result of local option rather than any clear national policy. The proportion of eleven-plus pupils awarded selective school places varied from about 10% to over 40% with wide variations often occurring between adjacent authorities. Unofficially there was a 'black list' of local education authorities with low selective entry percentages: for a child to be brought up in such an area meant only a slim chance of a grammar school education. Yet the Ministry made no real attempt, and perhaps did not have the inclination or the power, to equalise selective entry proportions throughout the country at a reasonable and considered level;

(c) the successful development of General Certificate of Education O-level courses by some secondary modern schools after 1952, when they were freed from the previous ban on their entering their pupils for external examinations. The subsequent results showed that many eleven-plus failures had academic potential which could be capitalised upon; by the end of the decade a few such pupils had even forced their way through to the universities. But only a minority of secondary modern schools were adequately staffed or equipped to run such courses effectively. The consequent waste of talent was bemoaned as well as demonstrated by both the Crowther (1959) and Newsom (1963) Reports, although their recommended solution was the improvement of the secondary modern schools rather than the abandonment of selection;

(d) the mounting concern over the sociological dimensions of the eleven-plus examination and the selective system. Because of the social distribution of intelligence and educational attainment it was inevitable, in spite of the formal equality of opportunity vested in the eleven-plus examination, that the middle class should continue to dominate the grammar schools whilst the secondary modern schools became the preserve of the working class. Evidence was produced to show that many working class children, fortunate enough to be selected for a grammar school education, either failed to meet requirements or in doing so became alienated from their own home background. Thus it was argued that eleven-plus selection tied the organisation of secondary education very strongly to differences in social class background and accordingly the selective system was castigated as an intolerably divisive influence in a democratic community. The recommended solution to this social problem was the comprehensive school.

Although forceful and considered counter-arguments were presented in defence of the grammar school and the retention of selection by Eric James, Harry Ree, G. H. Bantock and the Joint Four (a committee representing teachers in selective schools), the opposition to the continuance of the eleven-plus grew visibly stronger and was reinforced by the increasing objection to its backlash effect upon the work of the primary schools. In 1953, its reorganisation along comprehensive lines now complete, Anglesey achieved the distinction of being the first local authority completely to abandon the eleven-plus examination. The Labour party now closed its ranks and fully embraced the comprehensive cause; in 1955 comprehensive schools appeared in a Labour party election manifesto for the first time. In 1957 the Leicestershire Plan was launched, with the Conservative government's approval, to demonstrate the viability of a two-tier comprehensive system as an alternative to the very large all-through comprehensives pioneered by the London County Council. As a two-tier arrangement was much more compatible with the use of existing secondary school buildings and avoided the disadvantage of overpowering size, this experiment was a significant departure calculated to ease the way forward. In 1964 the Conservative government amended the 1944 Act to allow the West Riding authority to introduce the new middle school for the 9-13 years age group as another means of comprehensive reorganisation. Resistance was visibly weakening and the comprehensive tide was beginning to swell in Labour controlled areas: by the time the Conservatives fell from power in 1964 the number of comprehensive schools had risen to well over two hundred and now accounted for nearly 8% of secondary school pupils.

Given the developing context just described it was not long before the new Labour government of Harold Wilson decided the time was ripe to move from local option to a national policy in relation to secondary education. The result was Circular 10/65 on *The Organisation of Secondary Education* by which Mr A. Crosland, the Secretary of State for Education, exhorted all local education authorities to submit plans within a year for the comprehensive reorganisation of secondary education. This was followed later by Circular 10/66 which applied financial pressure by announcing that future secondary building programmes would only be approved so far as they were compatible with comprehensive reorganisation. In 1967 the government amended the financial arrangements for the voluntary schools to facilitate the co-operation of the churches in the reorganisation process. Meanwhile some 80% of the local education authorities made satisfactory responses to Circular 10/65 and only eighteen failed to respond in any shape or form. In 1970 the government determined to overcome the resistance of unco-operative Conservative-controlled authorities through new legislation and a bill was introduced to Parliament to accomplish this; at the same time the government received the Donnison Report which recommended that the direct-grant schools be given a straight choice between incorporation within the comprehensive system or independence and loss of State financial aid. The stage seemed set for a final showdown when the unexpected Conservative electoral victory later in the year radically changed the situation.

One of the first acts of Mrs Thatcher, the new Conservative Secretary of State for Education, was to withdraw Circular 10/65. It was replaced by Circular 10/70, the declared purpose of which was to restore the local education authorities' freedom of choice and action; to this end they were removed from any obligation to submit schemes of comprehensive reorganisation or to proceed with schemes already approved. This secured the position of those Conservative-controlled authorities which had previously responded to Circular 10/65 with delaying tactics or open resistance. But in practice it did not secure similar freedom for those authorities (a number of which were in fact Conservative-held) intent upon the completion or initiation of comprehensive reorganisation plans. Following the return of the Conservatives to office (1970) such plans were subject to a number of developments calculated to slow down the change from selection to comprehension. Firstly, the Department of Education and Science began to examine all plans school by school; this resulted in decisions being long delayed and to the partial approval of schemes. The latter result was particularly associated with Mrs Thatcher's refusal to approve the disappearance of nearly one hundred grammar schools; such refusal punctured the total scheme, required the retention of some selection and resulted in new comprehensives being little more than misnamed secondary modern schools. Secondly, and most significantly, the Conservative government combined its 'priority for primaries' policy with a determined attempt to deny capital funds to the secondary sector. Expenditure on secondary school building, beyond the separately financed programme for raising the school leaving age, was made strictly dependent upon establishing a need for 'roofs over heads', thereby gravely limiting the room for manoeuvre available for the promotion of satisfactory reorganisation. The White Paper *Education: a Framework for Expansion*, issued at the close of 1972, made it clear that the government did not intend to change this policy for at least two years. Already the National Foundation for Educational Research had shown that the first two years of Conservative rule had begun to slow down the change to comprehensive education, and later the National Union of Teachers, now fully committed to the end of selection, registered its protest by the publication of an official pamphlet called *What is Mrs Thatcher up to?*

However, the tide continued to run in favour of comprehensive reorganisation, the advent of a Conservative government having simply stiffened the resistance to it. The proportion of secondary pupils in comprehensive schools increased progressively from 8% to 40% between 1964 and 1972. But after 1970 the continued rise owed more to the impetus derived from the period of Labour rule than to the actions of the Conservative government. And to keep the situation in perspective it is necessary to appreciate that only one-third of the local education authorities completely abandoned the eleven-plus examination; late in 1972 one-third still operated selection procedures for all their eleven-year-olds, whilst one-third retained selection in one or more parts of their areas. Meanwhile the Labour party promised that, when it was returned to power, it would legislate to require all local education authorities to go completely comprehensive. Such a policy was supported by the National Union of Teachers.

Follow-up: Attempt to cover as much of the following ground as possible.
1 *Read* Bagley, J. J. and A. J. *The State and Education in England and Wales, 1833-1968*, Chapter 6
Curtis, S. J. and Boultwood, M. E. *An Introductory History of English Education since 1800*, Chapter IX
Barnard, H. C. *A History of English Education from 1760*, Chapters XXXII and XXXIV
Dent, H. C. *The Education Act 1944*, especially Parts I and II
Digest on 'Comprehensive Schools' in journal *Education*, 16 June 1972
2 *Consult* Maclure, J. S. *Educational Documents: England and Wales 1816-1968*; items 34, 37 and 48 are relevant.
Appendix I on Circular 10/65 *The Organisation of Secondary Education* (pages 333-5 of this book)
Appendix II on 'Arguments for and against the Comprehensive Organisation of Secondary Education' (pages 336-9 of this book)

3 *Clarify the following: the contents of the 1943 White Paper on* Educational Reconstruction; *the provisions of the 1944 Act concerning the central authority for education, local educational administration, the staging of education, the dual system and religious education; the significance of the 1944 Act in relation to equality of educational opportunity; the strengths and weaknesses of the 1944 Act in the light of developments since its passage; the post-war problems which made for difficulties in implementing the 1944 Act; the influences and developments which undermined support for selection at eleven plus; the contents of* Circular 10/65 *on* The Organisation of Secondary Education; *some of the arguments for and against the comprehensive organisation of secondary education.*

Chapter Eight
The Training and Employment of Teachers

Purpose: to emphasise the unsatisfactory nature of teacher education and training, conditions of employment and occupational status during the nineteenth century, to consider some of the most welcome and significant changes which have occurred since, and to review the recent situation in the light of the historical background so provided.

It is surely a truism that any system of education is only as good as the number and quality of the teachers it employs. In the long run the interests of education and the interests of the teachers are one and the same; the recruitment of well-qualified entrants on a sufficient scale, their satisfactory further education and training, and the provision of salaries and conditions of service calculated to sustain real professional status are all critical to the educational welfare of children as well as to the well-being of teachers. But the practical realisation of this axiomatic principle has involved a long and continuing struggle in relation to which a successful end is not yet in clear sight.

1 The History of Teacher Training Before 1944

It must be recognised that the nineteenth century was an age in which elementary education was not only in short supply, but also the majority of teachers providing it were neither trained nor certificated. Indeed many of the dame, common day and charity schools of the early nineteenth century were staffed by female child-minders and men who had failed at other trades or who treated teaching as a second source of income; most such persons had little or no education themselves and, at best, it was often a matter of the one-eyed leading the blind. It was only very slowly that the concept of a wholly trained and certificated corps of elementary schoolteachers emerged and gained acceptance. In this process a number of phases may be distinguished.

(a) 1805-39 The Monitorial Phase
The National Society and the British and Foreign School Society both supported a number of normal schools to provide senior pupils and other

people with a thorough working knowledge of Bell's or Lancaster's monitorial technique before going out to take charge of their own schools. But such training was of very short duration and made no attempt to raise the usually very low level of personal education of the individuals concerned.

(*b*) 1839-90 The Age of the Pupil-Teacher System

Because of its failure to serve as an effective vehicle for moral and social training, the monitorial system gradually suffered a decline in its popularity. In the 1830s David Stow developed the simultaneous system of class teaching in which an appropriately trained adult teacher directed the learning and moral development of a very large class of children. From his Glasgow Normal Seminary (established 1837) Stow's ideas spread south of the border and were particularly welcomed by Kay-Shuttleworth and the National Society. Encouraged by the new Committee of Council for Education, the National Society began to found new colleges and to transform its existing monitorial normal schools; between 1839 and 1845 over twenty such Anglican establishments emerged for the training of adults along the new lines. The great difficulty was that of obtaining satisfactory entrants of eighteen or over; the attempted solution to this problem was the introduction of the pupil-teacher system by Kay-Shuttleworth in 1846. Initiated by Minutes of the Committee of Council to provide competent teachers for grant-aided elementary schools, the pupil-teacher system incorporated two progressive features:

(i) the official selection and apprenticeship training of young persons who served as pupil-teachers from thirteen to eighteen years in specially chosen grant-aided schools. Required to teach all day, the pupil-teachers were dependent upon the headteacher for the improvement of their own knowledge and this had to be accomplished outside normal school hours. Periodically they were examined by one of H.M. Inspectors and were paid a small stipend to help maintain themselves;

(ii) the provision of Queen's scholarships for outstanding pupil-teachers to support their attendance at a two-year training college course. With the help of much increased State financial aid, the denominational colleges expanded in size and numbers to train these Queen's scholars; by 1859 there were thirty-four such colleges catering for some 2,500 students. The Education Department bestowed official certificates upon those successfully negotiating the final examinations, so giving rise to a growing elite of trained certificated elementary schoolteachers. Those pupil-teachers who successfully completed their apprenticeship, but failed to obtain one of the limited number of Queen's scholarships, could take the Department's examinations externally and so become an untrained certificated teacher. But many pupil-teachers were content to serve as completely uncertificated teachers and spent their lifetime in the schools in that inferior capacity. Under Kay-Shuttleworth's influence the Committee extended proficiency grants and limited pension rights to certificated teachers.

The pupil-teacher system, backed by the denominational training colleges, formed the base of the developing system of elementary education in the latter half of the nineteenth century, but its operation was gradually modified and even challenged by a number of developments.

(i) *The Revised Code (1862)*

The 'payment by results' system emphasised the aridity of the pupil-teacher system as the apprentices were increasingly committed to a taxing and narrow concentration upon drilling in the three Rs. The sharp reduction in the number of Queen's scholarships and the withdrawal of building grants checked the expansion of the denominational training colleges, whilst the associated restriction of their curricula finally scotched any hope of their providing their students with a more liberal education.

(ii) *1870 Education Act*

Because it resulted in a sudden and impressive rise in the number of elementary school pupils without providing for any means of expanding the supply of teachers, this measure placed the existing pupil-teacher system and training colleges under great strain. The number of pupil-teachers was rapidly increased and training college courses were shortened and certification manipulated in order to get bodies into classrooms. Nevertheless, there was a significant rise in the average size of classes being prepared for the Department's annual examinations.

(iii) *Development of Pupil-Teacher Centres*

The traditional dependence of pupil-teachers on the knowledge and energy (or otherwise) of their headteacher for raising the level of their personal education was recognised by some of the larger School Boards as a palpable weakness. Led by the Liverpool School Board they began to provide pupil-teacher centres at which, by evening and Saturday attendance, their apprentices could obtain a poor man's secondary education; in 1884 the Education Department authorised half-time attendance by pupil-teachers at such centres. Those able to attend the centres were soon achieving results in the Queen's scholarship examinations out of all proportion to their numbers.

(iv) *Report of the Cross Commission (1888)*

Whilst the Majority report admitted the need to improve the pupil-teacher system, the Minority report condemned pupil-teachers as persons who were 'badly taught and who taught badly' and called for the abandonment of the system. Furthermore there was general agreement upon the need to expand training college provision, especially on a non-residential and undenominational basis. The continuance of the Kay-Shuttleworth system was now being called into question.

(c) 1890-1914 The Emergence of the Modern System

This was a period of innovation and expansion during which the foundations of the twentieth century system of teacher education and training were laid by a number of critical developments:

(i) the development of day training colleges attached to universities and university colleges. This recommendation of the Cross Commission produced an immediate and full response and by 1900 there were sixteen such new institutions containing about 1,200 students. Apart from making a major contribution to the training of an increased number of certificated teachers, their development had a wider significance. They broke the denominational monopoly of teacher training and successfully challenged the assumption that only residential training was a satisfactory proposition. The development also ended the former complete isolation of the training colleges from the field of higher education. For the first time student teachers were able to undertake degree courses and the universities became interested in the development of educational theory. The new arrangements provided the earliest facilities for the professional training of graduates for secondary schoolteaching;

(ii) the development of municipal training colleges by Part II local education authorities as authorised by the 1902 Education Act. By the outbreak of the First World War there were twenty-two of these colleges helping to swell the number of training places available; some were day institutions, others partly residential, but all were non-denominational. The former Anglican domination of teacher training thus received a further setback;

(iii) the dismantlement of the pupil-teacher system in favour of a full secondary education for all intending elementary teachers. This course of action had been recommended in the Report of the Departmental Committee on *The Pupil-Teacher System* (1898) and had the full support of Robert Morant when he became Permanent Secretary to the Board of Education in 1903. The 1902 Act, which authorised the Part II authorities to develop State

E

secondary education and an associated system of scholarship places, provided the necessary basis for radical change. In 1903 Morant issued the first self-contained set of regulations for pupil-teachers and training college students; the minimum age for the apprenticeship of pupil-teachers was raised to sixteen for the express purpose of enabling them to obtain at least four years of full-time secondary education. In 1907 further regulations introduced the bursary system by which intending teachers were to continue their secondary education from sixteen to eighteen years pending direct transference to training college. Initially it was possible to serve for one year as a student teacher before going to college and in the remoter rural areas the revised pupil-teacher system continued to operate; but during the inter-war years these anomalies were destined to be gradually phased out;

(iv) the acceptance by the Board of Education in 1911 of a four year course for graduate certification. Since the 1890s students attending the day training colleges had found it a tall order to combine study for a degree with their professional training even when the time allowed was raised to three years. After lengthy resistance the Board conceded grant for the support of a consecutive three plus one arrangement for such students. Thereafter the University Education Departments rapidly assumed their modern form, concerning themselves with the provision of a year's professional training for graduates.

Thus by 1914 the basis for the modern pattern of teacher education and training had already emerged, with Morant having been the central figure in its development.

(*d*) 1914-44 The Consolidation of the Modern System

The inter-war period was one of consolidation rather than expansion and change in the field of teacher training. Only six new colleges emerged against the background of fluctuation and stringency in educational expenditure and the recurrent threat of unemployment amongst qualified teachers. But the Morant system became firmly established and received the approval of the Report of the Departmental Committee on *The Training of Teachers in Public Elementary Schools* (1925). Basically the new pattern rested on the concept of teaching as a professional occupation, entry into which would be dependent upon the completion of a full secondary education, matriculation and two years teacher training at a recognised college. Until 1926 the examination and certification of teachers remained the strict responsibility of the Board of Education, but in that year, following a recommendation of the Departmental

Committee, the examining function was devolved upon Joint Examining Boards on which the training colleges and associated regional universities were represented. Ten such Boards emerged to cover the country and all were in operation by 1930. This development did something to bring the universities and the training colleges into closer association to the benefit of the latter's status. In most cases however the relationship remained a limited rather than a full-blooded one; the colleges were still on the fringe of higher education rather than within it. Meanwhile, being in receipt of an increasing number of well-qualified ex-sixth formers, the colleges were beginning to move away from the wide and equal coverage of all the subjects of the elementary curriculum towards the further study in depth of one or two particular subjects along university pass degree lines.

The foregoing analysis is primarily concerned with the training of teachers for elementary schools. In the secondary sector the tradition that the possession of a degree was in itself a qualification to teach died very hard. But after 1890 there was a slow but steady growth in secondary teacher training, which gradually undermined the dominance of the untrained graduate in the secondary field. The Board's recognition of four-year courses in 1911 and the consequent shaping of the University Education Departments is something of an early landmark in this respect.

2 Teacher Employment; Status and Supply Before 1944

It is difficult to appreciate how onerous were the conditions of employment for elementary teachers, and how low was their status, before the First World War.

(a) Conditions of Employment

Highly unsatisfactory in the mid-nineteenth century when Kay-Shuttleworth's influence at least extended a pseudo-Civil Service position to the new certificated teachers, conditions of employment became even worse as a result of the Revised Code (1862) and the rapid expansion of elementary education consequent upon the 1870 Act. The deteriorating situation produced the National Union of Elementary Teachers, established in 1870, to fight for an improvement of the teachers' wretched lot. During the ensuing half-century the union campaigned upon control of entry to the profession, the registration of teachers, capricious dismissal, compulsory extraneous duties, admission to H.M. Inspectorate, the abolition of payment by results, the restitution and improvement of pension rights, better salaries and more favourable staffing ratios. In spite of some limited gains, the pre-war position was still so unsatisfactory that it helped to produce a growing recruitment problem after 1907 which forced the Board temporarily to suspend its attempt to eliminate unqualified persons from the schools.

(*b*) Status

The status accorded by contemporary society to those who taught in the elementary schools of the early and mid-nineteenth century was inevitably and deservedly low. But even later when the pupil-teacher system, college training and government certification, and the National Union of Elementary Teachers had come to wield a more professional influence, the status of elementary teachers continued to be undermined by a number of factors.

(i) Elementary teachers were drawn almost exclusively from the ranks of the upper working class. No respectable middle class family would allow its sons or daughters to lower themselves by entering elementary teaching. Thus in the highly class-conscious context of Victorian society their social origins proved a severe status handicap to elementary schoolteachers. This contrasted sharply with the much more favourable position of middle class graduates serving in the reformed public and endowed grammar schools.

(ii) The rapid expansion in the demand for elementary teachers following the 1870 Act resulted in a process of dilution. In quarter of a century there was a five-fold increase in the size of the total teaching force and this was achieved by lowering the standards of the certificate examination and various other expedients. At the turn of the century the staff employed in the nation's elementary schools consisted of the following categories:

Trained certificated (the elite)	32%
Untrained certificated (external)	25%
Uncertificated ex-pupil-teachers	28%
Article 68-ers	15%

Thus at the close of Victoria's reign, when the number of elementary teachers reached 110,000, over two-fifths of them were still uncertificated; and this ignores the existence of some 30,000 odd pupil-teachers whose services were essential to the manning of the schools. The Article 68-ers were a species of teacher officially recognised by the 1893 Code and employed upon the satisfaction of four conditions: that they were female, that they were over eighteen years of age, that they had been vaccinated and that they had received the (perfunctory) approval of a visiting H.M. Inspector. They were little more than a source of cheap labour, widely employed by the hard pressed voluntary schools and much resented by the rest of the aspiring profession.

(iii) Elementary schoolteaching became dominated by women, the proportion rising from 53% in 1869 to 75% thirty years later. This trend was strongly associated with the dilution process; at the end of the century less than one-quarter of female elementary teachers were trained and certificated compared with almost three-fifths of their male counterparts. The employment of female teachers was encouraged by the significantly lower cost of hiring their services. Meanwhile other reputable professions remained male preserves in a society still insisting that woman's only place was in the home.

(iv) the conditions of work (described earlier) were associated with low and variable salaries. Promotion prospects were poor as the number of headships was limited and entry to the Inspectorate barred to non-graduates. Since 1862 the elementary teacher had become the hired servant of his employer with his income subject to anxious individual negotiation; even the 1902 Act did not provide for the introduction of machinery for the agreement and payment of a national set of salary scales.

Little wonder that many skilled artisans looked upon the elementary schoolteacher with scant respect, whilst the middle class attitude was one of derision, a derision sharpened by the elementary schoolteachers' aspiration to join that very class.

The period 1916-22, during which H. A. L. Fisher was President of the Board of Education and wartime experience stimulated an unprecedented national interest in educational improvement, may be regarded as a turning point in the fortunes of the teaching profession. Five developments combined then or shortly thereafter immeasurably to improve the position and status of teachers:

(a) the establishment of the Burnham Committee (1920) for the negotiation of national salary scales and the passage of the Teachers' Superannuation Act (1918), which combined to provide elementary schoolteachers with much greater financial security;

(b) the post-war slump and the subsequently depressed economic conditions, which paradoxically benefited the teachers. Reasonably secure in their jobs and having refused to tie the Burnham salary scales to a cost of living index, they were able to improve their real incomes because retail prices fell more heavily than their salaries, even though the latter were subjected to the vicious Geddes (1922) and May (1931) Committee cuts;

(c) the unprecedently low birth-rate of the inter-war period and the surfeit of unmarried female teachers. This situation provided the opportunity for improving the teacher-pupil ratio which had been so unfavourable before the First World War. This situation also facilitated a marked reduction in the employment of uncertificated teachers;

(*d*) the long-term influence of Fisher upon the local authorities and the public at large. Taking advantage of the widespread interest in post-war reconstruction, he was able to elevate the importance of both education and the teacher in national life. He exhorted the teachers to improve their professional image and did all he could personally to improve their status. Some of the effect of this was lost in the economic troubles that later supervened but it was never completely dissipated;

(*e*) the rising standard of entrants to the profession once the Morant system became firmly established. By the 1930s it was no longer exceptional to find graduate teachers serving in the elementary sector, especially in the new secondary modern schools which were emerging as part of the Hadow reorganisation process.

But in spite of this welcome advance a serious dichotomy still divided the profession and weakened its claim to full status recognition; this was the distinction between elementary and grammar schoolteachers, reinforced by the Board's separate regulations for the respective sectors. Throughout the inter-war years, in spite of much talk about parity of esteem, they experienced different terms of employment and were allotted separate pay scales; the clear implication was that the elementary teacher was inferior in status to his secondary grammar counterpart. This could not but harm the cause of the profession as a whole, for the great majority of teachers served in the elementary field. Another weakness resulted from the Board's refusal to make an approved course of training and proper certification a strict condition of entry to the teaching profession; neither the exhortations of the National Union of Teachers nor the recommendations of the 1925 Departmental Committee had prevailed in this respect, and the employment of unqualified staff continued though on a declining scale.

3 Post-War Developments

In broad terms the post-war period has been one of early improvisation and later major expansion and change in the field of teacher training and supply. Whilst maintaining their connection with the local education authorities and the churches, the training colleges have strengthened both their association with the universities and their own independence, finally to take their place as a recognised sector of higher education. In relation to this basic context a number of particular developments and problems are worth considering.

(a) McNair Report on *Teachers and Youth Leaders* (1944)

The Departmental Committee set up under the chairmanship of Sir Arnold McNair investigated the supply, recruitment and training of teachers and through its critical recommendations did much to influence the future course of development in the field concerned. The prime concern of the report was the need to establish a truly national and co-ordinated system of teacher training to end the traditional isolation and lack of integration of the various training institutions, and to improve the supply and quality of teachers to match the new demands of the 1944 Act. Out of this concern arose the committee's specific recommendations:

  (i) the establishment of a Central Training Council to initiate the new administrative framework for a co-ordinated system of teacher training and to advise the Board on matters concerned with the supply, recruitment and training of teachers. Out of this was to emerge the National Advisory Council on the Training and Supply of Teachers.

 (ii) the setting up of Area Training Organisations on a regional basis to integrate the efforts of various colleges and to draw the universities more firmly into the business of teacher education and training. Two alternative schemes were suggested for the actual form which these Area Training Organisations should take. Half of the Committee recommended University Schools of Education consisting of an 'organic federation' of training institutions operating in a given area. The other half of the Committee favoured Joint Boards, which would maintain separate institutional identity to a much greater degree and which could be more easily developed from the existing Joint Examining Boards. Happily it was the first arrangement which won official support and came to characterise most of the Area Training Organisations and their associated Institutes (or Schools) of Education.

(iii) the adoption of various measures to increase the supply and improve the quality of teachers. The detailed recommendations made were calculated to facilitate the expansion of the teaching force by the minimum 25% deemed necessary and to raise the attractions and status of the teaching profession as a means to that end. They included the consolidation and improvement of teachers' basic salaries (with substantial additions for special qualifications and responsibilities), the recruitment of mature persons and an end to the disqualification of married women teachers, and the lengthening of the teacher training course from two to three years at the earliest possible juncture.

The report obtained immediate acceptance in principle and, with some refinements, was implemented in piecemeal fashion during the period 1945-60. Indeed, it became the basis of the post-war national system of teacher education and training in England and Wales.

(*b*) 1944 Education Act

This affected the over-all situation in several ways:

  (i) through associated regulations, it redefined 'qualified' teacher to end the sharp pre-war distinction between elementary and secondary teachers;

 (ii) it gave statutory authority to the Burnham negotiating machinery and required a single consolidated scale to cover the salaries of all teachers;

(iii) it secured teachers from dismissal on grounds of religion or marriage;

(iv) it specified the duties of the Ministry of Education and the local education authorities as to the training of teachers. Over-all responsibility was clearly lodged with the former, but the latter were committed to making a full contribution both financially and otherwise.

(*c*) Post-War Shortage of Teachers

In spite of a large increase in the number of training colleges during the first decade of peace, the unexpectedly high post-war birth rate, the high wastage rate amongst women teachers and stiff competition from industry for qualified people combined to produce an acute shortage of teachers. The situation was met by a series of improvised and palliative measures:

  (i) the Emergency Training Schemes for ex-servicemen and unqualified serving practitioners which added almost 40,000 to the total teaching force by 1952;

 (ii) the continuance of untrained graduate entry to the profession and the postponement of the introduction of three-year teacher training until 1960;

(iii) the development of special day training colleges for mature entrants combined with a national campaign to increase the number of married returnees and part-time teachers;

(iv) the enforcement of a Ministry quota scheme designed to ensure the fair distribution of available qualified staff;

(v) the reconstitution and progressive improvement of the Burnham salary scales for teachers.

Meanwhile the improving economic situation and the expansion of secondary education was preparing the ground for a more direct and positive assault on the problem.

(*d*) Expansion and Reform of Teacher Training

In 1958 a government White Paper announced a crash programme for expanding teacher training facilities to an extent that would facilitate the introduction of three-year courses in 1960 and thereafter make inroads upon the existing shortage. Under pressure from the National Advisory Council on the Training and Supply of Teachers and the Robbins Committee on *Higher Education*, the government progressively added to the initial programme so that during the 1960s the output of the colleges and University Education Departments more than doubled. This sustained expansion prepared the way for the raising of the school leaving age to sixteen in 1973 and gradually overcame the post-war shortage of teachers. Indeed it produced a situation which necessitated the reconsideration of the role of the teacher training colleges if a problem of over-supply was to be avoided in the later years of the decade.

(*e*) Continuing Official Concern for Teacher Training and Supply

Considerable time and energy was now devoted by various official advisory and investigating bodies to the issues and problems of this critical sector of the educational system.

(i) *The National Advisory Council on the Training and Supply of Teachers (established 1949)*

Issued many reports for the guidance of the Ministry and was largely responsible for the ultimate introduction of three-year training for certificate teachers. It also exerted a considerable influence upon how the colleges used the extra year. The Council stressed that the aim of the new three-year courses should be to produce well-educated teachers rather than technically competent practitioners; thus the colleges were to put the emphasis upon the wider education of their students rather than their mere professional training and so approximate more closely to the university ideal. It also exerted continuing pressure on the government in favour of the vigorous expansion of training college provision as the only satisfactory solution to the problem of teacher supply.

(ii) *Crowther Report on 15 to 18 (1959)*

Part VII on 'Institutions and Teachers' underlined the need for more training college places, for a further improvement in teachers' salaries and for an increase in the proportion of graduates (especially science and maths) in the profession.

(iii) *Newsom Report on Half our Future (1963)*

This drew attention to those aspects of teacher training which relate to the education of the average and below average ability 13-16 year olds. The need to prepare students for the raising of the school leaving age, for the continuing reform of curricula and method and for service in deprived areas received special emphasis. The continuing entry of untrained graduates into the profession was roundly condemned.

(iv) *Robbins Report on Higher Education (1963)*

This made several critical recommendations which did much to shape later development. The training colleges were to be renamed Colleges of Education and their stature and independence as institutions of higher education significantly increased. The former recommendation was accepted, whilst the latter was partially met by the 'Weaverisation' process (following the Weaver Report on *The Government of Colleges of Education*, 1966) which secured greater autonomy for the governing bodies of Colleges of Education. The Robbins Committee further recommended the introduction of a four-year B.Ed. degree course for college students and the planned expansion of over-all provision. Both recommendations were swiftly met.

(v) *Plowden Report on Children and their Primary Schools (1967)*

This paid considerable attention to teacher training and was highly critical of the existing situation. Having made many detailed recommendations with the particular needs of primary education in mind (e.g. the need to improve the mathematics/science qualifications and the sex balance of college entrants), the report emphasised that it was high time for a special inquiry into the whole business of teacher education and training. This contributed to the ultimate establishment of the James Committee to examine the existing arrangements for the education, training and probation of teachers; the recommendations of the James Report (1972) and the government's initial response to it are dealt with later in Chapter 11 (page 201 *et seq*.). It seems that the Colleges of Education now face a period of contraction and readjustment within the context of an increasingly integrated system of higher education.

4 Recent Arrangements in Relation to Teacher Training and Employment

The situation in this field has changed immeasurably for the better as a result of certain basic developments during this century. There has been the expansion of provision and the extension in the duration of courses, combined with the gradual shift in training emphasis from professional and technical competence to personal education and full development. The commitment to teaching has been progressively postponed, the logical extension of which is the recent questioning of the efficacy of monotechnic training colleges and concurrent courses. Teacher training and supply have been recognised as issues of national importance. The teaching profession has earned and been increasingly accorded a position of equal influence alongside the central and local education authorities within the educational system. The status of teachers has improved with their conditions of employment. The resultant situation may be considered in terms of various broad aspects.

(a) National Framework

Much greater co-ordination and integration of effort in the field of teacher training and supply has emerged in the post-war era. This is the result of and is exemplified by a number of developments:

(i) the clear identification of the Ministry's prime responsibility for the training and supply of teachers (section 62, 1944 Act);

(ii) the establishment of the National Advisory Council for the Training and Supply of Teachers, now in process of reconstitution, for co-ordination at the national level and for advising the Ministry;

(iii) the establishment of Area Training Organisations, centred upon about twenty University Institutes (or Schools) of Education, for the co-ordination of teacher training and related matters at regional level (the Institutes were responsible for training courses, standards, examinations and awards as well as for the promotion of advanced studies and research in education);

(iv) the setting up of the 'Clearing House' arrangements for the central co-ordination of training college admissions procedure.

(b) Colleges of Education

These institutions are still the main source of teacher training and supply and their number has recently risen to one hundred and sixty. Two-thirds of them are now State provided and maintained, but one-third are voluntary establishments (mainly Anglican and Roman Catholic). The majority of college students undertake the three-year certificate course, but a growing number now embark upon four-year B.Ed. degree and one-year postgraduate certificate courses. Special in-service courses have recently been developed on a widening front. The minimum entry requirements for a three-year certificate course are five G.C.E. O-level subjects, including English Language; but in practice one-third of college entrants now have two A-level subjects (giving eligibility for B.Ed. degree courses) and another one-third have one A-level subject. The curricula for certificate courses came under the control of each individual Area Training Organisation, nevertheless a fairly basic pattern emerged. All certificate students extended their personal education by the academic study of a principal and subsidiary subject; the extra year allowed much more depth to such study, especially in relation to the principal subject. All students were committed to the study and practice of education, spending at least thirteen weeks in the schools; this was the professional and pedagogic aspect of the course for which the Education Department was usually responsible and it was reinforced by a variety of curriculum courses concerned with teaching methods in different subjects. The tendency was for the latter courses to have low priority and prestige in the eyes of too many staff and students; recently this has led in many colleges to the development of a third distinct area of professional studies incorporating curriculum courses and other matters directly related to the actual business of teaching (e.g. the teaching of reading), and subsidiary subjects have been abandoned to facilitate the reform. The post-war period has witnessed a considerable change in the general tenor of college life. There has been the emergence of a much more liberal regime at teacher training institutions; the establishment of co-educational colleges and the growth of extra-mural and inter-college activities organised and run by the students themselves are a reflection of this change. However, the headlong expansion of teacher training provision was not calculated to secure satisfactory standards in relation to accommodation, library facilities and staffing ratios; in these respects the colleges continued to compare unfavourably with the universities.

(c) University Departments of Education

These remained the main source of trained graduates and the recent decision to disallow direct graduate entry after 1973 underlines their future importance. Exclusively concerned with the training of graduate teachers, they mount one-year courses consisting of lectures and seminars on various aspects of educational theory and considerable teaching practice in the schools. The staff concerned also serve the needs of the University Institute (of which the Department is, like the colleges, a constituent part) in relation to the development of advanced courses and educational research.

(d) Employment of Teachers

By 1970 the total teaching force in maintained schools reached one-third of a million. This was the result of the numbers having expanded fairly steadily and most impressively by 57% since 1950. Only 21% of such teachers were graduates, of which just over two-thirds had received professional training. In the maintained secondary sector 37% of the teaching staff were graduates, but this over-all percentage masked a much less favourable situation in mathematics and science than in arts subjects. Meanwhile graduates accounted for a mere 4·5% of the teachers in primary schools. Whilst the proportion of graduates in all maintained schools rose quite significantly during the 1950s, the following decade had witnessed no further improvement in this respect. The rest of the force consisted almost completely of certificated teachers; a campaign in the late 1960s had reduced the number of unqualified teachers to a minute level. In 1970 the training institutions turned out a total of almost 36,000 new teachers of whom about one-sixth were graduates; ten years earlier the output was only one-half of this figure. But the wastage rate continued to give serious grounds for concern as there was a turnover of 10% per annum amongst primary and secondary teachers. Of course, women were much more affected than men, the respective turnover rates being 13% and 6%. Many newly qualified female teachers were in employment for only a few years before marriage and child-bearing necessitated their withdrawal from the classroom to meet domestic responsibilities.

(e) Conditions of Service

These are now extremely favourable and would be unrecognisable to a teacher working at the turn of the century. They are negotiated between the local education authorities and the teachers' organisations, with a permanent Joint Committee responsible for ironing out any difficulties. The normal contract of employment for qualified teachers is an eminently favourable one. The teacher may terminate it at two months' notice, except during the summer when three months' warning is required. The teacher's security of tenure is very strong indeed; only 'gross misconduct' or 'dereliction of duty' (neither ever clearly defined, however) merit dismissal and in both cases the teacher has the right to be heard and represented by counsel. The projected Teachers' General Council, with prospective responsibility for disciplinary arrangements within the profession, is calculated to improve the position even further. In respect of serious illness the normal entitlement is to three months' full pay and three months' half-pay exclusive of holidays. No other profession does as well as teaching for holidays with pay. Although it is still widely held that schoolteaching compares unfavourably with other occupations demanding similar qualifications, the whole question of teachers' salaries remains a complex and difficult one. At least the 1944 Act gave statutory authority to the Burnham scales and the regular review of same became accepted practice; however, some would regard the Remuneration of Teachers Act (1965), which modified the negotiating arrangements so as to allow for direct government representation and for arbitration in the case of disagreement, as a retrogressive measure not calculated to improve the teachers' bargaining position. Finally it may be said that teachers are free from extraneous duties. Involvement in extra-mural activities is a voluntary matter and since 1968 teachers have not been compelled to undertake the supervision of school meals.

(f) Freedom of Teachers

Reasonable and appropriate freedom in the exercise of their professional role is now a deeply-rooted tradition in England and Wales, and the post-war years have reinforced this favourable situation for teachers. Such freedom is associated with and secured by a number of influences and developments.

(i) Teachers have come to enjoy considerable freedom in relation to curricula, syllabuses and teaching methods in both primary and secondary schools. This freedom cannot be said to be seriously threatened or impaired by the work of external examining bodies or the Schools Council—indeed, the latter body and the Certificate of Secondary Education Examining Boards are teacher-dominated organisations.

(ii) The 1944 Act secures teachers against any need to teach religious instruction or partake in corporate religious worship and in practice few secondary specialists are called upon to accept much responsibility for unfamiliar subjects.

(iii) The inspectorate, both local and central, is limited in its powers to that of guiding and assisting fully qualified teachers. The advice given and suggestions made may be rejected by the individual teacher. Thus the inspectorate must influence by persuasion rather than dictation.

The basic axiom is that teaching is a highly individual and professional matter which admits of no official strait-jacket (cf. other countries), and this view is accepted by all interested parties involved in English education.

(g) Teachers' Organisations

There are various, and certainly far too many, bodies officially dedicated to promoting the professional interests of serving teachers. Whilst dual membership and other complications make it virtually impossible to form a precise statistical picture of the state of the teacher unions, an impartial consideration of the available figures does give a rough and ready impression.

Teaching is an occupation in which there is no closed shop, in that any qualified person may teach without becoming a union member; nevertheless teachers are highly organised with over four-fifths of them being members of some union or association. Collectively the unions have a membership of well over 300,000 serving primary and secondary teachers, but fragmentation continues to be a serious weakness even though the field is dominated by the three largest organisations:

(i) *National Union of Teachers*

Since 1870 this body has been, and still remains, the most powerful of the teachers' organisations. Drawing its members from all sections of the profession, the National Union of Teachers accounts for approximately 55% of serving primary and secondary teachers. But its real strength lies in the primary sector and amongst women teachers; this lays it open to accusations of female domination. Whilst about 70% of primary teachers are members of the National Union of Teachers, the proportion for secondary teachers is somewhat below 40%. (Amongst male secondary teachers it takes second place to the National Association of Schoolmasters, see below.) Just over 70% of the serving members of the National Union of Teachers (in primary and secondary schools) are females, although the executive is usually dominated by male headteachers. However, this union, more than any other, stands for the common interest of all teachers and its sheer size has long ensured it a dominant influence in educational politics. The National Union of Teachers still enjoys an absolute majority on the teachers' panel of the Burnham Committee and has secured prior representation on the Schools Council. Its long established alliance with the Association of Teachers in Technical Institutions (involving reciprocal membership) extends its influence into the field of further education. Nevertheless it seems that the comparative strength of the largest union may have been weakening recently, although it is too early to be categorical about this.

(ii) *National Association of Schoolmasters*

Established in 1922 as the result of a breakaway from the National Union of Teachers, this body has the reputation of being the most militant of the teacher unions. Following rapid expansion during the 1960s the National Association of Schoolmasters encompasses some 14% of primary and secondary teachers; this rises to over 17% if the membership of its close ally, the Union of Women Teachers (formed in 1965) is added. Both these unions have shown a particular concern for representing the interests of long-serving career teachers. The main strength of the National Association of Schoolmasters rests upon the membership of non-graduate male teachers working in the non-selective secondary schools. The union now accounts for over one-third of male secondary teachers and can claim more importance than the National Union of Teachers in this limited field. Although it has secured places on the Burnham teachers' panel and the Schools Council, the representation is small and compares unfavourably with that of the Joint Four whose membership is about the same. Thus the National Association of School-masters can be expected to continue to press for an improvement of its position; in this respect an outright merger with the Union of Women Teachers would strengthen its hand and may be considered an interesting and likely future prospect.

(iii) *Joint Four*

This is a composite organisation joining together the Assistant Masters' Association, the Association of Assistant Mistresses, the Headmasters' Association and the Association of Headmistresses, all of which date from the late nineteenth century. The Joint Four embraces about 14% of serving teachers, although they are drawn almost exclusively from the secondary sector. The constituent unions are traditionally associated with the representation of the interests of graduate teachers working in selective schools; however, the comprehensive tide does not seem to have under-mined the strength or influence of the Joint Four and any future trend towards an all-graduate profession would surely work in its favour. Past experience has shown the Joint Four to be the least militant of the major teachers' organisations and, significantly, the constituent bodies are not affiliated to the Trades Union Congress. Nevertheless it enjoys fairly considerable representation on Burnham and the Schools Council. This is partly explicable in terms of its long-standing historical associations with the grammar schools and their largely graduate staffs.

The teachers' organisations wield their considerable influence through certain established channels. At the national level they are in continuing contact with the Department of Education and Science and with the Association of Education Committees; they also work through such nationally representative bodies as the Burnham Committees, the Schools Council and, until recently, the National Advisory Council on the Training and Supply of Teachers. At the local level the unions are in continuing consultation with the local education authorities, teacher representatives being co-opted on to the local education committees.

Follow-up: Attempt to cover as much of the following ground as possible.

1 *Read*   Curtis, S. J. and Boultwood, M. E. *An Introductory History of English Education since 1800*, Chapter XVI

Barnard, H. C. *A History of English Education from 1760*, Chapters XXI and XXVIII, pp. 252-8

Armfelt, R. *The Structure of English Education*, Chapter IX

Department of Education and Science *Trends in Education*, February 1970. Centenary issue: article by J. W. Tibble on 'The Education of Teachers', pp. 45-50

2 *Consult* Maclure, J. S. *Educational Documents: England and Wales 1816-1968;* items 6, 29 and 36 are relevant.

3 Clarify the following: the nature, strengths and weaknesses of the pupil-teacher system; the significance of the Cross Commission Report (1888) and the 1902 Act in the history of teacher training; the main grievances of teachers in relation to their conditions of work in the late nineteenth century; the factors which helped to raise the status of teachers after the First World War; the recommendations and results of the McNair Report on Teachers and Youth Leaders, 1944; the measures taken to deal with the acute shortage of teachers after the Second World War; the significance of the Robbins Report on Higher Education (1963) in relation to teacher training and supply; the present size and composition of the teaching force employed in maintained schools; the extent and nature of union organisation amongst teachers.

Chapter Nine
The Development of Educational Administration

Purpose: to review the historical and more recent growth of the central and local administration of education in England and Wales and thereby to promote a clearer understanding of the contemporary system of educational administration as it has developed since the 1944 Act.

The considerable subject matter involved in this particular study, which does much to set the stage for the next chapter, may be conveniently divided into three major parts; the over-all perspective, the development of central administration, and the development of local administration.

1 The Over-all Perspective

There are a number of basic points which can be made at the outset to help place the details of the history of English educational administration into some sort of over-all perspective.

(*a*) The growth of State involvement in educational development in England and Wales has passed through four main historical phases:

(i) the period of *State assistance*, 1833-70: during this phase the central government contented itself with the provision of a growing amount of financial assistance for the voluntary elementary schools and denominational training colleges, although such aid (especially after 1862) was increasingly tied to specific conditions and close inspection.

(ii) the period of *State intervention*, 1870-1900: finally convinced of the inability of the voluntary organisations to provide elementary schooling for the whole nation, the State intervened and through the agency of the School Boards at the local level proceeded directly to fill the gaps with elementary schools provided and maintained by moneys ultimately drawn solely from public sources.

(iii) the period of *State superintendence*, 1900-44: with the establishment of the Board of Education and the new local education authorities at the turn of the century, the State's activity in the field of educational development at last became co-ordinated and cohesive and was decisively extended beyond the elementary sector. But the local education authorities, established by the 1902 Act, enjoyed too wide a measure of freedom, especially in relation to other than elementary education, and the Boards' limited powers of superintendence proved inadequate to ensure reasonably uniform and satisfactory standards of provision throughout the country.

(iv) the period of *State control and direction*, post-1944: the 1944 Act considerably strengthened the powers of the central government at the expense of the local education authorities. The latter were categorically placed under the control and direction of the new Ministry of Education, so initiating a centralising process in the field of educational administration which subsequent developments have reflected and reinforced.

(*b*) The growth of central and local agencies for education formed part of the extension of government activity associated with the widening conception of the role of the State in English society. Before the twentieth century the concept of education as a comprehensive and cohesive service for the nation at large had not emerged; hence the State's involvement in nineteenth-century educational development was both piecemeal and unco-ordinated in character.

(*c*) The foundations of the present administrative system as related to education were laid at the turn of the century by the establishment of the Board of Education and the new local education authorities. Since then there has been a great increase in the work of the central and local agencies, together with associated changes in responsibilities and powers; but the essential structure based on the central-local partnership has remained virtually the same.

(*d*) The system of educational administration in England and Wales has always been primarily concerned with the problem of bringing the necessary financial support to educational development so as to ensure a sufficient supply of schools, teachers and equipment. The annual public expenditure on education has risen from a bare £20,000 in 1833 to a staggering sum of over £2,000 million in 1970; obviously the task of administering such moneys has gradually become a most complicated and onerous one. Critical to local influence on educational development is the percentage of the total cost borne by the local authorities; over most of this century the local rate contribution to the cost of State education has hovered between about one-half and two-fifths, with a long-term tendency to fall somewhat. Thus the proportion has always remained substantial enough to ensure for the local education authorities a continuing influence on government educational policy.

(*e*) Educational administrators have been only secondarily and decreasingly concerned with the supervision of curricula, examinations and teaching methods. For a whole generation the Revised Code (1862) served as a basis for developing this particular administrative role in very sharp form, but a strong reaction followed which was to lay the foundations of the professional freedom now enjoyed by teachers in England and Wales. In the 1890s the 'payment by results' system was finally phased out and a decade later Morant's *Handbook* and revised instructions for the Inspectorate ushered in a new era for the elementary teacher; in the 1920s the Board of Education was prevailed upon to transfer its responsibility for the curricula and examinations of the training colleges to professional bodies. Meanwhile in 1917, when the School Certificate examinations were launched, the Board delegated responsibility for their oversight and development to a pseudo-independent Secondary School Examinations Council. Similar arrangements were made in respect of the National Certificate examinations and awards developed in the field of technical education after the First World War. In the first half of the twentieth century there was a sufficient consensus as to what should be taught and how to allow the Board to withdraw its regulative tentacles with confidence, although as a safety-valve the local education authorities were made responsible for the control of secular instruction by the 1944 Act. The disintegration of the former consensus before the advance of modern primary methods and secondary innovation perhaps explains the setting up within the Ministry of a curriculum study group in 1962; initial teacher reaction was suspicious, but two years later the group was incorporated into the innocuous Schools Council with its teacher majority. Of course, part of the role of both Her Majesty's and local inspectors is the maintenance of satisfactory educational standards, but they tread warily in the pursuit of this objective because of the absence of any regulative framework within which to operate and the strong tradition of teacher freedom which has grown up.

2 The Development of Central Administration

NINETEENTH CENTURY: with effect from 1833 the central government took a varying but growing interest in the different fields of educational development. But the growth was piecemeal and conformed to no overall strategy, resulting in the emergence of several quite distinct central government organs to deal with educational matters. The work of these different bodies is best considered in terms of the main educational fields in which they operated.

Elementary instruction naturally absorbed the overwhelming share of the central government's interest in education during the nineteenth century. The responsibility for shaping and implementing government policy in this field was successively undertaken by two bodies:

(*a*) The Committee of the Privy Council for Education 1839-56

The establishment of this body in 1839 was the natural outcome of the introduction of annual State building grants for elementary schools six years earlier, grants which, however, had been rather loosely administered by the Treasury on the recommendations of the National Society and the British and Foreign School Society. The purpose of the new Committee was to secure more effective control over the use of the public money provided by Parliament and so justify the growth of State aid to elementary education. The Committee's constitution was somewhat peculiar: established by royal prerogative so as to avoid the religious difficulty, the Committee was not directly responsible to Parliament from whence it received its funds. The Committee was composed of four members (the Lord President, the Lord Privy Seal, the Chancellor of the Exchequer and the Home Secretary) all of whom sat in their capacity as Queen's Privy Councillors. It met only from time to time and its routine work depended very largely upon a full-time Secretary, who was responsible to, but not a member of, the Committee. Inspired by its first Secretary, Dr James Kay (later Kay-Shuttleworth), the Committee was responsible for some outstanding achievements:

(i) the development of a system of specific central grants as an effective administrative means of encouraging and shaping the growth of elementary education. The original building grants were gradually supplemented by various other grants designed to help defray current as distinct from capital costs; the ultimate result of this trend was the introduction of capitation grants in the mid 1850s. The Committee also made the grants available to bodies other than the National and British societies; the Methodist Church and the Catholic Poor School Committee became important beneficiaries. Meanwhile the Parliamentary grant for elementary education rose from £30,000 in 1839 to £369,000 in 1855.

(ii) the application of pressure upon the Anglican Church to accept the operation of a conscience clause in their grant-aided elementary schools. By the 1850s this policy was being made to stick and so presaged one of the important provisions of the 1870 Act;

(iii) the establishment of a central administrative machine capable of coping with the growing responsibilities and work load of the new agency. Kay-Shuttleworth's central office developed steadily so that by 1855 his successor had a staff of forty serving him at Whitehall. Meanwhile the central office had developed a professional arm in the shape of Her Majesty's Inspectorate; growing from the original pair (one for the Anglican and one for the Nonconformist schools) appointed in 1840, this body was composed of some thirty-odd inspectors by the mid 1850s, thus enabling the Committee to maintain closer contact with the grant-aided schools;

(iv) the introduction of the pupil-teacher system and the associated development of the denominational training colleges. Although the Committee failed to realise the establishment of a State normal school as suggested in its original terms of reference, it did set up and generously subsidise the system which was to provide the country with the great bulk of its elementary teachers down to the end of the century. Through its developing control of college curricula and certification the Committee underpinned the emergence of the first qualified elementary teachers.

(*b*) The Education Department 1856-1900

The establishment of this body arose out of the mounting Parliamentary criticism of the non-statutory Committee of Council which was not responsible to the House of Commons in spite of its growing demands on the public purse. Accordingly the Committee was reconstituted by statutory means: the post of Vice-President of the Committee of the Privy Council was created, the holder of this post being responsible to Parliament for the work and policy of a newly-formed Education Department. The former Secretary to the Committee now became Permanent Secretary to the new executive Department of State. For the rest of the century the Education Department formulated and implemented State policy in the field of elementary education; although the old Committee of Council continued to accept ultimate responsibility, the critical influence was that wielded by various individuals through the offices of Vice-President and Permanent Secretary.

In considering the work and influence of the Education Department during the period of its existence a number of striking points emerge.

(i) The Department came to exercise close control over the development of elementary education. Before 1856 the Committee had already assumed a position of immense potential power through its development of the specific grant system and its superintendence of the training of teachers. From 1860 the new Education Department gave much sharper expression to central influence and power by the publication of an annual Elementary Code of Regulations which laid down the conditions for the receipt of grant by voluntary and (later) Board schools as well as training colleges. This form of close control, affecting the curriculum, teaching methods and internal organisation of the institutions concerned, reached its height in Robert Lowe's Revised Code (1862) and was only very gradually relaxed during the subsequent 'payment by results' era. As explained in an earlier chapter, the results of such control were extremely double-edged, but on balance probably did more harm than good.

(ii) The 1870 Act greatly increased the importance of the Education Department. Not only was the annual Code given statutory force, but many new functions and powers arose from the appearance of the School Boards. As the new local authorities were untried and without precedent, the balance of power was heavily weighted in favour of the central body. The initial declaration of deficiency and the subsequent establishment of a Board in any school district was the responsibility of the Department. The raising of loans, the compulsory purchase of land for school building and the passage of attendance bye-laws by the School Boards were all subject to the approval of the officials of the Education Department. The central body was even given the power to dissolve and replace any School Board which it considered to be failing in its duty and this possibility was taken advantage of on a significant number of occasions.

(iii) The Education Department bore a growing administrative burden, resultant of having to deal directly and separately with over 2,500 School Boards, nearly 800 School Attendance Committees and some 14,000-odd voluntary managing bodies. The passing of the 1870 Act brought a particularly abrupt and large increase in the Department's work load. By the close of the century the permanent staff at Whitehall numbered almost 300, whilst H.M. Inspectorate had expanded to about 350 members. To increase the efficiency of its operation the Inspectorate had been reorganised on a territorial basis; this was facilitated by the abandonment after 1870 of the inspection of religious instruction so that any inspector could visit both Board and voluntary schools.

(iv) The constitutional arrangements related to the Committee of Council and the Education Department, especially in view of the latter's sudden accession of responsibilities and powers, remained anomalous and vulnerable to serious criticism. Meetings of the Committee became so rare that its continued existence seemed pointless. Practical decisions were recurrently taken by the Vice-President, but the strength of his position was undermined by his *de jure* subordination to the Lord President of the Council. The 1870 Act did nothing whatsoever to rationalise the situation. Various official enquiries condemned the existing arrangements and recommended the creation of one central authority for education headed by a single minister enjoying over-all responsibility and full status. By the time the Bryce Commission (1895) reported along similar lines the need for rationalisation had become a very pressing one.

(v) Given the failure of the 1870 Act to define the term 'elementary', the Education Department became party to the development of higher-grade schools and advanced evening classes by the larger School Boards. Liberal governments were happy that the Department should encourage such developments and Sir George Kekewich, its Permanent Secretary 1890-1900, was particularly well-disposed towards them. The introduction of Standard VII in 1882 raised the general level of work in the elementary schools and thus assisted higher-grade experiment; the 1893 Code altered the regulations governing evening classes in a way that facilitated the development of more advanced work by the School Boards. Both these departures were the responsibility of the Education Department and the consequent blurring of the limits of its jurisdiction added to the growing administrative confusion at the centre.

Technical and commercial instruction was another field in which the State interested itself from a fairly early date. The beginnings may be traced back to 1836, but the interest did not assume significant proportions until after the Great Exhibition of 1851. To promote the teaching of science and arts subjects of direct utility to industry and commerce, the *Department of Science and Art 1853-1900* was established under the auspices of the Board of Trade. Although placed under the jurisdiction of the Committee of Council and its Vice-President three years later, this new body managed to maintain a virtually independent existence down to the end of the century. Gradually the Department of Science and Art not only emerged as the central authority for technical and commercial education, but as such began to take a growing interest in the secondary field. Any brief consideration of the administrative nature and influence of this Department must include mention of the following noteworthy points.

(a) With effect from 1859 the Department of Science and Art operated a progressively refined 'payment by results' system which dispensed central grants to those institutions, classes and teachers successfully entering candidates for the Department's annual examinations. By the 1890s over 100,000 students were studying for these every year. The annual expenditure of the Department rose from £57,000 to over £770,000, its permanent staff at South Kensington expanded ten-fold and it developed its own branch of H.M. Inspectorate.

(b) In 1872 the Department introduced a special grant for organised science schools or classes which committed themselves to a three-year scientific and technical course absorbing at least 40% of the available teaching time. By 1897 there were many higher-grade schools and even some endowed grammar schools taking advantage of this financial opportunity.

(c) The Department placed an increasingly wide and liberal interpretation on its initial terms of reference. The range of subjects eligible for examination grants was gradually broadened from six to twenty-five, so that ultimately all secondary school subjects (excepting Classics) were able to benefit from the Department's support. This was another means by which it was rendering some financial assistance to the endowed grammar schools by the close of the century.

(d) Following the Technical Instruction Act (1889), the Department of Science and Art considerably increased its influence as it became responsible for advising the County and County Borough Councils upon the question of which subjects and institutions were suitable for 'technical' rate-aid. The influence wielded by the Department in this direction was again liberal in character, encouraging county interest in their local endowed grammar schools.

In spite of the considerable achievements of the Science and Art Department, its continued existence was condemned by the Bryce Report (1895); it was seen as a too specialised and independent body which required absorption into a single central authority for education.

Secondary education was a field in relation to which State intervention was threatened rather than realised during the nineteenth century. Following the Taunton Report (1868), the *Endowed Schools Commission* (1869-73) and the *Charity Commission* (1874-1900) acted as central government agencies charged with the responsibility of improving secondary provision by the redistribution of endowments and the reform of trust deeds and governing bodies. Although their powers were strictly limited to these pseudo-judicial functions, it seems that the revival of the endowed grammar schools owed much to these government commissioners. But the constitutional position of the Charity Commission was the most anomalous and unsatisfactory of all; it had no political head and its relationship to the other two departments lacked any sort of definition. Worst of all, the Charity Commission had no brief or means to develop secondary education beyond that sector supported by endowments. It was therefore never in a position to realise the ambitious hopes expressed in the Taunton Report.

TWENTIETH CENTURY: the establishment and development of a single and effective central authority for State activity in all sectors of education is the outstanding achievement of this period. This historical process centred upon the foundation and work of three bodies.

(a) The Board of Education 1900-44

Following the Bryce Report, which demanded the rationalisation of central administration, the 1899 Act created the new Board of Education by merging the Education Department, the Science and Art Department and the Charity Commission into a single body. It also established a Consultative Committee to advise the Board on matters referred to it. The President of the Board and his Parliamentary Secretary were to be the political heads of the new government department; unfortunately the President was accorded the salary and status of a junior minister rather than a full Secretary of State. The Board's permanent staff were all to be placed under a single Secretary, of which the first was the able, energetic Robert Morant. Under the Act the Board of Education was given the responsibility for the 'superintendence' of educational matters in England and Wales, but the nature of this particular role and the powers required to exercise it were not clarified. The actual history of the Board of Education not only illuminates the nature of its development but also displays an interesting balance of strengths and weaknesses.

(i) The Board was always beset by the double disadvantage of the low ministerial status of its President and the extreme vagueness of its superintendence role and powers. Looked upon as a stepping stone to higher office or a retreat for the mediocre, the Presidency was held by no fewer than nineteen politicians in forty-four years; only four of these can be held to have served education with any distinction. Meanwhile the 1902 Act had given the initiative for the development of other than elementary education to the new Part II local education authorities. The 1918 Education Act attempted to bolster the power of the Board by giving it the statutory right to require the submission of development schemes by Part II authorities, but the post-war economic difficulties and the shelving of so many of the Act's provisions robbed this of its potential significance. Gradually the weakness of the Board's position was recognised as a serious shortcoming in relation to the full implementation of national policy and the realisation of minimal standards of provision across the whole of England and Wales.

(ii) In spite of these handicaps, and inside a single decade, the genius of Morant built the Board into an effective government department capable of shaping national policy and leading the local authorities forward. He realised that, given vigorous leadership and its strong financial influence, the Board could make its presence felt sharply. Internally the Board was organised into elementary, secondary and technological branches; a little later Morant added the medical, legal and finance branches to develop further the specialist structure. In 1907 a separate Welsh Department was created. A year later the Board became a physical entity when the technological branch finally left South Kensington for Whitehall. Meanwhile the forging of the vital partnership between the new central and local authorities for education went rapidly ahead. Whatever its early shortcomings, this was the base upon which the conception and quality of State education was broadened and improved in the period before the Second World War.

(iii) The work of H. A. L. Fisher, President of the Board 1916-22, resulted in the further development of the central machinery and the basis of partnership at the close of the First World War. The 1918 Act introduced the percentage grant system (to replace the previous multiplicity of fixed and separate grants) and the development scheme arrangements which facilitated the growth of a closer and more constructive relationship between the Board and the local authorities. Fisher's establishment of the Burnham Committee and his concern for the status of teachers prepared the way for their recognition as the third vital partner in English education. Within the Board of Education the demands of the new Act necessitated some restructuring of its organisation. The specialist branches were overlaid by a territorial organisational pattern to allow the Board to deal more efficiently with the Part II authorities whose responsibilities ranged across the whole educational board; somewhat later the organisation of H.M. Inspectorate, significantly enlarged since 1902, was brought into line with this. The uneasy compromise continued until 1944 when much more thorough-going and unified territorial arrangements were introduced.

(b) The Ministry of Education 1944-64

The 1944 Act strengthened the central authority by replacing the old Board, with its vague superintendence role, by a new Ministry of Education charged with the duty of promoting the education of the people and of controlling and directing the local authorities to that end. As fully explained in the next chapter, the Act provided the Minister with the means of ensuring that the local authorities met the requirements of the Act and contributed effectively to the execution of national policy. Thus the 1944 Act recognised that education, though locally administered, is a national concern, and that consequently the powers of the central agency must be paramount. The shift in the balance of power within the educational system, to which the Act gave rise, seems to have been justified in the event; it is clear that the serious pre-war inequalities of educational opportunity between different areas have been much reduced over the last thirty years.

Although the tradition of consultation and co-operation between partners, firmly established by the old Board, has held firm, the centralising tendencies associated with the Ministry and its successor have found expression in many ways. Since 1944 the central authority has not only enforced the Burnham salary scales but has revised the negotiating arrangements to give itself much more influence upon the final outcome. The private sector has been subjected to central inspection and sometimes to more serious threats. The traditional independence of the universities has been eroded as their reliance on public funds has increased; in a very important sense they now come under the jurisdiction of the Department of Education and Science. After 1944 the required submission of development plans and their recurrent adjustment thereafter facilitated the routine exercise of central control over the local education authorities. The Local Government Act (1958), which replaced the specific percentage grant for education by a general fixed grant to cover all locally administered services, further increased the power of the Ministry by enabling it to place a ceiling on the educational expenditure of the local authorities. The issue of Circular 10/65 and the later introduction of a bill to require statutorily comprehensive secondary reorganisation were also indicative of this post-war trend.

(c) The Department of Education and Science 1964

The reconstitution of the Ministry twenty years after the 1944 Act was itself an expression of the trend towards increased centralisation. By the early 1960s the adequacy of the arrangements by which the universities received what had become immense sums of public money directly from the Treasury and yet were completely outside the jurisdiction of the Ministry of Education was being seriously questioned. Outside the universities there were many who favoured a single Minister assuming responsibility for all forms of education and civil science. But the Robbins Committee (1963) reported in favour of two separate ministries, one for those forms of education provided by the local authorities and one to serve the needs of the universities and scientific research bodies. In the event a compromise was effected which took the form of the Department of Education and Science: this new body assumed the functions and powers of the former Ministry of Education and Ministry of Science and was headed by a Secretary of State enjoying very high status. Initially, to meet the sensitivities of the universities, the Department was organised in two administrative units and there was to be a Permanent Secretary for each. However, within a year this plan was abandoned and 'Universities

(Finance and General)' became just another branch of the Department, although the institutions themselves continued to enjoy safeguards against serious interference with their academic freedom. A super-Ministry had been created in the interests of a closer supervision of university finance and development and in the hope of achieving greater integration of effort in the field of higher education.

3 The Development of Local Administration

NINETEENTH CENTURY: once it became involved, the central government was for many years content to further its growing educational commitment by direct contact with the schools and other institutions receiving State financial assistance. However, the growth of grant-aided elementary and technical education and the urge to expand it further ultimately made it necessary for the central government departments to reduce their administrative burden by the introduction of local agencies for State education. This could have been done by instituting a centralised system along Prussian or French lines, whereby the local agencies would have been run by government officials operating in the provinces. The 1870 Act rejected such a solution in favour of the involvement of local finance and responsibility in educational development in England and Wales. Out of this basic strategy, which for better or for worse has been followed ever since, there arose the first local education authorities.

(a) The School Boards 1870-1902

These were established under the 1870 Act in those deficiency areas where the voluntary organisations failed to meet the total need for elementary school places. Thus the 2,568 School Boards which gradually came into existence did not cover the whole country, nor were they in any way responsible for the denominational schools existing in their areas. Their job was to fill the gaps with public elementary schools, which they would thereafter administer and help to maintain. The School Boards were *ad hoc* bodies in that their responsibilities were strictly limited to the field of rate-aided elementary education in their own areas. They consisted of from five to fifteen members, varying according to the size of the population of the school district concerned. The School Boards were directly elected by the ratepayers through a cumulative voting system designed to ensure the representation of religious minorities. Under the 1870 Act the School Boards enjoyed a wide range of powers:

(i) to provide and maintain public elementary schools on the basis of central grants, parental fees and rate-aid. The latter could be obtained on annual demand from the local rating authorities which were initially the municipal borough corporations and the civil parishes; thus the School Boards used rate moneys without having the onerous responsibility of raising them;

(ii) to make attendance compulsory between five and thirteen years through the bye-laws, but subject to requirements laid down by the Education Department. The detailed nature of this power changed as a result of later legislation but was retained in substance. In areas where no School Board existed, School Attendance Committees were established for the purpose of framing and enforcing appropriate bye-laws;

(iii) to decide for or against religious worship and instruction in the Board schools, though subject to the Cowper-Temple and conscience clauses of the Act. Whilst it was usual for a School Board to opt for undenominational religious worship and instruction, a very tiny minority chose the purely secular alternative;

(iv) to remit the fees of necessitous children attending either Board or denominational schools in the area concerned. The power of remission in relation to poor children attending church schools was lost in 1876 and fifteen years later the Boards were in any case required to provide free elementary education on demand;

(v) to appoint their own full-time salaried officials and to delegate powers of control over individual schools to a body of managers. Clerk to the School Board was a normal appointment and from this office is descended the Chief Education Officer of today. But some of the larger Boards appointed local inspectors as well. Only London and Liverpool seem to have taken much advantage of the power to set up managing bodies.

Within the confused framework of local educational administration the School Boards aroused opposition and criticism. The denominational interests disliked them as the source of rate-aided competition. The endowed grammar school governing bodies objected to the development of the higher-grade elementary schools. Some of the new Technical Instruction Committees did not take too kindly to the provision of advanced evening work by certain Boards. Ratepayers were only too ready to accuse the more progressive Boards of extravagance and irresponsibility in the use of public money. Many of the small rural School Boards were palpably inefficient. Because their use of the rates to develop higher-grade and advanced studies was always questionable in law, the School Boards became increasingly vulnerable and were finally toppled by their enemies at the turn of the century. But meanwhile they had made universal elementary education a reality and the larger, more progressive Boards had set an example of dedicated public service which could not be lost upon the new local education authorities.

(b) The Technical Instruction Committees 1889-1902

Following the Local Government Act of 1888, which introduced the modern system of multi-purpose local authorities, these committees emerged as a result of two additional legislative measures.

(i) *1889 Technical Instruction Act*

This empowered the new County and County Borough Councils to raise a 1d rate to provide or support technical education. The councils were allowed to establish Technical Instruction Committees, wholly or partly drawn from council members, to undertake the responsibility.

(ii) *1890 Local Taxation (Customs and Excise) Act*

This made the proceeds of an increased duty on beer and spirits available to the councils, with the recommendation that it be used to promote technical education. Thus the Technical Instruction Committees were able to utilise the so-called 'whisky money' for promoting their work.

Although this legislation was only permissive, the majority of County and County Borough Councils established Technical Instruction Committees and by 1900 they were dispensing almost £1 million in aid of technical education. In any study of the short history of these committees a number of points are particularly noteworthy.

(i) There were wide variations in the degree of autonomy enjoyed by the Technical Instruction Committees and their full-time Directors or Secretaries. Some councils (e.g. London) gave them almost a free hand, whilst others (e.g. Manchester) limited their role to a strictly advisory one; over-all the arrangements approximated to the latter rather than the former position.

(ii) At first many Technical Instruction Committees placed a narrow interpretation upon technical education and focused their energies on the provision of instruction which met the needs of local industry and business. Later a much wider interpretation emerged, once experience had shown a sound secondary education to be the necessary foundation for advanced technical instruction. Such a development was encouraged by the policy and example of the central Department of Science and Art. Many Technical Instruction Committees granted aid to local secondary schools, obtaining representation on their governing bodies and even the right of inspection, and thereby began to influence their curricula, examinations and the like. The generous assistance received by a large number of endowed grammar schools from the London Technical Education Board was tied to the reciprocal provision of many scholarship places open to talent. Thus by 1900 many County and County Borough Councils had in practice become authorities for secondary as well as technical education.

(iii) The Technical Instruction Committees were of great potential significance because they were the offspring of the multi-purpose councils, which were thus able to prove themselves in the field of local educational administration, albeit in what seemed a narrow sector. But the widening of their role by the committees went far towards anticipating the Part II authorities of the 1902 Act.

By the close of the nineteenth century the administrative framework at the local level was even more confused than at the centre. The School Boards, the School Attendance Committees, the Technical Instruction Committees, the voluntary school managers and the governing bodies of the endowed grammar schools ploughed their supposedly separate but overlapping furrows, with conflict and disharmony the order of the day. In 1895 the Bryce Report made it clear that the proper development of secondary education was contingent upon the rationalisation of local educational administration.

TWENTIETH CENTURY: the development of a single type of local authority for all fields of State education is the outstanding achievement of this period. It has been associated with an increasing official concern to concentrate local responsibility for education in the hands of fewer and larger authorities. This historical process has taken place as a result of and within the framework of certain outstanding legislative enactments.

(a) The 1902 Education Act

As the main architect of this measure, Morant aimed at a unified structure of local educational administration based on the multi-purpose authorities established in 1888, dismissing the *ad hoc* approach to rationalisation as an inferior alternative. As already shown to some extent in Chapter 5, the 1902 Act included many far-reaching administrative provisions.

(i) The existing local agencies were replaced by three hundred and eighteen new local education authorities. The majority of these were Part III authorities (i.e. populous municipal boroughs and urban districts) charged with responsibility in their areas for elementary education only. The rest were Part II authorities which were also given powers for the development of 'other than elementary' education in their areas; these were the County and County Borough Councils which had previously given rise to the Technical Instruction Committees. Both types of authority were to delegate all except their financial powers to local education committees, the majority of members to be drawn from or nominated by the parent council; but the Act also required the co-option of professional people such as were representative of the various sectors of education. It was made possible for these committees to operate through a system of sub-committees and the Part II authorities in particular took full advantage of this.

(ii) The new local education authorities were given many administrative responsibilities. They were charged with the financial support and development of the former Board and voluntary elementary schools; the latter now received rate-aid in respect of their current costs, but were incorporated into the unified administrative framework with one-third of their managers being appointed by the local education authority. The Part II authorities were required (as far as they thought desirable) to develop secondary education, technical education and teacher training facilities and to take responsibility for the co-ordination of all forms of education. Subsequent legislation provided for the development of the School Medical Service by all the authorities and empowered them to introduce school meals.

(iii) The 1902 Act did not require the existence of a managing or governing body for all schools within the statutory system. Naturally the voluntary schools had managers, with a denominational majority to safeguard their special position, details of which have already been described. Non-provided secondary schools receiving financial support from the Part II authorities all had their governing bodies on which the benefactor was suitably represented. But the establishment of managing or governing bodies for the provided schools was very largely a matter for the discretion of the local education committees; generally speaking the county grammar schools were so privileged whereas the provided elementary schools were not.

Although the 1902 Act completed the foundations of a national system of educational administration, the subsequent history of the new local authorities showed the arrangements to suffer from certain serious weaknesses.

(i) The local education authorities were left with too much discretion, especially in relation to the permissive nature of their powers in respect of other than elementary education. The result was considerable variation in the attitudes and performances of the authorities on such matters as secondary development, Hadow re-organisation, teacher training, technical and adult education, and teachers' pay.

(ii) The existence of so many Part III authorities made for greater expense and produced a serious administrative dichotomy in the county areas, which consequently included numerous enclaves where elementary education was beyond the jurisdiction of the County (Part II) local authority. This arrangement, born of political expediency rather than administrative logic, gave rise to a number of difficulties. The organisation and co-ordination of scholarship examinations for the transfer of Part III elementary pupils to Part II grammar schools was not easy from the outset; the development of selective central schools by some Part III authorities later on tended to exacerbate the situation. The execution of Hadow re-organisation and the aspiration towards parity of esteem for the various secondary schools were not helped by the distinction between the two types of authority. Nor did the organisation and development of evening class work benefit; such work was the financial and administrative responsibility of the Part II authorities, but very often the buildings and the teachers were supplied by the Part III authorities with their separate accounts. Such problems affected, to a greater or lesser extent, over two-thirds of the county areas. The County Borough Councils (Part II) were, of course, quite unaffected, controlling both elementary and other than elementary education throughout their respective areas.

(b) The 1944 Education Act

This did much to increase the importance and improve the effectiveness of local educational administration, though at the price of some shift in the balance of power towards the central government. As the most important provisions affecting the local education authorities have already been dealt with at length in Chapter 7 (see page 98 *et seq.*), a short recapitulation must suffice. The Part III authorities were abolished, leaving the County and County Borough Councils with sole local responsibility for education. Their actual responsibilities were both extended and more strictly defined and they were required to organise provision in consecutive primary, secondary and further stages. They were to ensure that each and every school under their control had a properly constituted managing or governing body. The modification of the dual system (in terms of the arrangements for the controlled, aided and special agreement categories) required the local education authorities to extend increased financial aid to, and to readjust their relationship with, the voluntary schools. They were made responsible for ensuring the provision of compulsory religious worship and instruction in their schools. They were required to contribute to the development of teacher training facilities and to pay the Burnham salary scales. The Fisher percentage grant system was retained, but the exact formula was revised in favour of the local authorities. They were empowered to make grants for further study beyond the school leaving age. The Act also provided for the establishment of local education committees through which the authorities were to discharge all their non-financial educational functions; the continuance of work through sub-committees was allowed for as well. A new departure was the requirement that all local education authorities must appoint a chief education officer, the actual appointment made being subject to the approval of the Ministry.

Since 1944 there have been a number of developments which have had a bearing upon the nature and growth of post-war local educational administration.

(i) The immediate post-war years witnessed the establishment of a large number of divisional executives. In order to relate educational development to local circumstances in the large county areas, the 1944 Act allowed for (at the Minister's discretion) schemes of divisional administration. This also had the merit of buying off the opposition of those localities destined to lose their status as Part III authorities. The schemes, drawn up by the County authority and approved by the Minister, were to divide the county area into smaller administrative units and equip each of them with a divisional executive for the delegation of functions in respect of primary and secondary education. These executives were not directly elected bodies, being composed of County representatives, the nominees of the urban and rural district councils and other co-opted members. They were graced by their own divisional education officers. Under such schemes large municipal boroughs or urban districts (i.e. those with over 60,000 people or 7,000 pupils in 1939) could qualify for the status of excepted districts. Subject to consultation with the County authority and the Minister's approval, such towns could make their own schemes which might include the additional delegation of functions related to further education. In their case the local elected council became the divisional executive. Altogether some two hundred divisional executives were set up, including over forty excepted districts, to complicate the structure of local educational administration. Whilst they served as sources of local influence upon educational development, the divisional executives tended to raise the cost and reduce the pace of administration in the county areas.

(ii) The Local Government Act of 1958 introduced the rate support grant arrangement by which the central government gave a general fixed grant to each local authority towards the annual cost of all its services. The abandonment of ear-marked percentage grants for education has had two significant effects. It has inevitably weakened the position of the local education committees, faced as they were with a new need to argue for their fair share of the rate support grant. And, as far as it can be estimated, it seems that during the 1960s the new system resulted in a significant rise in the proportion of the total educational bill borne by the local authorities.

(iii) The London Government Act of 1963 changed the face of local educational administration in the greater metropolitan area. The measure abolished the London and Middlesex County Councils and introduced a two-tier system of local government consisting of the Greater London Council and the councils of the various inner and outer metropolitan boroughs. The outcome for educational administration was interesting as well as significant. The twenty outer London boroughs were given full status as local education authorities. But to maintain the continuity of educational development in central London, a special committee of the Greater London Council was given responsibility for education throughout that area. The *ad hoc* Inner London Education Authority, serving a population of almost four millions, was the result. In consequence of these new arrangements the total number of local education authorities in England and Wales rose to one hundred and sixty-four.

(c) The 1972 Local Government Act

By the 1960s it was increasingly felt that the organisational structure and geographical pattern of English local government needed to be radically reformed if it was to satisfy current and future needs. In the field of education there emerged a strong body of opinion that condemned the existence of so many different and small local education authorities and of the divisional administration arrangements in county areas. It was argued that 'bigger and better' local education authorities were the answer to the problem of promoting greater administrative and educational efficiency, especially in the special and post-secondary sectors. Both the Department of Education and Science and Her Majesty's Inspectorate presented such a viewpoint to the Redcliffe-Maud Commission when it reported (1969) to the government on the whole subject of local government reform. In revised form the recommendations of the Maud Report served as the basis for actual legislation three years later. The provisions of the 1972

Local Government Act were of far-reaching significance for local educational administration.

(i) Outside Greater London (which was unaffected) the total number of English and Welsh local education authorities was reduced from one hundred and forty-three to eighty-three. A few of the old county authorities (e.g. Rutland, Westmorland and Huntingdon-shire) were absorbed into larger local government units. Almost fifty of the existing county boroughs lost their former control of education as the result of absorption. The divisional executives and excepted districts were swept away. The total result was markedly to increase the average size of local education authorities and to abandon the requirement that they should delegate some of their functions in certain areas to minor representative bodies.

(ii) In the great conurbations (west Midlands, greater Manchester, Merseyside, west Yorkshire, south Yorkshire and Tyneside) a two-tier system of six metropolitan areas divided into thirty-six metro-politan districts was introduced. Local responsibility for education was devolved upon the latter rather than the former, although many critics insisted that some of the metropolitan districts were too small to develop satisfactorily the full range of educational services.

(iii) The rest of the country was covered by a two-tier system of forty-seven counties divided into approaching three hundred districts. But responsibility for education was lodged with the large county authorities. Whether they will work through area advisory com-mittees or simply through area offices, and whether they will extend increased importance to school managing and governing bodies, remains (1974) to be seen.

There is no doubt that the 1972 Local Government Act will prove to be a critical landmark in the history of educational administration in England and Wales. But it is difficult to foretell what its exact results will be. It is hoped and expected that the new arrangements will contribute to an improvement in the range and quality of local educational provision. The future role of local education committees and of governors and managers could be significantly affected. Finally, the emergence of fewer and much larger local education authorities might act as some sort of counterweight to the existing trend towards greater centralisation in education.

Follow-up: Attempt to cover as much of the following ground as possible.
1 Read Department of Education and Science *Trends in Education*, February 1970. Centenary issue: articles by H. C. Dent on 'The

Role of Central Government', pp. 31-38, and by G. Taylor on 'School Board to LEA', pp. 39-45

Gosden, P. H. J. H. *The Development of Educational Administration in England and Wales,* especially Chapters 6, 9, 10 and Conclusion,

2 *Clarify the following: the four main historical phases in the development of educational administration; the broad pattern of development in relation to the official supervision of curriculum, examinations and teaching methods; the main achievements of the Committee of Council for Education 1839-56; the most important features of the development of the Education Department 1856-1900; the nature and work of the Department of Science and Art; the distinction between central superintendence and control and direction as exemplified in the Board of Education and the Ministry of Education respectively; the nature and powers of the School Boards; the origins and significance of the Technical Instruction Committees; the distinction between the Part II and Part III local education authorities (1902 Act); the arrangements for divisional administration in county areas introduced by the 1944 Act; the difference between the percentage grant system 1918-58 and the succeeding rate support grant system of educational finance; the provisions and potential significance of the 1972 Local Government Act as related to educational administration.*

Chapter Ten
The Post-War Structure of the English Educational System

Purpose: to consider the administrative structure and institutional pattern of education in England and Wales during the post-war period and to identify the main elements and developments in the over-all contemporary framework.

1 The General Framework

A broad understanding of the English educational system may be obtained by initial reference to three important and illuminating matters: its unique features, the limits to centralised authority, and the layers of operation.

(a) Unique Features

The educational system in England and Wales is still distinguished from arrangements operating in other countries by a number of characteristic features:

(i) the existence of the private sector alongside the State system. Centred upon the prestigious and expensive public boarding schools, this sector has maintained the real substance of its independence from State control and continues to have an importance out of all proportion to the number of fee-paying pupils it serves;

(ii) the major contribution of voluntary organisations to the statutory system of education. The dual arrangements established in 1870 continue to operate in modified form; over one-fifth of primary and secondary pupils presently attend church schools and the religious (primarily Anglican and Roman Catholic) organisations enjoy a similar importance in the field of teacher training. In further education, including the Youth Service, various voluntary bodies contribute to the total provision organised by the local education authorities;

(iii) the distribution of power and responsibility within the State system. The development and continuance of a complicated mechanism of checks and balances ensures that the system of education in England and Wales is essentially dependent on the co-operative efforts of the central government, the local authorities, the churches and the teaching profession. The exact nature of the balance of power may be subject to change, but the basic principle itself is too deep-rooted to be vulnerable;

(iv) the marked degree of professional freedom enjoyed by teachers in the schools. In England and Wales there is the very strong tradition that curriculum, teaching methods and internal organisation are strictly professional matters which should be left to the teachers themselves to sort out. It is a tradition jealously guarded and developed by the teachers' organisations, but it is also a tradition which has been encouraged and even widened by some of the more progressive post-war local education authorities. Many headteachers now receive capitation allowances without any sort of restriction upon areas or percentages of spending; similar room for manoeuvre is quite commonly granted in relation to the allocation of teaching posts above Scale I. Some authorities operate a points scheme for ancillary staff and allow their schools to determine the number and nature of appointments made within their points entitlement. All this is calculated to permit and encourage the head and his staff to play a more positive role in relating available resources to the particular needs and circumstances of the school.

In different ways these features reflect a traditional and rooted objection to the centralised control of education in this country (cf. France).

(b) Limits to Centralised Authority

Although the central government has increased its power at the expense of other elements in the system, the threat of straightforward centralised State direction in the educational field is guarded against in a number of ways:

(i) the supremacy of the law. The central authority in education is just as subject to the law as it affects education as are other elements in the system. Legislation lays down the duties and powers of the central authority: palpably to neglect the one or exceed the other is to operate illegally;

Tameside

(ii) the central authority's wider responsibility and sensitivity to Parliament, the mass-media and public opinion. The introduction or amendment of legislation or regulations related to education is dependent upon the support of Parliament. New and existing policies are subject to questions in the House, to critical appraisal by the press and television, and to pressure from particular interested parties;

(iii) the continued distribution of power and responsibility between the central, local, institutional and professional levels. After all, education in England and Wales remains a locally provided and administered service, inclining the central authority to a policy of consultation and co-operation. Inevitably the system allows for the exercise of considerable discretion at the local level; the wide variations in

wherefore "control and direction

pattern and practice between individual local education authorities gives sharp expression to this fact. Nor can managing or governing bodies, especially in the field of further and higher education, be simply dismissed as mere ciphers. The dominant influence of the teachers in respect of various professional matters has already been referred to.

(c) Layers of Operation

In contemporary educational administration three layers of operation may be distinguished at both the central and local levels (see diagram, below).

The Basic Structure of Post-war Educational Administration

Layers of operation	Central structure	Local structure
Political Concerned with policy and decision making; carries ultimate public responsibility for educational matters. Personnel involved subject to political change both central and local.	*D.E.S.* *Secretary of State* (general policy, science & research, allocation of resources and other sensitive areas) Parliamentary Secretary (assists above) under- under- *Minister* *Minister* I II (higher & (schools) further) (*All* political figures)	*Local Education Committee* consisting of Chairman & Vice-Chairman, majority of Council members, minority of co-opted people. The L.E.C. undertakes the duties and exercises the powers of the multi-purpose local authorities in the field of education. They operate a sub-committee structure and delegate limited powers to schools. Managers Governors (primary) (secondary)
Administrative Concerned with the provision of information and advice to the political layer, and with the execution of decisions and the day-to-day working of the educational system. Personnel involved give continuity and stability to educational system.	Permanent *Civil Service* staff serving the D.E.S. at Whitehall. *Permanent Secretary* | Deputy | Branch Under-Secretaries Assisted by many other staff of lower grades.	Permanent *Local Government* officers, administrative & clerical staff serving the local authority in the field of education. *Chief Education Officer* | Deputy | Asst. Education Officers (variable division of responsibilities)
Advisory Links the administrative layer with the staff and institutions operating in the field, and provides a means through which information and advice can be amassed, sifted and communicated.	*Her Majesty's Inspectorate* *Central Advisory Councils* (for England and Wales) Standing Committees (e.g. N.A.C.E.I.C., N.A.C.T.S.T., Student grants) Special Committees (e.g. Albemarle, James) D.E.S. consultation with other interested parties.	*Local Inspectorate* (includes Advisers/Organisers) *ad hoc* sub-committees of the L.E.C. Consultation with teachers, churches, universities and other voluntary bodies and interested parties. *But* the Chief Education Officer acts as both filter and power-house for passage of information and advice to the L.E.C.

(i) *Political Layer*

Concerned with decision making in education and ultimately responsible for the development of policy and provision. The Department of Education and Science, on behalf of the central government, makes the major decisions in accordance with party political attitudes and professional advice. The local education committees, on behalf of their parent County or County Borough Councils, make what are increasingly less important decisions, coloured by local government politics, local needs and circumstances and local professional advice.

(ii) *Administrative Layer*

Concerned with the provision of information and advice necessary for the making of decisions and with the execution of those decisions and the day to day running of the system. Because the Department of Education and Science and local education committees usually take serious notice of the advice rendered by their leading administrators, the latter are placed in a position whereby they can often wield a critical influence upon the process of decision making. Thus at the local level the creative power behind dynamic development is generally that of the Chief Education Officer; the records of Sir Alec Clegg in the West Riding of Yorkshire and of many others testify to this. On the executive side some of the administrative tasks are purely routine and recurring (e.g. the maintenance of adequate provision, the allocation of funds and the payment of teachers' salaries), whilst others involve the implementation of new policy or schemes as related to such matters as comprehensive re-organisation, educational priority arrangements, or special immigrant facilities.

(iii) *Advisory Layer*

Encompassed by and works through the administrative layer, but to some extent can be separately distinguished. At both the central and local levels there are advisory bodies and staff concerned with maintaining contact between the administrative layer and the actual institutions and practitioners in the field. Such contact enables them to accumulate the sort of knowledge and experience which can be drawn upon for all sorts of purposes by the administrators who render advice or execute policy. The Department of Education and Science is helped in this respect by the wide-ranging work of Her Majesty's Inspectorate; but where there is a need for an intensive investigation and precise recommendations upon some major educational matter or area, the Department can call on the services of the Central Advisory Councils, certain standing committees and special *ad hoc* bodies which may be set up to report on a specific issue (e.g. Albemarle, James). Many, but not all, of the post-war local education authorities have come to employ their own local inspectors and advisers as a means of strengthening contact between the office and the man in the field. However, it must be understood that at the local level the Chief Education Officer and his administrative assistants also undertake such contact work to supplement the efforts of their advisory staffs. This of course blurs the picture somewhat, although the coming of much larger authorities may make for greater specialisation of function in future. In any case the Chief Education Officer, his Deputy or Assistant Education Officers will retain the role of actually addressing advice to the local education committee or its sub-committees.

Thus the English educational system involves, both at the central and local levels, an odd combination of amateurs and professionals, with the latter merely advising and executing whilst the former are responsible for actually making the major decisions. But because the decisions taken are often quite simply the result of advice given, the professional administrators enjoy much more power than it might at first appear.

2 The Department of Education and Science

Its direct line of descent is the Committee of Council for Education 1839-56; the Education Department 1856-1900; the Board of Education 1900-44; the Ministry of Education 1944-64.

(*a*) Powers and Responsibilities

These were considerably increased by the 1944 Act, under which the central authority has the duty 'to promote the education of the people of England and Wales' and 'to secure the effective execution by local authorities, under (its) control and direction, of the national policy' (Part I, Section 1). National policy is legally the policy which finds statutory expression in the 1944 Act, subsequent amending legislation and the regulations which the Department issues with Parliamentary approval to fill in the details related to the broad legislative requirements. The actual power of the central authority to control and direct is not easy to pin down in terms of either its exact source or its extent, but it may be said to consist in a number of mutually reinforcing elements.

(i) The 1944 Act emphasised the mandatory duties (rather than permissive powers) of the local education authorities. Under Section 99 of the Act, the Minister has the right to declare any local authority in default of its obligations, to issue appropriate directions and to enforce them, if necessary, by legal action (writ of *mandamus*).

He was armed with similar powers in respect of managing and governing bodies.

(ii) Under the enigmatic Section 68 of the Act, the Minister was given the power to decide that a local education authority is acting unreasonably, or proposes to do so, in a respect not directly covered by statute or regulation, and to intervene to give such directions as he thinks expedient. Again, such powers were to cover both managing and governing bodies as well. The exact legal implications of Section 68 are still a matter of conjecture; it has never undergone serious testing in the courts, for the threat of taking it that far has proved enough (e.g. in the Durham dispute of 1952, when the county local education authority attempted to enforce trade union membership on all its staff). On the face of it, Section 68 gives the Minister powers which are only limited by his/her interpretation of 'reasonable' and 'expedient'! The power seems so wide and unaccountable that Section 68 caused much concern and debate in 1944. Only Butler's persuasive arguments and the general belief that such power would not be abused secured its passage. In the event the worst forebodings have not been realised. The past tradition of central-local partnership, the view that Section 68 could only be invoked to prevent rather than to initiate a new development, and only in relation to a particular local authority, have combined to limit its practical significance. However, its use by Mrs Thatcher in 1970 to force Surrey education authority to retain selective school opportunities for children living in particular areas chosen for the first stage of comprehensive re-organisation, serves as a reminder of the potential of Section 68 as a source of power for the central authority.

(iii) Under Section 13 of the Act (as amended) the Minister has the negative power of approving or disapproving the opening, closure or transposition of individual schools. Thus the Minister can wield direct influence upon the process of school re-organisation. Conservative ministers used it with effect to stem the comprehensive tide before 1964; thereafter responsible Labour ministers used it to check unsatisfactory comprehensive arrangements by over-enthusiastic local education authorities. During her first two years of office, Mrs Thatcher took advantage of Section 13 procedure to save nearly one hundred grammar schools from comprehensive re-organisation.

(iv) Under Sections 100 and 111 of the Act, which authorise the central authority to clarify its broad legislative provisions by means of issuing Standing Rules and Orders, the Minister has the power to control by regulation. Such regulations relate to schools, further education establishments, teacher training colleges, scholarships and other benefits, the school health service, handicapped pupils and teacher superannuation. But the threat of bureaucratic rule by regulation is contained by the Act's requirement that the introduction of Standing Rules and Orders be subject to consultation and the final approval of Parliament. As a matter of policy regulations are kept to a minimum, but once authorised and issued they enjoy the force of law.

(v) Traditionally the central authority has wielded power through the purse, facilitated by the local authorities' heavy dependence upon central financial support. Failure to meet the conditions of grant made the local authority liable to financial penalty. Under the old specific percentage grant system, which involved ear-marked grants for education, such pressure could be directly and sharply exerted. Since 1958 the operation of the general rate support grant arrangements has blunted rather than removed this instrument of central power. The annual negotiations over the financing of all locally administered services presents the central government with the means of vetting and controlling major developments in education at the local level. It can be used, for instance, for instrumenting a priority for primaries policy and incidentally, thereby, for holding up comprehensive reorganisation. And the Local Government Act (1958) made the payment of block grants to local authorities contingent upon, amongst other things, the satisfaction of 'standards and general requirements prescribed for the administration of education'.

Further central influence is projected through the medium of circulars, memoranda and pamphlets, and is also exerted through Her Majesty's Inspectorate. But these means depend on the co-operative response of the local authorities, the teachers and the other parties involved; for example, a Department circular can only acquaint local authorities with the wishes of the central authority and has no statutory force, even though it is no light matter to ignore one. The submission of development plans for central examination and approval, made a mandatory requirement by the 1944 Act, is also worthy of mention; these relate to future provision and are mainly concerned with items of capital expenditure. However, this instrument of control is now really part and parcel of the central authority's financial power.

The responsibilities of the central authority are numerous and critical. Apart from the general duty to promote the education of the people and to develop policies calculated to achieve that end, the Department of Education and Science has a number of specific functions to perform:

(i) to set minimum standards of provision and to ensure that these are being met by the local authorities and others concerned;

(ii) to control the rate, distribution, nature and cost of educational building within the national context of available resources; on an annual basis, the Department must consult with the local authorities to agree upon the sum total of their educational expenditure for the coming year and the extent of the central government's contribution towards it (the latter is then actually paid as part of the rate support grant received by each local authority);

(iii) to determine the requirements to be met for recognition as a qualified teacher and to control the training, supply and distribution of such personnel (the Department is further responsible for the implementation of the Burnham salary procedures and scales and for the running of the teachers' superannuation scheme);

(iv) to support financially by direct grants certain institutions and activities that do not come under the jurisdiction of the local education authorities—the direct grant secondary schools, the denominational training colleges and some non-provided special schools fall into this category, and educational research is also directly financed by making central grants available for this purpose to university departments and other reputable bodies;

(v) to settle any serious disputes which may arise between any of the other elements which make up the educational system. Thus children are safeguarded against the effects of local authorities, managing and governing bodies, teachers' organisations, church bodies and parents failing to agree amongst themselves on any important matter.

However, in relation to the exercise of control and direction and the fulfilment of its particular responsibilities, it is also important to appreciate what the Department does not do. In contrast to the central authority in many other countries, it does not provide or run schools or any other educational institutions, it does not engage or employ teaching staff, it does not select or publish educational text books, it does not determine the curriculum or the teaching methods and it does not directly concern itself with external examinations. It is the other elements in the system which marshal the necessary resources for and determine the substance of the education actually provided.

(b) Internal Organisation of the Department of Education and Science

Basically one must distinguish between three groups of people.

(i) *Political Heads*
These are political appointments, subject to sudden change following elections and ministerial reshuffles. The political heads of the Department are responsible to the government and to Parliament for the policy and the conduct of their department, and are usually politicians with a marked interest in, if not direct experience of, the field of education. They formulate national policy, initiate any necessary legislation and press the claims of education within the government's total programme. During the period 1944-64 there were only two political appointees, the Minister of Education and his Parliamentary Secretary. But the establishment of the enlarged Department of Education and Science raised the number to include the new Secretary of State for Education and Science, a personal Parliamentary Secretary and two under-Ministers of State. The division of work amongst the political heads is a flexible one, although the Secretary of State deals with the most politically sensitive areas (e.g. general policy and allocation of resources) and the Ministers of State tend to devote their individual attentions to either further and higher education or to the work of the schools. Ultimate political responsibility for the Department resides of course with the Secretary of State.

(ii) *Civil Service Personnel*
The Department is served by some 3,000-odd Civil Service staff, headed by a Permanent Secretary and his deputy, who undertake various responsibilities according to grade, ranging from the direct provision of information and advice to the political heads to the maintenance of routine contact with the local education authorities and other bodies. The Permanent Secretary and his staff represent the executive arm of the Department, communicating national policy and control outwards from the centre. As the Civil Service staff are completely outside the political arena, they contribute a measure of continuity and stability to central educational administration.

(iii) *Her Majesty's Inspectorate*
This body is the professional arm of the Department and is composed of some five hundred officers organised on both a specialist and territorial basis. The Inspectorate serves as an administrative link with the local education authorities and as a professional link with the schools, other educational institutions and bodies. Its role is increasingly advisory and consultative, providing a two-way link between the central authority and the educational system at ground level; its essential functions are to help maintain satisfactory standards and to spread new and sound educational developments throughout the system by personal contact and the organisation of conferences and courses.

Special arrangements exist for the central administration of education in Wales. Whilst political responsibility for science and higher education is retained by the Secretary of State for Education and Science, such responsibility in respect of primary, secondary and special education lies with the Secretary of State for Wales. Both exercise their respective executive functions in relation to Welsh education through the Welsh Education Office in Cardiff, which has its own Civil Service staff.

(c) Vital Relationships for the Department of Education and Science

As a major government department it is involved in three critical relationships:

(i) *With Parliament*

The Department of Education and Science is responsible to Parliament for educational policy and its implementation. This responsibility finds clear expression in educational legislation and regulations, the financial estimates and in debates and questions on education in Parliament.

(ii) *With the Local Authorities*

The Department determines national policy and lays down minimal requirements whilst the local education authorities work within this set framework, consulting the Department when necessary and receiving guidance from it.

(iii) *With Other Interested Parties*

It is both traditional and desirable for the central authority to consult and develop a sound working relationship with such bodies as the teachers' organisations and the churches.

3 The Local Education Authorities

The direct line of descent is the School Boards 1870-1902; the Technical Instruction Committees 1889-1902; Part II and Part III local education authorities 1902-44.

(a) Structural Framework

Under the 1944 Act the local education authorities have operated within a framework distinguished by a number of structural features:

(i) Only the County and County Borough Councils were given the powers and responsibilities of local education authorities, although there was provision for divisional administration in the large county areas. But the 1972 Local Government Act has given rise to new arrangements based upon larger and fewer County and Metropolitan District local education authorities; the main victims of this change have been the divisional executives and the County Borough authorities. For further details, see Chapter 9, pages 154-5.

(ii) The local education authority is required to set up a local education committee, a majority of its members being drawn from the parent council and including co-opted members with experience in education and acquainted with the educational conditions of the area concerned. The parent council must consult its local education committee before exercising its educational functions, and may (and usually does) delegate its responsibilities and powers to the committee, excepting the borrowing of money and the raising of rates. Broadly speaking, such arrangements will continue to operate under the new local education authorities, although there are indications that the new parent councils may not be so disposed to grant their local education committees the same measure of autonomy and special influence as was the case before.

(iii) The local education committee is empowered to work through a system of sub-committees in order to cope with its wide-ranging and voluminous business. Initially the tendency was for local education committees, especially those serving large authorities, to establish a considerable number of standing sub-committees to deal with such matters as primary education, secondary education, further education, special services, sites and buildings, youth employment and finance and general purposes. But most authorities later adopted a reduced sub-committee structure involving much less specialisation. Such standing sub-committees do not normally work on a reporting back basis; the great bulk of their business passes through the local education committee 'on the nod'. The relationship between the local education committee and the parent council normally conforms to a similar pattern. Debate at the higher levels is only likely to be provoked by controversial matters of major policy such as comprehensive reorganisation. As education is by far the most expensive and important of the locally administered services, the amount of business to be done puts a premium on real delegation and routine working. This fact may safeguard such established relationships and procedures from any really marked changes under the new arrangements.

(iv) The local education committee, led by its chairman and vice-chairman, is supported by a full-time staff of principal local government officers and their administrative and clerical assistants. Firstly, there are those who are purely and directly concerned with education.

Outstanding is the Chief Education Officer or Director of Education, who is expected to identify the issues and marshal the business requiring the attention of the local education committee and to accept executive responsibility for the development of local provision. But he is the committee's major source of professional advice and often leaves the imprint of his own power and influence upon local policy and development. It is a statutory requirement that each local education authority appoint a Chief Education Officer; both he and his senior colleagues are recruited originally from the ranks of qualified and serving teachers. On the administrative side the Chief Education Officer is backed by a Deputy Education Officer and a third tier of Assistant Education Officers. In large authorities the third tier is differentiated into three levels and over-all the pattern of responsibility for Assistant Education Officers varies fairly widely and is subject to change. Quite distinct are the local inspectors, advisers and organisers who compose the Chief Education Officer's advisory staff. They are also drawn from the ranks of the teaching profession and operate as the main link between the local education offices and the schools and other educational institutions in the area. The development of teacher centres and the mounting of local courses for teachers come within their province of responsibility. Behind the Chief Education Officer and his professional staff are a large number of local government employees dealing with fairly routine administrative and clerical work at the education offices. Secondly, there are those who serve the local authority in its multi-purpose capacity; where appropriate the expertise of other principal local government officers and their assistants may be made available to the local education committee and its Chief Education Officer. For both these groups of professional administrators the 1972 Local Government Act must have been a most disturbing prospect. As the number of Chief Education Officers was almost double the number of new local education authorities, the competition for the top appointments was inevitably fierce. And should the comparative importance of the local education committees suffer under the reorganisation the new appointees may find themselves with less scope and influence than previously.

(b) Duties and Powers

The basic responsibility of the local education authorities is set out in general terms in Section 7 of the 1944 Act. This is 'to contribute towards the spiritual, moral, mental, and physical development of the community' by securing the provision of efficient primary, secondary and further education in the geographical area for which they are responsible. Particular duties and powers, with more emphasis on the former than the latter, are spelled out by subsequent provisions of the Act. The *duties* include:

(i) to make adequate and satisfactory provision of primary and secondary schooling suited to pupils' different ages, abilities and aptitudes;

(ii) to have regard to the need for nursery education and for the need to make special arrangements for the education of handicapped children;

(iii) to meet adequately and efficiently the local need for further education in its various forms;

(iv) to establish, maintain or otherwise assist Colleges of Education as directed by the central authority;

(v) to ensure that the premises and accommodation of all their schools and other educational establishments conform to official standards;

(vi) to contribute substantially, on the basis of an agreed formula, to the total cost of maintaining and developing the statutory system of education in its own area;

(vii) to draw up articles of management and instruments of government for provided schools and institutions and to secure the establishment of suitable managing and governing bodies to exercise the responsibilities laid down;

(viii) to ensure the implementation of compulsory religious worship and instruction (the latter according to an agreed syllabus) in all its county primary and secondary schools;

(ix) to support its own School Medical and School Meals services;

(x) to establish its own local education committee and to appoint its own Chief Education Officer.

The *powers* include:

(i) compulsorily to purchase land for the exercise of their functions;

(ii) to establish a new school or to cease maintaining an existing one, subject to Section 13 procedure;

(iii) to control secular education in the schools which they maintain—this acts as a safeguard against the exercise of professional freedom in favour of questionable or bizarre curriculum developments and may be used to rationalise the organisation of courses for older pupils in secondary and further education;

(iv) to control the appointment of teachers, though with reservations in respect of voluntary aided schools;

(v) to mount an inspection of any educational institution which they maintain or to request Her Majesty's Inspectorate to undertake one;

(vi) to grant scholarships, exhibitions, bursaries and other allowances for
further and higher educational study.

(c) Managers and Governors

The 1944 Act required that all primary schools have a body of managers
and that all secondary schools have a body of governors, the object being
to secure an individual identity for each school within any local authority
area. Primary school managers are appointed under articles of management drawn up by the local education authority. Secondary school
governors are appointed under instruments of government submitted
by the local education authority for the approval of the central authority.
Articles and instruments related to voluntary schools are the responsibility of the Department of Education and Science. Paradoxically, and
perhaps unhappily, the 1944 Act empowers the local education authorities
to encompass a number of schools with one managing or governing
body and this practice has been adopted by many of them.

In theory, the articles of management or instruments of government
demarcate areas of responsibility for the local education authority, the
managers or governors and the headteacher, although there are no
legislative guidelines in this respect. In practice, given the importance of
the local education authority and the strong tradition that the headteacher
must be allowed to run his own school in his way, the managers or
governors usually find themselves denied any clear and useful role. They
may play a subsidiary part in the appointment of staff and will normally
grace any important school occasion such as the annual prize distribution.
By and large they are mere figureheads, although if devoted to the
interests of their particular school they can be a source of strength in any
differences which may emerge between the head and the office. The
struggle over comprehensive education has sometimes demonstrated their
potential energy and influence.

It was not until 1968 that the local education authorities were statutorily required to draw up instruments of government for their Colleges
of Education; under the Weaverisation policy (see page 128) such
institutions were to have their own governing bodies (without an in-
built majority of local authority representatives) and their own academic
boards, so as to enjoy increased autonomy as befitted their enhanced status
in the post-Robbins period. The benefits of this development were later
passed on to the polytechnics and the Colleges of Further Education. In
the field of both financial control and other matters, the position of the
local education authorities in relation to these institutions has been
significantly weakened as their governing bodies and academic boards have
developed an increasingly important role.

4 National Associations

The English educational system, although centred upon the Department of Education and Science, is geared to consultation and co-operation on a continuing basis, so that national policy and practice in education becomes as far as possible the expression of a consensus of opinion distilled from various sources within the system. In this process certain bodies are especially important.

(a) Associations Representing the Local Education Authorities

For many years the County Councils' Association and the Association of Municipal Corporations represented the multi-purpose interests of the local authorities; given the primacy of education as the most expensive and important of the locally administered services, they always showed a strong interest in post-war educational developments. Both these associations maintained a standing Education Committee to handle the relevant business; they also secured nine and six places respectively on the management panel of the Burnham Committee. But it was the Association of Education Committees which undertook the specialist role by directly representing all the local education committees (*not* the local education authorities) of England and Wales. This Association held annual and other general meetings, but the major working responsibility fell upon the Executive Committee which met frequently and spoke on behalf of all the local education committees. The Executive Committee employed a full-time, professional adviser or Secretary; in this capacity Sir William P. Alexander became the dominant influence within and the chief spokesman for the Association. Through its permanent staff in London the Association of Education Committees undertook a number of important functions:

(i) to negotiate and consult with the central authority in relation to proposed legislation, regulations, circulars and other memoranda for general publication;

(ii) to submit evidence and present the viewpoint of the local education committees to various bodies undertaking inquiries directly or indirectly concerned with education (e.g. Maud, James);

(iii) to advise and represent particular local education authorities when at issue with the central authority, the teachers' organisations or other interested party;

(iv) to represent the local education committees on various national bodies concerned with education (e.g. the Schools Council);

(v) to take part in negotiations with the teachers' organisations on conditions of service and salaries. The Association secured six places on the management panel of the Burnham Committee and its Secretary usually presented the employers' case in the salary negotiations.

Given the new situation created by the 1972 Local Government Act and the state of flux arising from its implementation, it was thought expedient to couch the foregoing analysis in the past tense. Two new local authority associations, the Association of County Councils and the Association of Metropolitan Authorities, have replaced the old County Councils' Association and Association of Municipal Corporations. Each of these multi-purpose associations supports its own standing Education Committee, and there is the prospect of them joining together to form a central council of local education authorities (with equal representation from the two associations). This latter body would concern itself with major policy issues, parliamentary matters, salary negotiations and other critical considerations related to education in which the new local authorities have a sharp interest. Thus the established practice of having a national body to represent the local education committees directly may be discontinued. But there will be disadvantages if a central council of local education authorities replaces the Association of Education Committees. Such a council will be able to speak with one voice only if the Education Committees of its parent associations are already in agreement. And one of those parent associations will probably be dominated by the representatives of the large metropolitan areas which are *not* serving as local education authorities; this would hardly be favourable to the cause of education within the new total context.

(*b*) Associations Representing the Teachers

The most important of these are the Headmasters' Association, the Association of Headmistresses, the Assistant Masters' Association, the Association of Assistant Mistresses (together making up the Joint Four), the National Association of Schoolmasters, the Union of Women Teachers, the Association of Teachers in Technical Institutions, the National Association of Headteachers and the National Union of Teachers. Thus the teachers have no single organisation to represent their interests in the way that the Association of Education Committees has taken care of the interests of all the local education committees. This fragmentation is a reflection of the sectional interests traditionally existing within the teaching profession.

The teachers' organisations have two major roles to play and these sometimes come into conflict. Firstly, they operate as normal labour associations undertaking the role of ordinary trade unions, involving in certain cases affiliation to the Trades Union Congress. Secondly, they operate as professional bodies, looking upon themselves as repositories of professional knowledge and expertise and responsible sources of professional advice for the central authority and other interested parties. The National Union of Teachers is by far the largest and most influential of the teachers' organisations. It has a majority on the teachers' panel of the Burnham Committee and has its own permanent staff and head-quarters at Hamilton House in London. Like the Association of Education Committees, it has its own full-time Secretary and professional adviser; for many years Sir Ronald Gould distinguished himself in this capacity during the post-war era.

There are a number of particular functions which the National Union of Teachers, like its less important rival associations, attempts to perform:

(i) to negotiate and consult with the central authority in relation to proposed legislation, regulations, circulars and other memoranda for general publication;

(ii) to submit evidence and present the teachers' viewpoint to various committees of enquiry (e.g. James) and to undertake its own investigations and formulate policy recommendations with a view to influencing the government and public opinion; in the latter respect the annual conference and such reports as *The State of the Schools* (1963) provide important means of publicising the union's views;

(iii) to advise individual members and render them necessary and justifiable support in relation to their professional capacity;

(iv) to represent teachers on various national bodies concerned with education such as the Schools Council, the School Broadcasting Council, the National Foundation for Educational Research and the Central Industrial Training Council;

(v) to negotiate and consult with the Association of Education Committees (or other bodies representing the employers at national level) and individual local education authorities in relation to conditions of service and contractual arrangements. Through the Burnham machinery, the National Union of Teachers also wields an important influence upon the question of salaries.

For further information on the teacher's organisations, see Chapter 8, pages 132-4.

(c) Associations Representing Other Interested Parties

There are also national bodies or organisations concerned to look after the interests and to present the views of the various churches, the chief education officers, managers and governors, university teachers, staff in colleges and departments of education, students in further and higher education, vice-chancellors and principals of autonomous higher educational institutions and even parents. Many of these bodies have links with the Department of Education and Science, and where appropriate with the Association of Education Committees (or its successor), teachers' organisations and with each other. They are usually consulted when issues arise which relate directly to them.

Thus, with such representative bodies working in the background and smoothing the way by continuing contact, educational policy and practice can be formulated and implemented without the central authority having to rely on an overt demonstration of its power to control and direct.

5 The Present Institutional Pattern in English Education

The diagram on page 175 shows the basic institutional pattern of educational provision now existing in England and Wales. The following points are particularly noteworthy:

(*a*) The immediate post-war institutional pattern was rather simpler than the existing one. The 1944 Act enforced a rigid division at eleven-plus between primary and secondary schools, and the overwhelming majority of local education authorities chose to organise their secondary education along tripartite (grammar/technical/modern) or bipartite (grammar/modern) lines.

(*b*) Since the late 1950s the comprehensive tide has produced a more complex pattern, especially at the secondary level, with selective and comprehensive arrangements (each with their own sub-variations) now co-existing within the total national framework and even within the confines of a single authority. The middle school comprehensive alternative, authorised by the Education Act of 1964, has dismantled the established eleven plus dividing line and thus blurred the distinction between primary and secondary schooling in certain areas.

(*c*) The reorganisation of secondary education has proceeded very largely on the basis of four comprehensive alternatives laid down in Circular 10/65. These are the all-through 11-18 comprehensive school, the two-tier pattern with complete transfer from a junior to a senior comprehensive at 13 or 14 years, the 11-16 comprehensive school plus Sixth Form (or tertiary) college arrangement and the middle school pattern involving transfer at 12 or 13 years to senior comprehensives. Each of these possibilities has its strengths and weaknesses, but the most important single factor in determining which arrangements to adopt has been the nature of the existing school buildings and the cost of adaptation. For more detailed information, see appendix I, pages 333-5.

The Institutional Pattern of Educational Provision

Higher and Further Education

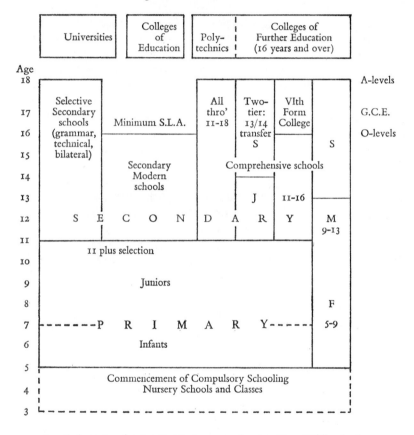

S = Senior comprehensive; J = Junior comprehensive; M = Middle school;
F = First school; S.L.A. = school leaving age.
This diagram is a modified version of that presented in the D.E.S. publication
The Educational System of England and Wales (1971), page 11.

(*d*) The diagram encompasses all the institutions composing the statutory system of education, but ignores the independent and direct grant grammar schools which account for about 6% of the total school population. The independent schools are completely within the private sector and receive no public moneys for their provision or maintenance; the direct-grant schools have a foot in both the private and public sectors of education, receiving grants direct from the central authority, but being in no way under the jurisdiction of the local education authorities.

(e) After 1944 the post-secondary sector was simply composed of higher education, virtually monopolised by the degree-awarding universities, and further education in all its sub-degree level forms provided by institutions under local education authority control. Only the fact that certain Colleges of Further Education prepared students for University of London external degrees blurred the distinction. But with the development of the Colleges of Advanced Technology in the 1950s and the growing aspirations of other major institutions, an increasing amount of higher education and degree level work was undertaken in the non-university sector. Since 1965 higher and further education have been developed on the basis of the so-called binary system. This consists of a public sector composed of the Colleges of Education, the new polytechnics and Colleges of Further Education, which have maintained direct links with both the Department of Education and Science and the local education authorities, and the autonomous sector centred upon the universities with their long tradition of academic freedom and self-government. However, recent trends have been in the direction of an increasing measure of autonomy for higher educational institutions in the public sector (Weaverisation process, see page 128) and a growing measure of public control over the universities and their development. The establishment of the Council for National Academic Awards in 1964 finally opened the way to the development of their own distinctive degree courses by non-university institutions.

(f) The new polytechnics have emerged as an attempt to rationalise the provision of higher education within the public sector. In 1966 a government White Paper launched the policy of concentrating full-time and sandwich courses of higher education within the further education system in a limited number of centres to be called polytechnics. At thirty such institutions up and down the country, the necessary staff and other facilities would be marshalled for the efficient and economic running of such courses. Much of the polytechnics' work is at degree level and the institutions enjoy a considerable measure of independence in spite of being located in the public sector.

(g) The Colleges of Education have served a number of masters in the post-McNair (1944) period. Whilst responsibility for teacher recruitment and training facilities has rested with the central authority and financial and administrative responsibility was lodged with the local education authorities (excepting the denominational training colleges which have operated as direct-grant institutions), the responsibility for the approval of courses and the validation of awards was undertaken by the universities working through the Area Training Organisations. As monotechnic institutions solely concerned with the training of teachers, the place of the Colleges of Education in the post-war system of higher and further education was never very clear, although the development of B.Ed. degree courses after 1964 enhanced their status and strengthened the university link. The Weaver Report (1966) led to a considerable loosening of the financial and administrative control formerly exerted by the local education authorities, and the James Report (1972) went on to recommend that the Colleges of Education should abandon their purely monotechnic role and become a third sector of higher education, breaking out of their former subordination to the universities in the process. But the latter suggestion was controversial and met with a mixed reception in the Colleges of Education themselves.

(*h*) The White Paper *Education: a Framework for Expansion* (1972) portends significant changes in the existing institutional pattern. The provision of nursery education for three- and four-year-old children, palpably neglected since 1944 and positively discouraged by Circular 8/60, received a new and high priority in the government's ten-year programme for educational advance. The expectation is that within a decade nursery education will be freely available on at least a half-time basis for all three- to four-year-olds whose parents wish them to have it; most of the extra places to be provided will be in the form of nursery classes attached to primary schools. But the major changes consequent upon this policy statement will take place in the field of higher education. Although the White Paper implies that the binary system will continue, the intention is to increase the comparative importance of the public sector and especially of the polytechnics. By 1981 no fewer than one-half of the full-time and sandwich course places in higher education will be in non-university institutions. The latter clearly face a decade of considerable expansion and reorganisation; the prior establishment of the Local Authorities' Higher Education Committee 'to consider and advise on the provision, co-ordination and future development of higher education in the local authority sector' fits in with this.

Given the intention to cut down the number of teacher training places by almost one-third, it is the Colleges of Education which face the greatest institutional upheaval. As a whole these formerly monotechnic institutions will be required to accept a substantial broadening of function, including the development of the new Diploma of Higher Education. Those Colleges of Education which expand and diversify, either unilaterally or on the basis of a merger, would ultimately be indistinguishable from a polytechnic or other advanced College of Further Education. Only a limited number of Colleges of Education, but especially the denominational ones, will continue to pursue their traditionally specialist role. As the Area Training Organisations are also to be dismantled, the result will be to draw the Colleges of Education firmly into the rest of the non-university sector of further and higher education. It is intended that Diploma of Higher Education courses should be developed by the universities as well as other higher educational institutions; conversely, especially given the government's declared intention to work towards a graduate teaching profession, the latter will continue to develop their degree level work apace. Some commentators see such developments as a potentially long-term dissolvent of the binary system itself.

Follow-up: Attempt to cover as much of the following ground as possible.
1 *Read* Department of Education and Science booklet *The Educational System of England and Wales*
   Burgess, T. *A Guide to English Schools*, Chapters 2, 3, 4 and 9
   Armfelt, R. *The Structure of English Education*, Chapters I, II and III
   Dent, H. C. *The Educational System of England and Wales*, Chapters 2, 3 and 12
   Alexander, W. P. *Education in England. The National System— How it Works*, Chapters I and VII
2 *Clarify the following: the distinguishing features of the educational system in England and Wales which make it unique; the distinction between the political, administrative and advisory layers in the functioning of the system at both the central and local levels; the extent of and the limitations upon the power of the central authority in education since 1944; the functions and the internal organisation of the Department of Education and Science; the composition and mode*

of operation of local education committees; the role of the Chief Education Officer; the duties and powers of the local education authorities; the identity and significance of the more important national associations and representative bodies operating within the educational system; the nature of the existing institutional pattern and any prospective changes in it.

Chapter Eleven
The Major Post-War Reports on Education

Purpose: to identify the most important of the many post-war reports on education and to provide a cohesive and summary analysis of their substance and main recommendations. Further, to assess the influence of these reports, both actual and prospective, upon educational development and practice in England and Wales.

In the history of English education there are numerous instances of official reports which achieved little or no direct impact upon contemporary development. On the other hand, many such reports have crystallised and reinforced developing ideas and attitudes, supported new and progressive practice, identified existing weaknesses and shortcomings and made critical recommendations which have done much to shape and colour later policy and development. During the nineteenth century the Royal Commission emerged as the major means of high-powered investigation into educational matters. Elementary education was examined by the Newcastle (1858-61) and Cross (1886-8) Commissions, both submitting reports which significantly affected the elementary schools and teacher training. The Royal Commissions which reported on the ancient universities, the public schools and the endowed grammar schools produced worthwhile if limited results. The report of the Bryce Commission on *Secondary Education* (1895) was epoch-making, providing the basis for the new administrative framework and system of State secondary schools introduced by the 1899 and 1902 Education Acts. From the turn of the century it was the Consultative Committee, set up to advise the new Board of Education on all educational matters referred to it, which became the main source of investigations and reports. Its most influential work was done in the inter-war years when, under the chairmanship of Sir W. H. Hadow, it reported on *The Education of the Adolescent* (1926) and *The Primary School* (1931); the former pointed the way towards secondary education for all, whilst the latter encouraged the paedocentric approach to the schooling of younger children. In a more limited field the Secondary Schools Examination Council also wielded influence; established in 1917 to supervise the development of the new School Certificate, it helped to shape curricula and examinations, first in the grammar schools and later in the wider secondary field. The Norwood

Report on *Curriculum and Examinations in Secondary Schools* (1943), not only increased the support for the tripartite organisation of secondary education, but also paved the way for the introduction of the General Certificate of Education examinations. The Beloe Report on *Secondary School Examinations other than G.C.E.* (1960) was a seminal document leading to the development of the Certificate of Secondary Education courses and examinations. Meanwhile the 1944 Act had replaced the Consultative Committee by two Central Advisory Councils (one for England and one for Wales) empowered to investigate and report upon any educational issue they or the Ministry thought fit. The Minister also had the right to use departmental and special committees to examine particular matters; he received reports from such new bodies as the National Advisory Council on the Training and Supply of Teachers, the National Advisory Council on Education for Industry and Commerce, the National Institute of Adult Education and the Standing Committee on student grants. As before, Parliamentary Select Committees could, and on occasion did, operate in the field of education. Given this welter of possibilities and the fast rising comparative importance of education, it is not surprising that the post-war era has produced a spate of educational reports. Between 1959 and 1972 virtually the whole of the educational system was covered by five major reports which must now be individually examined.

1 Crowther Report on Fifteen to Eighteen (1959)

Source

The Central Advisory Council for Education under the chairmanship of Sir Geoffrey Crowther.

Terms of Reference

To consider, in relation to changing individual and socio-economic needs, the education of young persons aged 15-18 years and to examine the interrelationship of the various stages of education. Thus the Council's brief was wide enough to allow a major review of the post-primary sector of the educational system, and in particular to facilitate a close examination of the secondary and further educational provision developed under the 1944 Act.

Dominant Themes

The report featured a number of themes or viewpoints which underpinned many of the detailed recommendations made:

(*a*) the conservative attitude towards existing institutional forms and other traditional practices. The report gave its qualified approval to the tripartite system of secondary education and was very lukewarm in its response to comprehensive schools. It conceived the future expansion and development of further education along similarly selective lines and even seemed to project this strategy into the structuring of an enlarged teaching profession. The academic Sixth Form with its traditional specialisation also received the backing of the report;

(*b*) the populist concern for the wastage of talent resultant of an excessively elitist system and a determination to check this in the interests of the nation's economic future. The Council expressed dissatisfaction over the fact that only 12% of the 16-18 years age group were in full-time education, which compared very unfavourably with some other advanced industrial countries: it urged that the proportion should be raised to 50% by 1980. The country's potential pool of trained manpower was being especially ill-effected by the failure of the educational system to capitalise upon the talent of the second quartile of adolescent ability, which represented 'the richest vein of untapped human resources' available to the economy;

(*c*) the progressive belief in the vital need for social justice in education, in terms of ensuring the provision of real opportunity for every boy and girl to pursue their education to the limits of their talents and desires. The Council felt that the education provided for the great mass of children was inadequate in both quality and duration; nor was it acceptable that contact between many young people and the educational system should be suddenly and completely severed at the completion of compulsory full-time schooling. It also drew attention to the serious educational disadvantage suffered by secondary modern pupils attending schools in decaying slum areas and new housing estates where all sorts of social problems were concentrated.

The institutional conservatism of the report was not welcomed in certain progressive circles; it savoured too much of the 'leaders and the led' approach. Although the Council thought them quite reconcilable, it may be said that there was an underlying conflict of principle between the first viewpoint and the other two as educational wastage of talent and social injustice cannot be divorced from institutional forms, especially when they include such critical determinants of opportunity as eleven-plus selection.

Main Recommendations

The earlier part of the report, whilst paying homage to the great post-war improvement in full-time educational provision for the most able 15 to 18-year-olds, dwelt upon the comparative neglect of the less able secondary school child and the early school leaver. The recommendations made in the first half of the report reflected the Council's concern for these young persons. Part Five of the report was concerned with the selective secondary schools and especially their expanding Sixth Forms; the Council was at pains to both support and temper the tradition of progressive specialisation for their able pupils. As previously indicated the Council was impressed by the grave wastage of talent amongst the second quartile of ability and this weakness received its close attention in the section (Part Six) on 'Technical Challenge and Educational Response'. It regretted that the 25% of the 15-18 year age group continuing in further education after leaving school amounted to 'neglected educational territory'. This was identified as the next major problem in English education requiring decisive action and a number of suggestions were made to improve the situation. The rest of the report dealt with institutional matters, teachers and the question of forward planning in education. The report's specific recommendations may be summarised as follows:

(*a*) that the secondary modern schools be improved by the intensified development of extended courses over a wider curricula range for those pupils prepared to stay on voluntarily. For a small minority G.C.E. O-level courses should be available and for a further third of modern pupils the possibility of a new external examination, operated on a decentralised basis, should be seriously considered. But the need to avoid burdening the least able with external examinations was forcibly underlined and a system of internal leaving certificates was suggested instead. The overall object was to give new hope and direction to the discredited secondary modern schools;

(*b*) that the minimum school-leaving age be raised to sixteen during the late 1960s. Such action it was claimed would be the best answer to the wastage of talent directly resultant of early leaving, as the educational system would be given more time to wield its beneficial influence at a crucial stage in adolescent development. Meanwhile, an immediate restriction of school leaving to Easter and July was urged as a means of making existing final year courses more viable and satisfactory;

(*c*) that the county colleges plan for the compulsory part-time continuative education of early school leavers be implemented as provided for under the 1944 Act. Such provision was to relate to the 16-18 years age group and was to be introduced on a phased basis at 'the earliest possible date'; this is explained by the fact that the raising of the school-leaving age was given first priority. In the interim

G

an intensive campaign for the expansion of day-release to a wider range of young workers on a voluntary basis was judged essential;

(*d*) that the Youth Service be recognised as a vital sector of the educational system for maintaining contact with and helping the less able early school leaver. The report deplored its continuing neglect and stated that 'in no other field of education can the expenditure of public money accomplish so much so readily'. But detailed recommendations for the improvement of the service were left to the Albemarle Committee's Report (1960);

(*e*) that early specialisation in the middle years of selective schools give way to a wider curriculum involving all pupils in aesthetic and practical subjects as well as the full range of English studies. Pre-specialisation for Sixth Form entry was condemned as an illiberal practice;

(*f*) that Sixth Form specialisation be somewhat diluted by limiting all pupils to a maximum of three A-level subjects and by making liberal use of minority time, so as to ensure the 'literacy' of science Sixth Formers and the 'numeracy of' Arts Sixth Formers. All Sixth Formers should share some common general course during minority time and this broad educational influence should be reinforced by giving more attention to extra-academic objectives such as all-round personal development and social responsibility;

(*g*) that curricula and examinations in further education be reformed to produce a coherent system of technician, craftsman and operative courses to replace the patchwork pattern which had grown up as a result of past piecemeal development;

(*h*) that a closer relationship be forged between the schools, industrial apprenticeship schemes and further education. In particular, the report urged the widening of day-release arrangements (preferably on a block or sandwich basis), especially for girls, hitherto largely neglected in this respect;

(*i*) that a wider range of full-time further education courses (currently concentrated on G.C.E. and commercial subjects) be developed. Conversely, the report urged the abandonment of the existing heavy reliance on evening classes for National Certificate and City and Guilds courses with their associated high failure rates. To remove a major source of student frustration and retardation, it was also recommended that block examinations be replaced by a single subject approach;

(*j*) that the average size of secondary schools be increased to provide a wider curricula choice for older pupils and that the number of secondary technical high schools with strong science Sixth Forms be expanded. Whilst the comprehensive school was recognised as a viable proposition when purpose-built, the report was unprepared to countenance any injury to existing efficient selective schools to make way for them; comprehensive schools were unproven and on balance the Council was unfavourably disposed towards them;

(*k*) that a larger and better qualified teaching force be developed to meet the expansion in full-time education recommended by the Council. Stress was laid on the importance of making the teaching profession more attractive to the well-qualified graduate, especially in shortage subjects such as mathematics and science. Financial incentives were suggested as a possible answer to the shortage and high turnover of teaching staff in the secondary schools of problem neighbourhoods;

(*l*) that long-term planning be applied to educational development and that it be insulated from political changes and economic vicissitudes. In spite of the obvious difficulties, the Council considered this to be a vital and practicable proposal.

Results

The Crowther Report occasioned more discussion than decisive action. There were only two direct results of the Council's labours. Firstly, the 1962 Education Act terminated Christmas leaving and thereby marginally raised the duration of compulsory schooling for some pupils. Secondly, the 1961 White Paper on *Better Opportunities in Technical Education* initiated the reform of the curricula pattern in technical education and the abandonment of block examinations. Less directly, the Report influenced a number of other developments. In the long term it contributed to the ultimate raising of the school-leaving age to sixteen years with effect from 1972-3. The emergence of the Certificate of Secondary Education examinations and the associated extended courses were partly the result of its influence. Its support of the Youth Service was not without effect. The expansion of full-time further education courses and the reorganisation of industrial training in 1964 also owed something to the Report. The growth of teacher training and supply during the 1960s was in line with the Crowther recommendations. However, all these developments owe as much, if not more, to other reports and influences contemporaneous with or subsequent to the Crowther submission.

On the other hand, the Report's support of the tripartite system of secondary education and the continuance of Sixth Form specialisation (in basic terms) were subjected to considerable criticism. The former position was soon increasingly challenged by the advance of comprehensive reorganisation, ironically enough in the cause of reducing the wastage of talent consequent upon eleven-plus selection. The latter standpoint, albeit qualified by a plea for the better broadening use of minority time, helped to perpetuate the strong university influence on Sixth Form curricula; it is significant that the attempts so far made to really change the curriculum arrangements for the 'new' Sixth Form (e.g. the Schools Council's 'Q' and 'F' proposals) have not got very far. A more radical approach by Crowther would have helped in this respect. Moreover, the Report's support of the county college scheme for the compulsory part-time continuative education of all early school leavers has come to nought; the Industrial Training Act (1964) has improved part-time educational opportunities for skilled and semi-skilled employees, but the young unskilled worker is as neglected as ever. The Council's concern for educational disadvantage in problem areas drew little official response until it had been reinforced by both the Newsom and the Plowden Reports. Finally, there was no long-term plan for the expansion recommended by Crowther; the politicians preferred to avoid the thorny problem of actually having to decide on a clear set of long-term educational priorities.

Perhaps the Crowther Report's greatest contribution to and influence upon English education was thematic rather than specific. It questioned the notion of a limited pool of ability and spotlighted the wastage of talent then taking place. This theme was inherited by the Newsom Report (1963) and fully developed in relation to higher education by the Robbins Report (1963). Such was the seed-bed for the principle of compensatory education as later developed in the Plowden Report (1967). The ripples of the Crowther outlook on the wastage of talent continue to work upon the developing educational scene.

2 Newsom Report on Half our Future (1963)

Source

The Central Advisory Council for Education under the chairmanship of Mr (later Sir) John Newsom.

Terms of Reference

To consider the education of 13- to 16-year-olds of average and less than average ability following full-time courses at school or in establishments of further education. Thus the Council's commission was not only largely limited to a consideration of the secondary modern field, but also involved the recoverage of ground already reviewed by the Crowther Report. The need for this specific investigation implied the failure of the secondary modern school as it had developed since the 1944 Act.

Dominant Themes

Not surprisingly, the Report intimated that much of secondary modern educational provision was unsatisfactory. But instead of interpreting its terms of reference widely and examining the efficacy of the selective system as such and seriously considering the comprehensive alternative, the Council was content to think in terms of limited recommendations that might afford the secondary modern idea a second chance of achieving success. Indeed, the Report saw the remedy, not in organisational change, but in terms of a new attitude by the official authorities and the general public to ensure that the secondary modern schools received their fair share of resources and respect. Whilst such a cautious approach was not calculated to win approval in progressive educational circles, paradoxically it threw up the critical message of the Newsom Report, which was that gross inequalities in educational provision existed at the secondary level and that there was a crying need to give the less able young adolescent a much better deal.

Main Recommendations

These may be summarised in terms of the major matters over which the Report expressed concern.

(a) School-leaving Age

This should be raised to sixteen years with effect from 1969-70 and the intention announced immediately. The extra year was to be school-based and the possibility of optional full-time attendance at a further education establishment was rejected. The aim of this recommendation was to check the wastage of talent consequent upon the heavy incidence of early leaving in relation to certain geographical areas and socio-economic groups.

(b) Problem Areas

Old, over-crowded industrial and slum areas, where school buildings and other facilities were especially unsatisfactory, should receive special treatment and support. But apart from insisting on new or improved accommodation and better staffing where the need was acute, the only concrete suggestion the Report could offer was the setting up of a working party and research facilities to consider the inter-related social and educational problems of such areas.

(c) Curriculum

Given the extension of the school leaving age, every secondary modern school was to provide a wide choice of fourth- and fifth-year courses, for which pupils should not be rigidly streamed. The extra year at school should be distinctly outgoing in character, which would require the schools to forge closer links with industry, the Youth Employment Service and further education. The Report recommended the direct use of vocational interest to stimulate pupils during the final year, and actual work experience was suggested as a possibility in this direction. The potential benefits for such pupils of short residential courses away from their homes was also underlined. The general object of final-year courses should be initiation into the adult world of work and leisure. More specifically the Report recommended the provision of factual knowledge and moral guidance on sexual matters, and the revision of the agreed syllabuses to allow a more relevant and imaginative approach to compulsory religious education. The need to involve pupils in the broadening experience of extra-curricular activity was strongly emphasised, even to the extent of suggesting that the normal school day should be extended and rearranged so as to absorb extra-curricular activities into the official timetable.

(d) Examinations

The Report urged caution in this field, stressing the need to resist pressure to extend external examinations to unsuitable pupils. It was suggested that all pupils should receive an internal leaver's certificate based on teachers' assessments and school records. The projected Certificate of Secondary Education examinations were given qualified approval, but the schools were warned against potential untoward side-effects such as the domination of curricula and the neglect of the least able pupils.

(e) Internal School Organisation

The existing situation was felt to be in need of liberalisation in the interests of improving human relationships within the secondary modern school. Greater attention to pupil responsibility and involvement (e.g. through school councils and the like) was needed to give senior pupils a sense of status and commitment. Staff-pupil relations needed to be closer and more adult, and it was thought that the abandonment of corporal punishment would contribute to this end. Every school should support a Parent-Teacher Association to forge and maintain links between the pupil's home and school.

(f) Material Resources

Attention was drawn to the inadequacy of the general accommodation, laboratory provision, library arrangements and facilities for practical subjects in far too many modern schools. The Council reiterated the plea for parity of treatment for the modern school to ensure that its material environment matched up to the new expectations of it. This should even extend to the provision of modern audio-visual aids and the facilities for using them.

(g) Staffing

The report voiced dissatisfaction with the existing training and supply of teachers for secondary modern schools. Too many schools, often in problem areas, faced unfavourable staff-pupil ratios and high rates of turnover. The training of teachers for 'Newsom pupils', especially in relation to work in difficult areas, required more deliberate thought and specific attention by the Colleges of Education. More Certificate student teachers should be equipped to teach with competence in more than one secondary subject area. The influx of untrained graduates direct from university or industry must be terminated; henceforth all teachers should be professionally trained. It was further suggested that the Colleges of Education should make a significant contribution to the professional training of graduates, thus sharing this role with the University Education Departments. Finally, the need for more generous ancillary staffing in the modern schools was also mentioned.

Results

These can only be described as rather disappointing, although the nature of the Report was partly to blame for this. In concerning itself with a reconsideration and restatement of the objectives and form of secondary modern education, the Newsom Report avoided the really important issue of whether the selective system should be condemned in favour of comprehensive secondary schooling. Whilst this cautious approach indirectly supported the organisational *status quo* and was thus acceptable to the Conservative government, it did much to rob the Report of potential significance. Instead it got bogged down in matters of curriculum reform detail and failed to throw up a priority list of clear, concrete operational objectives. In the event it was the general comprehensive tide rather than the Newsom recommendations that were to improve the educational prospects of the young adolescent of average and less than average ability. Where the secondary modern school continued to exist it rarely enjoyed the more generous treatment urged by the Report; no national policy emerged to stimulate the local authorities to action in this respect. Many comprehensive schools inherited the unsatisfactory accommodation and material facilities of the modern schools which they replaced. Secondary provision in problem areas continued to suffer from the shortcomings described by Newsom, but then an inter-departmental committee to investigate the situation further was hardly an inspired recommendation to make.

At best the Report crystallised the demand for the raising of the school leaving age, pointed the way towards Plowden's educational priority areas, brought rather more money to the improvement of modern school buildings in problem areas, sharpened the pressures for an end to the employment of untrained graduates (which came about between 1971-3) and encouraged the cause of curricula reform in secondary education. The latter issue was taken up by the newly established Schools Council (1964) which undertook a number of curriculum projects related to senior secondary pupils of average and less than average ability destined to stay on for an extra year. But in spite of the growth of teachers' centres and a patchwork of official encouragement for the preparation of courses suitable for those compulsorily staying on, the extent of such influence at ground level has been highly variable rather than impressive. All in all, it cannot be said that anything immediate and far-reaching followed from the Newsom Report: in the long run it will probably be remembered only for its connection with the raising of the school leaving age in 1972-3.

3 Robbins Report on Higher Education (1963)

Source

Special Committee appointed by the then prime minister (Mr Harold Macmillan) and under the chairmanship of Lord Robbins.

Terms of Reference

To consider the existing pattern of full-time higher education in Great Britain and, in the light of national needs and resources, to make recommendations for its future development. For the first time a powerful investigating body was commissioned to examine and report upon the whole field of higher education; the committee's attention was particularly drawn to the possible need for institutional and structural changes in the existing pattern.

Dominant Themes

The Report was characterised by a number of important and distinctive themes which underpinned and coloured its recommendations:

(a) the populist principle that a place in higher education should be available to every suitably qualified student desiring it. Pertinent international comparisons showed quite clearly that entry to higher education in Britain was much more restrictive than in certain other advanced industrial countries and the Robbins Committee accordingly argued for a major improvement in the scale of opportunity for higher education in this country. Such improvement would have to be subject to long-term planning and co-ordination if it was to be effective and sustained;

(*b*) the egalitarian principle that equal academic awards must be made for equal academic performances. This involved the rejection of the traditional idea that degree awards must remain the exclusive prerogative of the universities irrespective of the fact that non-university institutions were involved in work of equal standard and merit. The new principle was calculated to encourage the aspirations and to raise the status of both the training colleges and the major establishments of further education;

(*c*) the structural principle of delineating a co-ordinated sector of higher education within which all the institutions concerned would be financed through a central Grants Commission. The universities, although dominating the sector, would for the first time be brought under a significant measure of public control. Other institutions undertaking high level work would aspire towards ultimate university status or association and would escape the restrictive control of local education authorities. Thus, whilst the need for public control in higher education was acknowledged, the design was to develop an enlarged sector of various and largely autonomous institutions. Official influence was to be exercised through a new central government department and the new Grants Commission.

Main Recommendations

The following summary of the Report's specific recommendations is highly selective but must suffice.

(*a*) that the number of places in higher education should be progressively raised from 216,000 (1962-3) to 390,000 in 1973-4 and to 560,000 in 1980-1. The most impressive rate of expansion was to be enjoyed by the universities, with the institutions of advanced further education lagging well behind. The total projection was based on estimates of the number of appropriately qualified young people who would be seeking places ten and twenty years ahead; such an expansion was calculated to raise the proportion of the relevant age group undergoing higher education from 8% to 17%, though without relaxing the degree of competition for places. The Robbins' programme involved a marked increase in the existing rate of growth for higher education and a total long-term cost of £3,500 million;

(b) that the university should continue to be the 'model' institution and hence dominate the field of higher education. The large increase in the number of university places was to be achieved by the expansion of existing universities, the immediate foundation of six new universities and the translation of ten major colleges into technological universities;

(c) that the teacher training sector of higher education should enjoy both expansion and a rise in status. The latter object was to be achieved in various ways:

    (i) by renaming teacher training institutions as Colleges of Education now that the three year Certificate course allowed so much more scope for the development of a student's personal education;

    (ii) by introducing a four years Bachelor of Education degree course for appropriately qualified students in Colleges of Education;

    (iii) by establishing the colleges as University Schools of Education within the existing Area Training Organisation framework; each college would have its own governing body responsible to the University Senate for the degrees and certificates offered to its students. The Colleges of Education should be financed by ear-marked central funds channelled from the Grants Commission through the Area Training Organisations. The influence of the local education authorities in the teacher training sector would be much reduced, although they would retain some representation on the governing bodies of the colleges;

(d) that higher technological and advanced technical education must receive special attention if British industry was to remain competitive in the world at large. This sector of higher education had to expand considerably and attract students of a higher ability level than hitherto; moreover, it was vital that the long-standing inferiority of applied science to pure science should end. Various more detailed recommendations were made:

    (i) the need further to expand provision at Imperial College, London, the University of Manchester Institute of Science and Technology (U.M.I.S.T.) and the Royal College of Science and Technology, Glasgow (R.C.S.T.);

    (ii) the immediate establishment of two new technological universities, so as to provide five institutions capable of the very highest level of teaching and research in the technologies;

    (iii) the elevation of the Colleges of Advanced Technology to the status of technological universities with their own degree-awarding powers;

(iv) the encouragement of the National Colleges and the regional Colleges of Further Education to aspire to degree work in certain fields under the auspices of a new Council for National Academic Awards, which was to ensure the maintenance of standards;

(*e*) that staffing ratios and qualifications in higher education be improved, and the associated implications in relation to salaries, research facilities, secretarial assistance and general conditions of work be accepted;

(*f*) that higher education should be the responsibility of both university and non-university institutions enjoying a largely autonomous existence in terms of controlling their own staff, curricula, size, entrance requirements and academic standards. But at the same time the report emphasised the importance of ensuring a unified system of higher education subject to coherent central policy direction and co-ordination. The outcome was a compromise plan which, however, was more likely to protect the traditional independence of the universities than really to ensure proper central control in the national interest. The machinery of government as related to higher education was to be reorganised so as to transfer responsibility from the Treasury and the old University Grants Committee, to a new Ministry of Arts and Science supported by an enlarged central Grants Commission which would encompass both the universities and other autonomous higher educational institutions. Under such an arrangement a dichotomy would exist between the primary, secondary and further sectors of education (local education authority based) which would remain the responsibility of the Ministry of Education, and the higher education sector which would come under the jurisdiction of the new Ministry of Arts and Science. Given the need to treat the educational system as an organic whole, such a division of ministerial responsibility was extremely questionable and was rejected by one of the committee members, Mr H. C. Shearman, in an important note of reservation.

The cost of such far-reaching proposals was bound to be high and the Report made no secret of this. The financial implications were worked out in some detail and the committee judged the total cost to be well within the country's means, as well as a necessary investment if the socio-economic future of the nation was to be assured.

Results

The government quickly accepted the Robbins Report in principle and there has been an impressive record of action ever since. The recommended programme of expansion for the period 1963-74 was undertaken and even exceeded; in spite of an intent to cut back somewhat upon the rate of growth for higher education, the 1972 White Paper *Education: A Framework for Expansion* quotes a target figure of 750,000 places by 1981, which compares most favourably with the Robbins recommendation for a total of 560,000 by that time. Of course, the Robbins calculations upon the growth in the number of qualified students destined to seek places in higher education have proved too low; the result is that in spite of impressive expansion there has been no improvement (especially in relation to the universities) in terms of diluting the competition for entry into higher education. Given this situation and the awesome cost of higher education, the Robbins principle of a place for each and every qualified student desiring one remains (and is likely to remain) an unrealised ideal.

Whilst the foundation of six new universities did not materialise, the existing universities were required to expand and the development of scientific and technological higher education was assured by the transposition of the Colleges of Advanced Technology into full technological universities and by the further expansion of Imperial College, U.M.I.S.T. and R.C.S.T. The establishment of the Council for National Academic Awards in 1964 enabled the non-university institutions of higher education to develop their own degree work, especially in the scientific and technological field. Through such work these institutions could aspire towards ultimate university status.

The teacher training institutions were duly renamed Colleges of Education and they were allowed to develop B.Ed. degree courses within their Area Training Organisations. The latter development, involving a minority of students, has however been characterised by a number of anomalies (e.g. the availability or otherwise of honours awards) consequent upon a lack of central control or agreed practice. The University Schools of Education suggested by the Robbins Report were rejected because of the dilution of public control in the teacher training and supply sector which seemed a likely consequence of acceptance; the College of Education staffs had to be satisfied with greater representation on their governing bodies and an increase in the latters' responsibilities, whilst the local education authorities retained nominal financial and administrative control.

The machinery of government for higher education and its institutional structure were reorganised, but largely along different lines from those recommended by the Robbins Report. In accordance with the Shearman reservation, a super-ministry called the Department of Education and Science was created to encompass the whole educational system. The Secretary of State for Education and Science was supported by two under-

Ministers, one with basic responsibility for primary, secondary and special education under the control of the local education authorities, and the other concerned largely with higher education and other associated matters. To placate the universities, which were also made financially accountable to Parliament in 1968, the old Grants Committee was retained to act as a buffer between them and the new ministry. But in reality the traditional independence of the universities had been undermined in the interests of national control and co-ordination in the field of higher education. Meanwhile, the binary policy emerged by which the Labour government encouraged the development of non-university institutions of higher education under the auspices of the local education authorities. For this reason the expansion of the Colleges of Education, the regional Colleges of Further Education and the new polytechnics went ahead faster than university expansion. This policy implied the rejection of the Robbins axiom that the university was the 'model' for higher education to which other institutions should aspire. The Labour government was interested in developing a real alternative that might be more sensitive to national needs, more amenable to government control and free of any elitist tradition. The development of the so-called public sector of higher education within the binary framework was continued by the Heath Conservative government and the 1972 White Paper spoke in terms of no less than half of the total number of higher education students being placed in this sector by 1981. So it seems that the anti-Robbins binary system is here to stay.

4 Plowden Report on Children and their Primary Schools (1967)

Source
The Central Advisory Council for Education under the chairmanship of Lady Bridget Plowden.

Terms of Reference
To consider primary education in all its aspects and the transition to secondary education. It is noteworthy that the latter question became a less pressing one as mid-way through the Council's work the Labour government declared itself against the continuance of eleven-plus selection and in favour of comprehensive reorganisation.

Dominant Themes
The Report was characterised by three critical themes which underlay many of the detailed recommendations:

(a) the populist principle of compensatory education which insisted upon the need for positive discrimination in favour of socially disadvantaged children. The principle was in accordance with ideals of social justice and with the quest to reduce the wastage of talent, much of which was consequent upon the environmental factor. The compensatory principle could be most effectively applied at the nursery and primary stages of education;

(b) the progressive principle of paedocentricism which encouraged the further spread of modern child-centred and less formal methods of teaching and organisation in the primary schools. In this respect the Report was heir to the progressive tradition first expressed in the Hadow Report of 1931;

(c) the principle of equal treatment for all sectors of the educational system. It was no longer acceptable that the distribution of educational resources should be so much more favourable to secondary, further and higher education than it was to the primary sector. That the latter had been comparatively starved of support since the 1944 Act was hardly open to challenge.

Main Recommendations

These may be considered under several broad headings, some of which were used in the Report itself.

(a) The Home, School and Neighbourhood

The Report underlined the correlation existing between intelligence levels and educational attainments on the one hand and social class background, parental attitudes and wider environmental influences on the other. Attention was focused on the deprived areas, encompassing 10% of the population, where old school buildings, decaying housing, parental indifference and high staff turnover condemned thousands of children to social and educational handicap. Such was the basis for the Plowden demand for compensatory education as a new dimension in primary provision. Out of this basic demand there arose several particular recommendations:

(i) the need to identify and bring special help to 'educational priority areas', to be determined by such criteria as occupational structure, the housing situation, average family size, the proportion of coloured immigrants and the incidence of backwardness and truancy. Such areas, it was insisted, must be helped by the improvement of staffing ratios (via extra responsibility allowances of £120 per annum), the expansion of ancillary staff, top priority in school building and repair, full nursery provision for the three- to five-year-old group and the

forging of close links between the Colleges of Education and the schools involved;
(ii) the need to involve parents more directly and deeply in their children's education, especially in deprived areas where the school must bring the parents in rather than simply establish a Parent-Teacher Association and hope for the best. The introduction of parents to extra-curricular activity work and other such forms of non-professional help were suggested as a means of moving forward;
(iii) the need to recognise and act upon the experience of social welfare workers, especially in the deprived areas. Education Welfare Officers must assume a wider and more positive role and joint training courses for teachers and social workers be seriously considered.

(*b*) *The Structure of Primary Education*

In this context several far-reaching recommendations were made and elaborated upon:
(i) the immediate expansion of nursery education so that all the three-to five-year-old group could attend on a half-time basis, whilst some 15% could attend full-time where the need was demonstrated.
(ii) the reorganisation of the staging of primary education to accord with the Council's conclusion that twelve years was the best age for the transfer to secondary education. A new three-stage pattern was recommended, composed of the nursery school (3-5 years with at least half-time attendance), the first school (5-8 years) and the middle school (8-12 years). School entries were to be rationalised by requiring each child to commence the first school in the September following his fifth birthday, to be followed by a minimum of eleven years full-time schooling.
(iii) the abandonment of eleven-plus selection by intelligence and attainment tests. This was tantamount to a condemnation of tripartitism in favour of comprehension.

(*c*) *Curricula and Internal Organisation*

The progressive tide in primary education received considerable support from the recommendations made in this area. The report emphasised:
(i) the need for a broad, child-centred approach to primary education at the junior as well as the infant level. The report backed non-streaming, the experimental grouping of children, the open-plan approach, the integrated day and individualised learning procedures. Characteristically it stated: 'A (primary) school is not merely a teaching shop, it must transmit values and attitudes. It is a community in which children learn to live first and foremost as children and not as future adults';

(ii) the need to cultivate a friendly atmosphere in the primary school, with sound discipline being founded on the satisfactions of learning experiences rather than upon 'outdated sanctions and incentives'. In particular, the Report condemned outright the use of corporal punishment in primary schools and recommended its abandonment;

(iii) the need to review the position of religious worship and instruction in the primary school. The Report was critical of the compulsory basis established by the 1944 Act and of the agreed syllabuses which limited the freedom of the teacher in this sector of the curriculum. The desirability of any sort of positive religious instruction for primary schoolchildren was also seriously questioned. In a separate 'Reservation on Religious Education', six members of the Council went as far as to reject religious education as altogether unsuitable for the primary stage and recommended its displacement by informal moral education resting upon the atmosphere of the school and the personal influence of the staff (i.e. the humanist approach).

(d) Staffing

The Council's consideration of this important area produced a number of critical recommendations:

(i) that the shortage of primary teachers (estimated at about 20,000) and the excessive preponderance of women (i.e. 75% of the total) must be tackled by such means as a selective quota system, persuasive influence exerted by the Colleges of Education and the reform of the Burnham points system to provide better financial prospects for men in primary education;

(ii) that teacher aides (i.e. trained ancillaries) should be accepted and introduced to assist qualified teachers in the infant and junior schools, both inside and outside the classroom;

(iii) that the existing system of teacher training should be subjected to a full-scale investigation. Meanwhile the Colleges of Education should make a conscious effort to increase the proportion of students training for primary work (especially men), ensure that intending primary teachers are fairly represented on B.Ed. degree courses, strengthen their direct contact with the primary schools and raise their contribution to the training of graduates. For official consumption the Council urged an end to untrained graduate entry, the stiffening of college entry requirements to meet the current weakness in basic mathematics and science qualifications, the improvement of arrangements for the probationary year and much more attention to the question of in-service education and training.

(e) Buildings

In this respect the Report's major recommendation was that a special sum of £50 million to £70 million should be provided over the period 1971-8 'to rid the primary schools of their worst deficiencies'. More flexibility and expedition was called for in the procedures related to the financing and authorising of minor works.

(f) Status and Government of the Primary Schools

The Report insisted on equality of status and treatment for primary and secondary education, especially in relation to class sizes, buildings and equipment, per capita allowances and the Burnham points system. The latter discriminated against the primary schools in respect of headteachers' salaries and the distribution of above-scale special posts. It was also considered that the government of primary schools could be improved by allowing headteachers and their staff to wield more influence upon decisions affecting them; this would involve better representation on the local education committees and fuller consultation. There was a need to ensure that primary school managers were committed persons interested in education as such; all such managing bodies should include parents of children attending the school concerned.

In conclusion, the Plowden Report stated that 'the primary schools are giving good value for the inadequate amount of money spent on them'. Because teachers were too few and too mal-distributed they were unable to do a really effective job. What was needed was a programme of action, and accordingly the Report submitted its list of priorities to improve the situation: educational priority areas, teachers' aides, new and improved primary school buildings, the extension of nursery education and the re-staging of primary schooling, in that order of urgency. The whole operation was finely costed to allay exaggerated fears on the financial front.

Results

The Plowden Report has wielded a significant, but nevertheless limited, influence upon educational development in England and Wales. Much remains to be done before its recommendations are anywhere near fully implemented. On the issue of teachers' aides the steadfast opposition of the teachers' organisations, fearful of the prospect of dilution and the problem of demarcation, ensured the shelving of this particular recommendation. The Plowden plea for the abandonment of corporal punishment also proved a professionally controversial matter; although certain individual local education authorities were stimulated to take unilateral action in this direction, the government has been unprepared to grasp this nettle for fear of alienating the teachers' organisations which are opposed to the legal abolition of corporal punishment in State schools. In the field of home-school relations the government has similarly failed to take the initiative and give strong official support to some of the Council's objectives. There is still no requirement that all primary schools must support a Parent-Teacher Association, nor is the universal representation of parents on school managing bodies yet a statutory matter. In spite of the Council's original terms of reference, the Labour government's secondary reorganisation policy was crystallised before the submission of the Report and supported the continuance of eleven-plus transfer from primary to secondary school as the basic policy. But the possibility of transfer at other ages was later fully conceded, so opening the way to Plowden re-staging: the result was that a growing number of local education authorities adopted the middle school pattern of comprehensive reorganisation. Yet, as the government did not back the Plowden scheme as the one to be generally applied, the end result was to introduce further variation and confusion into the organisation and staging of compulsory schooling. The Plowden desire to lengthen the years of infant experience has not been a necessary result of the changes which have taken place. At best the Plowden Report has contributed to the idea that the middle years of schooling (between eight and thirteen) should be seen as a whole rather than disturbed by transfer between two very different educational worlds at the age of eleven. Whether the middle school will make a distinctive and worth-while contribution to English education remains to be seen.

The Plowden principle of positive discrimination and compensatory education was accepted as an ideal and much lip-service has been paid to it, but so far it has not been decisively applied in practice. Initially economic difficulties were allowed to limit action to the matter of school buildings. The government acceded to the Plowden demand for an additional £7 million to £10 million per annum for building renewal and it is in this direction that educational priority area policy has made its most significant mark. Only later was the programme somewhat broadened to embrace staffing (including the derisory £75 per annum special allowances) and equipment, and combined with a wider urban aid policy for relieving social deprivation in selected areas. Between 1968 and 1972 the government sponsored five action research groups working in the schools of seriously deprived areas in order to map out the most effective way ahead for dealing with educational disadvantage in such places. The completion of the Halsey project has not drawn any particularly significant response from the government. At present the educational priority area policy lacks both conviction and funds, being based on additional help for particular schools rather than for whole deprived areas. The policy has not been given the resources and the priority it needs if it is to have a chance of real success. Nor does the ten-year programme outlined in the 1972 White Paper *Education: A Framework for Expansion* include educational priority area policy as one of its major themes.

However, the Plowden Report acted as the long-awaited catalyst in the field of nursery education. Circular 8/60 had severely restricted the efforts of the local education authorities in this direction, but during the period 1967-71 the proportion of three- and four-year-olds receiving proper nursery education rose from $5\frac{1}{2}\%$ to $8\frac{1}{2}\%$, although most of the expansion involved took place in deprived areas. Meanwhile day nurseries continued to develop and the play-group movement emerged as a national concern. The campaign for a decisive government response to the Plowden recommendations grew progressively stronger until the 1972 White Paper announced the withdrawal of Circular 8/60 and a new State initiative in the sector concerned. The declared object over the succeeding ten years was to be the provision of free nursery education for all three- and four-year-old children whose parents wished them to have it; for some 15% of the children, with priority for those in deprived areas, such provision would be on a full-time basis. The prospects for nursery education are thus better than ever before and the Plowden Report can claim much credit for this. The Report also strengthened and encouraged the progressive camp in primary education. As the eleven-plus retreated the primary tide continued to flow in favour of de-streaming, experimental grouping and the integrated, child-centred approach to learning; the acceleration of this process provoked strong criticism in the Black Paper *Fight for Education*, edited by C. B. Cox and A. E. Dyson (1969) and increased traditionalist fears for the maintenance of educational standards. Meanwhile, the issue of religious education in the primary school remains unresolved, with the government obviously reluctant to stir up hidden passions on this matter. Finally, the Plowden Report served as the basis for the Heath Conservative government's 'priority for primaries' policy, which may in the long-term raise both the quality and status of this sector of the educational system.

5 James Report on Teacher Education and Training (1972)

Source

A special Committee of Inquiry appointed by the Secretary of State for Education and Science, under the chairmanship of Lord James of Rusholme.

Terms of Reference

To consider the existing arrangements for the education, training and probation of teachers and to make recommendations for their improvement. The Committee's attention was drawn particularly to the content and organisation of courses, the monotechnic nature of the Colleges of Education and the prospective roles of various higher educational institutions in the field concerned.

Dominant Themes

The appointment of the James Committee was prompted by the mounting criticism levelled at the system of teacher education and training which had developed out of the McNair (1944) and Robbins (1963) Reports. The need for such an investigation was also explicable in terms of the changing wider context. As a result of the dramatic expansion of teacher training during the 1960s, the prolonged post-war problem of teacher shortage was within sight of solution and the new spectre was one of developing over-supply: it was time seriously to consider the future use and possible redeployment of the resources invested in the teacher training institutions. Inevitably this would have to be looked at in the even broader light of the continuing rise in the demand for higher education as such by suitably qualified persons. Working against this over-all backcloth the James Committee struck a number of dominant themes in its Report.

(*a*) The traditional concurrent approach to teacher education and training for Certificate and B.Ed. degree students was largely condemned in favour of a consecutive arrangement. The Committee felt that in the great majority of cases acceptance for teacher training should be conditional upon the prior completion of a full course of higher education, although not necessarily to degree level. This became the basis of the Report's 'first cycle' proposals.

(*b*) The formal distinction between certificated and graduate teachers, entrenched in the shape of quite separate three-year concurrent courses for certificate purposes and one-year consecutive courses of professional training for university graduates, was viewed with disfavour because of its divisive influence within the teaching occupation. The Report supported the idea of an all-graduate profession based upon a common pattern of actual training for teaching. This became the basis of the Report's 'second cycle' proposals.

(*c*) The palpably unsatisfactory nature of the existing probationary year arrangements was fully recognised by the Committee and the need for major reform emerged as an important theme within the Report's consideration of the newly proposed 'second cycle'.

(*d*) The view that no pre-service training course can equip a person for all the responsibilities and demands he is going to face in the school situation was stressed. Therefore, the Committee insisted, a generous programme of in-service training for teachers must be developed. This emerged as one of the really outstanding themes of the Report and found detailed expression in its 'third cycle' proposals.

(*e*) The Colleges of Education should be allowed and encouraged to manage their own affairs to a much greater extent, developing as a third autonomous sector of higher education alongside the universities and polytechnics. The Committee felt that they lacked sufficient scope and stature under the post-McNair pattern of organisation and control: the academic supremacy of the universities, wielded through the mechanism of the Area Training Organisations, and the continuing financial and administrative ties with the local education authorities were seen as stifling and no longer appropriate. This viewpoint found expression in the Report's recommendations for the reform of the machinery of government.

Main Recommendations

These may be considered in relation to three very broad areas with which the Report concerned itself.

(a) Organisation of Courses

It was basically recommended that the concurrent approach to teacher education and training be abandoned in favour of three consecutive stages or cycles (see diagram, page 204).

(i) *First cycle* This was to be concerned with raising the level of students' personal education so as to qualify them for selective entry into the second cycle. Thus the first cycle would include the widening range of three-year university and C.N.A.A. degree courses and their accepted equivalents, but would also embrace a new two-year course leading to a Diploma in Higher Education. The proposed diploma course, entry to which would ultimately require a minimum of two A-levels, was to be unit-based, combining a study of general options for breadth and two special subjects for depth. The range and character of the general and special options would vary between different colleges. The diploma would qualify its holders for entry into teacher training and in certain cases for transfer to degree courses; for some students it would be a sub-degree terminal qualification prior to entering into full-time employment in occupations where the diploma would obtain credit. The initial development of the new Diploma in Higher Education was to rest with the Colleges of Education and the polytechnics.

The Organisation of Teacher Education and Training
(as recommended by the James Report, 1972)

First cycle	Second cycle	Third cycle
Personal Education	*Initial training*	*In-service Arrangements*
University degree courses	Specialised and functional training at a professional institution; curriculum courses dominant; minimum of four weeks teaching practice	*Entitlement:* release with pay on a scale equivalent to one term in every five years of service, such release to relate to substantial approved courses
C.N.A.A. degree courses		*Actual courses:* to vary widely in duration, content and form; all designed to extend teacher education and professional competence, including courses for degrees, higher degrees and additional professional qualifications
New joint Hons. degrees (including education)	School-based induction on reduced time-table; attendance at a professional centre (20% time); professional tutors to give guidance	*Organisation:* school-based professional tutors to arrange release programme, co-operating with professional institutions and centres which would mount the courses or activities
Dip.H.E.-based degree courses		
S G S S G		
Dip.H.E. courses		
S G S S G		
Year 1 | Year 2 | Year 3	Year 1 | Year 2	Career in teaching

Entry - - - normally two 'A' levels.

Selective entry   Licensed teachers   Registered teachers : B.A.(Ed)

Dip.H.E. = Diploma of Higher Education   S = Special options   G = General options
C.N.A.A. = Council for National Academic Awards.

(ii) *Second cycle* This was to be concerned with pre-service training and induction, with an 'unashamedly specialist and functional' emphasis 'aimed at professional preparation'. The first year of the second cycle would be spent in a professional institution (i.e. College of Education, polytechnic Department of Education, or a University Education Department). Curriculum-type courses were to dominate this year so as to ensure that the practical demands of classroom teaching obtained top priority; conversely, the study of educational theory was to be contracted and reduced to a rudimentary level. This was to be combined with a minimum of only four weeks' teaching practice in the schools! At the conclusion of the first year, teaching competence would be assessed and successful students would be recognised as 'licensed teachers'. The second year of the second cycle was to be largely school-based. The newly-licensed teacher would be accepted as a full member of staff whilst enjoying a reduced timetable and the opportunity to spend one-fifth of his working time receiving help through the medium of professional tutors and professional centres dedicated to the task of providing effective and sustained probationary assistance. Following the successful completion of this year the student was to be awarded the B.A.(Ed.) degree and recognised as a 'registered' teacher; thus all teachers would become graduates having undertaken a minimum four year course of education and training.

(iii) *Third cycle* This was to be concerned with in-service education and training and aimed at ending the existing overdependence on initial training. Teachers were to be entitled to paid release for in-service purposes on a scale of not less than one term in every seven years. Such release would relate to substantial courses lasting at least four weeks and to the whole range of activities designed to extend the teacher's personal education or professional competence. The local education authorities and the schools themselves were to facilitate the release of staff for third cycle work; in this respect the improved teacher supply situation would soon allow for a 3% to 5% incidence of release at any one point in time.

(b) *Professional Tutors and Centres*

The new departures related to induction and in-service education and training would depend on a national network to support them. The Report recommended that every school should have a professional tutor serving as a member of its staff. The tutor's responsibility would cover the oversight of teaching practice students and licensed teachers in their probationary year, as well as the organisation of the in-service release arrangements in respect of his colleagues. In very large schools such tutors would require a much reduced teaching load in order to fulfil this new role satisfactorily. They would operate as links between the schools and the professional centres concerned with the provision of courses for both probationary and serving teachers. Some Colleges of Education, polytechnic and University Education Departments would encompass the functions of professional centres as well as undertaking first cycle and initial training work; indeed, they would be the main providers of third cycle full-time courses and the major centres of curriculum development. But other professional centres would need to be developed by the local education authorities, with the existing teachers' centres providing a starting point for this. Some Colleges of Further Education and some large schools would also have to operate as professional centres. The number, distribution and size of professional centres would depend on local circumstances; the particular role of any one centre would vary, especially in densely populated areas, with regional co-ordination and rationalisation of pertinent courses. It was not envisaged that there would be much need for the establishment of new purpose-built centres.

(c) New System of Government

It was recommended that the system of Area Training Organisations be replaced by a system of fifteen Regional Councils topped by a National Council for teacher education and training. Thus the special responsibility and role of the universities would end, though they would continue to be associated with the new system through representation on the regional bodies, the provision of external examiners and their involvement in second and third cycle work. The recommended arrangements were deliberately calculated to enhance the status and independence of the colleges, 'inviting them to take a lead in the development of new and broader patterns of higher education'. Each college would be directly represented on the regional councils which would take over from the universities the role of approving courses and validating professional awards. It was suggested that responsibility for the development of the new Diploma in Higher Education might also be met in this way. The planning and financing of teacher education and training would work on a three-tier basis, involving the Department of Education and Science, the National Council and the fifteen Regional Councils: the latter would include representatives of the local education authorities, the teachers, the C.N.A.A., the Open University and the central Department as well as one from each of the professional institutions.

Significantly, the Report concluded with a 'Note of Reservation' submitted by two of the seven Committee members. It expressed serious disagreement with the majority opinion on a number of vital matters.

Firstly, it criticised the notion that the Diploma in Higher Education combined with the award of the unconvincing B.A.(Ed.) was the right road towards an all graduate profession; instead, the long-term solution must be for all intending teachers to pursue three-year first degree courses and for the colleges to be given the opportunity to contribute to this. Secondly, the urge to sever the established academic ties with the universities was sharply questioned; it was suggested that the integration of the Colleges of Education into the system of higher education would be better served if their courses and awards were validated by the universities and the C.N.A.A. rather than the new and untried Regional Councils. In a word, the academic connection with the universities was a source of strength rather than a cause of frustration for most Colleges of Education.

Results

It is too early to do more than prognosticate upon the significance of the James Report. However, the White Paper on *Education: a Framework for Expansion* (1972) gave some important leads upon the extent to which the James' strategy is to be followed during the present decade. On the positive side the government accepted the James' recommendations on in-service training and vowed to provide a 3% level of release by 1981. The reform of the probationary year along James' lines was affirmed. The need for professional tutors and centres to support these developments was acknowledged. The Diploma of Higher Education received the government's enthusiastic support as a two-year sub-degree level course which would widen opportunities and could be developed by all higher educational institutions. The White Paper also supported the replacement of the Area Training Organisations by a new system of regional bodies for the government and administration of teacher education and training.

But there were important respects in which the White Paper ignored the James' recommendations. The cyclical pattern of consecutive stages, which would have separated teacher education from teacher training, failed to receive official support; this allowed greater flexibility and was favourable to the continuance of the concurrent approach. Although the White Paper backed the James' objective of an all graduate teaching profession, it chose a different path for reaching the desired goal. The award of a bogus B.A.(Ed.) at the close of the second professional cycle was rejected in favour of more credible three-year B.Ed. degree and four-year Honours B.Ed. degree courses incorporating both academic and educational studies. To give uncommitted students room for manoeuvre, the three-year courses were to be so devised that the first two years of study could lead to the new Diploma award. Certificate courses were to be gradually phased out as the new degree courses developed. Finally, the White Paper came out in favour of academic validation remaining the responsibility of existing and reputable bodies (i.e. the senates of universities, the academic boards of polytechnics and Colleges of Education and the C.N.A.A.).

The need to redeploy the resources invested in teacher training and the prospect of the Colleges of Education diversifying their role in the field of higher education, both implicit in the James Report, were forcibly elaborated in the White Paper. In the light of its ten-year programme the government estimated that the teaching force needed to be increased by only 10% by 1981. This would involve a gradual contraction of about one-third in the number of training places required in the Colleges of Education. Whilst some of the excess capacity would be absorbed by the development of probationary and in-service education and training, many Colleges of Education would face an uncertain future and the need to widen or change their role. The distinct teacher training sector with its traditionally monotechnic institutions would gradually merge into the wider public sector of further and higher education. Thus the Colleges of Education are to enjoy no respite; after a decade of headlong expansion and much change, the White Paper promised a further decade of most difficult adjustment to new policies and a changed context.

Follow-up: Attempt to cover as much of the following ground as possible.

1 Read   Corbett, Anne. *Much to do about Education*: a critical survey of the fate of the major educational reports, published by the Council for Educational Advance in booklet form

Lello, John. *The Official View on Education*: a summary of the major educational reports since 1944. Chapters 1 and 8 are especially helpful

Curtis, S. J. and Boultwood, M. E. *An Introductory History of English Education since 1800*, Chapter XVII

Government White Paper, *Education: A Framework for Expansion* (1972) issued by Her Majesty's Stationery Office

2 Consult Maclure, J. S. *Educational Documents: England and Wales 1816–1968*; items 40, 42, 43, 46, 47, 49, 50 and 52 are relevant

The original reports (Crowther, Newsom, Robbins, Plowden and James) as issued by Her Majsety's Stationery Office

3 Clarify the following: the various sources of official reports on education; the list of significant educational reports submitted since 1850; the terms of reference, the dominant themes, the outstanding recommendations and results of each of the major post-war reports on education; the development of any themes which figure in more than one of these reports, e.g. wastage of talent, social deprivation and educational disadvantage, expansion of educational opportunity; the basic contents of the White Paper on Education: A Framework for Expansion *(1972) and their significance for later development.*

Chapter Twelve
The Development of Technical and Further Education

Purpose: to trace the growth of technical and scientific instruction during the nineteenth century and the emergence of the wider sector of further education in the twentieth century, indicating the factors which condemned education for industry and commerce to inferior status for so long and the influences and developments which have ensured the ultimate recognition of its vital importance to the nation's future.

1 The Beginnings of Technical and Scientific Education

(a) The Legacy of the Past

As late as 1800 there were virtually no facilities which were seriously concerned with the provision of technical or scientific instruction. Indeed, there had never been any deliberate or sustained attempt to provide such facilities to any significant degree. The parlous situation in the middle of the Industrial Revolution was reflected in both sectors of education.

(i) In higher education, centred on the ancient universities, the public and endowed grammar schools, the Classics were still quite dominant, mathematics held a lowly position and there was no place for mundane instruction in technical and scientific subjects. Only the Dissenting academies and the more variable private academies and schools had shown a developing interest in education for commerce and industry, though the eighteenth-century academies were rapidly losing their vigour by the close of the Napoleonic era.

(ii) In elementary education, centred on the dame, common-day, charity schools and schools of industry, the situation was obviously very different but no more promising. True, amidst all the shortcomings, there was in some schools considerable vocational stress on industrial and domestic occupations; very poor working class and pauper children were taught to spin, sew, knit, plait, cobble, garden, plough and undertake other menial tasks. But, whilst this may have served some directly useful purpose and cultivated habits of industry, such instruction was limited to narrow practical experience in simple processes and never aspired to anything approaching technical or scientific education. In any case, the latter depended on a previous mastery of the three Rs, which very few elementary schools were capable of providing at that time.

(b) The Mechanics Institutes

The Industrial Revolution changed the nature of the economy, creating new occupations and positions, some of which required minimal mechanical, technical, or scientific understanding if industry was to function effectively. The propertied manufacturing class was interested in the diffusion of useful knowledge and was prepared to support an extended education for a minority of the lower orders if it was designed to meet specific economic needs within the existing class structure. This really meant a preparedness to promote the distribution of cheap instructive literature and to project elementary education forward within narrow technical and scientific limits in order to render a minority of key workers more knowledgeable and productive.

In 1799 George Birkbeck, Professor of Chemistry, following visits to the local workshops which provided his department at the University of Glasgow with its scientific apparatus, launched a course of evening classes in science and mathematics for skilled artisans. The classes were continued by his successor and in 1823 the workmen currently attending formed the Glasgow Mechanics Institute to 'instruct artisans in the scientific principles of arts and manufactures'. Birkbeck, then working as a physician in London, reacted by founding the second Mechanics Institute in the metropolis and by initiating the publication of a periodical, *The Mechanic's Magazine*. Lord Brougham supported the movement and it spread quickly, drawing its financial resources from members' subscriptions and the donations of sympathisers. The main beneficiaries of the movement were the new artisans (e.g. engineers and mechanics) and other skilled craftsmen. By 1850 there were over six hundred Mechanics' Institutes with more than half a million members, concentrated mainly in the urban, manufacturing districts of London, south Lancashire and the West Riding. Yet the Institutes were only a limited rather than an unqualified success; most of them failed to sustain their original purpose and their prosperity was short-lived. This has various explanations.

(i) The Institutes failed to attract ordinary working men in really large and growing numbers. This is accounted for by the fact that the minimal elementary education necessary to take advantage of the Institutes was far from sufficiently widespread, whilst the subscription fees seem to have been rather high as well. Nor did the contemporary conditions of life, characterised by long working hours and economic insecurity, dispose the urban proletariat to make an enthusiastic response to these new institutions.

(ii) There was a gradual shift of interest from scientific and mechanical matters to a widening range of popular lectures and recreational activity that savoured of adult education rather than technical instruction. This was associated with the incursion of a growing number of clerks and other lower middle class persons into the Institutes.

But not all the Mechanics' Institutes were adversely affected by such influences; in the West Riding the majority of them prospered in their original purpose and in the later nineteenth century some developed into important technical institutions. Even though the movement as a whole had faltered by the middle of the century, it was not without significant results for the longer term.

(i) The Institutes prepared the way for the technical institutions and trade schools of the future. The London Mechanics' Institute formed the basis for the later development of Birkbeck College which ultimately became part of the University of London. The technical colleges which emerged in Leeds, Bradford and Huddersfield in the late nineteenth century had their original roots in the Institutes.

(ii) The Institutes established the questionable tradition of separating scientific and technical education from practical craft instruction, in that their courses emphasised the former and ignored the latter. The influence of this tradition was to persist well into the twentieth century.

(iii) The Institutes probably helped to initiate the process by which a growing body of influential public opinion began to recognise the close connection between industrial strength and the promotion of technical instruction.

(iv) Those Institutes which were gradually transposed into middle class literary and philosophical societies and the like, contributed a strand to the slow evolution of adult education in the later nineteenth century.

(c) Scientific and Technical Teaching in the mid-Nineteenth Century

In spite of the progress of the Industrial Revolution and the developing relationship between science and industry, and in spite of the work of the Royal Institution (founded in 1800 to stimulate teaching on 'the application of science to the common purposes of life') backed by Sir Humphry Davy and Michael Faraday, established educational institutions showed great reluctance to embark upon the teaching of scientific and technical subject matter. Not until the 1860s were Oxford and Cambridge developing pure science studies with any real commitment or effect. The Clarendon Report (1864) revealed that Rugby was the only public school to have introduced science teaching; the Taunton Commission (1864-8) found an equally unsatisfactory situation in relation to the endowed grammar schools. The elementary schools had made negligible progress in terms of widening their curricula to include simple science. And with the Mechanics' Institutes clearly in decline there were as yet few hopeful signs pointing towards the development of new institutions that might fill the void. This dismal situation on the eve of the Great Exhibition was explained by a number of factors.

(i) The university ideal was still that of the cultured Christian gentleman pursuing knowledge for its own sake. This traditional attitude, reinforced as late as 1852 by J. H. Newman's *The Idea of a University*, involved a marked disdain for scientific and technical instruction with its utilitarian ends. The Victorian engineer or applied scientist did not go to university; he emerged from the old craft apprenticeship system, learned by experience and improved his own knowledge. In career terms the ancient universities limited themselves to serving the needs of the old-established professions.

(ii) Given their long connection with the older universities and their entrenched Classical tradition, the poor response of the public and endowed grammar schools is not surprising. The great majority of their staff were not interested in science and were unable to teach it; this situation could only change in the wake of reforms and new developments at the university level.

(iii) The foundations for extended technical education were still not there at the elementary level. As late as the 1840s about one-third of working class men could not sign their own name on the marriage register. The provision of elementary education was not only still in limited supply, but was usually inefficient and narrowly conceived. The Revised Code (1862) was temporarily to destroy the small but growing interest in elementary science in some of the better schools and training colleges.

(iv) The attitude of industry and the public at large to the actual or potential importance of formal scientific and technical instruction was one of complacency. The last century had thrown up so many outstanding inventors, engineers and industrialists who had enjoyed little or no formal education that the *laissez faire* reliance on self-made men to carry the economy forward seemed fully justified by the event. Of course, the managerial and technological structure of British industry was still relatively simple and it had not as yet been subjected to any serious foreign competition. Britian's industrial pre-eminence and the success of the Great Exhibition were not calculated to produce a really critical outlook.

2 Progress in the Later Nineteenth Century

Clearly, by the middle of the nineteenth century, far too little had been done for the development of scientific and technical education in Great Britain. The Great Exhibition (1851), whilst it expressed Britain's industrial supremacy as the 'workshop of the world', showed that in certain respects some Continental countries were pushing ahead in applied science and technology. The second half of the century witnessed remarkable progress compared with the preceding fifty years. The cause of science teaching and technical instruction gathered strength during the third quarter of the century, but it was not until the 1880s and 1890s that rapid and sustained advance was made. Throughout the period the way forward involved a hard struggle within a total context composed of both favourable and unfavourable influences.

(a) Factors Encouraging or Retarding the Growth of Technical Education

(i) The advance towards universal elementary education and the revision of the Revised Code to include elementary science in the curriculum both helped to provide a much better basis for extended technical education. Since scientific and technical instruction had acquired the low status of useful knowledge there was no social objection to such instruction being made available to the working class; however, this was double-edged in that it militated against the traditional educational institutions moving away from those studies so long associated with higher social status and ensured that, as far as they did, they would emphasise the study of pure science rather than its applications.

(ii) The difficulties experienced by British industry from the onset of the Great Depression in the mid 1870s and the associated growth of competition in overseas markets, strengthened the hand of those who argued the link between technical education and economic power. For instance, the Royal Commission report on *The Depression of Trade and Industry* (1886) identified shortcomings in relation to educational provision in general and technical education in particular as a factor contributing to the prevailing ills.

(iii) The final collapse of the old apprenticeship system in the face of factory production and technological change created a growing vacuum which organised technical instruction could help to fill. The 'New Model' skilled craft unions saw such classes as a service to the aspiring worker. But their interest was more practically oriented than disposed towards the underlying scientific principles.

(iv) the indifference of most employers towards technical education proved a dead-weight in two important respects. As so much depended on local initiative, the lack of interest shown by those most likely to gain from the promotion of technical education acted as a serious brake upon extending provision. Skilled workers, foremen and managers were hardly encouraged to take advantage of existing facilities and stimulate their growth if employers continued to put all their faith in on-the-job training. The apathy of British industrialists compared most unfavourably with the attitude of their German counterparts in this respect. There seems to be no simple explanation of the situation, the effects of which were to spill over into the twentieth century; the complacency and practical traditions born of the age of easy industrial supremacy, and the rise of joint-stock enterprise which increasingly placed management responsibility in the hands of cultivated (but not scientific or technically-minded) individuals, no doubt had much to do with it.

(v) During the latter half of the nineteenth century those interested in and concerned with the development of science pressed its claims for much fuller recognition as an area of prior importance to national life. A small but vociferous minority produced a veritable 'scientific movement', which had as one of its main purposes the acceptance of scientific and technical studies as a major sector of educational provision. In this respect the 'scientific movement' was not only part of the wider utilitarian challenge to the traditional curricula of secondary and higher education, but was a source of support for new institutional developments. The movement drew its strength from the personal influence and writings of its many outstanding members, amongst whom the Prince Consort may be seen as an early inspiration and figurehead. The impact of Charles Darwin and his theory of evolution aroused not only controversy but also a real interest in science. The Christian Scientists emerged to reconcile Darwin with Genesis, and they went on to acclaim scientific knowledge as the means to medical advance and environmental progress. Herbert Spencer, an engineer and scientist who turned to writing on philosophy and education, was perhaps the most extreme protagonist of the claims of science. He declared the purpose of education to be the preparation of the individual for 'complete living'; he then argued, though sometimes rather speciously, that a broad education in science was the best single means to this end. Thomas H. Huxley, a doctor and naturalist, brought a more balanced and cogent attitude to the support of science and technical teaching; he acknowledged the importance of the humanities whilst demanding a proper place for scientific studies. He argued the case for the latter, not simply along utilitarian lines but also in terms of the spirit and wonder of science. Sir Lyon Playfair combined the roles of academic scientist and man of affairs. Trained in Germany, he became an expert in industrial chemistry, held a Chair at Edinburgh University, helped to organise the Great Exhibition, served on many investigating bodies and finally entered politics as a Liberal member of Parliament. Until his death in 1898 he never tired of advancing the cause of the 'scientific movement'. A comparable figure was Sir Bernhard Samuelson, a machinery exporter turned engineer and ironmaster, who set an exemplary record for his fellow employers in terms of the time and energy he devoted to promoting the growth of technical education. He also entered politics as a Liberal and was an outstanding member of various commissions set up to investigate educational matters; as the first Englishman to engage himself in a serious comparative study of technical education in other countries, he was able to make telling comparisons with real authority. It was through the able and persistent efforts of such individuals that the cause of scientific and technical education gradually, but never fully, overcame the apathy and resistance which beset its early growth.

(vi) With *laissez faire* beginning to retreat before the rising tide of collectivism, the State gradually increased its interest and involvement in technical education. The foremost expression of this was the establishment and development of the Science and Art Department, supplemented much later by the creation of the local Technical Instruction Committees; through these agencies an increasing amount of public money was made available for the support of technical education. The period is also punctuated by a considerable number of official investigations into the field of scientific and technical education. Indeed, the area enjoyed the attentions of two Royal Commissions as well as that of various other lesser bodies. The Devonshire Commission Reports on *Scientific Instruction and the Advancement of Science* (1872-5) served to underline the progress being made abroad and to encourage the expansion of science teaching in the elementary schools, training colleges, public and endowed grammar schools, and other higher educational institutions. But these Reports resulted in no direct and dramatic government initiative. A decade later the Samuelson Commission Report on

Technical Instruction (1884) reinforced the arguments of the previous commission and also made its own particular recommendations. The amount of basic science, rudimentary drawing and craft work provided in the elementary schools was to be increased. The higher-grade schools, with their more advanced and modern curricula, were to be positively encouraged. It was recommended that local authorities be given the power to establish State secondary and technical schools and that rate-aid be made available for the purpose. Finally, the Report stressed the need for more technical colleges of a high standard if Britain was to catch up with developments on the Continent. The most direct, though somewhat delayed, result of the Report was the Technical Instruction Act (1889).

However, the interest and help of the State had its limitations, and not only financially. The official policy was very much to equate technical education with the study of science rather than with any sort of trade training. It was presumed that the place for practical instruction was the workshop; many manufacturers supported this view in order to ensure the protection of trade secrets. Hence the Science and Art Department consistently refused to make funds available for practical trade classes, and they were also expressly excluded from the potential benefits of the Technical Instruction Act. Yet it was in the field of direct vocational training, given the decline of the apprenticeship system, that the greatest working class need and interest existed. The result was that this field was left very largely to voluntary initiative and effort.

(*b*) Development of Science in Education

The second half of the nineteenth century saw the study of science gain a much more important place in education at all levels. This was the result of a number of developments:

(i) the work of the Department of Science and Art (see also Chapter 9. pages 142-3). Established in 1853 as the central agency for the encouragement of technical and commercial education, it was from the outset responsible for those institutions at South Kensington which developed into the Royal College of Science, the Royal School of Mines and the Royal College of Art. Through its 'payment by results' system the Department supported the development of municipal schools of science launched by voluntary initiative, transposed many higher-grade and some endowed grammar schools into organised science schools and encouraged the progressive School Boards to develop advanced evening classes. Its special examinations for teachers, qualifying them to undertake the instruction of candidates for the Department's ordinary examinations, was the main source of supply for competent staff. The Department was later joined in its particular field of operation by the Technical Instruction Committees (see also Chapter 9, pages 149-50); both were primarily concerned with promoting the academic study of science subjects, which led naturally to their growing interest in the secondary sector as a whole. The support of the higher-grade schools helped to promote the idea of a different sort of secondary education biased towards science and technical studies. The connections slowly forged with the endowed grammar schools contributed towards the advance of science to a proper place in their curricula, though the influence of the Taunton Commission and Henry Armstrong's heuristic method (emphasising scientific habits of mind and procedures) were probably even more important here;

(ii) the work of the Education Department. Its revision of the 'payment by results' system to allow the introduction of elementary science and practical subjects, its acceptance of the development of higher-grade schools and its support after 1893 of advanced evening classes combined to make a significant contribution to the general advance;

(iii) the emergence of the new civic universities (see also Chapter 13, pages 247-8). Beginning with Owens College, Manchester, and resultant of a mixture of private benevolence, municipal and local business support, there grew up a number of new institutions which gradually acquired the status of universities or university colleges by the turn of the century. Nearly all of them showed a marked interest in pure and applied science, as most of them were established in the centre of industrial areas and initially to serve local needs. In 1889 the persuasive tongue of Lyon Playfair procured the introduction of limited State financial support for these institutions. Meanwhile the older University of London was expanding and continuing to develop its early interest in promoting the study of pure and applied science; by the late nineteenth century its earliest constituent part, University College, could lay claim to being the country's outstanding centre of education for engineering. Progress at the ancient universities, especially Oxford, was slower and leaned heavily towards the pure rather than the applied sciences.

(c) Development of Technical and Further Education

The encouragement and expansion of science teaching made only a limited contribution to the cause of technical and further education as we would understand it today. Much of it was restricted to the elementary and secondary school levels and the emphasis was placed upon the academic study of pure science. Even where the Science and Art Department supported the development of clearly technical subjects (e.g. steam power, mechanical drawing, building construction), a textbook approach was encouraged; the result was always to stress theoretical principles rather than practical applications in relation to the subjects taught. Hence the efforts already considered did little or nothing to provide the technological or trade training required by works managers, supervisors, foremen and artisans in search of practical knowledge and craft skills. Until about 1880 this need went almost completely unsatisfied, but thereafter the growth of vocationally oriented courses was impressive and based upon three outstanding developments.

(i) In 1880 the wealthy metropolitan Livery Companies founded the City and Guilds of London Institute for the Advancement of Technical Education. This body developed an increasingly widespread system of subsidised evening classes following syllabuses leading to City and Guilds examinations. By the end of the century over sixty subjects were offered, the majority of which were of a technological or craft nature. Within a year of its foundation the Institute had also established Finsbury Technical College; armed with generous laboratory and workshop facilities, this became a model institution in the provision of both day and evening courses for artisans and those holding intermediate management positions in local industry. In 1884 the even more ambitious Central Technical College was opened at South Kensington. Here the emphasis was on the teaching of applied science at a high level and its courses were designed for engineers, industrial chemists, works managers and technical teachers. Grants from the Institute helped to stimulate the growth of technical education outside of London. The new lease of life found by some of the old Mechanics' Institutes owed as much to the encouragement of the City and Guilds as to the later interest of the Technical Instruction Committees.

(ii) The London polytechnics were another most significant development dating from 1880. In that year Quintin Hogg, a prosperous City merchant with some long-standing interest in working class youth and artisans' clubs, opened the Regent Street Polytechnic. This act of private philanthropy achieved such initial success that eight other polytechnics were established and thriving by the close of the century. The movement was facilitated by the City Parochial Charities Act (1883) which released a considerable amount of endowed income for their support. The Livery Companies and the City and Guilds Institute were a further source of financial help. After 1889 the London Technical Education Board took the new polytechnics under its wing, so making both rate-aid and whisky money available to them. Initially the polytechnics provided social and recreational facilities as well as a widening range of vocational trade classes and were clearly aimed at the metropolitan working class. But under the influence of Sidney Webb, chairman of the London Technical Education Board, they gradually developed a wider role; advanced technical courses were developed on a full-time day basis, evening courses for general education were begun and some students were even prepared for University of London external degrees. By 1900 the term 'polytechnic' was a very apt description for the majority of these developing institutions in the field of further education.

(iii) The 1890s witnessed a quite remarkable increase in attendances at the evening schools run by the School Boards. At the outset of the decade the restrictive regulations which had hitherto severely limited the work and the appeal of these institutions underwent radical revision. The original age limit was removed and elementary subjects were supplemented by both advanced and vocational studies. The introduction of various commercial and practical subjects brought a ready response from those engaged in the clerical and skilled manual occupations. Of course, the rise of the first generation to enjoy compulsory elementary education provided a favourable base for such a development. In 1900 almost half a million evening class students enrolled to further their education.

3 Development of Technical and Further Education 1900-45

Following the vigorous growth of technical and further education during the last quarter of the nineteenth century, the next forty-odd years would, on the face of it, seem to have offered a favourable context for accelerated progress. The expansion of post-primary and secondary education provided a stronger potential basis for an improved system of technical and further education, the 1902 Act rationalised local educational administration and established the Part II authorities with their power to develop all sectors of other than elementary education, and Britain's serious economic difficulties during the inter-war period served to underline the technical, scientific and competitive weakness of industry. Yet, in fact, the years between the turn of the century and the Second World War were a 'period of relative quiescence' in the development of technical and further education; such is the apt descriptive phrase used by S. F. Cotgrove in his illuminating work *Technical Education and Social*

Change. Within this broad and disappointing context we must now examine the features of development and the various factors which combined to limit the progress made.

(a) Nature and Extent of Development

Compared with the years before 1900 and after 1945 the intervening period was one of much less rapid growth, punctuated by very few new or dramatic developments in the field of technical and further education. The emphasis was on the consolidation, reorganisation and co-ordination of existing arrangements, although by the close of the period the stage was being set for more vigorous development. In these respects the following features are noteworthy.

(i) The reform of central and local educational administration 1899-1902 ended the former fragmentation of responsibility for the development of technical and further education. The concentration of that responsibility in the hands of the technological branch of the Board of Education and the Part II authorities facilitated the better co-ordination and rationalisation of provision. The establishment of the Association of Teachers in Technical Institutions (1904) and the Association of Principals of Technical Institutions (1921) also made for more cohesion.

(ii) The confusion arising from the previous piecemeal and unco-ordinated development of technical courses and examinations was tackled with some considerable success. Many of the new Part II local education authorities in Lancashire, Cheshire and the West Riding replaced single subject arrangements by 'grouped' courses of related subjects in their evening institutions; in 1910 Morant gave official central support to this policy and three years later the course system was adopted by the London County Council. As the Board of Education gradually phased out the old Science and Art examinations, a co-ordinated system of regional and national examinations for technical and commercial education slowly emerged. Before the First World War the more progressive local authorities developed the work and importance of regional examining bodies such as the Union of Lancashire and Cheshire Institutes and the East Midland Educational Union; drafting syllabuses and mounting examinations appropriate to local circumstances, they were however linked with each other and such organisations as the City and Guilds Institute through a system of joint committees. But it was not until 1921 that the most significant breakthrough of all took place, when the Board of Education and the Institute of Mechanical Engineers combined to launch the National Certificate courses and examinations. The

221

declared purpose was to make available courses which would lead to a nationally recognised technological qualification combining both practical and theoretical studies. National Certificates were offered at Ordinary level after three years part-time study and at the Higher level following a further two years of successful effort. By 1945 there were such courses in mechanical and electrical engineering, industrial chemistry, naval architecture, building and construction, textiles and commerce. Although the growth of the scheme was steady rather than spectacular, its long-term significance was great: it gave the more aspiring technical institutes the opportunity to develop courses approximating to university degree level in certain areas and attracted increased interest from those industries calculated to benefit.

(iii) The rate of growth for technical and further education was not very impressive. In forty years the number of students involved just more than doubled, but the late nineteenth century tradition of part-time evening attendance stood firm. On the eve of the Second World War some 96% of those in attendance at institutions of further education were completely dependent upon evening study. In the absence of widespread interest from employers and with the failure of Fisher's compulsory continuation school scheme, the development of day-release arrangements for young apprentices proved very slow and limited. The growth of full-time day courses was even more disappointing in its extent; within the very limited expansion that took place professional and commercial subjects fared better than their technical counterparts. Of course, there was the development of the junior technical schools, officially recognised by the Board of Education in 1913, and providing full-time day classes for post-elementary 13- to 16-year-olds awaiting skilled apprenticeships in engineering and other such industries. Although these new schools fed a high proportion of their ex-pupils into further technical education, they were really part of the developing secondary sector and never accounted for more than thirty thousand pupils all told.

(iv) The contribution of the universities to the growth of higher education in science and technology did not develop very impressively. Although the establishment of the University Grants Committee (1919) and the provision of more generous State financial assistance gave a fillip to university development as such in the immediate post-war years, the inter-war period was one in which science and technology actually lost ground at this level. In 1939 the number of students taking science and technology was virtually the same as in 1922; the proportion of the total number of university students engaged in such studies fell from 32% to $27\frac{1}{2}$%. Some long-term compensations were to be found, however, in the work of the Department for Scientific and Industrial Research (set up by the government in 1916), the creation of the Imperial College of Science and Technology and its incorporation in the University of London in 1908, and the development of the Royal College of Science and Technology, Glasgow, and the distinctive Faculty of Technology, University of Manchester; all these institutions stood out as centres of progressive influence and development in the field of higher technological education and research.

(v) It was only with the advent of Lord Eustace Percy to the Presidency of the Board of Education (1924-9) that the central authority began to show real concern for the development of technical and further education. He was responsible for a number of searching inquiries into various aspects of further education for industry and commerce and conducted a personal crusade against the under-employment and low status of the technical colleges. In 1928 the Malcolm Committee Report on *Education and Industry* deplored the overwhelming dependence on evening classes and urged the expansion of full-time and part-time day courses as a matter of national importance. Employers were exhorted to give much more support to the development of day-release arrangements for young employees. The financial climate engendered by the world economic depression gravely limited the results of such reports, but also underlined the growing need to strengthen the bases of British industry in an increasingly competitive world. In the later 1930s the Board of Education returned to the theme. It issued a report on *Co-operation in Technical Education* (1937) calculated to bestir the Part II authorities into making a new and major drive in the field of further technical education. The government confirmed its serious intent by making no less than £12 million available for the purpose. But before the preliminaries were complete the Second World War intervened.

(vi) The developing system of further education continued to embrace much more than technical courses and became even more diffuse in character during these years. As post-primary and secondary provision was improved the demand for evening continuative education in general subjects slackened, but was more than compensated for by a growing interest in non-vocational courses and recreational activities. In 1924 adult education emerged as a distinctive sector and central grants were made available for its support. The contribution of the Workers' Educational Association (founded in 1903), the emergence of the Women's Institutes and Townswomen's

The Development and Structure of the English Educational System Morris.

Henry

Guilds, the development of community centres in newly established urban areas and of the Cambridgeshire village colleges are all worthy of study within the process of diffusion but limits of space preclude anything more than passing reference to them here.

(b) Factors Militating against Progress

It is clear that the development of technical and further education during the period concerned was inhibited by the adverse influence of a number of critical factors.

(i) Following the 1902 Act, the policy of Morant was to encourage the new local education authorities to give top priority to the development of State secondary grammar schooling and the expansion of teacher training facilities. After the First World War it was the growth of post-primary education and the movement towards secondary education for all which consumed most of the interest and energies of the Board and the local authorities. Given the economic difficulties of the inter-war period and the public disinclination to spend really large sums of money on education, it was inevitable that progress should vary considerably between different sectors competing for limited and unreliable resources. Technical and further education was the major victim of this situation. Before 1918 the central authority contributed nothing to capital expenditure in this field and maintained a grant system designed to perpetuate the evening class tradition. After 1918 Fisher's day continuation schools, which would have added a new dimension to further education, were the main casualty of the Geddes axe; even the new percentage grant system did not work to the significant advantage of technical and further education. It was only at the close of the period that there were real signs of a prospective shift in policy and the distribution of available funds.

(ii) The classical and liberal tradition in English education continued to wield its pernicious influence upon the fortunes of technical and further education. By the close of the nineteenth century the latter had already been branded as inferior to a liberal education provided by traditional institutions; these enjoyed a strong connection with the high status professions and other black-coated occupations. During the inter-war years the fact that a liberal education became the key to obtaining secure employment exacerbated this situation. Thus the development of the State secondary grammar schools brought only very limited benefits for technical and technological education. The grammar schools oriented their pupils towards the arts and humanities, the black-coated occupations and the universities. Very few grammar school leavers were attracted to technical college courses; at the university level they had been conditioned to ascribe higher status to arts than science subjects and to pure sciences than to technological studies. The secondary technical school never enjoyed the prestige or support given to its grammar counterpart; in 1938 there were twenty grammar school pupils for every one in a technical school, which testifies to the tardiness with which this new institution had been developed since before the First World War. Thus the technical colleges were dependent on former senior elementary and secondary modern pupils for about 80% of their enrolments; this gravely inhibited the development of technical and technological studies at the higher levels. Even the attitude of the Labour movement towards technical and continuative education seems to have been influenced by the liberal tradition and its connotations. It favoured the extension of the more prestigious secondary grammar opportunities to the working class and secondary education for all became its vital goal as a means to breaking down social barriers. Many Labour and trade union leaders also suspected that progressive employers had ulterior motives in their support of continuative technical instruction as a means of expanding the pool of skilled labour and so reducing wages. Thus the development of technical and further education in its existing form lacked vigorous support from one powerful source from which it might have been expected.

(iii) The apathetic attitude of employers and employees also acted as a very serious brake on progress. The former were most at fault: not until the 1930s was there any pressure from industry itself for the expansion and improvement of further technical education. Of course, the general malaise which overcame much of British industry was hardly calculated to throw up a rising demand for more technical and scientific manpower; the basic response to the economic difficulties was to bolster up the declining staple industries rather than vigorously to develop the new and more sophisticated ones. The prosperity of the Edwardian era lulled too many British industrialists into the complacency which the Great Depression had previously diluted but not dispelled. In relation to the majority of industrial employers the period concerned was characterised by an indifference to scientific research and its application to industry, a continued reliance upon on-the-job training and a corresponding scepticism directed towards the benefits of theoretical technical instruction, and a preponderance of managers and directors without scientific or technical qualifications. Given that promotions were usually made from the shop floor as a result of practical experience or based upon nepotism and influence, there was far too little incentive for employees to undertake courses leading to vocational qualifications not held in high esteem by their employers. In this context it is not surprising that it was the opposition of employers that tipped the scales against Fisher's compulsory day continuation classes in the early 1920s and it was their lack of interest that made the development of day-release courses such an uphill struggle. The vigorous and effective growth of technical and technological education must rest upon the co-operative efforts of both industry and the institutions concerned; it was only on the eve of the Second World War that the necessary partnership and mutual interest began to show real signs of developing.

4 The Post-War Era: from Indecision to Expansion

Considered as a whole the post-war period has been one of remarkable expansion and development in technical and further education; since the late 1950s this sector of the educational system has enjoyed greater priority and support than it ever received before. Compared with the situation existing on the eve of the Second World War there has been impressive progress on almost all fronts. Evening class attendances have increased very substantially, although the largest growth relates to recreational subjects and activities. But much more significant is the considerable shift towards day-time work in the technical and further education colleges. Full-time and sandwich courses at the higher levels and part-time day-release and block courses at lower levels have at last come into their own and now account for well over half of the total student hours worked in this sector of education. Within this latter context the major colleges have developed an increasing amount of advanced work and since 1964 have been able to mount their own internal degree courses, albeit subject to the approval and validation of the Council for National Academic Awards. Some outstanding technical colleges, originally designated as Colleges of Advanced Technology, have developed into full technological universities; a number of regional colleges have provided the basis for the formation of the thirty polytechnics in which the higher and really advanced work in the further education sector is now being concentrated. At the lower levels the much greater interest and support shown by employers, duly sharpened by the Industrial Training Act (1964), has facilitated the great post-war expansion in day-release arrangements, especially for male apprentices in certain manufacturing industries. Meanwhile the post-war years have seen a four-fold

Nationalised Industries influence.

rise in the number of university students and the proportion undertaking undergraduate or postgraduate courses in pure and applied sciences has increased significantly. Certain universities have embarked upon the development of degree courses in business and management studies; these will supplement the earlier and more narrowly conceived courses leading to the Bachelor of Commerce degree.

The progress just reviewed has, of course, taken place within a total context which has proved much more favourable and stimulating than its pre-war counterpart. Firstly, further education has enjoyed much more official interest and encouragement than was the case in the early decades of this century. The shortage of trained manpower during the Second World War, and the economic price of industrial weakness in the sharply competitive post-war world, gradually convinced the government that the country's very survival depended in part upon the development of a really satisfactory system of scientific, technological and technical education. The period is punctuated by innumerable official reports concerned with the various aspects of further education and from the late 1950s a new and unprecedented drive began, with an emphasis on the expansion of courses which would draw the most direct and significant economic benefits in relation to the needs of industry and commerce. Secondly, the lessons of the world economic depression, the wartime years and the struggle for post-war markets were not lost upon industrial employers and mangement. Their interest in research and development and its industrial applications grew quite markedly and produced a much greater demand for scientists, technologists and technicians. This post-war trend has acquired growing strength from the emergence of nationalised industries and large-scale private corporations with their divorce of ownership and control; here actual business management has passed increasingly into the hands of professional administrators with the requisite background in science, technology and commercial matters. Out of this has grown a much closer partnership between industry and the local authorities and other bodies for the effective development of further and higher education to subserve the needs of the economy. As the pre-war apathy of employers towards further education receded, employees became that much more interested in the prospect of obtaining the sort of vocational education and training that now began to bear a significantly closer relationship to their pay and promotion prospects. The gradual development of a more generous policy in relation to students seeking grants for full-time or sandwich courses in the further education sector also stimulated recruitment. Thirdly, the introduction of secondary education for all and the development of stronger Science Sixth Forms provided a broader and much improved base for the expansion of technical and further education. By the early 1960s the post-war birth-rate bulge was favourably affecting the further education sector as the secondary schools turned out a significantly enlarged 15-18 years age cohort. Finally, the gradual reduction in the average working week and the consequent expansion of leisure time operated as an important factor in the growth of evening institute work in recreational and similar activities. The extended emancipation of women and the growing trend for mothers to return to work later in life combined to increase recruitment to full-time and part-time day courses in general subjects.

However, the development of technical and further education after the Second World War was not without its problems and shortcomings. It can be argued that, despite all the advances made, the further education sector continues to fail the early school leaver of less than average ability and aspiration. The 1944 Act's provision for compulsory part-time day education at so-called county colleges has not materialised and shows no signs of doing so; thus thousands of young people continue to sever all connection with the educational system once they leave school for the largely philistine world of employment. Adolescents employed in unskilled and some semi-skilled occupations do not enjoy day-release arrangements to attend vocational courses and the failure of the county colleges has denied them the extended general, social and recreational education intended by the Act. As the incidence of day-release for young female employees is still disproportionately very low, girls have been the chief sufferers in this respect. The situation has been exacerbated by the fact that until the Albemarle Report (1960) the Youth Service was palpably starved of official interest and support and clearly emerged as the Cinderella of further education; even now it does not enjoy any real priority and its development seems to lack any clear sense of direction. Compared with other advanced industrial countries, technical and commercial education at the lower levels is still too dependent upon part-time day and evening work with which is associated considerable wastage. The field of adult education, providing non-vocational and cultural courses for mature persons, is also an aspect of further education which has received more lip-service and less real support than many would deem desirable; like the county colleges and the Youth Service it has suffered from the fact that it offers no direct economic benefits such as those that may be claimed on behalf of education for industry and commerce. Finally, it must be stressed that the post-war period has not been one of steady advance in the field of technical and further education; indeed the year 1956 forms something of a major watershed and any detailed analysis must take this into account. The first post-war decade was one of limited progress in which, in spite of some important long-term developments, there was a lack of a clear and vigorous policy in relation to technical and further education. Thereafter, however, government policy was clarified and the sector concerned began to enjoy a priority and support hitherto denied it. The catalyst was the government's growing apprehensions over the educational system's failure to produce the scientific and technological strength to sustain our economic position alongside the United States, the Soviet Union and other advanced industrial nations.

(*a*) Period of Limited Progress and Indecision 1945-55

This began auspiciously enough with the Board of Education reiterating its new and ambitious pre-war programme for technical and further education in the 1943 White Paper *Educational Reconstruction*. Accordingly the 1944 Act made it the duty of every local education authority to provide adequate facilities for further education and required all of them to submit schemes of development calculated to achieve this to the new Ministry of Education. Meanwhile, a special committee under the chairmanship of Lord Eustace Percy was set up to investigate the existing provision of higher technological and advanced technical education in England and Wales and to make recommendations for its future development on a co-ordinated basis. The Percy Report on *Higher Technological Education* (1945), having underlined the serious threat of a post-war shortage of scientists and technologists to meet the needs of industry and criticised the lack of any concerted attempt to effect a real partnership between the universities and technical colleges in this field, warned the government that a failure to cure the deficiencies could positively endanger Britain's position as a leading industrial nation in the post-war world. It went on to make a number of far-seeing *recommendations* designed to secure the necessary improvements:

(i) the development of an appropriate administrative and advisory framework to facilitate the effective and co-ordinated growth of higher technological and advanced technical education. This was to involve the establishment of about ten Regional Advisory Councils, representing universities, major technical colleges, local education authorities, the Ministry and industrial interests, to cover the whole of England and Wales and to undertake the promotion and co-ordination of suitable courses within each region. Each Council was to be backed by a Regional Academic Board to oversee both courses and examinations and to secure the maintenance of satisfactory academic standards. This structure was to be topped by a National Council of Technology for co-ordination between regions and for rendering advice to the Ministry on all major issues related to the field concerned. It would also be responsible, either directly or through an associated National Academic Board, for the moderation of examinations and the validation of awards designed to have national currency;

(ii) the adoption of an over-all strategy for the production of trained manpower to ensure the complementary integration of university and technical college contributions. The Report recommended that the universities should remain the source of scientists whilst the technical colleges would continue to help train craftsmen and technical assistants on a part-time basis; but both the universities and certain technical institutions should contribute to the supply of technologists, thus blurring the distinction between further and higher education;

(iii) the designation of a limited number of major technical colleges for the development of technological courses to degree and post-graduate standards. However, out of respect for the long tradition of university monopoly in the awarding of degrees, the Percy Committee shrank from the principle of equal awards for equal work and recommended the institution of a new Diploma in Technology qualification to attract recruits to such courses. These Colleges of Advanced Technology were to be supplemented by National Colleges serving the needs of certain small but sophisticated industries for highly educated and trained personnel; this would involve the economic concentration of all the necessary expert staff and costly facilities at one centre;

(iv) the development of much closer links between industry and those concerned with the actual provision of higher technological and advanced technical education. Accordingly the report emphasised the need for greater support from industrial interests and their full representation on all the pertinent bodies.

When the Barlow Report on *Scientific Manpower* (1946) confirmed the broad conclusions of the Percy Committee and insisted upon the need for the universities to double their output of scientists within ten years, all seemed set for a very rapid advance. In fact, the way forward proved more difficult than expected, with a number of unfavourable factors operating to hold up progress. Firstly, during the immediate post-war years of austerity the Attlee Labour government was forced to work to a strict order of priorities; within the context of the limited resources available for education, priority was given to the raising of the school leaving age and the development of secondary education for all. Conscious of the commitment to introduce the expensive county college scheme, there was a short-term disinclination to spend large sums on other aspects of further education. Whilst the local education authorities dutifully submitted their ambitious schemes for the development of further education, the government refused to authorise the necessary capital expenditure. It could be argued that, given the country's urgent economic needs, such a policy was based on a set of false priorities. Secondly, the Churchill Conservative government 1951-5, which appointed Miss Florence Horsburgh as Minister of Education and denied her a Cabinet position, was responsible for some serious short-term cuts in educational expenditure and was slow to develop a sense of urgency in relation to technical and technological education. Finally, the field of further and higher education was particularly sensitive to new developments because of the existence of strong vested interests as represented by the universities, the local education authorities, the professional institutes and the aspiring front-rank technical colleges; amidst the conflicting pressures it took the central government a whole decade to arrive at a clear and decisive policy for expansion.

Nevertheless, by 1955 limited progress had been made both in the growth of technical and further education and in preparing the ground for the new drive which was to follow.

(i) The Regional Advisory Councils and Academic Boards were established within two years of the Percy Report's publication. A year later the National Advisory Council on Education for Industry and Commerce was set up to advise the Ministry; it was soon mounting useful investigations into various aspects of vocational further education and kept pressing on the government the need for more vigorous action in the field of higher technological and advanced technical education. Its reports provided a basis for the critical White Paper of 1956.

(ii) In line with the Percy Report a number of National Colleges, enjoying direct government and industrial support, were established for aeronautics, horology, rubber technology, metallurgy, leather-making, heating and ventilating, food technology, and art and design.

(iii) In 1952 the government initiated special 75% grants to encourage the growth of advanced technical education in those colleges approved for such courses by the Regional Advisory Councils. Three years later it set up the National Council for Technological Awards to oversee the introduction and development of Diploma in Technology courses in such colleges. Meanwhile, the expansion of the university output of scientists and technologists had managed to meet the minimum requirements of the Barlow Report.

(iv) The growing interest of the larger employers in further technical education found expression in an impressive expansion of day-release attendance which involved over 350,000 young employees by 1955. Thus the initial breakthrough in this field, achieved by

Ernest Bevin as Minister of Labour in the wartime Coalition government, was being further developed as industry became more responsive.

(b) Period of Priority and Expansion 1956-72

From 1956 education for industry and commerce benefited from a new sense of urgency and direction at Whitehall. Those sectors of further and higher education able to make a direct contribution to the strengthening of the economy through the expansion of trained manpower began to enjoy unprecedented priority and support. The ensuing years were punctuated by government White Papers, official reports and actual legislation which served as the basis for development and expansion in the field concerned.

1956 *White Paper on Technical Education* In this the Eden Conservative government set out a comprehensive five-year programme for the development of scientific, technological and technical education. Whilst the universities were to continue their expansion of science and technology graduates, the further education sector was substantially to increase its work in higher technological and advanced technical education. This led to the designation of ten Colleges of Advanced Technology to support a broad range of high level courses, including the new Diploma in Technology and postgraduate studies. Four- to five-year sandwich courses, combining theoretical study with industrial experience, were the recommended means to higher technological qualifications. In relation to technical education at the lower levels the White Paper ambitiously urged that the number of day-release students should be doubled within five years, a target which industry was to fall well short of. Finally, the need for a rationalisation of the use of resources in further education was emphasised; to that end a subsequent Ministry circular initiated a process of national reorganisation into local, area, regional and advanced technology colleges with each type of institution playing a fairly definitive and distinct role.

1957 *Jackson Report on The Supply and Training of Teachers for Technical Colleges* In the wake of the White Paper this made appropriate recommendations for the expansion of full-time and part-time technical college staff, the improvement of conditions of work and an increase in the incidence of professional teacher training. Significantly enough the number of full-time staff trebled during the next decade.

1959 *Crowther Report on 15 to 18* Having identified the system of further education as the critical sector for realising the potential of the second quartile of ability, this Report went on to express dissatisfaction with it. The major weakness was the low proportion of students on full-time courses and the continued over-reliance on part-time evening attendance with its associated high wastage rates. Furthermore, the piecemeal development and proliferation of courses in technical education had produced a confused pattern which was in need of rationalisation: it was suggested that the basic strategy should be the development of distinct courses and examinations for technicians, craftsmen and operatives. The danger of devoting too much attention to the production of higher level scientists and technologists was underlined; this would lead to an imbalance in the output of trained manpower. At all levels it was important to develop block release and sandwich courses to replace the much less satisfactory day-release and evening attendance for serving apprentices and other young persons. The Report's dominant theme was the wastage of talent consequent upon the partial failure of further education to give the second quartile of ability a really satisfactory educational deal; this sector was described (in spite of the new drive) as 'neglected educational territory' and a top priority if the country's economic needs were to be met adequately. An official response to some of these criticisms was soon forthcoming.

1960 *Anderson Report on Grants to Students* By introducing equality of treatment for all students following higher level courses, this Report facilitated a marked increase in the number of grant awards to students pursuing full-time or sandwich courses in the further education sector. Without this the Colleges of Advanced Technology and the regional colleges would have been placed at a considerable disadvantage compared with the universities.

1961 *White Paper on Better Opportunities in Technical Education* This confirmed the government's continuing concern, initiated a major reorganisation of courses for technicians, craftsmen and operatives and promoted the further expansion of industrial release though preferably on a sandwich or block basis. The details were developed in a ten point programme in which complete reliance upon evening attendance for technical courses was roundly condemned. The need to increase the output of trained manpower at intermediate and lower levels was accepted as a matter of urgency.

1963 *Robbins Report on Higher Education* Set up to review the existing pattern of full-time higher education throughout Great Britain and to make recommendations for its long-term future development, the Robbins Committee made a major and almost immediate impact. As the result of some onerous and well-substantiated international comparisons, the Committee warned the government that 'vigorous action is needed to avert the danger of a serious relative decline in this country's standing'. Such danger was especially apparent in the economic field and accordingly the Committee gave considerable attention to higher technological and advanced technical education in both the university and further education sectors. The actual *results* of some of the recommendations made have been impressive.

(i) The number of university students doubled in the decade 1962–72 and the proportion of postgraduates rose significantly. Science and technology courses and research particularly benefited from this expansion. The three premier university institutions of science and technology in London, Manchester and Glasgow grew considerably and the Colleges of Advanced Technology were translated into full technological universities and substantially increased their intake.

(ii) The advanced sector of further education has enjoyed an even higher rate of growth and a deserved rise in comparative status. The Robbins Report recommended the development of degree level work in suitable fields by the National Colleges, the regional Colleges of Further Education and even some of the area colleges. It further suggested the replacement of the National Council for Technological Awards by a new Council for National Academic Awards with a much wider function and power, including the right to grant degrees to students pursuing approved courses or research in non-university institutions. Established by royal charter as a self-governing body in 1964, the Council for National Academic Awards quickly won the support and respect of the further and higher educational world; within five years there were over fifty non-university colleges offering C.N.A.A. degree courses and the students engaged upon them were growing fast. Whilst the Council's initial interest was very largely in the promotion of degree level courses in science, technology and engineering, it soon began to widen its role to encompass and encourage advanced work in the other sectors of further education. Its work has finally ended the traditional university monopoly of degree work and has raised the aspirations and levels of work of many Colleges of Further Education.

(iii) The development of degree and postgraduate courses in business and management studies, an area of serious weakness in English higher education, also received a marked stimulus from the interest and concern of the Robbins Committee.

1964 *Industrial Training Act* In spite of the exhortations of the 1956 White Paper, the recommendations of the Carr Report on *Recruitment and Training of Young Workers in Industry* (1958) and the criticisms of the Crowther Report (1959), the existing apprenticeship arrangements and the extent of industrial release had remained inadequate for the needs of a highly industrialised society. The new Act was designed to expand the pool of trained manpower, to improve the quality of industrial training and to distribute the cost of this fairly between all the firms concerned. The Minister of Labour was empowered to establish Industrial Training Boards to undertake responsibility for organising efficient training at all levels of employment in the industry concerned and for administering a levy fund scheme to finance the operation. Wherever substantial training was involved the Boards were required to provide industrial release for attending a suitable further education course. About thirty such Boards now cover virtually the whole of industry and commerce; under their influence the proportion of young employees obtaining industrial release rose from 18% in 1963 to 25% in 1969. Whilst many existing courses were incorporated in the Boards' training schemes, others were amended and new ones devised to meet the needs of the Act. The whole development has been co-ordinated and overlooked by the Central Training Council, which has provided a much needed focus for the problems and requirements of technical training and education at the intermediate and lower levels.

1966 *White Paper on A Plan for Polytechnics and Other Colleges* Whilst it accepted many of the Robbins' principles and the need for an urgent and integrated expansion of higher education, the new Labour government rejected the Robbins' strategy of concentrating degree work in universities and other autonomous institutions in favour of the development of a binary system. Official policy became one of expanding higher education in both the university-centred autonomous sector and the local education authority controlled public sector, with the latter enjoying the fastest rate of growth. This policy was calculated to increase the proportion of higher level work undertaken by the further education sector and it was considered vital to concentrate such work, and the requisite staff and facilities, in a limited number of outstanding institutions. Some thirty polytechnics were designated to fulfil this need; in a sense they replaced the old Colleges of Advanced Technology but were intended to pursue a broader role and encompass a wider range of courses, especially at degree level under C.N.A.A. auspices. The polytechnics were usually developed from existing regional Colleges of Further Education already concerned with a large amount of advanced work; sometimes they were based upon mergers between two or more reputable institutions lodged in the same urban area. They not only developed the humanities and the social sciences, but even entered the field of teacher training in a small way.

The future of technical and further education seems promising. The country's recurrent post-war economic difficulties have gradually produced the firm conviction that British industry cannot remain competitive unless the educational system makes an adequate contribution to the production of trained manpower. Whilst the primary and secondary schools have obviously a basic role to fulfil in this respect, it is in the field of further and higher education that the need must be ultimately met. The White Paper on *Education: A Framework for Expansion* (1972) portends a further impressive expansion of full-time higher and further education, even though the rate of growth up to 1981 is not intended to match that of the 1960s. However, it is significant that the ten-year programme envisages that the number of students enjoying a higher education in non-university institutions will ultimately equate with the number in the established universities. Thus the further education sector will grow more quickly than the universities and the polytechnics have been singled out for the fastest expansion. Many Colleges of Further Education may be expected to become involved in the development of the new Diploma of Higher Education, which would tend to increase the comparative importance of non-vocational studies in these institutions. The Council of National Academic Awards expressed a willingness to validate such Diploma courses and this was welcomed by the government. Although the White Paper did not blandly say so, it seems that the binary system will be retained for the foreseeable future.

Follow-up: Attempt to cover as much of the following ground as possible.

1 *Read* Department of Education and Science *Trends in Education*, February 1970. Centenary issue: article by J. A. R. Pimlott on 'Continuing Education', pp. 50–5

Curtis, S. J. and Boultwood, M. E. *An Introductory History of English Education since 1800*, Chapters XII and XIV

Barnard, H. C. *A History of English Education from 1760*, Chapters X, XVI, XX and XXX

Lowndes, G. A. N. *The Silent Social Revolution*, Chapters IX, XVIII and XIX

2 *Consult* Maclure, J. S. *Educational Documents: England and Wales 1816–1968;* items 15, 17, 26, 27, 28, 38, 39, 41, 43, 45, 47 and 51 are relevant

3 *Clarify the following: the state of scientific and technical education at the outset of the nineteenth century; the significance and limitations of the Mechanics' Institutes movement; the factors favourable to the growth of science teaching and technical instruction in the later nineteenth century; the institutions which promoted the teaching of science at various levels 1850-1900; the institutions contemporaneously developing technical and further education on a largely*

part-time evening basis; the extent and nature of the development of technical and further education between the 1902 and 1944 Education Acts; the outstanding features of the marked progress achieved in scientific, technological, technical and further education since 1945; the post-war influences which produced an increasingly favourable context for such progress; the relationship between the long-term post-war advance and the recommendations of the Percy Report on Higher Technological Education *(1945); the significance of the* White Paper on Technical Education *(1956); the results of the Robbins Report (1963) for higher technological and advanced technical courses in the university and further education sectors; the importance of the Industrial Training Act (1964); the origin and development of the binary system of higher education.*

Chapter Thirteen
The Development of University Education

Purpose: to consider the history of university education in England and Wales during the nineteenth and twentieth centuries and to emphasise the marked extent to which State support for and influence upon university development increased after the Second World War.

Since 1800 the number of university institutions existing in England and Wales has risen from merely two to the impressive total of almost forty. In the nineteenth century the process of change at home and the growth of Empire abroad produced a growing demand for more civil servants, colonial administrators, lawyers, doctors, schoolmasters, financiers, scientists and technologists. The rise of an expanding wealthy middle class and the beginnings of women's emancipation reinforced the need to improve and increase existing university provision. The contemporary response to this situation was the reform and expansion of the ancient universities of Oxford and Cambridge and the development of other university institutions in both England and Wales. Between the close of the nineteenth century and the eve of the Second World War the semblance of a national policy for university education gradually emerged; at the outset a reluctant government acceded to pressing requests for financial help from the new universities, but, with the later and increasing recognition of the importance of university education to the nation's life and well-being, the State's interest had become much more positive by the inter-war period. Yet it was not until the coming of the nuclear and space age which grew out of the Second World War that the strong tradition of providing university education for only a tiny minority was finally challenged and broken down. Faced by powerful economic and social pressures, successive post-war governments contributed to an unprecedented and mounting State-sponsored expansion of university education in Great Britain.

1 The Reform of Oxford and Cambridge
(a) Condition at the Turn of the Century
The traditional monopoly of university education in England and Wales enjoyed by Oxford and Cambridge at this time would have been more

acceptable if these mediaeval foundations had been in better shape. Following the Restoration they had both entered upon a period of marked decline during which they became increasingly removed from the mainstream of national life. Although the extent of their decay has sometimes been exaggerated, the sort of intellectual vigour displayed by the Scottish universities and the Dissenting academies during the eighteenth century was certainly lacking at Oxford and Cambridge. Given their strong connection with the established State and Church, the ancient universities were infected by the political corruption and the ecclesiastical indolence of the Hanoverian age; the associated deterioration in the condition of the public and endowed grammar schools also wielded an adverse influence upon their fortunes. Yet, whilst external factors played a part, the unsatisfactory nature of university life at Oxford and Cambridge was basically the result of the oligarchic, conservative and leisurely ethos of the institutions themselves. Far too few of those holding influential positions within the ancient universities in the late eighteenth century were concerned to stop the rot and thus the growing need for improvement and reform was largely ignored. Against the backcloth of a society being changed by the forces unleased by the Industrial Revolution at home and the French Revolution abroad, the grave shortcomings of the ancient universities assumed even larger proportions and began to attract mounting criticism both from within and without. The major shortcomings which were identified must now be analysed.

(i) The constitution and government of the ancient universities had become far too oligarchic, anachronistic and resistant to change. The Elizabethan statutes for Cambridge (1570) and the Laudian statutes for Oxford (1636) had facilitated the process by which the wealthy constituent colleges came to overshadow the corporate life of the universities. Effective power was concentrated in the hands of a few heads of colleges who dominated the Caput at Cambridge and the Hebdomadal Board at Oxford. It was the colleges which accommodated and educated the undergraduates and to whom the latter owed their loyalty. The leisurely practice of residential tutoring rested on a collegiate system of closed fellowships, appointment to which often owed much to patronage or nepotism and offered the prospect of a relaxed and comfortable academic life. The university, as such, simply conferred degrees and charged the appropriate fees for so doing. True, the university appointed to the professoriate which traversed all the colleges, but lacking the endowed wealth of the latter it could rarely afford to offer satisfactory emoluments for such positions: the influence of the university professors was also seriously undermined by the fact that attendance at their lectures was not only voluntary but quite unrelated to obtaining the degree qualification. The need was for a reassertion of the corporate character of the universities at the expense of the separate colleges and a marked rise in the comparative importance of the professoriates.

(ii) The ancient universities were distinguished by their social and religious exclusiveness. The expense of residence at most of the constituent colleges was such that only the sons of the aristocracy, gentry and very wealthy merchant families could afford to go up to Oxford or Cambridge; the limited number of scholarships available were generally restricted to the products of particular public or endowed grammar schools. The formal social distinctions made between various undergraduates were associated with collegiate privileges for the idle rich who made up a large proportion of the students. They were even excused from the examinations leading to the award of a degree! Meanwhile, religious discrimination was strictly maintained in the interests of the Church of England and its monopolistic claims in the field of education. The ancient universities were open only to members of the Anglican Church, with the Dissenters and Roman Catholics rigorously debarred from graduation by making subscription to the Thirty-nine Articles a prior requirement. Once the repeal of the Test and Corporation Acts (1828) and the passage of the Catholic Relief Act (1829) removed the civil disabilities under which the non-Anglican sections of the community had laboured for so long, the religious exclusiveness of the ancient universities inevitably came under increasing pressure.

(iii) The academic standards and outlook of the ancient universities were palpably unsatisfactory, as was exemplified by the nature of their curriculum and examinations. At Oxford the old scholasticism vested in the study of the Classics, Aristotelian philosophy and mediaeval logic still held sway, whilst at Cambridge there was too much emphasis upon outmoded mathematical studies. Entrance examinations to the various colleges were still virtually unknown and at Oxford graduation was based on a minimum of thirteen weeks' residence, submission to the Anglican tests and success in quite farcical oral examinations. Natural science and other modern subjects, such as were developed in the eighteenth century Dissenting academies, were almost totally neglected. The former importance of the ancient universities in training for the law and medicine had been largely lost. What work went on at Oxford and Cambridge was confined to the teaching of undergraduates; postgraduate study was a rarity and neither university made a significant contribution to extending the frontiers of knowledge through research work. Exclusive seminaries for the training of Anglican clergymen and the finishing of wealthy gentlemen, the ancient universities were singularly unreceptive to the changing needs of a society which they were founded to serve.

Given the condition of the ancient universities (and Oxford was worse than Cambridge), it was inevitable that they should become a cardinal object of the reform movement during the nineteenth century. Liberal reformers inside the universities combined with more fierce external critics (e.g. Sir William Hamilton and the *Edinburgh Review*) to initiate change; in the third quarter of the century the State intervened to both stimulate and direct the impetus towards self-improvement.

(*b*) Internal Reforms in the Early Nineteenth Century

As any real changes in the constitution of the universities and the administration of religious tests could only be accomplished by statutory means, the success of the minority of reformers emerging within Oxford and Cambridge before 1850 was limited to the field of curriculum and examinations. At Oxford degrees were no longer awarded without examination and the latter now took the form of written papers. A new premium was placed upon real scholarship by the introduction (1807) of Honours degrees in both Classics and mathematics, giving rise to the opportunity to obtain a 'double first', a distinction first achieved by the future Sir Robert Peel. In 1850 Honours schools of natural science and law with history (later separated) were introduced to offset the recurrent criticisms directed at the narrowness of the curriculum. At Cambridge the original tripos in mathematics was supplemented by a second tripos in Classics (1824) for Honours candidates; a quarter of a century later new triposes in natural science and moral science were also instituted. A minority of college fellowships were thrown open to all comers, thus facilitating the appointment of outstanding Honours men to such positions. Professors were now required to lecture even if their role still bore little or no relation to the examination system.

But the overall impact of these limited reforms must not be exaggerated. The Classics and mathematics still dominated undergraduate studies and the Pass degree represented a low level of academic achievement. Many students did not present themselves for degrees, attending the universities for social rather than academic purposes. Even the progress made encountered considerable resistance from certain heads of colleges, and by 1850 it was quite clear that the strength of the conservative oligarchy was too great to expect any reform of constitutional or religious matters from within.

(c) State Intervention and Further Reform

Dissatisfaction with both the pace and extent of change amongst liberal reformers inside and outside the ancient universities, sharpened by the rise of the High Church Tractarian movement at Oxford, led the new Whig prime minister, Lord John Russell, to initiate the process by which the power of the State was thrown on to the scales to weight the balance in favour of decisive reform. In 1850 Russell advised Queen Victoria to appoint royal commissions to inquire into the state of Oxford and Cambridge; her favourable response began a period of thirty years during which the ancient universities were subjected to a great deal of official investigation, debate and legislation. The Royal Commission Reports on Oxford and Cambridge (1852) were made in the face of much conservative opposition but successfully re-established the government's right to interfere in the affairs of the ancient universities. There followed the Oxford University Act (1854) and the Cambridge University Act (1856), the consequent establishment of statutory Commissions to ensure the execution of the reforms provided for, the numerous legislative attempts finally to end the Anglican monopoly culminating in the University Tests Act (1871), yet another Royal Commission to report on the finances of Oxford and Cambridge (1873), the Universities of Oxford and Cambridge Act (1877) and the inevitable statutory Commissions to carry out its provisions. This sustained series of governmental interventions, inspired by Whig and Liberal ministries, proved a powerful catalyst and in cumulative fashion produced some far-reaching results.

(i) The government of the ancient universities was remodelled to break the power of the conservative oligarchies which had previously dominated the Hebdomadal Board and Caput. The reconstituted Hebdomadal Council at Oxford and Senate at Cambridge were much more representative bodies designed to promote rather than resist change. Their potential for reform was increased by the annulment of restrictive founders' regulations and earlier statutes. The prior importance of the university administration was reasserted by the diversion of some of the endowed wealth of the individual colleges to common purposes. The professoriate was expanded, better paid and enjoyed a marked rise in its comparative importance. University buildings, libraries and museums also profited from the tapping of college revenues. College fellowships were awarded on merit and the practice of holding some of them for life was abolished; the traditional requirement that college fellows should be celibate and ordained was withdrawn.

(ii) The social exclusiveness of the ancient universities was diluted to some extent by making entry less heavily dependent upon high birth or propertied wealth. Scholarships were increased in number and thrown open to unrestricted competition; but the new emphasis upon attainment played into the hands of the rejuvenated and expanding public and endowed grammar schools serving the wealthy middle class and consequently the intake was not significantly broadened by this means. But meanwhile the expense of an education at Oxford or Cambridge was reduced by the resurrection of the old practice of students living in halls of residence or private lodgings rather than in the colleges. The gradual replacement of costly aristocratic pursuits by organised games and other team activities also contributed to a reduction in the financial pressures of university life.

(iii) The religious exclusiveness of the ancient universities, and of Oxford in particular, was finally ended by the University Tests Act of 1871. Outside the field of theological studies, religious restrictions were completely removed in respect of matriculation, graduation, fellowships, lecturing posts and other university offices. Although Oxford's divinity degree maintained its particular connection with the established Church into the early twentieth century, the opening of the ancient universities to non-Anglicans was a critical landmark in the process of secularisation which transformed these national institutions from conservative seminaries into modern universities.

(iv) The further widening of the curriculum and a reappraisal of teaching methods were closely associated with the other reforms. The system of Honours schools and triposes was extended to include new subject areas such as English language and literature, oriental and modern languages and theology. Both Oxford and Cambridge established separate history schools which were soon attracting some of the ablest talents. There was a gradual revival of the study of law and medicine. The establishment of the Clarendon Laboratory at Oxford (1868) and the famous Cavendish Laboratory at Cambridge (1873) symbolised the onset of an era in which the ancient universities gave growing recognition to the contemporary importance of scientific studies. The rise of science was most marked at Cambridge and excited favourable comment from an investigating Commission which reported immediately after the First World War. Oxford's strong attachment to the humanities proved more resistant, however, and the development of science made slower progress there. Meanwhile, the more fluid situation and the interest in reform produced by governmental intervention led to a major improvement in teaching methods. On the one hand, the conservative but purposeful influence of John Henry Newman inspired the resuscitation of the collegiate tutorial system with its ideal of close contact between fellows and undergraduates inside a well-knit residential community. On the other hand, the influence of Mark Pattison, drawing much of its substance from the Scottish and German universities, favoured the promotion of specialisation, higher scholarship and research as distinct from the function of providing a broad education for undergraduates. The life and work of the ancient universities benefited from both of these influences in the later nineteenth century. Inside the constituent colleges tutors applied much more time and energy to their work, whilst students could take advantage of the growth of the professoriate and the lecture system within the wider university framework. The closer connection between these two aspects of development was reflected in the growth of research activity and the greater interest displayed by college dons in higher scholarship in specialist areas. Oxford and Cambridge gradually accepted a much broader concept of the functions of a university.

The later nineteenth century also witnessed other progressive developments which were only tenuously connected with the official reform movement at Oxford and Cambridge. In the 1870s the ancient foundations launched the University Extension movement whereby the erudition of Oxford and Cambridge dons was made available to large classes of adults in various provincial centres. Conducted in the evening, mainly during university vacations, the lecture courses provided drew a largely middle class clientele which included many women. Almost simultaneously, beginning with the foundation of Girton College at Cambridge (1873), the ancient universities opened their doors to women and embarked upon the long road that was ultimately to lead to the accordance of full equality of status in respect of degree awards, fellowships and other important matters.

By the close of the nineteenth century the universities of Oxford and Cambridge had been transformed beyond recognition and had once again taken up their rightful position within the mainstream of national life, providing the country with many of its administrators, lawyers, schoolmasters, clergymen and other professional people. They were also developing a growing reputation for scholarship and research, although still mainly concerned with the teaching function. However, the development of science, especially in its applied forms, had been undertaken to only a limited degree and the social composition of Oxbridge undergraduates remained fairly exclusive. Moreover, continued reliance upon only two centres of higher learning for the satisfaction of the nation's developing needs during the nineteenth century was no longer acceptable. Thus the reform of Oxford and Cambridge was parallelled by the growth of new institutions of higher education in England and Wales.

2 The Rise of the Modern Universities

(a) The Actual Process of Growth

By the onset of the second quarter of the nineteenth century the formerly vigorous Dissenting academies had fallen victim to earlier political reaction and to their own increasingly sectarian character, whilst the ancient universities still showed too little inclination towards internal reform. The response to this situation, drawing particular support from liberal and radical opinion and from Nonconformist, secularist, scientific and business interests, included the long process by which new institutions were developed to meet the needs of an expanding middle class for higher education. The process of growth may be considered as follows.

(i) *University of London*

This complex institution had its roots in the establishment of University College in Gower Street (1827) and of King's College in the Strand (1829). The former represented a radical protest at the exclusiveness of Oxford and Cambridge and was characterised by low fees and an absence of religious tests; the latter was the Anglican counter-stroke to the radicals' metropolitan initiative. A common element, however, was their disposition towards a wide and modern curriculum which included medicine and science subjects. Both colleges sought the right to award their own degrees, but attempts to merge them for this purpose failed completely. The compromise solution was the foundation of the University of London as such in 1836. Under its charter the new university was constituted as an examining body empowered to confer degrees upon students prepared by affiliated institutions. University and King's Colleges were the first to affiliate, but within twenty years they had been joined by many other, and usually far less worthy, institutions. In 1858 the University of London became a purely examining body when the need for affiliation was abandoned. For the next forty years the University of London was exclusively concerned with the administration of an external degree system of examinations available to any student who paid his fees, irrespective of mode or place of study. The resultant lack of real contact between the university and the teaching institutions ultimately led University and King's Colleges to press for the creation of a new and distinct metropolitan teaching university of which they would be constituent parts. The ensuing discord dominated the scene during the later years of the century and taxed the efforts of two government investigating bodies to resolve it. The Reports of the Selborne (1889) and Cowper (1894) Commissions finally led to the University of London Act in 1898. By this measure the existing institution was reconstituted as both an examining body and a teaching university: in its former role it continued its external examination arrangements divorced from the responsibility for teaching, whilst in its latter capacity it now became responsible for its own internal students who attended courses at over twenty constituent colleges. Thus the University of London remained a source of degree awards for aspiring colleges and private students both in this country and in various parts of the overseas Empire. But it also emerged as a formidable teaching university able to claim an Edwardian pre-eminence in medicine, technology and the social sciences. By the outbreak of the First World War the amorphous teaching University of London included the new Imperial College of Science and Technology (1907) and the London School of Economics (1895) amongst its constituents. Following the pre-war Haldane Report (1913), the University of London Act in 1926 provided for greater administrative cohesion and unity by means of a faculty organisation based upon schools which were usually co-terminous with particular specialist institutions (e.g. the medical schools). Contemporaneously, with the acquisition of a large acreage in Bloomsbury, the long process of physical concentration began.

(ii) *University of Durham*

This ecclesiastical foundation originated in the desire of the wealthy chapter of Durham Cathedral to protect its revenues from the possibility of Whig depredation. Accordingly a local residential university was endowed for the study of theology and the arts: subject to religious tests and modelled on the Oxford pattern, the new institution received its charter for conferring degrees in 1837. In spite of developing an association with the Newcastle College of Medicine (founded 1834), the university was struggling to survive by the middle of the century. Government intervention in the shape of the Durham University Act (1861) and the University Tests Act (1871) widened both curricula and entry and prepared the way for a more auspicious period of development. The newly established Newcastle College of Science accepted affiliation (1874) and the University of Durham became a federal association of three autonomous parts. However, the federal arrangements did not work too well and ultimately the University of Durham Act (1908) reconstituted the institution into two constituent divisions enjoying considerable autonomy but bound by a single Senate. The Durham part, with its residential and humanities tradition, continued to resemble the Oxbridge model and ethos. The Newcastle part, composed of the colleges of medicine and science and later to emerge as the unitary King's College, bore much more likeness to the civic universities growing up in the northern industrial and commercial centres. Although the story of the University of Durham does not fit the normal pattern for the development of the modern universities, it afforded the first example of a federal approach to the problem of achieving real university rank and stature.

(iii) *Provincial Civic Universities*

During the latter half of the nineteenth century, beginning with the foundation of Owens College in Manchester, there arose no fewer than ten English university colleges incorporated to undertake studies up to degree level. The institutions concerned were established in Manchester (1851), Leeds (1874), Bristol (1876), Nottingham (1877), Birmingham (1880), Liverpool (1882), Reading (1892), Sheffield (1897), Exeter (1901) and Southampton (1902). The roots of these provincial institutions usually lay in local medical schools, colleges for scientific and technical instruction and university extension classes which had developed earlier. Generally speaking they were located in the centres of densely populated industrial towns, were non-residential and took the Scottish and German universities as their main source of inspiration. The typical pattern of development involved the foundation of a local College of Science by private benefaction, its gradual growth by the absorption of the local medical school and any university extension classes in arts subjects, leading perhaps to municipal support before or after incorporation as a university college. Thus these institutions developed a modern and widening curricula, and some came to embrace a day training college for teacher training. Initially much of the work was undertaken on a part-time evening basis and was often at sub-degree level. However, as university colleges they placed increasing emphasis upon full-time courses leading to London external degrees and aspired to the right to enjoy full university status themselves. For many years the Privy Council was not disposed to grant new degree-conferring powers except within a federal framework calculated to give the necessary range and stature to the institution concerned. Thus when Owens College, Manchester, failed to acquire full university status for itself during the 1870s, it was content to become the first constituent part of a new federal Victoria University (1880) which later absorbed the university colleges of Liverpool and Leeds. But the federal framework proved restrictive and during the 1890s became a growing source of conflict between the constituent parts, all of which remained very interested in the prospect of a separate charter. Meanwhile, the reconstitution of the University of London at the close of the century, which was calculated to weaken its former links with provincial institutions, introduced a new consideration for the Privy Council to take into account. Thus, when the university college at Birmingham, which had refused to join the federal Victoria University as a junior partner, applied for full status, it was acceded to as a result of the changed situation and the influential support of Joseph Chamberlain. The repercussions were almost immediate and certainly far-reaching. Within a decade six of the former university colleges acquired a royal charter as full universities; the incorporation of the University of Birmingham (1900) was followed by the elevation of Manchester (1903), Liverpool (1903), Leeds (1904), Sheffield (1905) and Bristol (1909). Thus by the outbreak of the First World War England was served by ten full universities as well as four reputable university colleges.

(iv) *University of Wales*

The emergence of a national university for Wales was seriously hindered by the prior establishment of the Anglican St David's College, Lampeter (1828), and its later acquisition of the right to confer its own theological and arts degrees. But Welsh Nonconformity ostracised this outpost of the established Church and in the second half of the century a campaign developed in favour of a quite separate and truly national university. In 1867 Hugh Owen and some other leading enthusiasts took advantage of a bankruptcy to purchase cheaply a large hotel in Aberystwyth; converted for scholastic as well as residential use, this building opened as a university college five years later. The hard financial struggle which followed resulted in Welsh members of Parliament pressing the Westminster government for aid. When the Aberdare Commission reported on *Intermediate and Higher Education in Wales* (1881) it recommended the foundation of two grant-aided university colleges for the Principality. The outcome was the establishment of the University College of South Wales at Cardiff and the University College of North Wales at Bangor (1883-4); the university college at Aberystwyth was retained to serve central Wales and each of the three institutions benefited from a State grant of £4,000 per annum. In 1893 the three colleges were drawn together to form the federal University of Wales with its own degree awards. Nevertheless, in spite of these encouraging developments, student numbers grew only slowly and it was not until after the First World War and the addition of the Swansea Technical College and the Cardiff School of Medicine that the University of Wales began to achieve real importance.

(b) Underlying Factors and Associated Features

The growth and nature of the modern universities may be more fully understood if one examines the underlying factors and associated features of their development prior to the First World War.

(i) Basic social and educational changes in the middle and later years of the nineteenth century provided an increasingly favourable platform for the rise of the modern universities. The expansion of the lower middle class and the increasing number of upper working class aspirants was producing a growing demand for higher educational opportunity, especially from the ranks of the Nonconformist community. The growth of municipal pride in the large provincial industrial towns and their association with very wealthy local industrialists provided a potential source of funds for the establishment of civic institutions devoted to higher education. The resuscitation of the endowed grammar schools and the development of higher-grade elementary education and advanced evening class tuition after 1870 gradually increased the number of students who were qualified to undertake a university education, even if their financial circumstances and occupational interests precluded them from entry to Oxford or Cambridge.

(ii) A particular aspect of Victorian change which bore upon the higher educational scene was the beginnings of the movement for the emancipation of women. This produced a limited but insistent demand that they should enjoy full rights of entry into university education and be able to obtain degrees and academic appointments. Whilst the way ahead at Oxford and Cambridge proved a long and difficult one, the rise of the modern universities and the growth of higher education for women went hand in hand. Although the foundation of Queen's College (1848) and Bedford College (1849) for women aroused much contemporary metropolitan scorn, the University of London adopted an increasingly sympathetic attitude towards their cause and in 1878 opened its degrees to women. This allowed the provincial university colleges, which usually welcomed women students from the outset, to make their London external degree courses available to them. The federal universities of Victoria and Wales were both quick to open their courses and degrees to women. In 1913 the University of London distinguished itself by appointing the first female professor to hold office in England and Wales.

(iii) The rise of the medical profession and the growing recognition of the importance of public health during the nineteenth century was another stimulus associated with the early development of the modern universities. The licensing powers conferred upon the Society of Apothecaries at the close of the Napoleonic Wars led to the establishment of medical schools in the metropolis and eight provincial towns. Those that were set up in Leeds (1826), Newcastle (1834), Manchester (1836), Liverpool (1838), Bristol (1840) and Birmingham (1841) later made a seminal contribution to the emergence of university colleges in the localities concerned. The creation in 1858 of the General Medical Council with its wide statutory powers sharpened the trend towards the standardisation of entry requirements for the profession and increased the importance of university studies in relation to medical training. The expansion of the medical schools and teaching hospitals of the modern universities was a feature of the late Victorian and Edwardian era.

(iv) The rapidly growing and changing economic needs of the country was also a most powerful underlying factor in the rise of the modern universities, especially as Oxford and Cambridge, even when reformed, responded to this particular stimulus to only a limited extent. The foreign threat to Britain's industrial supremacy was first clearly demonstrated at the Paris Industrial Exhibition of 1867; subsequent Royal Commissions investigating the state of scientific and technical education and the causes of the later depression of British trade and industry acknowledged the superiority of American and German manufacturing techniques and relevant educational provision. The need to strengthen the facilities for scientific and technical instruction was underlined and influential figures such as Lyon Playfair, Bernard Samuelson, Matthew Arnold and Sir Charles Dilke stirred up more public interest in the issue. Some wealthy industrialists began to see higher education with a utilitarian emphasis as an investment field worthy of their support. From their earliest days the new university colleges showed prior interest in the development of studies calculated to be of fairly direct benefit to local industries. Thus the Newcastle College of Science emphasised mining subjects, the Yorkshire College of Science at Leeds pushed textile studies, the Sheffield College of Science developed metallurgy, the University College of Liverpool offered commercial subjects and Birmingham Science College served the instructional needs of the west Midlands metal industries. Earlier Colleges of Sciences often formed the core of the university college at the time of incorporation, although later development usually reduced the comparative importance of pure and applied science studies. Many such colleges were initially established as the result of private benefaction by wealthy local business men. Owens College at

Manchester, the Mason Science College at Birmingham and the Firth College at Sheffield were all originally named after their founders. The University College of Bristol benefited greatly from the interest and generous financial support of the Wills tobacco family. Thus the modern universities inherited a strong connection with local and regional industry which ensured that they were always much more amenable than Oxford or even Cambridge to the development of scientific, technological and other utilitarian studies. They offered themselves as the potential source of the new meritocratic elite and intermediate personnel required by an increasingly specialised economy at the turn of the century.

(v) Another important strand in the rise of the modern provincial universities was the University Extension movement inspired by Miss A. J. Clough, a northern schoolmistress and feminist, and James Stuart, a fellow of Trinity College, Cambridge. During the 1870s the universities of Cambridge, London and Oxford successively offered their services for the support of evening and vacation courses largely in arts subjects undertaken by adult classes in the provincial towns. The response was so strong and the work involved so substantial that the resultant classes were seminal to the emergence of university colleges at Leeds, Bristol, Sheffield, Nottingham, Reading and Exeter. Where the University Extension classes were merged with an existing College of Science the result was to give a greater breadth and balance to the institution's curriculum, thus improving its ultimate chances of obtaining full university status.

(vi) The tradition and example of the Scottish universities proved a potent influence upon the constitutional and pedagogic development of the modern English university. Only in relation to the University of Wales was the federal system of organisation of lasting significance. The constitutions of other modern universities approximated to the Scottish model of a Vice-Chancellor as academic head, a university Council with a lay majority to govern matters of general policy, and a university Senate composed of academics responsible for the organisation of studies on a faculty basis. The modern universities developed overwhelmingly along non-residential lines and the lecture rather than the tutorial dominated the teaching process. A wide and progressive approach to curriculum development, which had characterised the Scottish universities since the eighteenth century, also owed something to influence from north of the border.

3 The Emergence of a National Policy for University Education

(*a*) The Beginnings of State Financial Support

The aspiring university colleges, some of which were to emerge as fully-fledged 'redbrick' universities in the early twentieth century, were faced with very serious financial difficulties during their early struggle for survival. Private benefactions, municipal support and students' fees proved insufficient to meet the high cost of adequate staffing, accommodation and facilities. Inevitably the institutions concerned turned to the State for support and in doing so sowed the seeds of national policy and a sense of unity in the field of university education. Hitherto the State had restricted itself to *ad hoc* interventions in the affairs of particular universities whenever such action seemed vitally necessary; in responding to the cry for help the State was to be inexorably drawn into a concern for university development as a whole. Faced with the need to develop an effective working relationship with their new paymaster, the universities and university colleges began to draw closer together. The first phase of this process worked itself out during the forty years prior to the conclusion of the First World War.

(i) The appeals for help by Owens College at Manchester and the University College of Aberystwyth during the third quarter of the nineteenth century were rejected on the grounds that it had never been government policy to render financial assistance for the promotion of higher education. But the subsequent payment of State grants to the Welsh university colleges following the Aberdare Report (1881) created a precedent which resulted in an intensive campaign by their English counterparts for similar treatment.

(ii) In 1889 the Salisbury government reluctantly succumbed to the pressure and granted £15,000 per annum to be distributed between University and King's Colleges, London, and the more fully developed provincial university colleges. Reading and Southampton had to wait until 1902 for inclusion and the wealthy University of Durham did not benefit fully until eight years later. The initial claim had been for a total annual grant of £50,000 and this was justified in terms of the assistance being 'calculated to contribute largely to the material prospect of the country'. The veracity of this argument gradually gained increasing support in government circles and the size of the grant rose accordingly; although only £27,000 in 1902, it had passed the £150,000 mark by the outbreak of the First World War. Nevertheless, the overwhelming proportion of requisite funds for university development were still forthcoming from other sources.

(iii) For many years the government was content to dispense the universities grant through a series of *ad hoc* committees, but following the recommendations of the Haldane Report (1905) a standing Advisory Committee was set up for the purpose. As the Treasury grant had for some time been supplemented by funds allocated by the Board of Education for teacher training and other strictly professional courses, this Advisory Committee transferred its allegiance from the Chancellor of the Exchequer to the President of the Board in 1910. Thus the stage was set for the future emergence of the permanent University Grants Committee after the war. The principle of 'block' grants for recurrent expenditure, which avoided any detailing of expenditure items and was calculated to protect the universities from undue influence, had already been clearly established.

(iv) At the close of the Edwardian period the modern universities began to benefit from yet another source of State funding. In 1909 a Development Commission was established for the promotion of scientific research likely to benefit agriculture and fisheries. In 1913 a similar government body was set up to further the cause of medical research. And finally, in 1915, under the stress of war the Department of Scientific and Industrial Research (D.S.I.R.) was created to encourage projects calculated to increase Britain's military and economic strength. All three bodies possessed considerable funds and they were to prove a real boon to the development of university postgraduate research. Significantly it was in 1917 that the doctorate degree was instituted for such work.

(v) The growing sense of unity and common purpose which developed among the modern universities as a result of their financial dealings with the State gradually found clearer expression on the eve of the First World War. Not only did the Committee of Vice-Chancellors and Principals emerge as an informal means of co-operation and collective consultation with government bodies, but the Federated Superannuation Scheme for Universities was launched to provide nationwide pension arrangements for university staff and thus facilitate the interchange of personnel. At this stage Oxford and Cambridge stood apart from such developments and continued to rely on their own financial resources.

(*b*) The Establishment of the University Grants Committee

The First World War had a considerable impact upon the fortunes of the universities and helped to shape their later development. Although their teaching function was severely contracted during the hostilities, their major contribution to wartime research and development served to underline their national importance. The stage was set for a further rise in the comparative importance of scientific study and research during the inter-war years. But this was a costly prospect, especially against the backcloth of capital deterioration and the inflationary erosion of endowment incomes during the war. Moreover, the universities faced a tremendous backlog of applicants seeking entry after the demobilisation: with Lloyd George's government having promised 'to make Britain a fit country for heroes to live in', the universities were clearly expected to accommodate the sudden rise in demand for places. Thus, when H. A. L. Fisher, the President of the Board of Education, called a meeting to consider the enlargement of the State grant it drew representatives from all the British universities, including Oxford and Cambridge. The critical outcome of the ensuing discussions was the establishment of the University Grants Committee (1919) as a permanent body responsible for assessing the financial needs of university education and advising the government upon the application of the moneys made available. Over the next half-century or more this committee was to exercise a decisive influence on university development in Britain and it is worth noting the features associated with its early operation during the inter-war period.

(i) The composition of the original University Grants Committee consisted of an eminent part-time chairman and ten academicians no longer actively connected with the recipient institutions. Those appointed were expected to combine an awareness of and a sympathy for the needs of the universities with a recognition of the proper claims and necessities of the State.

(ii) The new committee was deliberately placed under the Treasury rather than the Board of Education. The government felt that university sensitivities to the prospect of enhanced grants being accompanied by a growth of State interference would be best allayed if the committee reported to a department concerned purely with financial matters. This, however, had the long-term effect of divorcing the State's interest in university education from the development of the statutory system of education as a whole.

(iii) The principle of inspection without control was accepted by the committee and the government from the outset. The universities were visited and the grants awarded on a quinquennial basis, each institution being left to use its own block sum as it thought fit. However, the University Grants Committee could make known its views through the informal contacts resulting from regular visits or through its own official reports. For instance, the 1930 report expressed concern over the tendency to neglect the improvement of salaries and libraries in favour of the expansion of curricula; yet there was no inclination or attempt really to press the matter.

(iv) Under the auspices of the University Grants Committee, the Treasury grant for university education leapt to £1 million immediately after the First World War, and within twenty years this sum had more than doubled. During the inter-war period the Treasury grant was the largest single source of university funds, accounting for about one-third of their total income. Private benefactions and student fees continued to contribute very substantially to university finance.

In 1919 the University Grants Committee had been set up to undertake the difficult task of promoting university development within the framework of enlarged State grants and a tentative national policy without threatening the established principle of university autonomy. The combination of sympathy and efficiency with which it pursued its role had, by the eve of the Second World War, won the complete confidence of both the universities and the central government. Thus the ground was well prepared for the critical extension of the work and influence of the University Grants Committee during the post-war period.

(c) Other Developments during the Inter-War Period

The years between the wars constituted a period of consolidation and steady growth rather than one of dramatic advance in university education. There was no impressive rise in the number of university institutions: the University of Reading received its full charter (1926) and new university colleges were established at Leicester (1918) and Hull (1928). The aspirations of the pre-First World War university colleges of Nottingham, Exeter and Southampton towards fully independent status remained unrealised. But at existing university institutions there was considerable activity in the re-siting and extension of buildings and facilities, which included the provision of new science laboratories and halls of residence. This was associated with a significant rise in the number of full-time university students; with the influx of subsidised ex-servicemen the pre-war figure of 21,000 shot up to 33,000 in 1920 and by the eve of the Second World War had gradually increased to about 50,000. The great majority of students passing through the universities during the inter-war period were dependent on private means, but the opportunities for receiving public financial support were expanding quite apart from the special arrangements for ex-servicemen. The system of State scholarship awards for university attendance was introduced in 1920 and the number of scholarships offered by the universities themselves was increased, but their benefits were restricted to several hundred quite outstanding candidates. The Board of Education and the local education authorities further developed their grant support for suitable students prepared to pledge themselves to a teaching career in State schools; many able but poorer grammar school pupils obtained a university education by this means prior to the Second World War. Thus there emerged the beginnings of a more generous system of student grants.

The elitist character and liberal tradition of university education in England and Wales remained very strong during the inter-war years. State secondary grammar education remained the preserve of the better off and the extremely talented; the overwhelming majority of entrants to Oxford and Cambridge continued to be drawn from the private sector. Although the comparative importance of scientific studies and research increased, the Newmanian belief in the pursuit of knowledge for its own sake as the university's prime function might even have strengthened its hold. The continuance of applied science and technological studies as part of the university curriculum was not generally welcomed. Neither the University Grants Committee nor the increasingly influential Committee of Vice-Chancellors and Principals was keen to forge links with the major technical colleges or the teacher training colleges. Although some of the universities developed a limited association with the latter institutions through the Joint Examining Boards set up in the 1930s, they failed to respond to the overtures of Lord Eustace Percy and the Association of Teachers in Technical Institutions to accept the major technical colleges as partners in higher education. Thus the status and development of technological and advanced technical education continued to suffer and the problem was left to fester until after the Second World War.

4 The Era of Post-War Expansion and State Initiative

(a) Factors Favouring Growth After 1945

By producing a radical change in the context of national life and in the climate of public opinion, the Second World War had a critical long-term effect on the future of higher education in Britain. The post-war era featured a number of influences and developments which combined to challenge the narrow elitism and parsimony of the inter-war years and to promote a remarkable expansion and diversification of university education.

(i) *Social*

The powerful egalitarian tide unleashed by the wartime struggle underpinned the transition from political to social democracy and the marked extension of the welfare state. Equality of educational opportunity was demanded as an essential means to the achievement of social justice; the traditional practice of confining university education to a tiny social and meritocratic elite stood condemned. In order to build such a 'brave new world' out of the ashes of war the State assumed a much wider and more positive role, sustained in this respect by the strength of public support for a collectivist approach to the nation's post-war needs and problems. The State, which implemented the Beveridge proposals for social security, nationalised many of the country's major industries and launched the National Health Service, was inevitably disposed to show that much more interest in the relationship between the universities and the community at large. After the war the universities were increasingly seen, not merely as seats of academic learning, but as highly significant national institutions with a major contribution to make to overall progress. As such they deserved and received much more generous State financial backing.

(ii) *Educational*

The 1944 Act provided a much better basis for the growth of university education. The introduction of secondary education for all and the raising of the school leaving age, leading gradually to a marked rise in the number and proportion of Sixth Formers, greatly increased the supply of potential university students. Indeed, as more and more Sixth Formers came to regard a university course as the natural sequel to their schooling the demand for places grew rapidly. Such a development was facilitated by the liberal system of student grants instituted by the 1944 Act and operated by the local education authorities. In the wider sense, Butler's measure completed the establishment of the system of State education (primary, secondary and further) which had begun more than a century earlier; thus the need for the State to both encourage and co-ordinate the future development of higher education became a more pressing one.

(iii) *Economic*

Given her comparative lack of natural resources and the serious wartime loss of overseas investments, the economic future of Britain in a sharply competitive post-war world depended more than ever before upon the nation's capacity to invest in and capitalise upon human talent. At the highest level the need was to expand and realign university provision to supply the extra scientists, technologists, economists, administrators and managerial personnel required to sustain an increasingly sophisticated economy. The importance of the universities was exalted, not only in government circles and the nationalised concerns, but also in the board rooms of private industry. The direct recruitment of graduates into the higher echelons of industry and commerce rapidly gained ground at the expense of the tradition of on-the-job training for promotion to management. Industry's growing dependence on scientific and technological expertise placed a much higher premium upon a satisfactory supply of suitably qualified university graduates. The expansion of university education, if properly shaped, was seen as a national investment calculated to yield important economic benefits.

(iv) *International*

The post-war era witnessed an unprecedented growth of university education in those advanced industrial countries which were recognised as Britain's main rivals in the twin fields of economic power and political prestige. During the period 1950-64 the number of university students was trebled in France and the Soviet Union and more than doubled in West Germany, Japan and the United States. The increase for the United Kingdom (roughly 60%) was much less impressive and, in terms of the number of places provided, she fell to the bottom of the league. Such onerous comparisons were drawn by the Robbins Committee on *Higher Education* (1963) to stimulate a greater sense of urgency and to justify the further rapid growth of British university education.

(v) *Political*

Although certain post-war educational issues emerged as bones of political contention, it is significant that both of the major parties, whether in or out of government, have responded to the influences already described by consistently supporting the expansion of the universities. The initial political impetus arose out of a series of reports upon post-war reconstruction submitted during the years 1944-6; they covered agriculture (Loveday), medicine (Goodenough), dentistry (Teviot), teacher training (McNair), scientific manpower (Barlow), technological education (Percy) and social studies (Clapham), but shared common ground in their pleas for much increased university provision. The Labour ministry of Clement Attlee responded willingly and began the process by which successive governments authorised mounting State financial aid to sustain the expansion of the universities, albeit later within a widening system of higher education.

(*b*) State Initiative and Influence

Faced by a formidable array of social needs and economic problems, the post-war State took the initiative and in the national interest began to exert a much more positive influence upon the development of the universities. Inevitably the maintenance of an acceptable balance between their traditional autonomy and the claims of the government became an increasingly difficult exercise. The ever closer relationship between the State and the universities found expression in a number of ways.

(i) The universities gradually became overwhelmingly dependent upon the receipt of public funds for their maintenance and development. Soon after the Second World War the grant dispensed through the University Grants Committee was raised to over £5 million: twenty-five years later the figure had passed the £250 million mark and the Committee's grant accounted for close on 90% of total university income. Even when the erosion of money values by post-war inflation is taken into account, the growth of State financial assistance for the universities was remarkable in its proportions. Over a quarter of a century the result was to raise the university share of public expenditure on education from a tiny fraction to well over one-tenth of the total.

(ii) The state's inclination to assume a more positive role in the development of university education was implicit in the way in which the University Grants Committee's terms of reference were broadened in 1946. This body, rapidly to assume the importance if not the nature of a major government department, was henceforth to concern itself with 'the preparation and execution of such plans for the development of the universities as may from time to time be required in order to ensure that they are fully adequate to national needs' (*Hansard*, vol. 426, 30 July 1946). Of course, the government thought in terms of progress through partnership and the Committee was to proceed only on the basis of the fullest consultation with the Committee of Vice-Chancellors and Principals and individual university authorities. The University Grants Committee was significantly enlarged and its composition changed to include serving members of the university fraternity. Thereby better equipped for its post-war task, the Committee resumed its quinquennial mode of operation in 1947. The recurrent grants were made to cover a five-year period following quinquennial visitations and negotiations between the Committee and the Treasury. Although the grants were dispensed in block form, the amount awarded to an individual university was based upon previous detailed discussions and in practice left much less freedom for manoeuvre in the expenditure of the grant than might be imagined. Non-recurrent grants for capital development were tightly controlled from the start; these were determined annually by the Committee on a strict system of national priorities and were subject to Treasury approval. Nevertheless, the University Grants Committee continued to act as a buffer between the universities and the State and, in the absence of a government department directly responsible for university affairs, the universities continued to enjoy a large measure of real independence. But the growing need for a co-ordinated system of higher education made it necessary to strengthen the administrative links between the universities and the central government; in 1964 the affairs of the University Grants Committee were transferred from the Treasury to the newly created Department of Education and Science with its own universities branch. Four years later the accounts of the Committee and individual universities were opened to public inspection as a condition of grant receipt. Following the emergence of the binary system with its 'autonomous' and 'public' sectors, the 1972 White Paper underlined the fact that henceforth the universities would be allowed to continue their expansion only within the wider context of a co-ordinated system of higher education boasting an increasingly important non-university area of development. All higher educational institutions were faced with the prospect of growing government pressure for a reduction of unit costs to help facilitate further development. Thus there has been a gradual erosion of the former independence of the universities as the financial and administrative influence of the State upon their development has grown; yet the university sector has never been better provided for and the University Grants Committee continues to render a fair degree of protection against too much government interference.

(iii) The dependence of the universities upon the State was also increased by the growing support given to postgraduate work by the research councils and other government bodies and by the developing post-war system of student grants. In 1960 the Anderson Committee's Report on *Grants to Students* recommended that suitably qualified persons accepted for university first degree or equivalent courses (including teacher training) should receive mandatory awards. This was provided for by the 1962 Education Act and made for both greater uniformity and more generous provision; subject to a parental means test most university undergraduates received local education authority grants to cover their tuition fees and personal maintenance during term time. By the early 1970s grants for university students alone were costing the country some £50 million per annum.

(c) The Process of Expansion

The simplest and most significant yardstick of post-war university expansion is the growth in the number of students. Following the early impetus derived from the influx of ex-servicemen, the pre-war figure of 50,000 was gradually raised to 118,000 on the eve of the Robbins Report

(1963). The latter (for details, see Chapter 11, pages 190-5) initiated a period of more intensive growth and by 1971-2 the total had risen to 236,000. The 1972 White Paper planned for a target of 375,000 full-time university students by 1981, maintaining the proportion of postgraduates at about one-sixth. Although this involved some reduction in the prospective rate of growth, the Robbins programme for university expansion 1963-81 would in the end be significantly exceeded.

Whilst the remarkable expansion taking place after the Second World War was partly accommodated by the growth of the pre-war universities, a major contribution was made by the establishment of many new university institutions with full degree awarding powers. In the latter process three main stages may be distinguished:

(i) the emergence of the younger civic or 'redbrick' universities based on the pre-war university colleges which were now granted fully independent status. Thus Nottingham (1948), Southampton (1952), Hull (1954), Exeter (1955) and Leicester (1957) were added to the list of full universities. In 1963 the University of Newcastle-upon-Tyne became a separate entity when King's College finally ended its long association with the University of Durham;

(ii) the foundation of new 'whitebrick' universities following the success of the experimental University of Keele. The latter institution began its life in 1949 as the University College of North Staffordshire, but broke new ground by awarding its own sponsored degrees from the start. It quickly acquired the necessary stature and repute for the sponsorship arrangements to be withdrawn and for full independent status to be granted (1962). Thus emboldened, the University Grants Committee backed the idea of according full powers to new university institutions from the very outset. In the wake of the Crowther Report (see Chapter 11, pages 181-6), which had emphasised the growth of the Sixth Forms and the growing competition for university places, new foundations were established at Brighton (University of Sussex 1961), Colchester (University of Essex 1961), York (1963), Norwich (University of East Anglia 1963), Lancaster (1964), Canterbury (University of Kent 1965) and Coventry (University of Warwick 1965). They were carefully sited in relatively open country and enjoyed spacious accommodation and generous facilities from the beginning. Deliberately set apart from the great conurbations, the 'whitebrick' universities developed in settings more comparable with those of Oxford and Cambridge than those of the 'redbrick' institutions;

(iii) the elevation of the Colleges of Advanced Technology into full technological universities following the recommendation to that effect made by the Robbins Report (1963). Aston (Birmingham), Bath, Bradford, Brunel, City, Loughborough, Salford and Surrey Universities all emerged in this way during the 1960s. Meanwhile, the University of Manchester Institute of Science and Technology had achieved independent status and the Glasgow Royal College of Science and Technology had been translated into the University of Strathclyde. Thus the traditional objection to technologically-based institutions being granted university status was finally cast aside in spite of the continued opposition of conservative academicians.

All these developments produced a growing need for a rationalisation of university applications procedure and the co-ordination of university entry requirements. In 1961 the Universities' Central Council on Admissions was set up to deal with these problems on a continuing basis.

(d) Curriculum and Related Matters

Although the university sector of education came to be composed of a growing number of full status institutions with very different origins and backgrounds, the post-war period was featured by a number of general trends in the field of curricula outlook and development.

(i) The claims of science and technology at both undergraduate and postgraduate levels were increasingly acceded to as the post-war influence of the University Grants Committee gathered strength. In 1953 the sum of £15 million was earmarked for the capital development of Imperial College of Science and Technology; three years later the Committee issued a clear statement which supported the place of technological studies in the universities and encouraged a relative increase in their importance. The translation of the Colleges of Advanced Technology into full technological universities was another consequence of the breakdown of the restrictive liberal tradition which had dominated university education before the Second World War. By the late 1960s over one half of all university students were on science-based courses. However, the liberal tradition remained sufficiently strong to ensure that those university institutions vitally interested in science and technology developed their strengths within a broader setting. Thus the technological universities offer economics, business and sociological studies and have not ignored the humanities.

(ii) The post-war proliferation of specialisms has produced something of a reaction in the shape of new degree courses designed to avoid the narrowness of the traditional Honours approach. The pioneer in this respect was the University of Keele with its four-year degree course composed of a compulsory foundation course for all students, followed by an arrangement which continued to blur the arts-science divide during the final three years. The 'whitebrick' universities went on to develop a variety of progressive patterns, although the integrated degree course was not rejected in favour of the open-ended American 'credit' system. The University of Sussex forsook the orthodox faculty and departmental pattern of organisation in favour of Schools of Studies which would allow students to undertake an Honours course in a combination of subjects. Thus the study of history, language and philosophy could be associated in the schools of English, European, American, African or Asian studies. East Anglia and other new universities also joined the quest for a new and better mix which would combine breadth with depth in degree studies.

(iii) The post-war development of university teaching methods was towards a convergence of pattern. The Hale inquiry (1962), commissioned by the University Grants Committee, reported in favour of a combination of the different teaching approaches; lectures, seminars, tutorials and practical work with groups of variable size were all recommended as potentially beneficial. In the event, Oxford and Cambridge tended to move away from the one-to-one tutorial system whilst the 'redbrick' universities placed increasingly less reliance upon mass lectures. The 'whitebrick' universities have favoured the discussion approach based on relatively small sets of students. Continued faith in the benefits of communal life has found expression in the efforts made by most universities to offer a reasonable proportion of residential places; overall about one half of university students have the opportunity to reside in constituent colleges, halls of residence and hostels. However, the 1972 White Paper expressed concern over the high cost of residential places and favoured an increase in the proportion of home-based students.

(e) The Open University

This is perhaps the most revolutionary of all the post-war developments in university education. Such a possibility was first seriously mooted in public by Harold Wilson in 1963. Three years later a government White Paper developed the idea of 'a University of the Air' and led to the establishment of a special planning committee under Sir Peter Venables. The latter's report was accepted and the Open University received its charter as an independent degree-awarding institution; its first students were enrolled in 1970 and within three years totalled over 40,000. Receiving its funds largely by direct grant from the Department of Education and Science, the Open University displays a number of progressive and interesting features.

(i) Its open character is distinguished by the lack of formal entry requirements and the absence of any time limits for the successful completion of its degree courses. The cost is comparatively low and there is the possibility of students obtaining the reimbursement of some of their expenses from the local education authorities. The Open University is primarily aimed at mature adults who may, for a variety of reasons, be interested in and capable of undertaking a part-time, home-based degree course. Thus as an institution it was thoroughly populist in conception.

(ii) Its degrees are awarded on a cumulative credit system. A single credit is given for the successful completion of any one-year course; a maximum of two courses may be attempted in a given year. Six credits qualifies the student for an ordinary degree, but a total of eight is needed for an Honours award. For those who have already completed other courses of a higher educational nature there is a system of credit exemptions (maximum of three) to expedite progress. The normal student must first undertake foundation courses in any two of four main areas—'Mathematics', 'Understanding Science', 'Literature and Culture', and 'Understanding Society'. Thereafter the student has complete freedom of choice in relation to a wide range of courses offered by the faculties of Arts, Mathematics, Science, Technology, Social Sciences and Educational Studies. Thus the necessary additional credits may be accumulated within a particular faculty or along inter-disciplinary lines.

(iii) Its system of instruction is based on a combination of correspondence materials, radio and television broadcasts, tutorial and counselling help, local audio-visual study centres and short residential summer schools. The novelty and strength of the Open University lies, not in the introduction of such methods of tuition, but in drawing them together into an integrated and viable whole. Student performance is evaluated by continuous assessment, including examinations.

(iv) Its organisational framework has both central and regional dimensions. Walton Hall, at Milton Keynes near Bletchley in Buckinghamshire is the seat of the Vice-Chancellor, the Council and the Senate of the university and the location of a growing campus to accommodate many full-time academic and administrative staff. But equally important are the thirteen regional offices spread across the United Kingdom which co-ordinate the work of the Open University at the provincial level. Part-time tutors and counsellors who staff the local study centres and maintain personal contact with students come under the watching brief of full-time staff based at the regional offices.

(v) It has an interest in the development of post-experience and postgraduate courses. The former are a new departure, leading in some cases to a special certificate award, designed to help the working adult improve his skills or knowledge in a particular field through a short six-months' course. Postgraduate degrees are offered for original work leading to the submission of a satisfactory thesis. Thus the Open University is not simply concerned with undergraduate studies.

In its early years schoolteachers accounted for some 30% of the Open University's student population with professional, technical and clerical occupations accounting for a similar proportion. As the working class share of university entry had not risen significantly since the inter-war period (remaining at roughly one-quarter or rather more), many hoped that the Open University would be less dominated by the middle classes. The initial signs are not too encouraging in this respect.

Follow-up: Attempt to cover as much of the following ground as possible.
1 *Read* Curtis, S. J. and Boultwood, M. E. *An Introductory History of English Education since 1800*, Chapter XV
  Barnard, H. C. *A History of English Education from 1760*, Chapters III, IX, XIV, XXII and XXVIII
  Berdahl, R. O. *British Universities and the State*, Chapters III, IV and V
  D.E.S. Reports on Education, No. 56 of June 1969 *The Open University*
2 *Clarify the following: the shortcomings of the ancient universities in the early nineteenth century; the major reforms effected at Oxford and Cambridge during the middle and later years of the century; the nature and development of the University of London; the growth and character of the provincial 'redbrick' universities prior to the First World War; the origins of State financial support for university education; the significance of the University Grants Committee and its developing role; the nature and extent of progress in university education during the inter-war years; the factors favourable to the post-war expansion of university education 1945–70; the means by which the State strengthened its influence upon university development after the Second World War; the extent and direction of post-war university expansion (including the Open University).*

Chapter Fourteen

Schools' Curricula and Examinations

Purpose: to consider the development of curricula and examinations in the schools of England and Wales in terms of their changing nature and inter-relations, and, further, to relate this development during the nineteenth and twentieth centuries to the wider and unfolding context of pedagogic theory, institutional forms and socio-economic forces.

In the last analysis the real substance of education resides in the curriculum, by means of which the educational system is finally brought face to face with its numerous charges in the school setting. The nature of the curriculum wields a decisive influence upon what and how a child learns in school, and thereby goes a long way towards determining the benefits or otherwise of a formal education. The curriculum has its basis in a more or less conscious appreciation of the aims of the educational process; these are subject to both institutional differentiation and marked chronological change. In terms of subjects and syllabuses to be studied, learning activities or experiences to be engaged in and the methods of teaching to be used, the curriculum formulates the knowledge, skills, attitudes and values with which the school equips its pupils. The maintenance of a proper standard and pattern of work in relation to the curriculum may be secured by means of inspection or examinations or both. External examinations for schools have, over the last century or so, enjoyed great prominence; they have been used to raise or maintain standards of work in the schools, to solve administrative problems related to finance or selection and to promote or retard upward social mobility in the emerging meritocracy of the twentieth century. Whilst wielding a beneficial influence in certain respects, they gave rise to the serious and continuing danger of an externally controlled and standardised curriculum rendered insensitive to the needs of the pupil and the changing demands of society. To explore all these related matters in greater detail it is advisable to consider the curricula traditions of the public elementary and the secondary grammar schools separately, before passing on to an analysis of the modern developments which have gathered momentum and force over the last half-century.

1 The Elementary Tradition

Rooted in the class consciousness of Victorian society, the cheap and inferior traditions of the public elementary school were not seriously challenged until the early twentieth century, or officially and finally abandoned until 1944. This tradition, given clear expression in the curricula and examinations associated with the elementary school, is explicable in terms of a variety of nineteenth-century influences which only began to give ground in Edwardian times. It was in relation to the schooling of working class children aged seven to twelve years that the tradition of meanness established itself and became entrenched. From an early date the tradition was, however, diluted by the richer and more liberal heritage which shaped the development of infant education. Later on the growth of post-primary schooling added another more wholesome and promising dimension to the original tradition, thereby contributing to its gradual modification.

(a) Basic Influences

The development of the elementary school curriculum was conditioned by a number of critical influences which bore upon it during the nineteenth and early twentieth centuries.

(i) *Social*

The narrow, utilitarian curriculum of the Victorian elementary school, with its strong emphasis on the basic skills and social conditioning, reflected the determination of the propertied classes to deny the children of the poor and their teachers more than the minimal learning required to equip them for their humble station in life and to encourage an acceptance of the existing social fabric. The elementary school was a charitable institution designed to provide a very limited education for the children of those parents who could not afford to secure it independently; the middle classes were increasingly prepared to bear the cost as they recognised the contribution which such schools could make to the 'gentling of the masses' and the production of a more effective labour force. But cheapness and cost efficiency were the hallmarks demanded of these schools which had their roots in the charity schools and the schools of industry of the eighteenth century. At a time when all parents of any substance were expected to pay in full for any education received by their children, it was thought quite intolerable that philanthropic or public effort should secure anything but a markedly inferior schooling for the less fortunate or industrious sections of the community. Because they met these essential requirements, the monitorial and 'payment by results' systems were welcomed by those paying for the development of elementary education. Hence the Victorian elementary schools were inevitably characterised by large classes, spartan accommodation and facilities, a narrow and rudimentary curricula and a strict and repressive discipline. Even the teachers, with their working class background and restricted education and training, were successfully conditioned to accept the limits of their role. Indeed their long compliance with the stern requirements of the Revised Code gravely inhibited their capacity to take advantage of the more favourable climate which emerged at the turn of the century. By this time some of the basic assumptions which had differentiated the elementary school on purely social grounds were being challenged; in 1904 the elementary schools were officially recognised as a vital public service to the community at large rather than a charitable provision for working class children. As egalitarian influences wrought a gradual change in social attitudes and the collectivist philosophy wormed its way into political life, the image and work of the elementary school began to take on a more wholesome character. With the Hadow Reports of 1926-33 the process of finally abandoning the narrow social traditions of the elementary school for the developmental rationale of the modern primary school began in earnest. The curriculum was at the very centre of the changes which ensued, although more publicity has been given to the associated reorganisation of institutional forms.

(ii) *Economic*

Initially the needs of the Victorian economy reinforced the bare and narrow outlook upon elementary schooling. Employers were interested in securing the early employment of young persons who had acquired pronounced habits of industry and a working knowledge of the three Rs. Even in the later nineteenth century the nature of the economy was such that this was enough for the great bulk of the labour force. But meanwhile, amidst this economic context, there were those who were determined to protect the youngest children from the rigours of both industrialism and the typical elementary school; the result was the growth of a separate and much more enlightened native tradition of infant education. Much later the developing demands of both industry and commerce promoted the growth of post-primary education, first provided by the large School Boards in their higher-grade elementary schools and subsequently by the local education authorities in their central and junior technical schools. From 1880, in spite of much official indifference to or disapproval of such outgrowths, the national system of elementary education persistently developed various forms of post-primary schooling. This is explicable in terms of an increasingly industrialised society drawing into existence a type of school geared to providing a vocationally oriented secondary education fitted to the needs of more able young persons entering responsible employment at the age of fifteen or thereabouts. The quest was for an alternative to the secondary grammar school with its traditionally academic curricula. Such post-primary experiments involved the provision of much advanced instruction and a considerable broadening of the curriculum; both these developments were calculated to modify the original elementary tradition for the better.

(iii) *Institutional*

The basic elementary tradition was also conditioned by a number of unfavourable institutional limitations and influences. The duration of elementary schooling operated as a critical limiting factor upon the curriculum. In the middle of the nineteenth century the average school life was only two years; at its close it was still only six years. Even the benefits of the Hadow reorganisation process for senior elementary pupils after 1928 were undermined by the maintenance of a minimum school leaving age of fourteen throughout the inter-war period. Her Majesty's Inspectorate, with its literary background, wielded its early influence in favour of non-manual instruction on a limited front. The teaching of practical skills, formerly associated with the schools of industry, were squeezed out and the claims of physical and aesthetic education almost completely ignored. The die was finally cast by the Revised Code and the institution of the 'payment by results' system; designed to simplify the problem of dispensing central funds to grant-aided elementary schools and to raise the level of proficiency in the three Rs, this system placed a curricula strait-jacket upon the elementary schools which lasted for over thirty years. It was not until the turn of the century, with the abandonment of 'payment by results', the official encouragement of practical subjects and physical activity and the issue of the enlightened 1904 Elementary Code, that the institutional context became distinctly more favourable. Even then there were important residual limitations. The provision of a significant number of scholarships after 1907 for the transfer of able elementary pupils to secondary grammar schools was double-edged; whilst the preparatory tradition (hitherto centred in the private sector) was preferable to the original elementary one, it encouraged the teachers to concentrate on the needs of those pupils with scholarship potential. From the outset the demands of the emergent eleven plus examination had a distorting effect upon the curriculum of the junior classes and also became associated with the tendency to treat many senior elementary pupils as a rump, to be occupied by simply re-treading ground already covered. Happily, this latter phenomenon, officially described as 'marking time', underlined the need to give much fuller consideration to the curricula needs of the senior elementary pupil. Herein lies one of the seeds of the Hadow reorganisation and the abandonment of the elementary tradition. But, in spite of the Hadow Reports, the Board of Education continued to maintain separate sets of Elementary and Secondary (Grammar) Regulations; this helped to ensure that the secondary modern schools inherited part of the old and inferior elementary tradition.

(iv) *Pedagogic*

What passed for educational theory in the nineteenth century was also largely disposed to reinforce the aridity of the elementary tradition. The Lockian philosophy and associationist psychology of the time combined to justify an exclusively teacher-centred approach to education in which the child mind was conceived as an empty receptacle to be filled with the essentials of knowledge and the basic moral precepts. Effective learning was held to depend upon the teacher's capacity to curb the child's presumed predilections toward indolence and mischief and to present his lesson material in a systematically organised form conducive to initial assimilation and subsequent 'stamping in'. Thus the ideal teacher was the strict disciplinarian who demanded the children's constant attention and who built up their knowledge in associationist fashion by moving step by step from the simple to the complex. The question of motivation was completely ignored (apart from the sanction of fear) and the child was expected to learn by passive reception and response. The resultant regime was inevitably characterised by an unimaginative reliance on sequential rote-learning and drill methods; initially applied to the three Rs, this barren approach was later applied to other subjects of the developing elementary curriculum. Pioneered by the monitorial system, encouraged by the Revised Code and propagated by the denominational training colleges, such a pedagogy was peculiarly ill-designed to stimulate the pupil's interest in his own education.

However, by the early twentieth century various progressive influences in the field of educational theory were combining to challenge and erode the insensitive and misguided pedagogy of Victorian times. Indeed, infant education had developed a separate tradition from the early nineteenth century, based on the child-centred naturalism of Rousseau and Froebel, but adjusted to native conditions. This liberalising influence was cut off from the elementary school by the Revised Code; but after 1900, enriched by the work of the McMillan sisters and the influence of Maria Montessori, the infant tradition was able to infect the schooling of older children to some degree. Meanwhile, the ideas of Herbart, as interpreted by Sir John Adams in his *Herbartian Psychology as Applied to Education* (1897), began to wield a beneficial influence upon the elementary tradition itself. Although the Herbartian approach remained basically impressionist, the teacher was exhorted to know the child as well as the subject and to recognise the importance of sound psychology as a basis for effective teaching. The teaching of all subjects, even science, in an exclusively verbal and mechanical way was condemned; conversely the need to capitalise on the child's interest and experience and to relate one subject to another was underlined. By the time of the First World War the forces making for curricula and pedagogic change had been reinforced by the influence of Dewey and the pragmatic school of educational thought from across the Atlantic. The followers of Dewey stressed the social purposes of education; bookish learning was rejected in favour of practical pursuits, vocational studies and co-operative activities within a democratic school community. The emphasis was placed on learning by doing, based on a problem or project approach to the accumulation of useful experience. Traditional teaching methods were frowned upon and experiments involving a much more positive role for the learner were encouraged. By the inter-war period the 'New Education' movement was, in eclectic fashion, affecting practice in the elementary schools. The influences described made their mark on the tone and the recommendations of the Hadow Reports 1926-33 and thus received a degree of official blessing.

(b) The Core of the Elementary Tradition

This centred itself on the education of the seven- to ten-year-old children, who suffered most from the restricted curriculum and teaching methods of the elementary school. The monitorial system was not designed to cope with infants or to provide the individual tuition and training in practical skills which had been features of the earlier and smaller charity schools and schools of industry. Thus the monitorial school's stock in trade was mechanically to impart the rudiments of reading, writing and cyphering to children of over six who were unlikely to attend for more than two years. State involvement initially worked in favour of better provision, especially after 1846 when the aided schools began to benefit from specific grants and the pupil-teacher system. A decade later inspectors' reports were able to point to a small number of elementary schools with a comparatively liberal curricula, where the three Rs were supplemented by such subjects as grammar, history, geography, drawing, needlework and the inevitable religious instruction. However, the benefits of this were limited to the tiny minority who stayed until the age of twelve and most elementary schools were much more restricted in their scope. In 1861 the Newcastle Report publicised the fact that even the three Rs were being inefficiently taught to those pupils whose schooling was typically short in duration. The need, it seemed, was to cut out the curricula frills and concentrate exclusively on the basics.

From the Revised Code of 1862 until the end of the century, the curriculum of the elementary school was largely determined by grant earning considerations. What subjects were taught, to which children and by what means was decided by close reference to the regulations of successive Codes. Lowe's original design was to focus attention on instruction in the three Rs (together with needlework for girls) by tying two-thirds of the possible grant earnings to the results of annual examinations in these subjects. Pupils were to be assessed on the basis of Standards I-VI and the Code laid down a schedule of examinable work for each standard (see diagram, page 273). The immediate result was to stimulate the drilling of the younger and less proficient pupils to a satisfactory mastery of the three Rs and to destroy interest in more ambitious designs. Infants were exempt from the system, whilst no grants were payable for pupils over twelve. It was only gradually that Lowe's system was relaxed and it was the younger children who gained least from the changes. The study of 'specific' subjects, first introduced in 1867, was reserved for the older pupils. In 1871 military drill appeared and choral singing was added in the following year; both these activities could claim to have disciplinary benefits. In 1875 grants were offered for 'class' subjects undertaken by the whole school from Standard II upwards. Thereafter the younger children were taught grammar, geography, history and elementary science; however, any particular school was limited to two 'class' subjects and there was a strong tendency to apply the established drill methods to their teaching. Linear drawing was also introduced for all boys as a result of a recommendation of the Cross Report (1888). As the 'payment by results' system was being phased out at the close of the century, Her Majesty's Inspectorate identified the lower standards as the least satisfactory part of the elementary system.

The institution of the block grant for elementary schools (1900) opened the way to a more liberal approach. Henceforth the Board of Education was happy to place the responsibility for the curriculum squarely on the teachers, convinced that the oversight of the Inspectorate and the prevailing consensus of professional opinion was sufficient insurance against any bizarre developments. Accordingly the Elementary Code of 1904 recast the aims of the elementary school to embrace the physical, mental and character development of its pupils and the associated

Examinable Work required of Standards I–VI under the Revised Code (1862)
(as reproduced in the Board of Education report for 1910–11, page 7)

	Reading	Writing	Arithmetic
Standard I (6–7 years)	Narrative in monosyllables.	Form on blackboard or slate from dictation, letters, capital and small manuscript.	Form on blackboard or slate from dictation figures up to 20. Name at sight figures up to 20. Add and subtract figures up to 10 orally from examples on blackboard.
Standard II (7–8 years)	One of the narratives next in order after monosyllables in an elementary reading book used in the school.	Copy in manuscript character a line of print.	A sum in simple addition or subtraction and the multiplication table.
Standard III (8–9 years)	A short paragraph from an elementary reading book used in the school.	A sentence from the same paragraph slowly read once and then dictated in single words.	A sum in any simple rule as far as short division (inclusive).
Standard IV (9–10 years)	A short paragraph from a more advanced reading book used in the school.	A sentence slowly dictated once by a few words at a time, from the same book but not from the paragraph read.	A sum in compound rules (money).
Standard V (10–11 years)	A few lines of poetry from a reading book used in the first class of the school.	A sentence slowly dictated once by a few words at a time, from a reading book used in the first class of the school.	A sum in compound rules (common weights and measures).
Standard VI (11–12 years)	A short ordinary paragraph in a newspaper or other modern narrative.	Another short ordinary paragraph in a newspaper or other modern narrative slowly dictated once by a few words at a time.	A sum in Practice or Bills of Parcels.

Handbook of Suggestions (1905) officially disavowed any need for uniformity of practice in relation to curricula or teaching methods. Of course, it was pointed out that 'freedom implies a corresponding responsibility in its use'; in particular, every elementary teacher was expected to have a sound knowledge of the contents of the Board's handbook. Therein, the consensus curriculum was identified as English, arithmetic, history, geography, nature study, music, drawing, handwriting, handicrafts, needlework, housecraft, gardening and physical exercise. Although the approach was still subject-based, the breadth was such as to include considerable opportunity for practical work and aesthetic education. Unfortunately the conservatism of the teachers and the distraction of the scholarship examinations after 1907 militated against full and rapid advantage being taken of the Board's new policy. Significant improvements in the education of younger children had to wait upon the diffusion of new educational ideas and a change in organisational forms. The free place examinations and the rise of central schools encouraged the establishment of distinct junior departments in the elementary schools. It was then a short step to the Hadow arrangement of a separate primary stage of education, in relation to which the particular needs of junior children aged seven to eleven years would at last receive real consideration.

(c) Infant Development

Prior to 1870 many small children were sent to the largely inefficient and squalid dame schools inherited from the eighteenth century. But at the same time a growing number were able to attend new infant schools pioneered by such progressive spirits as Robert Owen, Samuel Wilderspin, David Stow and the Reverend Charles Mayo. To some extent indebted to the continental ideas of Rousseau and Pestalozzi, they shared an appreciation of the importance of understanding the nature of the infant as a basis for providing appropriate care and attention. Their schools combined sound habit training with open-air play activity, simple nature study, singing and rhymes and the learning of letters by such means as 'picturing out'. Thus in the first half of the nineteenth century the developmental tradition, based on a prior concern for the needs and interests of the child at a particular stage in its natural development, took root in the field of infant education and from the outset contrasted very favourably with its austere elementary counterpart. As the aided elementary schools accepted more infants they tended to treat them separately and this policy was encouraged by the Inspectorate. Accordingly they were exempt from the operation of Lowe's examinations, which allowed the infant teachers much more freedom than their colleagues and left the door open for the markedly child-centred ideas of Froebel further to develop the existing infant tradition. The 1870 Act, in specifying the age of five years as the starting point for compulsory attendance purposes, made the infant schools and departments an integral part of the national system of elementary education. This was of great potential importance, for the rich infant tradition, though held at bay for nearly forty years by the 'payment by results' system, was ultimately and inevitably able to infect the rest of the elementary school in an upward direction. Strengthened by the accession of Montessori's ideas and the nursery school movement in the early twentieth century, the infant tradition clearly influenced the reports of the Hadow Committee. Here lay the main source of the principle that education should be seen in terms of activity and experience rather than of knowledge to be acquired and facts to be stored. In 1931 Hadow recommended that henceforth it should underpin the approach to curricula and teaching methods in the reorganised junior schools for the seven-to eleven-year-olds.

(d) Post-Primary Development

The tendency for the elementary system to produce post-primary out-growths of a pseudo-secondary character was another development which helped to leaven the basic tradition. From the middle of the nineteenth century there were always some certificated elementary teachers who were interested in and capable of carrying their pupils well beyond a mere mastery of the three Rs. The beginnings of such development were cut short by the Revised Code (1862), but its later modification allowed for a rising amount of post-primary instruction. Grants were offered for a growing range of specific subjects, including algebra, geometry, English literature, French, German, botany, mechanics, physical geography and commercial studies, for pupils in Standard IV and above. In 1882 a new Standard VII was added for the twelve- to thirteen-year-olds. Out of these developments emerged the higher tops and higher-grade schools designed to provide more advanced schooling for those older pupils who were prepared to stay on. Most higher-grade schools catered for pupils of twelve and over, combining Standards VI and VII work with advanced science courses financed by the Science and Art Department. The majority of them registered as organised science schools and developed a marked vocational orientation based on the study of mathematics, practical geometry, physics, chemistry, machine construction and drawing. Pupils in the upper standards of ordinary elementary schools certainly benefited from the downward influence of the higher-grade movement: in the 1890s the Education Department introduced special grants for teaching the older pupils such practical subjects as manual instruction, cookery, laundrywork, household management, dairywork and gardening. The Inspectorate was also encouraged to take an increasingly critical view of the use of rote-learning methods in relation to the widening curricula of the upper standards.

The abolition of the School Boards and Morant's determination to enforce a rigid distinction between elementary and secondary education administered a temporary check to post-primary growth during the Edwardian period. But the development soon reasserted itself in the form of the new central and junior technical schools which had begun to emerge by the onset of the First World War. The central schools, although developed under the Elementary Code, were for pupils between eleven and fourteen or fifteen and provided an improved general education along practical lines, with an industrial or commercial bias that was never directly vocational. Their purpose was to prepare fairly able senior elementary pupils for immediate employment in workshops, warehouses and offices without the need for special intermediate training. The 1918 Act, which raised the minimum school-leaving age to fourteen and required the local authorities to provide both advanced and practical instruction for senior elementary pupils, encouraged the rise of the central schools. In 1926 their rationale and curriculum was recommended as the basis for the development of Hadow's 'new' secondary modern schools. The curricula of the junior trade, technical, commercial and art schools had a much stronger vocational flavour, although the continuance of the pupil's general education was not neglected. The junior technical school for thirteen- to sixteen-year-olds emphasised the manual skills and scientific principles related to a particular group of industries; accordingly much time was given to mathematics, science, drawing and practical instruction. Thus, under the regulations for technical institutions, there developed a post-primary dimension that was strongly vocational. The Hadow Report (1926) also accepted this as a worthwhile development and recommended its close association with the reconstituted secondary system of education.

2 The Secondary Grammar Tradition

Originally based on the Classics and later upon a liberal education rooted in the humanities, this tradition dominated the English conception of secondary education until well into the twentieth century. Indeed, until 1944 the terms 'secondary' and 'grammar' were officially regarded as synonymous. From the early nineteenth century the grammar tradition was questioned and refined, but also perpetuated, by a variety of influences that bore upon it. Its development was characterised by considerable curricula change and an associated growth of external examinations. These matters must now be considered in some detail.

(*a*) Operative Influences

These may be analysed on the same four-fold basis previously applied to the elementary tradition.

(i) *Social*

The grammar school has always drawn great strength from the fact that the education provided has been accepted as socially prestigious. In the nineteenth century a grammar education was largely restricted to those of considerable means and social standing; its links with the ancient universities, medicine, law and the Church reinforced its pretensions in the public eye. Appropriately, the curricula of the public and endowed grammar schools was calculated to differentiate their products clearly from others who might have managed to obtain some sort of elementary, technical or private education. Hence the grammar tradition centred on the provision of a liberal education of lengthy duration which emphasised learning for its own sake rather than a vulgar concern for vocational knowledge and skills. Because the Classics fitted so well into this class-conscious framework, they were able to muster much support for their retention; later on the concept of a liberal education found expression in the provision of a sound general education with a marked literary bias. The latter development, facilitated by the Secondary Regulations of 1904 and reinforced by the School Certificate examination (1917), was in accord with certain social forces at play in early twentieth century English society. As the State system of secondary education developed after 1902, the influence of graduate teachers and aspiring parents worked in favour of an academic curriculum with its social prestige and economic benefits. As a sound general education was the minimum requirement for entry into the professions and other white-collar occupations, the State secondary schools were under considerable pressure to ignore technical and vocational education of a practical character. Once the free-place system began to widen secondary opportunity, the Labour movement was insistent that able working class children should receive a proper grammar education rather than any vocationally oriented alternative.

The rise of the middle classes and the emancipation of women were two other important social factors wielding considerable influence upon the development of the secondary grammar tradition. In the early nineteenth century the middle class, with its largely utilitarian and modern frame of mind, criticised the Classical curriculum of the public and endowed grammar schools and gave support to the more progressive private academies and schools. The subsequent broadening of the grammar school curriculum was partly attributable to middle class pressure, although the claims of a thoroughly vocational approach were successfully resisted. Meanwhile, the growth of higher education for women and secondary schooling for girls reinforced the process of broadening the curriculum. Unfettered by tradition and prejudice, the girls' high schools, which grew markedly in number after 1868, were responsive to new ideas from the outset and readily accepted reforms in curricula and methods of teaching. They showed an early recognition of the need to allow older pupils a choice of curricula pattern and of the importance of aesthetic and practical subjects. The early growth of professional training for secondary teachers rested upon the interest and support of their headmistresses.

(ii) *Economic*

The changing nature and needs of the economy exerted an influence upon the development of secondary provision, but the impact on the grammar tradition was limited rather than marked. In economic terms the quasi-vocational type of secondary schooling pionered by the higher-grade schools and other post-primary developments offered the most direct benefits, but down to 1944 the grammar tradition successfully resisted serious incursions of this sort. Of course, the economic factor helped slowly to undermine the position of the Classics in favour of a more broadly based general education. Indeed, the increasingly important tertiary occupations found such a general education a most suitable basis for the further training of their employees and therefore supported the academically oriented School Certificate examinations of the inter-war period. In contrast to commerce and the professions, manufacturing industry was largely content to rely on early recruitment and on-the-job training, even for those destined to hold responsible positions; the result was that the grammar tradition was not put under any great pressure to change its face from this source. The late nineteenth-century tendency, emanating from the work of the Science and Art Department and the Technical Instruction Committees, for technical instruction to infiltrate the grammar tradition was checked after 1900 and the two developments went their separate ways. But the economic factor embraced a concern for the claims of scientific education as well as technical instruction and in this respect helped to bring about real change. Under the direct pressure of the 'scientific movement', drawing strength from the growth of foreign competition, the grammar curriculum granted a significant place to the study of pure science subjects. This development was facilitated by the fact that such studies of a non-vocational nature could be fairly easily incorporated into the basic conception of a liberal education. Similarly, the study of modern languages, albeit with their prospective commercial utility, could be absorbed without difficulty.

(iii) *Institutional*

The largely static and unsatisfactory condition of the grammar school curriculum in the first half of the nineteenth century was partly the result of founders' statutes determining both the studies undertaken and the methods of instruction used. The advantage of endowments made the grammar schools less susceptible to outside pressures than private establishments wholly dependent on paying custom. However, from the 1860s various institutional pressures combined to produce piecemeal and limited curricula reform. The influence of the Clarendon (1864) and Taunton (1868) Reports and the subsequent work of the Schools Commissioners appointed to reform both governing bodies and trust deeds, slowly served to widen the curriculum and raise standards of staffing and attainment during the last quarter of the century. But it was not until after 1902 that the grammar tradition became subject to the strong influence of a single central institution. With the launching of the State system of secondary education, the new Board of Education opted for the 'grammar' model and determined to regulate the curriculum to ensure the provision of a sound general education. Morant's decision to abandon the pupil-teacher system and use the new secondary schools as a preparation ground for teacher training certainly put a premium on the mounting of academic courses compatible with the basic grammar tradition. The Secondary Schools Regulations of 1904 were drawn up accordingly and throughout the inter-war period the Board was content to secure the situation by supporting the development of a School Certificate examination calculated to ensure the neglect of practical and vocational subjects in the grammar school curriculum. In spite of the Hadow reorganisation, the Board continued to issue separate and distinctive regulations for the State grammar schools; this also helped to insulate them from quasi-vocational and other non-academic influences.

But the main single institutional influence to affect the development of the grammar tradition was that of external examinations. From the middle of the nineteenth century public examinations developed rapidly as a means of countering patronage and influence, of raising standards of competence, of controlling entry to various occupations and of searching out the sort of talent upon which the nation's future was increasingly recognised to depend. A major aspect of this development was the growth of external examinations for secondary schools. The ancient universities, which benefited from the use of written examinations to reform themselves, began to set external examinations for secondary pupils in 1858.

K

Over the next half-century several University Examining Boards developed both matriculation and certificate examinations which were embraced by most of the public and grammar schools as a goal for their pupils. Meanwhile, various professional occupations designed their own entry examinations for secondary pupils. The result was double-edged; whilst the curriculum was broadened in response to the examiners' interest in a sound general education, the existence of so many different syllabuses and requirements made for serious difficulties in the organisation of the teaching. In 1917 agreement reached between the University Examining bodies and the Board of Education resulted in the introduction of the School Certificate and Higher School Certificate examinations. Enjoying national currency from the outset, they combined to entrench the grammar school's preoccupation with an academic curriculum and to encourage the development of Sixth Form specialisation. Throughout the period the trend was towards external examinations exerting a quite decisive influence upon the nature of secondary grammar curricula and teaching methods; this influence was latterly supportive of traditional forms rather than progressive change.

(iv) *Pedagogic*

A critical influence which supported the maintenance of a grammar curriculum at once both academic and common to all pupils was the faculty psychology of the nineteenth century. This held the human mind to be composed of separate faculties, all of which could be trained to a high level of efficiency as the result of sustained and appropriate mental exercise. The ultimate product was the trained mind which could then turn itself successfully to any activity. The proponents of faculty psychology further believed that there were certain forms of study which were eminently suitable for the training of the various faculties. Initially they emphasised the prior position of the Classics (especially Latin) for developing the powers of memory and verbal accuracy; later on mathematics was enthusiastically approved for its potential in developing reasoning powers and the sciences were accepted for their capacity to develop the power of observation. Conversely, practical and vocational subjects were rejected as narrow and incapable of supporting the sort of mental training that was transferable to other areas. It was not until the turn of the century, when educational psychology began to assume a scientific basis and the transfer of training theory was upset, that faculty psychology began to suffer a decline in influence. By the inter-war period the ideas of Dewey were challenging the notion of a hierarchy of secondary subjects and pressing the claims of non-academic activities. But as late as 1938 the Spens Report, in so many ways progressively disposed, strongly supported Latin as the second language for any respectable grammar school and even bemoaned the serious decline in the study of Greek.

Reforming headmasters made a growing impact on the development of curricula and methods. Outstanding in this respect were Thring of Uppingham and Sanderson of Oundle whose combined headships spanned the years 1853 to 1922. Edward Thring pioneered the development of English and aesthetic subjects such as music and art as integral parts of the grammar tradition; his influence was also responsible for the acceptance of a wide range of extra-mural activities as an essential part of a healthy school life. His book *The Theory and Practice of Teaching* (1883) helped to stimulate the beginnings of interest in matters of technique and professional training among the reluctant schoolmasters. Sanderson was an opponent of sedentary classroom studies who stressed the importance of pupil interests and motivation. His school developed both science and workshop practice, whilst a more creative approach was applied to the teaching of English, history and geography. By the early twentieth century the University Education Departments were emerging to add their weight in favour of greater enlightenment. To the prospect of professional training for secondary teachers they gave a new respectability. Whilst supporting the provision of a sound general education as the grammar school's basic role, they contributed to a considerable improvement of teaching methods in the various academic subject areas.

(*b*) Changes in Curricula and Method

In the mid-nineteenth century the Classics and associated elements of history and geography dominated the secular curriculum of the public and endowed grammar schools. In 1937 the majority of grammar school pupils entered for the School Certificate examinations offered English, French, mathematics, history, geography and at least one science subject; half of the entrants offered Latin or art which completed the basic curriculum designed to afford a sound general education. Thus a century of development simply broadened the essentially academic basis of the grammar tradition. Although the position of Classics was irreparably damaged by the virtual disappearance of Greek, the influence of official policy and university matriculation requirements ensured the widespread retention of Latin. Meanwhile, the study of English, in terms of both language and literature, secured a prime place in the curriculum; initially the emphasis was on formal grammar and philology, but gradually the literary and creative dimensions received more attention. History won early recognition as a subject worth adding to the original Classical core, but for many years its teaching suffered from too much rote-memory work at the intermediate stage. However, Dr Keatinge's source method and the professional influence of the Historical Association helped to improve the situation in the early twentieth century. Geography slowly established itself as a basic subject, although it was not until after 1900 that a major transformation of substance and method made it a worthwhile field of study. By the time of the First World War, English, history and geography had clearly emerged as the new 'humanities' core of the grammar curriculum. In complementary fashion, mathematics emerged as a vital subject and developed its several distinct branches; the abandonment of Euclid, which had supported a highly abstract and syllogistic approach to mathematical study, opened the way to beneficial changes of substance and method pioneered in the Edwardian period. It was not until the 1880s that the natural sciences began to make rapid headway in the grammar schools. At first their teaching suffered from a verbal approach encouraged by the written examinations of the day; the result was a sharp reaction in favour of H. E. Armstrong's 'heuristic method' which expected the pupil to assume the position of the scientific discoverer. Of course, whilst emphasising the practical nature of the sciences, this proved too ambitious and finally led to a more reasonable compromise in the inter-war years. The study of science was developed through its separate disciplines, with chemistry, physics and biology enjoying widespread support. Modern languages, especially French and to a much lesser extent German, became the third essential element in the developing curriculum. In this field the introduction of the direct method after the turn of the century was double-edged; it stimulated the first serious interest in the question of how best to teach foreign languages, but generally proved too demanding for all but the best teachers and ablest pupils. Yet here were the seeds of the modern audio-visual technique of language teaching. In the late nineteenth century drawing forced its way into the curriculum of some grammar schools: subsequently and predictably it was creative art rather than linear drawing that won a significant place in a general education. Other subjects to establish their presence in the broadened curriculum were religious knowledge and music. Of the various practical subjects, which later laid claim to inclusion, only domestic science for girls assumed any importance prior to the Second World War.

(c) The Development of Secondary Examinations

The growing influence of external examinations on the grammar school curriculum, initiated in the late nineteenth century, finally crystallised itself in the shape of the School Certificate after the First World

War. The process may be considered in terms of three successive developments:

(i) *The Emergence of the University Examining Boards*

It was the Oxford and Cambridge Local and the University of London Matriculation examinations, dating from 1858, which first affected the secondary schools. Half a century later there were eight University Examining Boards, the most important addition being that of the Northern Universities' joint body in 1903. The attraction of qualifications and certificates enjoying wide public esteem, and the policy of the Charity Commissioners to make external examinations obligatory for the reformed grammar schools, ensured an expanding custom. Initially the university bodies set their examinations without reference to the schools, with a particular interest in establishing their own matriculation requirements. Later on they developed school leaving certificate examinations that took account of the school context and were associated with a system of inspection. Their reputation was such that the competition of such bodies as the College of Preceptors, founded and controlled by teachers, ultimately proved unavailing. Their influence both raised the standards of work and widened the curriculum of the schools concerned. But the fact that each university body worked independently without provision for any sort of equivalence combined with the growth of Civil Service and professional entrance examinations to produce a jungle of alternatives for the schools to face. This posed serious difficulties for the organisation of viable courses to suit different needs.

(ii) *The Incursion of the Board of Education*

Once the State began to develop its own system of secondary schools, the University Examining Boards were forced to take account of the policy of the Board of Education which immediately exercised its right to control the curriculum in aided schools. The 1904 Secondary Schools Regulations required the grammar school to provide a general education based on a minimum four-year course of graded instruction commencing at about twelve years of age. The course was to provide for the study of English language and literature, history, geography, mathematics, science, at least one foreign language, physical exercises and either manual work or housewifery. The initial three humanities subjects were to receive a combined total of not less than 9 hours per week. Mathematics and science were allocated a minimum of $7\frac{1}{2}$ hours, of which at least 3 hours were to be devoted to the latter. A single foreign language received $3\frac{1}{2}$ hours, whilst two obtained 6 hours; where a second language was studied, the omission of Latin needed the Board's express approval. No pupil was to be presented for external examinations below the age of fifteen years and the whole framework was guaranteed by general inspections. Although the University Examining bodies had to work within the set context, the Board's rejection of the quasi-vocational curricula of the higher-grade schools in favour of a strongly academic orientation was most acceptable. But the problem of so many unco-ordinated examinations for secondary schools remained; this the Board referred to the Consultative Committee for a solution and a far-reaching report was submitted in 1911. The report's main recommendations underlined the pressing need for rationalisation and identified the existing University Examining Boards as the best available means for the establishment of a State-sponsored system of secondary examinations. This set the stage for prolonged negotiations between the Board of Education, the universities and certain other interested parties.

(iii) *The Establishment of the School Certificate (1917)*

Once the majority of professional bodies accepted the principle of equivalence and the University Examining Boards agreed to co-ordinate their activities, the Board of Education was able to launch the School Certificate and Higher School Certificate examinations. The former was designed for pupils of sixteen years and was underpinned by the ideal of a sound general education. Accordingly the award of the certificate was tied to success in a minimum of five subjects, including at least one from each of three groups—the humanities, foreign languages and mathematics/ science. A fourth group, including art, music, domestic science and other practical subjects, was recognised by the Board, but was accepted for certification purposes only slowly and reluctantly. In the 1930s it became possible to secure a School Certificate which included two Group IV subjects; but as many pupils found success in a foreign language beyond them, the group system itself came under growing criticism. Meanwhile, the situation was exacerbated by the fact that the examination was from the outset used for matriculation as well as school leaving purposes. The strictly academic subjects, if passed at credit level, counted for university entrance requirements. As matriculation was a well known level of attainment before 1917, many employers demanded it from secondary school leavers and headteachers were under considerable parental pressure to organise the curriculum so as to present this possibility to the pupils. Thus the School Certificate, the basic pattern of which conformed to the desires of the universities, came to exert a dominant and over-academic influence upon the curriculum of schools whose range of ability was now widening. Thus in 1938 the Spens Report recommended the severance of the School Certificate from the question of matriculation and more freedom of subject choice for entrants. The

Secondary School Examinations Council, set up in 1917 to oversee and co-ordinate the work of the eight examining bodies on behalf of the Board, instrumented these changes on the eve of the Second World War. At last the long preoccupation with a rigidly academic and general education was under serious challenge.

The Higher School Certificate, based on specialised examinations in the Classics, modern studies or science and mathematics, contributed to the steady growth of grammar school Sixth Forms during the inter-war period. But the curriculum conflict between those aiming at university entrance and other Sixth Formers was already emerging and led to the introduction of subsidiary subjects.

3 Modern Developments

During the last half-century, and especially in the post-war years, the whole question of curriculum and examinations moved to the very centre of the educational stage. The issues involved enjoyed more attention and concern than ever before and the result was a large number of new and quite major developments in the field concerned.

(a) Changing Context

Social, economic, institutional and pedagogic factors now came to exert a growing influence in favour of progressive change. Curriculum and examinations could not be unaffected by the introduction of secondary education for all, the raising of the school leaving age to fifteen and then sixteen, the substantial increase in voluntary staying on and the impressive growth of Sixth Forms. The constraints of the tripartite system and the eleven plus examination were of critical importance for many years; the rise of the comprehensive tide and the retreat of the eleven plus were even more significant. Equality of educational opportunity was increasingly seen in terms of an open system of education providing a broad and varied curriculum which would encourage and enable the individual pupil fully to extend himself without the constriction of premature examinations or rigid curricula patterns. The ideal was to subordinate both curricula and examinations to the needs and interests of the pupil; such an outlook inevitably challenged the traditional academicism of the grammar schools and the dominant influence of the universities on secondary examinations. Educational theory widened its dimensions and increased its stature. The developmental approach to learning, essentially child-centred in its basis, drew much of its growing strength from educational psychology. Philosophy of education showed much more interest in the social aims of education and their curricula implications. Sociology of education and curriculum development gradually emerged as new and influential disciplines. The three year certificate course ultimately gave the training colleges the time to infect many of their students with progressive ideas related to curricula and method. At a higher level many official reports, notably those of Hadow, Spens, Norwood, Crowther, Beloe, Newsom and Plowden, gave considerable attention to curriculum matters. Two critical results were the displacement of the School Certificate by the General Certificate of Education and the development of the Certificate of Secondary Education for less able pupils. Finally, the new found concern for curricula reappraisal found expression in the establishment and work of the Schools Council for the Curriculum and Examinations (1964).

(b) Rise of the Modern Primary School

The primary school for five- to eleven-year-old children, institutionally the product of the Hadow reorganisation process, inherited the mixed legacy of three different traditions. The elementary tradition emphasised a narrow and formal approach based on the three Rs, the preparatory tradition associated with the educational ladder stressed academic preparation for the subsequent secondary stage, whilst the developmental tradition of the infant schools rested upon a paedocentric concern for the nature and needs of the child at particular stages of growth. The rise of the modern primary school is, to a large extent, the story of the gradual triumph of the developmental tradition over its less wholesome counterparts. The Hadow Report on *The Primary School* (1931) struck a futuristic and progressive note when it insisted that junior schooling should be seen in terms of activity and experience rather than of knowledge to be acquired and facts to be stored. A recognition of the educational needs and interests of childhood and a prior concern for general all-round development were to underpin the curriculum. The report stressed the need for much more creative and expressive activity; simple craftwork, drawing, painting, poetry, music, dance and drama were identified as areas of outstanding potential in this respect. The efficiency of subject-centred teaching was brought into question and qualified support was given to the topic or project approach. But it was emphasised that the mastery of the three Rs remained indispensable and should be secured by regular and systematic practice. The importance of adequate space, equipment, library facilities, audio-visual aids, playing fields and outside visits to the prospective success of the 'new' junior school was also made plain.

The broadening and humanising process in primary education, drawing its main inspiration from the 1931 report, made slow but sure headway, in spite of certain obstacles being placed in its way. The influence of the eleven plus examination and the logistical priority given to the later stages of education after 1944 were both unfavourable. The widespread adoption of streaming in the junior schools produced a certain rigidity which encouraged the continuance of the traditional class-teaching approach. But after 1960 the retreat of the eleven plus, the work of the Schools Council, the influence of the Plowden Report and new departures in school design combined to quicken the pace of change. The policy of 'priority for primaries' in terms of resources, introduced in 1970, and the final emergence of a much improved staffing situation were also calculated to help. Thus the modern primary school is increasingly characterised by the integrated day, the project approach, unstreamed classes, open-plan arrangements, junior school French, group activities and individualised learning techniques. Its generally happy atmosphere is a stark contrast to the austerity of the old elementary school.

(c) Secondary Curricula and the G.C.E. Examinations

The principle that secondary examinations should grow out of the curriculum, which the Board of Education had subscribed to as early as 1918, remained an unrealised ideal throughout the inter-war years. The group-based School Certificate came to determine the grammar school curriculum in a very rigid way; the outcome was a strongly academic stereotype, favoured by the University Examining Boards with their matriculation interests, but far too demanding and unsuitable for the majority of pupils. It was the gradual recognition of the serious defects and distorting influence of the School Certificate which paved the way for the introduction of the much more flexible, subject-based General Certificate of Education. But the new examinations did not prove ideal and wielded an adverse influence upon the curriculum in other directions. For the abler pupil the former rigidity of secondary courses gave way to a developing and disturbing imbalance. This broad course of change may be illuminated by reference to a number of developments.

(i) *Spens Report on Secondary Education (1938)*

This accepted the Hadow principle that the purpose of secondary education is to provide for the needs of pupils entering and passing through the stage of adolescence. The idea that the grammar school curriculum should be designed to give a foundation course for Sixth Form work and perhaps university entry was firmly rejected. The relegation or neglect of creative, practical and vocational subjects was severely criticised. The recommended curriculum strategy was that of a wide-ranging common core of subjects for the eleven- to thirteen-year-old pupils, followed by differentiation through options according to pupil interests and strengths. Inevitably the report underlined the need to alter the shape of the School Certificate and to detach it from the question of matriculation requirements. This set the stage for a more intensive investigation of the whole area by the Secondary School Examinations Council.

(ii) *Norwood Report on Curriculum and Examinations in Secondary Schools (1943)*

This gave clear and almost unqualified expression to the principle that examinations should follow the curriculum and not determine it. On the curriculum it echoed the views of Spens: although strongly in favour of tripartite arrangements, the Report insisted upon the need for each type of secondary school to provide a variety of courses within it. But its recommendations for the future of secondary examinations were much more radical than Spens. Firstly, it was suggested that there should be a planned move to a system of internal examinations for sixteen-year-old secondary pupils. Such examinations would be conducted by the teachers themselves on the basis of syllabuses and papers designed by them; the main guarantee of standards would be the oversight of an enlarged inspectorate. Secondly, it was recommended that for an interim period the School Certificate should continue in a much modified form. The University Examining Boards were to operate through sub-committees containing a strong contingent of teachers and pupils were to be allowed to offer any number and combination of subjects. Finally, the existing Higher School Certificate was to be abolished in favour of a new dual arrangement. An eighteen plus qualifying external examination would be provided for the majority of Sixth Formers; a separate selective examination would be mounted for scholarship purposes. Both would be based on a narrow range of chosen subjects studied in depth. Thus in the Norwood Report lay the seeds of a more flexible and teacher-controlled examination system, but also of a secondary curriculum weakened by lack of balance and too much specialisation.

(iii) *Adoption of the General Certificate of Education*

The Ministry's decision to exclude the University Examining Boards from representation on the reconstituted Secondary School Examinations Council (1946) seemed to portend the onset of really radical reforms. In the event, however, the Norwood policy was seriously compromised because neither the Ministry nor the teachers were prepared to support an internal system of examinations for the grammar schools. The need to maintain standards and the external currency of any certificate offered finally won the day; in this respect their inhibitions simply reflected the attitudes of employers, parents and pupils. In 1947 the die was cast. A new General Certificate of Education (G.C.E.) based on external examinations was to replace the old School Certificate. Although the University Examining Boards were to administer the examinations at Ordinary, Advanced and Scholarship levels, they were to be bound by much more flexible arrangements designed to benefit the pupil and free the curriculum. The G.C.E. was to be a subject examination with no conditions laid down in respect of the number or nature of the subjects to be taken. A pass in only one subject would secure a certificate. Individual as distinct from class entries were permissible. Papers could be taken at more than one level at a single sitting. It was possible to by-pass the Ordinary level and take only the Advanced papers in any given subject area. But the removal of the restrictions formerly associated with the group-system was to some extent counter-balanced by the raising of the qualifying pass standard from 33% to 45%. The new examinations were first held in 1951; although they bestowed considerable benefits and enjoyed a rapidly growing custom, they were soon beset by their own problems and shortcomings in relation to the curriculum.

In spite of all the good intentions, the G.C.E. developed something of the character of the School Certificate. The universities adjusted their matriculation requirements to correspond to five Ordinary levels, including English language and mathematics or an approved science and a foreign language, and two Advanced levels. For the ablest pupils this became the minimum target and inevitably affected the schools' approach to the curriculum. The less academic grammar pupils were once again the main sufferers. But once the growth of the Sixth Forms made competition for university places increasingly cut-throat a further distortion emerged. The rising demands of the universities in a sellers' market put a high premium on narrow specialisation; the temptation was to rush able pupils through Ordinary level on a restricted front in order to allow three years' intensive study of two or three Science or Arts subjects. The ideal of a general education gave way to the competitive advantages of an imbalanced curriculum. The Advanced level qualifying examination became an instrument of selection, with growing emphasis being placed upon an expanding body of detailed factual knowledge. In this context the needs of the non-university Sixth Former were largely neglected. Although the Crowther Report (1959) drew attention to the deteriorating situation and insisted on the need for more university places, it was unprepared to make any radical attack upon Sixth Form specialisation as such. The better use of minority time was a palliative rather than a solution and so the problem of the Sixth Form curriculum was left for the Schools Council to grapple with later on.

(*d*) Secondary Curricula and the C.S.E. Examinations

For many years the central authority and the teachers concerned con-
curred in the view that the secondary modern schools should remain
free of external examinations so as to ensure the unrestricted development
of their curriculum. The Hadow Report (1926) recommended that this
curriculum should afford a general education, characterised during the
final two years by a practical and realistic bias. However, the secondary
modern school was not to concern itself with any directly vocational
work. Thus from the outset it lacked the academic prestige of the
grammar school or the utilitarian appeal of the technical school. Unable
to find a distinctive and meaningful curriculum for itself, the modern
school began to content itself with a diluted and truncated version of
grammar school courses. In search of a clear goal and determined to earn
some measure of public esteem, a growing number of modern schools
began to enter their pupiils for external examinations and by the 1950s
this tide was running strong. In 1955 the Ministry abandoned its policy of
discouraging G.C.E. entries from the secondary modern schools. But
as only a few modern pupils were able to reach the standard required,
others were entered for external examinations run by such bodies as the
College of Preceptors, the Royal Society of Arts and the Union of
Lancashire and Cheshire Institutes. The attractions of these national and
regional examinations served to nullify the Ministry's policy of encouraging the modern schools to develop purely local examinations on an
internal basis. Alarmed by the growing influence of examining bodies
over which it had no control, the Ministry was forced to consider the
prospect of an officially sponsored system of external examinations. The
Crowther Report (1959) supported such an idea and meanwhile the
Secondary School Examinations Council considered the possibility. The
resultant Beloe Report on *Secondary School Examinations other than G.C.E.*
(1960) was the turning point. In conjunction with the more specific
proposals of the Lockwood Report of two years later, its main recommendations provided the basis for the development of the Certificate
of Secondary Education (C.S.E.) Designed for pupils of average ability
completing a five-year course in secondary modern and comprehensive
schools, the C.S.E. system of examinations was characterised by a
number of radical features.

(i) From the outset the new system was teacher controlled. Although
the governing bodies of the fourteen Regional Examining Boards
included representatives of local education authorities, Area Training
Organisations, further education and employers, the actual conduct
of the examinations was delegated to committees of serving
teachers.

(ii) The Regional Examining Boards and their executive committees adopted a flexible approach by offering the schools and their teachers three major options. Under Mode 1 pupils could simply be entered for external examinations based on syllabuses set and published by the Boards. Under Mode 2 the Boards set examinations on syllabuses devised by the schools, either individually or on a group basis. Under Mode 3 the syllabuses were determined and the examinations set and marked internally by the schools, subject only to the external moderation of the Board.

(iii) To allow and encourage pupils of less than average ability to take isolated papers, the C.S.E. examinations were run on a subject rather than a group basis. The growing range of practical and vocational subjects offered and the development of course assessment, project work, objective and oral testing as part of the examining procedures ensured that the C.S.E. did not become a pale replica of the G.C.E. Even the traditional pass/fail concept was abandoned; a five-point scale (Grades 1-5) was used to categorise results, with those falling below the minimal standard being ungraded. For comparability purposes the C.S.E. Grade 1 was soon equated with a G.C.E. pass at Ordinary level.

Responsibility for admission requirements and for the maintenance and co-ordination of standards was vested in the Secondary School Examinations Council. The comparability of results between the different Regional Boards was safeguarded by statistical means and by inter-regional liaison. The C.S.E. examinations were well received and the prospect of the raising of the school leaving age in 1972-3 helped to draw mounting support. As a revolutionary departure designed to provide less able pupils with a worthwhile examination goal without the usual backlash effects on the curriculum, the C.S.E. deserved and obtained an enthusiastic response from the schools. The growth of public interest and confidence in a system which implies that teachers can be trusted reliably to assess their own work has, however, been somewhat tardy rather than really encouraging.

(e) The Schools Council for the Curriculum and Examinations

One of the most notable post-war events in the development of English education was the establishment of the Schools Council in 1964. The nature and role of this influential body may be considered in terms of its origins, constitution and actual work in the related fields of curricula and examinations.

(i) *Origins*

During the first half of the twentieth century a large measure of consensus existed upon what should be taught in the schools, allowing the central authority to accord considerable curricula freedom to the profession. But this consensus then began to give way before the rise of modern methods in the primary sector and innovation in non-selective secondary schools. In this new context the Secondary School Examinations Council found the exclusion of the curriculum from its direct terms of reference a serious embarrassment. In 1962 a Curriculum Study Group was set up within the Ministry to offer information and guidance to both the schools and the Examinations Council. A mixture of interest and suspicion then led to the appointment of a Working Party, led by Sir John Lockwood, to consider the desirability and possible form of new co-operative machinery for both curriculum and examinations. The Lockwood Report resulted in the establishment of the Schools Council which took over the functions of the Examinations Council and the Curriculum Study Group.

(ii) *Constitution*

The Schools Council is an independent body equally financed by the central and local education authorities. The constitution requires that each of the Council's main committees must include a majority of teachers nominated by their associations. This is to ensure that the potential influence of the Schools Council rests upon a professional basis acceptable to serving teachers. The organisation of the Schools Council consists of a complex structure of inter-related committees. Ultimate responsibility for policy is lodged with a large Governing Council, which is backed by a Programme Committee responsible for the determination of priorities. There are three Steering Committees concerned with the curriculum and its development: as they relate to the age ranges two to thirteen years, eleven to sixteen years and fourteen to eighteen years respectively, their interests obviously overlap. The second Steering Committee also operates as the co-ordinating body for secondary examinations. There are two committees exclusively concerned with examinations. The First Examinations Committee embraces both the G.C.E. Ordinary level and the C.S.E. by means of separate sub-committees. The Second Examinations Committee is concerned with school examinations beyond the sixteen plus level. There are also some fifteen Subject Committees ranging from English to the social sciences; these are interested in both the curriculum and examinations as they relate to particular subject fields. Finally, there is a Publications Committee and a number of separate committees for Wales.

(iii) *Curriculum Development*

The Schools Council's main interest is in the review and reform of the curriculum, in accordance with the principle that each school must retain both freedom and responsibility for its own work. Although there are dangers in the existence of a central body with a vested interest in change, this is counter-balanced by the Schools Council having to proceed by persuasion. In its first ten years of life, aided to a significant degree by the Nuffield Foundation, the Council straddled the whole field of curriculum development and closely related matters with a spate of working party enquiries and sponsored projects. The latter were most numerous in relation to the teaching of English, the humanities and the sciences; many emerged from the Council's major programme of work concerned with preparation for the raising of the school leaving age. An official Curriculum Development Project (e.g. Nuffield Secondary Science) is often a most ambitious and prolonged affair. An initial investigation of aims and practice in a particular area of the curriculum is followed by the creation of new materials by a Council team of teachers and professional aides. The materials are then put on trial in pilot schools and revised according to reactions and experience. Before being published for general use, the project and its materials are introduced to a wider audience through special courses and conferences. The final possibility is that of later evaluation and modification in the light of feedback from ordinary users. The Field Officers appointed by the Council and the teachers' centres provided by the local education authorities operate as a two-way link between head office and the schools.

It is both too difficult and too early to evaluate the impact of the Schools Council upon curricula and teaching methods. Whilst it is obviously a major source of influence in favour of change, many of its ideas are either costly to implement, unsuitable for large classes, or too emancipationist to attract the average teacher. The sheer output of papers and projects may also be calculated to overawe rather than inspire many of the Council's potential customers.

(iv) *Examinations*

Apart from presiding over the introduction of the C.S.E. examinations in 1965 and securing their regional comparability and national currency during the early years of development, the Schools Council concerned itself with the exploration of other needs and possibilities associated with secondary examinations.

A high priority was given to the reform of Sixth Form curricula and examinations. Convinced of the need to broaden the curriculum and make it more suitable to the widening range of Sixth Form abilities and aspirations, the Schools Council forged close links with the Standing Conference on University Entrance to tackle the problem. Following the rejection of the initial 'Q' and 'F' recommendations in 1970, the Joint Working Party produced its 'N' and 'F' proposals three years later. This scheme provided for an eighteen plus examination based on a normal programme of five subjects, two of which might be studied in greater depth. Whilst the Normal level would secure breadth, the Further level would allow limited scope for specialisation. A parallel proposal was that a new Certificate of Extended Education should be introduced at Sixth Form level to cater for the needs of pupils previously obtaining C.S.E. Grades 2-4. This would be based on seventeen plus examinations conducted under the three Modes already developed by the C.S.E. Boards. If these ideas materialise the Sixth Form curriculum will change very considerably in the years ahead.

The prospect of a common system of examining at sixteen plus gradually emerged as the Council's other major concern. The co-existence of the G.C.E. Ordinary level and C.S.E. examinations had its drawbacks: pupils were forced to make an early choice of course, separate teaching groups were generally required and teaching time was lost because of the long summer examination season. The Council's First Examinations Committee addressed itself to the problem as early as 1966, but its initial reaction was that a common system of grading and certification was all that could be hoped for. This failed to satisfy the C.S.E. Boards and in 1970 the Schools Council finally accepted in principle that there should be a single examination system at sixteen plus. A year later a special Working Party produced recommendations for the reshaping of examinations at this stage and laid down a time scale for their implementation. Subject to satisfactory feasibility studies, the new examinations were to be launched within six years. The prospect seemed to be that of the more academic tradition of the G.C.E. losing ground to the more progressive and teacher-centred procedures of the C.S.E.

(f) Impact of Educational Technology

Another important influence upon the development of the curriculum and teaching methods over the last half-century has been the growth of a widening range of technical devices and apparatus available to the teacher in school and classroom. The film-strip projector, the record player, the radio, the tape-recorder, the television set, the overhead projector, the language laboratory and even video-tape equipment are amongst the resources now to be found in some schools, although their high cost obviously prevents provision on any really generous scale. Singly, the most significant has been the contribution of educational broadcasting.

From its earliest days the British Broadcasting Corporation has provided special radio broadcasts for schools and since 1957, together with the Independent Broadcasting Authority, it has developed school television programmes as well. The whole field of schools broadcasting has always rested upon the closest co-operation between the authorities concerned and the educational world. The output of programmes is now very large and wide ranging, covering all the various age groups and most of the subjects of the curriculum. Most schools make some use of educational broadcasts, although timetable complications at the secondary level ensure that it is the junior schools which are most involved. But programmes prepared for the raising of the school leaving age may well produce some shift in this respect. Originally the aim of schools broadcasting was to enrich and supplement the work of the teacher, but the advent of television has raised the prospect of direct teaching through the medium and of the teacher accepting a very subordinate role. Future development must concentrate upon diffusing the benefits of schools broadcasting, whilst guarding against the danger of relegating the teacher to the educational sidelines.

Follow-up: Attempt to cover as much of the following ground as possible.
1 *Read* Department of Education and Science *Trends in Education,* February 1970. Centenary issue: article by D. Lawton on '100 Years of Curriculum Change', pp. 18-26

Wardle, D. *English Popular Education 1780-1970,* Chapter 5
Department of Education and Science Reports on Education: No. 29 on 'The Schools Council' (February 1966), and No. 47 on 'The Certificate of Secondary Education' (June 1968)
2 *Clarify the following: the social determinants of the nineteenth century elementary curriculum; the relationship between the economic factor and post-primary developments; the early twentieth century progressive influences in the field of pedagogic theory (e.g. Dewey); the impact of 'payment by results' on elementary curricula and teaching methods; the significance of the 1904 Elementary Code and the associated* Handbook of Suggestions; *the nature of the nineteenth century tradition in infant education; the place of the higher-grade, central and junior technical schools in the development of the curriculum; the social basis of the grammar tradition; the institutional forces favouring the nineteenth century reform and the early twentieth century consolidation of the grammar school curriculum; the importance of faculty psychology as a conservative force in the grammar tradition; the changes in curricula and method in the grammar*

school during the half century prior to the First World War; the significance of the 1904 Regulations for Secondary Schools; the origins, nature and influence of the School Certificate examinations; the importance of the 1931 Hadow Report for the development of the modern primary school; the recommendations of the Norwood Report *on* Curriculum and Examinations in Secondary Schools *(1943); the nature and weaknesses of the G.C.E. examinations; the radical features distinguishing the C.S.E. examinations; the origins and functions of the Schools Council.*

Chapter Fifteen
Current Issues and Future Prospects

Purpose: to identify and explore some of the current issues in English education which are likely to prove matters of continuing concern in relation to future development.

In contemporary society educational development contains the seeds of its own future expansion. The acceptance of secondary education for all and the progressive raising of the school-leaving age provides a widening platform for the growth of further and higher education. As education becomes the key to upward social mobility and consumes more and more public money, its comparative importance within the total framework of national life and government rises inexorably. Although the basic issues related to educational development may remain much the same, they change their form and tend to emerge in sharper relief as education assumes overwhelming social and political importance.

1 The Economics of Education

The major problem for the forseeable future will be that of finding the money to sustain educational development, simply in terms of meeting present commitments and accepted policies. During the 1960s education did exceptionally well under both Conservative and Labour governments ultimately surpassing defence as the largest single item in public expenditure. Rising from £800-odd million to over £2,200 million in a single decade, educational spending increased considerably faster than expenditure on the rest of the social services and its share of the gross national product jumped from 4·2% to 6·3%. The core of the mounting cost problem was the rapid growth of further and higher education, in relation to which expenditure quadrupled 1960-70. With the *per capita* cost of a university place rising beyond £1,000 per annum, the acceptance of the Robbins principle of providing higher education for all suitably qualified applicants had very serious cost implications. The proportion of eighteen-year-olds entering higher education rose from 7% to 15% during the 1960s; extrapolations based on the recent growth in the number of school leavers with two A-levels suggest that some 22% of the age group could well be demanding entry by 1980. Meanwhile the growth of public interest in the need to expand nursery education raised the prospect of another source of pressure upon short resources. By the early 1970s some critical questions were being posed by the continuing rise of educational expenditure.

(a) Can the country afford to maintain its present policies, especially for higher education, let alone embark upon new developments? In the 1960s it was strongly argued that education was a major investment item upon which the economic strength and social well-being of the country depends. But this simple faith seems to have lost some of its former conviction and support: there is a more acute awareness of the need to contain educational expenditure in the interests of limiting the burden of taxation and of more fully developing other social services. Only with a sustained rate of national economic growth markedly greater than has hitherto been achieved can such sharp conflict be avoided, and the omens in this respect remain distinctly unfavourable. Thus the question of basic alternatives must be faced and argued out at the highest political levels.

(b) What should our educational priorities be? The major choice lies between the pattern of the 1960s and a new scale of priorities favouring the majority of pupils who will continue to leave school at sixteen. As the expansion of higher education benefits only a minority and involves such high *per capita* costs, a strong case may be argued for shifting the emphasis to pre-school, primary and special education. Plowden's compensatory principle might then receive more than much lip-service and mean support.

(c) How can the educational system be made more cost effective? It is now vital to obtain full value for money and to achieve a reduction in *per capita* costs, especially in the expensive field of higher education. Governments will inevitably bring the universities, the local education authorities and the teachers' organisations under increasing pressure in this respect. The case for larger local authorities, home-based higher education, student loans, sub-degree courses, tertiary colleges, large secondary schools and open-plan primaries is to a significant extent economic. The danger is that the quality of education suffers in the quest for cost savings by administrators and politicians. In particular, because of the potential backlash effects upon corporate ethos and learning climate, the economies of large-scale plant may well be a concept which is quite inappropriate to both primary and secondary education.

Given the context just described, it is now vital for educational development to be considered as a whole and subjected to long-term planning. This need was spotlighted by the Crowther Report as early as 1959, but it was not until seven years later that the Department of Education and Science established its own planning branch. Although it does not cover the whole field in depth, the 1972 White Paper, in laying down a ten-year programme for educational development, sets an important precedent for the future. Concerned with matters of scale, organisation and cost, it has attempted to grapple with the financial problem. The resources devoted to education are planned to grow at a slower rate (3·4% per annum in real terms) than they did during the 1960s (5·2%). There is also some shift in emphasis in favour of the schools sector and to the disadvantage of higher education. The expansion of pre-school education is to enjoy a high priority, but the Robbins' principle will probably come under further strain. It is doubtful whether the planned increase in higher education places will match the growth of demand. In any case the achievement of the set target (750,000) is dependent on a significant lowering of unit costs. The decision to raise the non-university contribution to one half by 1981 and to develop the two-year Diploma of Higher Education is calculated to help in this respect. Moreover, the government clearly expects the universities to accept less favourable staffing ratios and to raise their proportion of home-based students. Thus for sheer cost reasons the White Paper contains more of the letter than the spirit of Robbins. Given the steady fall in the birth rate since 1964 and large output of teachers in the 1960s, the government also intends to conserve money and other resources through a sharp reduction in initial teacher training places; the resultant saving can then be re-deployed within the wider field of higher education to help relieve the pressure there. Clearly, the financing of education has become, and will remain, a highly complex and intractable problem.

2 The Distribution of Power and Responsibility

The English educational system, providing a national service which is locally administered, has long been based on a distribution of power and responsibility between the various elements composing it. Happily or otherwise, the balance of power and the respective rights and responsibilities of the different interested parties have not been too clearly defined. Since 1944 the growth of central power and the growing pressure from other elements for a greater say in what goes on have combined to make a re-examination of this area a matter of current and future concern. Various issues are involved:

(a) the question of the proper functions and powers of the central government in relation to overall policy and planning, finance, university development and student grants, the private sector, the organisation of schooling, curricula and examinations, educational priority areas and other such critical matters. The case for greater central control continues to draw increasing strength from the need to plan educational development as a whole and from the growing proportion of total expenditure met from national taxes;

(b) the question of the appropriate size and powers of the local education authorities. Although the reorganisation of local government provides for fewer and larger local education authorities in the interests of a more efficient service, there is the suspicion that many of the thirty-odd metropolitan districts will prove too small and weak in relation to the needs of special and higher education. But to shift educational responsibility to the metropolitan area level is to court the danger of remoteness. What are the implications of larger local authorities for the central/local balance of power and for the role of the local education committee? The Department of Education and Science has intimated a preparedness to allow more responsibility to larger Maud-type authorities (see page 154). Hopefully, the latter have formed the Local Authorities Higher Education Committee to represent them in consultations with the central government over the financing and organisation of higher education. Meanwhile, current interest in focusing the decision-making responsibility of the new authorities on top management teams does not augur too well for the future influence of education committees and chief education officers as such. At the national level this is reflected in the real prospect of the Association of Education Committees giving way to a central council of local education authorities (see page 172). Such developments would not be in the best interests of education;

(c) the question of the composition and responsibilities of managing and governing bodies. The Weaver Report (1966) and the subsequent Education Act (1968) led to the reform of the internal government of the Colleges of Education; inevitably the polytechnics and Colleges of Further Education were drawn into and benefited from the process of change. The composition of their governing bodies was broadened to include academic staff and the former degree of administrative and financial control wielded by the local education authority was significantly reduced. Given the reluctance of many authorities to loosen their grip, this developing shift in the balance of power will remain a source of contention in the future. There are signs that the reorganisation of higher education in the public sector, consequent upon the 1972 White Paper, could and may be used as an opportunity to reassert a greater degree of local education authority control. Meanwhile, there is the prospect of the focus of attention being switched to the managing and governing bodies of the schools, the majority of which have hitherto been denied a clear and positive role. Already there are strong demands for a broadening of their composition and an accession to their powers. It may be that the new local government pattern, destined to make the 'education offices' that much more remote, will both present and encourage greater possibilities in this direction.

(*d*) the question of the rights and responsibilities of teachers and their organisations within the total framework. The main issues arising relate to the representation of teachers on local education committees and governing bodies, the form and responsibilities of the prospective General Teachers' Council, the control of curricula and examinations and the democratisation of decision-making at school level. The nature and operation of the Burnham machinery for the negotiation of teachers' salaries promises to be another bone of contention in the years ahead. All these issues are, of course, simply part of the larger and vital question of the professional status (or otherwise) of the teaching occupation.

(*e*) the question of parental rights in relation to the education of their offspring in State schools. By common consent Section 76 of the 1944 Act has failed to secure such rights in proper measure and there has been growing pressure for an improvement in the situation. This is likely to continue, with the emphasis being placed upon the right of choice between schools, parental representation on managing and governing bodies and the universal establishment of Parent-Teacher Associations. To some extent the ground has already been prepared for change in this area: the play-group movement, the successful exertion of collective parental pressure upon the secondary plans of some authorities and the emergence of nationally representative bodies to safeguard and promote parental interests have combined over the last decade to underline the potentialities of parental interest and power.

(*f*) the question of student rights in institutions of further and higher education where they undertake full-time study. The critical issues are those relating to student grants, the financing and administering of student unions and the representation of students on governing and other internal bodies. The difficulty is to decide how far and in what ways students are to be given a share of power, and whether this should infringe upon specifically academic matters. The National Union of Students may be relied upon to present and push the 'student case', in militant fashion when deemed necessary, on all these issues.

3 The State and the Private Sector

The State system of education has never enjoyed a monopoly in Britain. Today some 6% of children attend independent schools, their parents paying fees to obtain what they believe to be a superior education. This private sector is composed of public schools, preparatory schools and other independent schools, all of which have had since 1957 to register with the central authority and some of which seek and obtain recognition as efficient. Also associated with the private sector are the direct grant schools which fill anything up to 75% of their places with fee-paying pupils, although one-quarter of their annual intake must be drawn from State maintained schools to qualify them for direct grants from the Department of Education and Science. Taken together these schools afford an alternative to the State system for those parents who can afford the fees. As a result of endowments and high fees some of them are able to give a better education and provide improved chances of university entry; others are said to be inferior to State schools and even educationally harmful to the children attending them.

Whilst the private sector does accord with the right of the parent to spend his money as he so desires and to choose the schooling appropriate to his child, it is inevitably a source of educational privilege and class consciousness and may be construed as a critically divisive influence within society. The favourable staffing ratios, the generous provision of facilities, the 'above Burnham' salary scales and the long established connections with Oxford and Cambridge enable the outstanding public and direct grant schools to offer better prospects of educational and occupational advancement than are usually open to children passing through the State system. Moreover, those influential parents who use the fee paying places at public and direct grant schools have no incentive to interest themselves in the State system and its improvement. Thus the continuance of the private sector provokes the wrath of those dedicated to the democratic ideal of real equality of educational opportunity. The National Union of Teachers has declared the only acceptable solution to be 'for all independent schools either to be fully integrated into the local authority system or to go out of existence' (*Into the Seventies*, page 33).

The problem of the independent schools is a highly controversial and continuing one, which various investigating bodies and governments have tried unsuccessfully to solve. The Fleming Report (1944) and the first Report of the Public Schools Commission (1968) both failed to resolve the difficulty posed by the independent schools: unprepared to recommend their abolition or forcible incorporation in the State system, the commissioners resorted to suggesting impracticable solutions acceptable to neither side. When the Public Schools Commission turned to consider the direct grant schools, with Donnison replacing Newsom as its chairman, the second Report (1970) was much more positive and calculated to bring about change. It was recommended that the direct-grant schools be given a straight choice between full incorporation within the State system of secondary education or the withdrawal of their State grants. The majority of the schools concerned made it clear that, faced with such alternatives, they would go it alone and join the ranks of the public schools. But the immediate threat was soon removed by the Conservative electoral victory in 1970.

It is difficult to gauge what the future holds in store for the public and direct-grant schools. Whilst they may rely on continuing Conservative support, the official attitude and intentions of the Labour party can only be viewed by them with fear and apprehension. If the Labour leadership, given a sufficient majority in the Commons, can steel itself to implement a policy which will be bitterly attacked as a gross violation of individual parental rights, the direct grant system will be scrapped and even the independent schools may find that their days are numbered.

4 The Organisation of Education

Since 1944 the external organisation of the State system of education, in terms of its basic stages and differentiation by institution within particular stages, has become increasingly confused and unsatisfactory. The result is a continuing need for rationalisation in the interests of educational opportunity, administrative sense and cost efficiency. The present organisational pattern consists of broad divisions into primary, secondary, further and higher education; to a considerable extent the institutional pattern is elitist and hierarchic at both the secondary and post-secondary levels. The introduction of middle schools has blurred the primary/secondary division laid down by the 1944 Act, the growing minority of pupils switching from secondary schools to Colleges of Further Education for A-level courses is a source of duplication and waste, whilst the distinction between further and higher education has never been made clear. Within the secondary stage the existence of direct grant, grammar, technical, modern, bilateral and a variety of comprehensive schools has produced innumerable patterns of secondary provision amongst the different local education authorities. The overall confusion is now such that somewhere in the country children are being transferred from one school or stage to another at every age during the compulsory years of schooling except six and fifteen. In a modern community characterised by a high degree of geographical mobility, such a patchwork of different arrangements is palpably unsatisfactory. Out of this context emerge a number of issues of obvious or potential importance for future development:

(*a*) the long-term question of producing a much more uniform staging and institutional pattern on a national basis. This has already been raised in a limited form by the local government reorganisation, where new and larger authorities faced the need to integrate the different patterns inherited from their predecessors. In the years ahead the 'model' recommended by Sir William Alexander may well attract growing support: it affords a clear and successive pattern of nursery (3-5), primary (5-11), secondary (11-16), tertiary (16-18) and higher (18+) stages. The cost of further reorganisation and the reluctance of secondary teachers to have their Sixth Formers hived off into separate institutions are the major obstacles to such long-term rationalisation.

(*b*) the future of nursery education in terms of its extent, the age range concerned, and full- or part-time character. The 1972 White Paper has opened a new era in this field, taking the Plowden proposals as the basis for its ten-year programme. But the official emphasis on priority for deprived areas, half-time provision in nursery classes of three- to five-year-olds and the integration of day nurseries and play-groups must obviously be subject to future experience and reaction. Pre-schooling could well become an educationally sensitive area in the years ahead.

(*c*) the age of school entry and leaving. There is a growing body of opinion which favours September as the only entry date and July as the only leaving date; such an arrangement would rid the infant schools of three separate annual intakes and end the disruption of final year secondary courses by Easter leavers. Beyond this there is the remote possibility of raising the school-leaving age once more or of implementing the old county college plan (see page 98) to complement the developing system of industrial training and release for early school leavers.

(*d*) the future of secondary education in terms of comprehensive re-organisation and Sixth Form arrangements. The abolition of the eleven plus examination and associated selective schools remains a major bone of political contention, but time and tide both favour the comprehensive system, which will almost certainly be made a statutory requirement by a strong, determined Labour government.

Meanwhile the widespread incidence of wasteful arrangements for expensive A-level courses places a growing premium upon the tertiary or Sixth Form college as an exercise in cost efficiency. The tendency for a growing proportion of sixteen year olds to transfer to Colleges of Further Education to do their A-levels adds to the waste and strengthens the case for a separate tertiary stage.

(e) the whole question of the organisation and government of higher education. This is virtually a sector in itself as it involves the continuing argument over the efficacy of the binary policy, the best means of planning for the development of higher education as a whole, the special status of the universities and their Grants Committee and the future of the Colleges of Education. Whether the binary system is likely, in the long term, to give way to a comprehensive approach to higher education is difficult to judge. Neither the Conservative White Paper nor declared Labour policy seem to threaten the binary approach, but nevertheless the universities must expect their traditional autonomy to undergo further erosion in future years. The economic factor and the need fully to rationalise the development of higher education at all levels make this inevitable. In the non-university sector of higher education the integration of the polytechnics, Colleges of Advanced Further Education and formerly monotechnic Colleges of Education into a viable whole will present sufficient problems in itself.

5 The Curriculum and Other Related Matters

In the widest sense the curriculum encompasses the aims and content of education, means of assessment, teaching methods and internal school organisation. These are the matters which bear most obviously and directly upon the nature of the educational process at classroom level. Therefore, they are now generally regarded as areas which should be left in the hands of the teachers rather than be subject to legislation or regulation. But there the consensus ends. In recent years, encouraged by the work of the Schools Council and the developing link between progressive attitudes and promotional prospects, the wind of curriculum change has been blowing strong and the odds are that it will continue to do so with even greater force. One clear result of this has been to produce sharp conflict between the progressive and conservative elements within the profession. Although the rate or extent of contemporary curricula change is impossible to assess, its general direction is amenable to description and comment.

(a) The Primary Sector

As already shown in the previous chapter, the infant schools were the seed-bed of the progressive child-centred approach to learning. Following the 1931 Hadow Report the ideas and methods involved began to make slow headway in the junior schools that fed the developing tripartite system. But it was not until the 1960s that the pace of change visibly quickened and began to affect the majority of primary schools. By this time the retreat of the eleven plus examination, the expansion of teacher training and the interest of the Nuffield Foundation and the Schools Council were providing a more favourable context for progressive advance. In 1967 the Plowden Report lent its considerable weight to the movement away from traditional forms and methods. Thus the 'good' primary school has become almost officially associated with a number of progressive features:

(i) a marked emphasis upon the aesthetic and socio-emotional aspects of education rather than a dominant concern for cognitive development and a mastery of the basic skills of reading, writing and arithmetic;

(ii) an inter-disciplinary approach to much of the curriculum based on topics, projects and activities arising out of the children's natural interests and experience. To ensure the requisite flexibility this is usually associated with the abandonment of timetabling in favour of the integrated day;

(iii) an internal organisation based on mixed ability classes instead of streaming. Such an arrangement puts traditional class teaching at a discount and involves the expectation that the teacher will develop group and individualised learning procedures which will allow each child to progress at his own pace in a non-competitive atmosphere. The emphasis is on the organisation of learning resources and individual guidance rather than formal class instruction and exercises;

(iv) an open-plan arrangement calculated to end the former isolation of each primary class, to allow for the most economic use of available space for the widened range of junior activities, to dilute the 'mother hen' tradition in favour of a limited team-teaching approach and to afford a more favourable context for the development of group and individual projects. The official faith placed in open-plan design as an ideal vehicle for the progressive strategy finds expression in the growing proportion of new primary schools built on the appropriate lines.

Whether the progressive primary school is better or worse than its traditional counterpart is, in the last analysis, simply a matter of opinion. The so-called 'Plowden Club' is convinced that it is much better; the Council for the Maintenance of Educational Standards is equally convinced that it is considerably worse. The report of the National Foundation of Educational Research on *Streaming in the Primary School* (1970) showed that mixed ability classes did not depress academic standards and probably promoted more desirable attitudes. Two years later its report on *The Trend of Reading Standards* showed that there had been a significant decline since 1964 in the competence of the average eleven-year-old; the conservative faction then ascribed most of the blame to progressive methods and their comparative neglect of direct and sustained instruction in the basic skills. But such controversy, though likely to continue, generates more heat than light. The two types of school are not only artifacts which defy any clear operational definition; they serve different educational aims and the evaluation of methods can only make sense in relation to common goals. Even where there is a shared and agreed goal, it is extremely difficult to isolate the influence of progressive or traditional forms and methods from other variables. The fact is that the quality of primary education depends more upon the ability and dedication of the teacher than upon the particular methods used, although the progressive approach is likely to make greater demands on both these qualities. The future need is for an impartial examination of the present aims and practice of primary education to identify the best way forward; such an exercise would demand considerable time and a realistic appreciation of the extent to which certain pedagogic styles depend on favourable staffing ratios, an abundance and variety of resources and a home background that encourages and supports self-reliance and initiative. It is time to take stock instead of pushing even further ahead.

(b) Secondary Sector

Since the early 1960s the comprehensive tide, the introduction of the new middle schools, the influence of the Schools Council, the development of the C.S.E. and the raising of the school-leaving age to sixteen have combined to loosen the conservative fabric of secondary education and encourage curricula change. Although progressive ideas and methods still struggle to make headway in secondary education, their rate of advance is seemingly faster than ever before. The direction of current, and possibly future, change can be shown by reference to a number of its developing features:

(i) a greater concern for the needs and interests of the less able secondary pupils as recommended in the Newsom Report (1963). This has found expression in a widening variety of extended courses which the larger comprehensive schools are particularly well able to support. The development of the C.S.E. examinations and of the curricula schemes for the raising of the school leaving age, both involving greater opportunity for the study of practical and vocational subjects, have involved a deliberate rejection of traditional forms;

(ii) a shift from the old emphasis upon an academic and competitive ethos to a new quest for a social and co-operative atmosphere. Whilst the majority of comprehensive schools are meritocratic, eliminating the injustices of the eleven plus but maintaining the essentials of the traditional outlook, a minority of egalitarian comprehensives are attempting to blaze a new secondary trail characterised by mixed ability groups, inter-disciplinary studies and team-teaching, generous provision for counselling and pastoral care, and the democratisation of staff-pupil relations and the machinery of school government. Pioneered within the State system by Albert Rowe at the David Lister Comprehensive School in Hull, this approach is now being developed to a very marked degree at Countesthorpe Upper School in Leicestershire;

(iii) a steady increase in the degree of teacher control over external examinations and thus over the details of the secondary curriculum. Whilst the C.S.E. has been teacher-dominated from the outset, improved representation within the machinery of the G.C.E. examining bodies has increased professional influence where it still matters most. For examining at sixteen plus the future seems to hold two main possibilities: either the fusion of the C.S.E. and the G.C.E. Ordinary level into a single external examination, or a radical switch to an internally based system such as recommended by the Norwood Report (1943). The alternative would be to retain the present dual arrangements with their difficulties and shortcomings. Whatever happens, the development of greater variety in examining procedures, pioneered by the C.S.E. Boards, is likely to continue. The two problems that loom large and will resist easy solution are those related to the Sixth Form and the least able pupils. The Schools Council hopes to broaden the Sixth Form curriculum by the judicious reconstruction of the associated examinations. The problem of finding an assessable goal for the least able or motivated secondary pupils, so as to avert any sense of institutional rejection, has not been really faced as yet. To claim that they are non-examinable offers no solution in the present social context.

Of course, the process of change in the secondary sector will be held up by the grammar tradition, whether outside or inside the comprehensive system. But once again internecine conflict makes no sense. Presuming that the State system of secondary education will ultimately become wholly comprehensive, the need is to ensure that what is worthwhile in the grammar tradition is absorbed and that future curricula change is measured rather than sweeping in character.

6 The School and the Community

Historically the schools of England and Wales developed in isolation from the local communities they were designed to serve. The schools were set apart to get on undisturbed with the job of teaching children their letters to a basic or academic level. Those aspects of the developing educational system which had wider connotations and afforded links with the community at large, such as the school welfare services, the Youth Service, the Youth Employment Service and adult education, were regarded as peripheral matters. Philosophically, education for individuality was preferred to education for community living; the meritocratic ideal overshadowed its egalitarian counterpart. Their strong professional, rather than democratic, outlook disinclined the majority of teachers to open the schools to parents or to forge strong links with the local community. But this situation is now being challenged by the radical viewpoint that school and community development are essentially inter-dependent and should be considered as a whole. Such an approach, it is claimed, offers very considerable economic, social and educational bene-fits. In recent years this viewpoint has found practical expression in a number of developments which have taken place along two basic lines:

(*a*) the growing recognition of the vital importance of home background and neighbourhood influence upon the educational progress and prospects of the child. Post-war urban redevelopment has sharpened the tendency for particular socio-economic groups to concentrate homogeneously in certain areas of housing. The advent of the neighbourhood comprehensive with its local catchment area ensures that more and more schools fall into the confines of this pattern. The result is that a significant minority of children are socially and educationally disadvantaged by the environment in which they live. The decaying centres of large cities present the worst problem: the children are from poor working class or immigrant homes, many are emotionally disturbed, and they suffer from a high turnover of teachers and unsatisfactory school premises. As many post-war sociological studies have shown, the formal equality of educational opportunity offered by the 1944 Act had little or no meaning for children brought up in such areas. Accordingly the compensatory principle has won growing support; it urges that educational pro-vision and communal development in disadvantaged areas should receive prior and favoured treatment and that the interest of the parents in their children's schooling should be enlisted by all possible means. The development of educational priority area policies, the new interest in the expansion of nursery provision, the continuing concern for more parental involvement and the establishment of a special Urban Aid Programme are the major outcome. The belief is that if sufficient resources are devoted to a policy of positive discrimination in favour of socially disadvantaged children, they will then be able to hold their own both inside and outside the educational system. But discrimination on the educational front alone is palpably not enough; it must relate to the local community as such in which the social disadvantage has its ultimate roots. This means that parlous funding and *ad hoc* half-measures, which have so far dominated this new scene, are likely to be self-defeating;

(*b*) the increasing interest in the school as a centre for community development irrespective of the socio-economic nature of the area concerned. The beginnings of the community school date back to the Cambridgeshire village colleges of the inter-war period, but it is only in recent years that the concept has excited fairly widespread interest. Although still ill-defined, the concept rests on the general idea that the life of the school and of the local community should be much more closely related for the benefit of both. Obvious cost advantages accrue from the joint financing of facilities put to common and intensive use by both the school and the wider community. Direct parental involvement in nursery provision and to a lesser extent in primary work, in school governance and parent-teacher organisations and in the work of local education committees are all socially desirable if community development is to take on a real 'grass roots' character. The effects of bringing school pupils into closer contact with active members of the adult community can only be educationally beneficial to both sides. Of course, it is in areas of new development that the community school approach finds its best opportunities. An outstanding example of the concept at work is afforded by the Abraham Moss Centre of north Manchester, designed to meet the needs of two thousand pupils and students by day and about half that number during the evening. The whole campus encloses a large 11-18 comprehensive school, a College of Further Education, an adult education centre, a sports and recreation complex, a district library, a Youth Club and a small residential block. Catering needs are provided for and the location of the redeveloped site is well related to local housing, shopping and transport facilities. The hope is that under a co-ordinated manage-ment interested in forging strong links with parents, voluntary organisations and the public at large, the Centre will become the heart of community life and foster a new sense of local identity and involvement. The wider significance of the Centre is one of basic principle, for it cannot be taken as any sort of practical model outside the great cities. Elsewhere the community school concept will usually have to find expression, as it already has done, in far less grandiose forms. It might simply involve the development of nursery and primary education on a co-operative and participative basis along lines pioneered by the play-school movement and the educational priority area projects.

The current interest in relating school and community rests upon the sort of egalitarian ideals which are more likely to attract Labour than Conservative political support. The extent to which the developments just reviewed can hope to win a really important place within the English educational system seems to depend on the party factor. The community approach did not figure large in the 1972 White Paper; even the expansion of nursery provision, depending on the form it takes, could result in less rather than more parental involvement. There is no real sign that the educational priority area policy and the loosely associated Urban Aid Programme are being taken really seriously. As long as the prime concern of educational policy makers is to maximise the opportunity for talent and ambition to find its reward, the context will remain unfavourable to the compensatory and community principles. They will, however, continue to press their claims and can no longer be ignored.

Behind the basic issues of contemporary and future educational development lies the whole spectrum of political and professional opinion. The consensus of earlier times, when education did not enjoy its present importance, has given way to considerable conflict as expressed in the comprehensive and Black Paper controversies. Central governments of one colour and local authorities of another work less easily together in the field of education. Teachers take up contrary positions upon such matters as raising the school leaving age and the school curriculum. Much of educational opinion has become polarised into two opposing camps. The traditionalists hold an elitist or meritocratic view of education; they conceive education in academic terms and emphasise its selective function; they are somewhat less demanding upon public funds for education; they oppose any widespread dispersion of power within education; they support the retention of the private sector and the State grammar schools; they bemoan the gradual erosion of the independence of the universities and their previous monopoly of higher education; they equate progressive developments in the field of curricula and examinations with the lowering of standards; they condemn the use of education for social engineering purposes and are unconvinced that compensatory education is not a misuse of short resources. The progressives hold a populist or egalitarian view of education; they conceive education in developmental terms and emphasise its socialising function; they make heavy demands upon public funds for educational purposes; they favour the democratisation of the power structure in education; they condemn the private sector and support the comprehensive reorganisation of State secondary education; they favour a comprehensive approach to higher education and are critical of the special position still enjoyed by the universities; they oppose the traditional forms of curricula, teaching method and internal school organisation; they see the school as an integral part of the local community and enthusiastically support the principle of compensatory education. To a considerable and unfortunate extent this division of educational opinion is mirrored politically. Of course, the analysis is simplistic because it hinges on the two ends of the spectrum; there are many traditionalists who are more liberally disposed than others and there are many progressives who are more conservatively inclined than their colleagues. But clearly there is a rift and a lack of real consensus upon which future educational development might be based. This does not mean that advances will not take place in the years ahead; what it does mean is that a clear and consistent underlying rationale, as befits the development of a national system of education, may be found wanting.

In some respects there are more favourable omens for the future. Education has firmly established itself as the chief of the social services and enjoys an allocation of resources roughly commensurate with its importance. There is little prospect that education will be left seriously short of funds and the recent fall in the birth rate, presuming it continues, should give more room for financial manoeuvre. The prospect of an all-graduate profession and the development of in-service education and training also augurs well for the quality of the service. The serious interest in the reform of curricula and examinations is a healthy sign so long as innovation is never allowed to become an end in itself and change is encouraged rather than imposed. The children of the first post-war generation are now entering the schools and this should go hand in hand with a growth of parental interest in education. Finally, the religious issue, which bedevilled English educational development for so long and remained threatening until the passage of the 1944 Act, now seems to be largely dormant. Although the legislative provision for compulsory religious worship and instruction in all maintained schools may excite controversy again, it is unlikely to emerge as a matter of major and bitter concern. The dual system continues to be a source of minor irritants (e.g. the ability of voluntary aided grammar schools to spike local comprehensive plans), but they should prove susceptible to removal by negotiation.

Follow-up: Attempt to cover as much of the following ground as possible.
1 *Read* National Union of Teachers *Into the Seventies*

National Association of Schoolmasters *Thoughts on a New Education Act*

Anderson, H. and others *Education for the Seventies*, Chapters 1, 2, 5 and 8

Bander, P. *Looking Forward to the Seventies*; this book provides a wide selection of relevant articles by different writers

2 *Clarify the following: the implications of the mounting cost problem for future educational development; the particular issues related to the distribution of power and responsibility in English education; the case for and against the abolition of the public schools and the direct grant system; the current anomalies and future prospects in relation to the organisational and institutional pattern of education; the direction of progressive change in the curriculum, methods of teaching and internal organisation of primary and secondary schools; the concept of the community school and its possible forms of expression; the contrast between the traditional and progressive outlooks upon contemporary educational matters; the factors which are favourable to continued educational advance.*

Essay Writing

Students undertaking courses concerned with the historical development and/or contemporary character of the educational system in England and Wales are usually required, at some time or other, to demonstrate their grasp of the subject by submitting written answers to formal essay questions. The need to cultivate a capacity for essay writing in the field concerned may relate to ordinary assignments given during term time, to arrangements for continuous assessment, or to the sitting of formal examinations at the end of the course. What follows is an attempt to help the student to meet this particular need with an adequate measure of success.

The Essential Attributes of Sound Essay Writing

A really satisfactory standard of essay writing in response to particular questions on the development and system of education in England and Wales depends upon the student paying attention to a number of vital considerations.

1 Standard of English

It is axiomatic that essay answers should be communicated in clear and otherwise satisfactory written English. Yet too many students, sometimes obsessed by the urge to deposit on paper as much material as possible, take insufficient care in this respect; the result is often a lack of clarity in what they write and even a quite unintentional perversion of what they mean to say. Thus there is a need for the use of proper sentences and paragraphs, the avoidance of notational forms and abbreviations, the precise use of technical terms, the cultivation of a wide and exact general vocabulary, the provision of correct spelling, punctuation and grammatical usage and, finally, the use of the appropriate tenses. Many students, including some working for degree awards, are unable to make use of the semi-colon and colon; this restricts their capacity to manipulate written language and may result in the recurrent misuse of the comma. There is no simple blueprint for raising the standard of English in essay writing. It can only be done by a conscious long-term effort by the individual student. Certain working habits can help a great deal. Firstly, the student should pay closer, even deliberate, attention to the above matters in the course of his general reading; the usual practice is for students to use the literature in the field concerned exclusively for purposes of substance. Secondly, the student should always be prepared to consult the dictionary to improve his spelling and vocabulary. Thirdly, the student should read his own essay answers before their submission; the return of marked scripts should then be capitalised upon by taking note of any errors or criticisms of English style as well as weaknesses of substance and structure.

2 Relevance

This is an absolutely critical requirement and yet is the most common source of difficulty and weakness. To be strictly relevant the essay answer must be tied very closely and consistently to the exact terms of the set question. All students undertaking formal essay assignments should take an oath to answer the set question, the whole question and nothing but the question! It is one thing to accumulate knowledge mechanically and thereupon to regurgitate it very much in its original form; it is quite another to develop the wider understanding and flexibility of mind which enable the student to select the material relevant to the answering of a specific question. Most essay questions, if they are worth their salt, are deliberately calculated to sort out the thinkers from the 'parrot-learners'.

The first stage in the production of a relevant essay answer is concerned with question interpretation. The student must read the set question very carefully and exercise his judgement upon the limits of the question and upon what exactly is being asked for. He must guard against the danger of grasping at a single name, term or phrase; every single word in the question is potentially vital because it can affect the slant or limit the nature of the task.

e.g. 'No one contributed more to the cause of elementary education in nineteenth century England than Sir James Kay-Shuttleworth.' Discuss.

This question is not simply concerned with Kay-Shuttleworth. It requires some consideration to be given to the contribution of *other* nineteenth century pioneers, such as W. E. Forster, before any satisfactory conclusion can be reached.

e.g. What were the benefits and limitations of the 1870 Elementary Education Act?

Whilst the student may well have geared his studies to a consideration of the causes, provisions and results of the 1870 Act, the question does not ask for them as such. The causative aspect is largely irrelevant, but a knowledge of the provisions and results should enable the student to draw out the benefits and limitations of the Act, which is what the question is asking for. This of course will require penetrative thought rather than simple regurgitation if the answer is to be consistently relevant.

The second stage is concerned with the business of sticking to the question once it has been interpreted correctly. Unless care is taken the student can easily, simply by following his nose or his predigested notes, lose his sense of direction and begin to unload irrelevant material. There are two possible safeguards against this. The first is to plan the answer broadly before putting pen to paper, ensuring that each major aspect of the intended answer does bear on the question. The second is to refer back recurrently to the question whilst writing the answer to ensure that one is still on the rails.

3 Balance

Obviously a thoroughly relevant essay answer must cover all the ground delineated by the terms of the question. But it is also important to achieve a proper balance so that each major aspect of the question receives its rightful share of attention. Sometimes the appropriate balance is openly declared by the wording of the set question.

e.g. Discuss the origins, the aims and the results of Circular 10/65 concerning the reorganisation of secondary education.

Obviously a satisfactory answer to this particular question will provide a balanced coverage of origins, aims and results. The main danger, especially under examination conditions when pressed for time, is that of getting bogged down in the historical antecedents of Circular 10/65, leading to the comparative neglect of the equally important aims and results. The student should consciously divide his time and energies on a roughly equal basis between the three aspects concerned and thereby obtain a satisfactory balance. Not all questions are so straightforward, however. Sometimes the right balance can only be judged as a result of effective question interpretation; the main aspects of the answer are not openly declared and the student must exercise judgement upon what will constitute a balanced response to the question.

e.g. Analyse the distribution of powers and responsibilities between the various elements which compose the present system of education in England and Wales.

The key to obtaining a proper balance in the answer is an appreciation of what is encompassed by 'the various elements'. The most important elements are the central authority, the local education authorities and the teachers; each of these deserves considerable attention. Other elements, such as managing and governing bodies, voluntary organisations, the universities and parents, will require summary mention as well.

4 Structure

Once the student is clear as to what the question is asking (relevance) and what are the main matters to be covered in the answer (balance), he is in a position to provide the essay with a clear structure. The satisfactory structuring of essay answers involves their systematic organisation into cohesive paragraphs, with each paragraph presenting a particular aspect or important sub-aspect of the answer. Thus any sound essay answer will contain the following broad divisions:

(*a*) an appropriate *introduction* which quickly sets the stage for a direct assault upon the set question. (Beware of long-winded and wasteful introductions; keep the introductory paragraph short (120-140 word maximum) and ensure that it really prepares the ground for what follows.)

(*b*) the *heart of the answer* which should be appropriately paragraphed and tied directly to the set question.

e.g. To what extent did the 1870 Act contribute towards the achievement of universal, compulsory, unsectarian and free elementary education in England and Wales?

The heart of the answer to this particular question would be made up of four separate paragraphs equating with each of the four main aspects:

(i) universal aspect = how far did the Act bring about adequate provision?

(ii) compulsory aspect = how far did the Act help to promote compulsory attendance at elementary school?

(iii) unsectarian aspect = how far did the Act contribute towards the provision of undenominational religious worship and instruction and the dilution of the 'religious difficulty' in elementary education?

(iv) free aspect = how far did the Act bring about free elementary education?

(*c*) a suitable *conclusion* to round off the answer and to deliver a final judgement where called upon to do so, as in the question under discussion. Concluding paragraphs should be kept short (100-120 words), but should draw together the main strands developed in the heart of the answer.

5 Depth and Accuracy

An essay answer may be relevant, well-balanced and satisfactorily structured yet be lacking in depth and accuracy. The latter attributes are necessarily dependent upon a fairly detailed knowledge of the subject built up gradually as a result of tuition, personal reading and effective revision. The fashionable denigration of factual knowledge should be treated with suspicion. This does not mean that facts should be labouriously amassed for their own sake; rather it is a matter of identifying fundamental educational developments and issues and clothing them with sufficient factual material to avoid shallowness of treatment and argument. A good essay answer, except in its introduction and conclusion, will not simply rely upon a series of generalised statements however sound they may be. In the heart of the answer any generalisations made will usually require elaboration or substantiation in detail. Such detail must of course be accurate. If one is to draw upon the provisions of the 1870 Act to help establish its significance there is no substitute for a thorough and detailed knowledge of each major provision; a reliance upon vague recollections will result in lack of depth and downright inaccuracy. Of course, there are facts and facts and the need for absolute precision is a variable one. It is not important to know every single significant date in the history of educational development, nor is it a sensible use of energy to try to absorb very much statistical material, however illuminating it may be. Concentrate rather upon the broad chronological sequence in relation to outstanding historical landmarks or processes and upon the significant developments and relationships which may be illustrated statistically. Do not try to be clever by quoting precise details that you are unsure of, for example the date of the free-place regulations (1907), or the number of School Boards ultimately established (2,568); where possible check such details out, or under examination conditions avoid committing yourself unnecessarily on such comparatively trivial matters.

To summarise then, a sound essay answer to a specific question will be characterised by an acceptable standard of written English, by sustained relevance, by a balanced and structured coverage of the subject concerned and by sufficient depth and accuracy. Finally, remember that preparation for and the writing of essay answers is not an end in itself; rather it affords a means of stimulating wider reading and study in depth in relation to any given sector of the course, and is calculated to develop a disciplined capacity for seeking out and selecting relevant material and for organising and presenting it in a satisfactory written form. Thus its educational benefits transcend the limits of any particular subject area.

Some Specimen Essay Questions

1 How was the nineteenth century development of elementary education in England and Wales affected by social, economic, political and religious influences?

2 Discuss some of the main obstacles to the development of a satisfactory system of elementary education in England and Wales during the first half of the nineteenth century.

3 Describe the condition of English elementary education in 1800 and consider critically the efforts made to improve the situation prior to the 1870 Act.

4 Examine the basic influences and contemporary climate of opinion which led up to and shaped the form of the 1870 Elementary Education Act.

5 'The 1870 Elementary Education Act was essentially a compromise measure.' Discuss this statement.

6 To what extent did the 1870 Act contribute towards the achievement of universal, compulsory, unsectarian and free elementary education in England and Wales?

7 Evaluate the contribution of the School Boards to the development of education in England and Wales. Account for their abolition.

8 By what means and to what extent was upper and middle class schooling reformed and expanded during the nineteenth century?

9 Discuss the recommendations and estimate the significance of the Taunton (Schools Inquiry) Commission Report on secondary education (1868).

10 What was the significance of the Bryce Commission Report on *Secondary Education* (1895) to the over-all development of education in England and Wales?

11 What were the problems that prompted the Education Acts of 1899 and 1902? To what extent did the legislation provide a satisfactory solution?

12 Evaluate the contribution to English educational development of *either* Sir James Kay-Shuttleworth *or* Sir Robert Morant.

13 How was the conception of State education progressively broadened between the Education Acts of 1902 and 1944?

14 Discuss the importance of H. A. L. Fisher's work as President of the Board of Education 1916-22.

15 Show how the Spens (1938) and the Norwood (1943) Reports reinforced and refined the recommendations of the Hadow Report on *The Education of the Adolescent* (1926).

16 Trace the rise and explain the nature of the post-war controversy over the organisation of secondary education in England and Wales.

17 Account for the rise and for the decline of the selective approach to the organisation of secondary education.

18 Critically assess the contribution of the 1944 Act to the development of a better system of education in England and Wales.

19 Discuss the origins, the aims and the results of Circular 10/65 concerning the reorganisation of secondary education.

20 Examine the processes by which the modern primary school has arisen out of the earlier system of elementary education.

21 What aspects of the education, training and employment of teachers in the nineteenth century combined to depress the occupational status of elementary school teaching?

22 Identify and comment upon the main developments in the field of teacher training and supply since the submission of the McNair Report (1944).

23 Discuss the development and role of the central authority in English education during the period 1833-1939.

24 Describe the administrative muddle existing in English education at the close of the nineteenth century and show how it was largely overcome by the acts of 1899 and 1902.

25 Analyse the distribution of powers and responsibilities between the various elements which compose the present system of education in England and Wales.

26 Discuss the view that educational administration in England and Wales is based upon the principles of consultation and co-operation between all interested parties.

27 Explain the exact nature of the functions and powers of the Department of Education and Science in the contemporary English educational system.

28 Discuss the influence upon educational thought and provision in England and Wales of *either* the Newsom (1963) *or* the Plowden (1967) Report.

29 Examine the significance of the Robbins Committee Report (1963) to the development of higher education in Britain.

30 What were the influences and agencies responsible for pushing forward the cause of scientific and technical education between the time of the Great Exhibition and the outbreak of the First World War?

31 Examine the major influences and developments which improved the fortunes of technical and higher technological education after the Second World War.

32 How and why was the period 1850-1914 one of major reform and development in the field of university education?

33 'The position and scope of university education has undergone revolutionary change since the end of the Second World War.' Discuss.

34 Identify and discuss the main developments which have taken place in secondary school curricula and examinations during the present century.

35 Explain the origins and the role of the Schools Council and assess its importance to educational development in England and Wales.
36 Consider the mounting influence of economic considerations upon the post-war development of education in England and Wales.
37 Discuss critically the present position and future prospects of the independent and direct grant grammar schools, making reference where appropriate to the reports of the Fleming Committee (1944) and the Public Schools Commission (1968-70).
38 Describe and explain the significance of the changes that have taken place in the institutional pattern of English education since the passing of the 1944 Act.
39 Analyse the way in which successive Education Acts since 1870 have attempted to solve the religious problem in English education.

A Few Model Answers in Summary Form

1st Question 'The 1870 Elementary Education Act was essentially a compromise measure.' Discuss this statement.

Interpretation of the Question

The question requires a response to the affirmative and palpably true statement that the 1870 Act was a compromise. Therefore any sound answer must be based upon the identification and elaboration of those features of the Act which represented a compromise between the principles of voluntary provision and State intervention.

Structuring the Answer

The following arrangement would prove satisfactory.

(a) Introduction (para. 1)

Brief description of pre-1870 situation and contending forces in elementary education. Stress the inadequacy of provision and the mounting agreement that serious improvement was necessary. Point to the sharp division upon *how* to achieve this by reference to the National Education Union representing the voluntary cause and the Birmingham Education League expressing the radical/secular viewpoint. Thus the Gladstone government passed a measure, the 1870 Act, which was a compromise between the demands of the two main pressure groups.

(b) Heart of the Answer

This should be devoted to identifying and explaining the compromise features of the Act.

Provision of Places (para. 2): the object of universal provision was to be achieved via the compromise of a 'dual system' involving the co-existence of denominational and State elementary schools. The six months 'period of grace' allowed the churches the first opportunity to meet existing deficiencies; with the aid of building grants over a million extra denominational places were provided. Thereupon School Boards, elected by the ratepayers, were established in deficiency districts to provide public elementary schools; in 'filling the gaps' the School Boards ultimately added a further two million school places. By 1900 the voluntary organisations and the School Boards were of roughly equal importance in the provision of universal elementary schooling.

Control of Elementary Schools (para. 3): a compromise was effected by leaving the church schools under the local control of their own voluntary managing bodies and completely outside the jurisdiction of the School Board, whilst the new Board schools came under the public control of trienially elected School Boards. In areas where voluntary provision was 'sufficient, efficient and suitable', School Boards were not even established; in areas where they were established the School Boards were subject to much closer supervision by the central Education Department than were the voluntary organisations.

Financial Arrangements (para. 4): these were based on an uneasy compromise that was not calculated to last. Whilst both the voluntary and Board schools were to receive central grants under the 'payment by results' system and were permitted to charge parental fees, the introduction of rate-aid was reserved for the benefit of the School Boards. Denied rate-aid on the ground that public opinion would not stand for the use of local taxation to support denominational instruction, the church schools were expected to rely on donations as a third source of income. This disadvantage was compensated to some small extent by raising the level of central grants and by permitting the voluntary schools to claim the fees of necessitous children from public funds.

The Religious Difficulty (para. 5): a long-lasting compromise over the question of religious worship and instruction was achieved by two critical clauses of the Act. Explain the conscience and Cowper-Temple clauses and resulting situation. The voluntary schools were permitted to continue giving denominational religious teaching but subject to the right of parental withdrawal. The Board Schools were limited to a choice between undenominational religious teaching (subject to the conscience clause) and the abandonment of religious teaching altogether. Thus the arrangements reflected an attempt to satisfy the denominationalists, the Nonconformists and the secularists. *Compulsory Attendance* (para. 6): for two reasons the 1870 Act was a compromise in this respect. It did not include a provision making attendance at elementary school compulsory on a national basis. But it did authorise the new School Boards to enforce attendance between five and thirteen years through the passage of local bye-laws. This system of local option provided an unsatisfactory half-way house between voluntary attendance and outright compulsion.

School Fees (para. 7): the 1870 Act even included a considerable element of compromise in relation to this thorny matter. On the one hand parents were generally expected to pay fees for their children's elementary education; this was justified in terms of cost and parental responsibility. On the other hand, the Act provided for the payment of poor children's fees out of public funds and set an upper limit on the fees to be charged by the School Boards.

(c) *Conclusion* (para. 8)

Clearly the 1870 Act was essentially a compromise measure even though, in relation to provision, finance, attendance and fees, it pointed in a direction calculated to erode the compromise nature of its own provisions. By the standards of the time the Act was a radical departure, but fell far short of the revolutionary programme advanced by the Birmingham Education League.

2nd Question Show how the Spens (1938) and Norwood (1943) Reports reinforced and refined the recommendations of the Hadow Report on *The Education of the Adolescent* (1926).

Interpretation of the Question

It may not be immediately obvious that any sound answer to this question must fall into three clear parts. One cannot relate Spens and Norwood to the Hadow recommendations without first stating the latter. Thus the Hadow Report should be given basic consideration first. Secondly, the Spens Report must be related to Hadow in terms of how it reinforced and refined the Hadow recommendations. Thirdly, the same exercise must be undertaken for the Norwood Report. An alternative and more sophisticated approach, based upon a linear analysis of each Hadow recommendation, is possible but lacks the simplicity of the course of action suggested.

Structuring the Answer

The following arrangement would prove satisfactory.

(*a*) *Introduction* (para. 1)

The nineteenth century saw the development of two separate and parallel systems of elementary and secondary education conceived on a class basis. Even the 1918 Education Act did not break down this traditional arrangement; the only inroad upon the two-track system was the narrow educational ladder which had developed slowly in the wake of the 1902 Act. The great majority of working class children still went through the elementary system only. However, the 1918 Act had at least required the local education authorities to provide advanced and practical instruction to meet the particular needs of senior elementary pupils aged eleven to fourteen years; this pointed the way towards future and more radical change.

(*b*) *Heart of the Answer*

This should deal with the Hadow Report (1926) and go on to relate the Spens and Norwood Reports to it.

Hadow Report (para. 2): the Consultative Committee under Sir W. H. Hadow was commissioned by the MacDonald Labour government to report on the education provided for senior elementary pupils who were not transferred to grammar schools (i.e. about 93% of the eleven to fourteen age group). It made a number of far-reaching recommendations:

   (i) the provision of secondary education for all. This would involve the abandonment of the separate systems of elementary and secondary grammar systems in favour of a continuous educational process divided into primary (5-11) and secondary (11+) stages through which all children would pass;

  (ii) the raising of the school leaving age to fifteen years as soon as possible to provide a viable minimum of four years for the secondary stage;

 (iii) the organisation of secondary education for all along selective lines so that eleven plus pupils of different abilities and aptitudes might receive an education appropriate to them. A basically bipartite framework, composed of secondary grammar and new secondary modern schools, was suggested. The grammar schools were to be academically oriented with a minimum leaving age of sixteen. The modern schools were to develop from existing central schools and senior elementary classes; they were to give a general education eleven to thirteen years, with a more practical orientation during the final two years. Beyond this the development of the junior technical schools was to be encouraged, but not as an integral part of the new secondary stage; they were to receive a small number of transfer entrants at thirteen to undertake three-year courses preparatory to an industrial apprenticeship (e.g. in engineering);

(iv) the mounting of selection examinations/procedures at eleven plus and thirteen plus by the local education authorities to channel pupils into and between the appropriate secondary schools. Written examinations and intelligence tests were recommended as the means of selection.

(v) the accordance of parity of esteem to all secondary schools. The modern schools were to be seen as different from, not inferior to, their grammar counterparts.

Spens Report (para. 3): the Spens Report on *Secondary Education* (1938) was especially concerned with the grammar and technical schools, but did consider the total context as it had developed since the Hadow Report (1926). The Hadow selective strategy for the development of secondary education for all was confirmed by Spens and the need for parity of esteem between the different types of school reiterated. As the 1936 Education Act had provided for the raising of the school leaving age there was no need to reinforce that particular recommendation. But the Spens recommendations also refined the Hadow Report in certain important ways:

(i) the abolition of fee-paying places in State grammar schools to throw them completely open to entry by merit. About half of the existing places were held by fee-payers;

(ii) the replacement of the basically bipartite strategy of Hadow by a clearly tripartite approach to secondary organisation. The Spens Report recommended that some of the junior technical schools (13-16) be translated into new technical high schools (11-16+) to form part of the main stream of secondary education. By providing a liberal education with the study of science and its applications as its core, the technical high school was seen as a real selective alternative to the academic grammar schools.

(iii) selection at eleven plus to be supplemented by an open-ended thirteen plus transfer system to serve as a safety-valve for late developers and initial misplacements. To make this a viable proposition all secondary schools should follow the same basic curricula for the eleven to thirteen age group.

The Spens Report also considered the claims of the multilateral school (the precursor of comprehensives) as an alternative to the emerging selective pattern, but the verdict was unfavourable and pro-Hadow.

Norwood Report (para. 4): the Norwood Report on *Secondary Schools Curricula and Examinations* (1943) ventured well beyond its terms of reference and also registered opinions upon the organisation of secondary education for all. The Norwood viewpoint was strongly selective and served to reinforce the Spens tripartite case and thus the broad Hadow strategy. Indeed, this Report argued that all potential secondary pupils fall into three psychological categories (the academically, technically and practically minded) and that selection procedures could reliably distinguish between them prior to channelling eleven plus children to grammar, technical and modern schools. Thus the authorities could rest happy that the Hadow reorganisation process begun in 1928 was the correct path to follow. To some small extent the Norwood Report recommendations also refined the Hadow strategy. The Spens concern for a fairly uniform curriculum during the initial two years of secondary education to support an effective system of thirteen plus transfers was reiterated and further elaborated. The case for teacher assessments as the prior instrument of 11+ selection was also made.

(c) Conclusion (para. 5)

The Spens and Norwood Reports greatly reinforced and to some extent refined the Hadow Report of 1926. The fact that eleven plus selection and the tripartite system of secondary education blossomed in the wake of the 1944 Act, even though it did not require the local education authorities to organise on selective lines, was largely the result of these three Reports conditioning so many people to think in such terms.

3rd Question What aspects of the education, training and employment of teachers in the nineteenth century combined to depress the occupational status of elementary school teaching?

Interpretation of the Question

Obviously the need is to identify and elaborate the shortcomings of the nineteenth century elementary teachers' education, training and conditions of employment which militated against the acceptance of elementary school teaching as a professional occupation. Only a consistently critical theme will make for a thoroughly relevant answer. The danger is to find oneself paying homage to various improvements in the education, training and employment of elementary teachers made during the nineteenth century. This of course would amount to irrelevance as no improvement as such could help to depress their status; thus the slant must be to stress the limitations and weaknesses of any improvements that took place. The approach to the question must also be analytical, involving the successive scrutiny of the three areas of concern provided by the question itself. A chronological approach (which is the line of least resistance for too many students) is not only inappropriate but dangerous, as it is much more likely to occasion thoughtless irrelevance than an analytical response.

Structuring the Answer

The following arrangement would prove satisfactory.

(a) *Introduction* (para. 1)

The concept of a properly educated and professionally trained corps of elementary schoolteachers enjoying reasonable conditions of employment made only limited progress during the nineteenth century. It is hard to appreciate how low were the levels of personal education and training and how onerous and degrading the working conditions of those who manned the elementary schools at that time. The result was low salaries and an occupational status which fell below that of skilled artisans; this legacy presented the teachers with a long and up-hill struggle for recognition as a genuine profession during this century.

(b) *Heart of the Answer*

This should be devoted to an analysis of shortcomings and depressive influences in relation to the three areas quoted.

Personal Education (para. 2): throughout the nineteenth century elementary teachers were drawn from the ranks of the working class. They were denied a secondary education and some received little elementary education either. Stress their low threshold of personal education by reference to the following matters:

  (i) the general lack of education of those employed in the dame, common-day, charity, industrial and Sunday schools of the early nineteenth century;

 (ii) the monitorial schools which used a mechanical system of rote-learning to offset the shortage of adequately educated schoolmasters;

(iii) the weaknesses of the pupil-teacher system and the associated voluntary training colleges during the latter half of the nineteenth century. Stress the craft apprenticeship character of the pupil-teacher system, with raising the level of personal education receiving low priority and being dependent on ability and interest of the headteacher. Show that pupil-teacher centres which developed in the later nineteenth century were available to only a limited proportion of pupil-teachers and worked on no more than a half-time basis. Emphasise the narrow and illiberal nature of training college courses, especially after the introduction of the Revised Code (1862), which did little to improve the personal education of the students involved.

Not until Morant scrapped the pupil-teacher system in the early twentieth century did prospective elementary teachers begin to enjoy a proper secondary schooling and an opportunity to realise a satisfactory level of personal education.

Professional Training (para. 3): this was inadequate in both its incidence and nature. The pre-monitorial schools were staffed by persons who received no training whatsoever. The monitorial schools, at best, were run by adults who had received several weeks of training in the application of the monitorial techniques; the senior monitors simply learned on the job. After 1846 the pupil-teacher system and associated training colleges effected an improvement, but serious weaknesses remained:

(i) the pupil-teacher's five-year craft apprenticeship (13-18) was dominated by on-the-job experience which lacked professional direction;

(ii) fewer than one third of the elementary teaching force won Queen's Scholarships and enjoyed a training college course. Three categories of teacher emerged with a diminishing measure of professional training; they were trained certificated (the elite), untrained certificated and untrained uncertificated ex-pupil-teachers. Under the pressure of expansion in the late nineteenth century the infamous and completely untrained Article 68-ers were introduced;

(iii) even those who attended a training college for two years underwent a very restricted form of professional training concerned with the mastery of rote-learning techniques and Herbartian object lessons. Residential domestic chores and denominational influence favoured the promotion of servility rather than professionality.

Such was the ill-repute of the training received by elementary teachers that it reinforced the prejudice of secondary schoolmasters against any form of professional as distinct from academic preparation.

Conditions of Employment (para. 4): in the early nineteenth century the assorted mass of unqualified elementary teachers suffered the conditions many thought they deserved—wretched accommodation, primitive facilities, inadequate materials, large classes and an insecure livelihood. The improvements wrought by Kay-Shuttleworth were later overshadowed by the ill-effects of the Revised Code (1862), which introduced the 'payment by results' system, and the 1870 Act, which initiated an immense expansion of the school population whilst ignoring the question of teacher supply. The worsening situation produced the National Union of Elementary Teachers (1870) which campaigned intensively for an improvement in the situation. It fought against dilution, capricious dismissal, compulsory ex-traneous duties, payment by results and large classes. It pressed for admission to the full Inspectorate, better salaries and the restitution of pension rights. The Union's efforts met with only very limited success and most of the symptoms remained to depress the morale and the status of the elementry teacher down to the end of the century.

(c) Conclusion (para. 5)

The major shortcomings and poor conditions just described ensured that Victorian society accorded a rather low status to elementary school-teachers. This situation was then reinforced by the refusal of middle class families to countenance the possibility of their sons or daughters entering the occupation: thus even at the close of the nineteenth century elementary schoolteachers were being recruited almost exclusively from the respect-able working class.

4th Question Examine the significance of the Robbins Committee Report (1963) to the development of higher education in Britain.

Interpretation of the Question

To examine the significance of any major educational report one must possess a working knowledge of the relationship between its recommen-dations and results. In the last analysis an educational report derives its significance, not so much from its detailed findings or underlying principles, but from the nature of its concrete recommendations and their subsequent influence upon development. Thus the question demands an analysis of the main recommendations of the Robbins Report and the actual results which flowed from them; by this means one may gauge the significance of the report up to the present time. As some of the recom-mendations were related to higher education as a whole whilst others were directed towards particular sectors of it, it would seem sensible to incorporate this consideration into the structure of the answer.

Structuring the Answer

The following arrangement would prove satisfactory.

(a) *Introduction* (para. 1)

Brief description of higher educational scene at outset of 1960s. Mention the post-war growth of Sixth Forms and the developing bottle-neck in spite of university places having doubled in number; the restricted nature of higher educational opportunity in the United Kingdom compared with other advanced industrial countries; the continuing shortage of teachers; the development of the Colleges of Advanced Technology and the introduction of three-year teacher training courses to provide genuine higher education outside the universities and the consequent need for a co-ordinated policy and structure. It was against this backcloth that the prime minister appointed the Robbins Committee (1961-3) to consider the situation and, in the light of national needs and resources, to make recommendations for future long-term development.

(b) *Heart of the Answer*

This should be devoted to identifying the main recommendations of the Report, both general and particular, and assessing their significance in terms of subsequent results.

Expansion of Higher Education (para. 2): spotlight the significance of Robbins' recommendations and results in terms of three matters:

(i) enunciation and acceptance of the Robbins principle that every qualified person should be able to obtain a place in higher education. Thus the Report shattered the traditional concept of a fixed pool of higher educational ability in favour of a much more expansive and populist approach to higher education.

(ii) the idea of planned and co-ordinated development based on a progressively revised ten-year programme for the provision of higher education so as to equate supply with demand. Subsequent events, culminating in the 1972 White Paper, have reflected the growing support for such a strategy.

(iii) recommendation and acceptance of a specific programme of expansion for the succeeding decade. The total number of places in higher education was to be raised from 216,000 to 390,000 in the period 1963-74. In fact, the subsequent expansion exceeded this commitment. Within eight years the pre-Robbins figure had more than doubled and in 1972 the government set a new target figure of 750,000 to be reached by 1981. Thus the Robbins Report, whilst underestimating the rate of increase in qualified candidates, initiated a remarkable expansion of higher education.

Structure of Higher Education (para. 3): show strictly limited significance of Robbins in this context by contrasting the Report's recommendations with subsequent developments.

(i) Robbins recommended a unitary system of higher education made up of the universities and other increasingly autonomous institutions aspiring to the university model and status. A closer relationship with the central government was to be developed by means of a new and distinct Ministry of Arts and Science.

(ii) the emergence of the binary policy and the establishment of the Department of Education and Science were *not* compatible with Robbins. The first divided higher education into distinct 'autonomous' and 'public' sectors and rejected the notion of the university as necessarily the model. The second brought higher education within the ambit of the same government department responsible for primary, secondary and further education. The Robbins concern for the autonomy of higher educational institutions was subordinated to the need for greater public influence and control.

But the Robbins' insistence on the need for an integrated (if not unitary) higher educational structure and for parity of status in terms of equal awards for equal performance (through C.N.A.A. degrees especially) was fully met.

Technological Education (para. 4): underline the significance of Robbins' contribution to the expansion and elevation (economic argument) of advanced technical and technological studies. Illustrate this by reference to the translation of the Colleges of Advanced Technology into full-scale technological universities and the establishment of the Council for National Academic Awards to stimulate degree level work in the major Colleges of Further Education. Also mention further subsequent growth of Imperial, Manchester and Glasgow Colleges of Science and Technology within the university sector.

Teacher Training (para. 5): here the significance of the Robbins Report was very considerable. It was recommended that the number of teacher training places should be more than doubled within a decade and this was achieved with time to spare; the post-war shortage of teachers was largely overcome by 1972, necessitating a switch to a policy of contraction. The expansion after 1963 facilitated a general improvement in staffing ratios and the raising of the school-leaving age. The status of the teacher training institutions was raised by renaming them Colleges of Education (emphasising the broader nature of the minimum three-year course introduced in 1960) and by launching B.Ed. degree courses for the ablest students. However, the Robbins recommendation designed to draw the training colleges more closely to the universities and to make them autonomous of the local education authorities was rejected.

The Universities (para. 6): here Robbins recommended major and dominant expansion within a framework calculated to safeguard the universities traditional independence as well as recognise the claims of the State. A massive expansion did follow and within eight years provision was doubled; Robbins support for six new universities was, however, ignored in favour of growth based on existing institutions. But the dominant place and secure independence of the universities envisaged by the Robbins Report fell foul of the government's binary policy and interest in greater State control.

(c) Conclusion (para. 7)

The Robbins Report was clearly a watershed in the development of higher education in Great Britain, even though some of its recommendations were ignored and an anti-Robbins structure has emerged. It marked the major divide between the old elitist and the new populist patterns of higher educational opportunity. It initiated a co-ordinated and programmed approach to higher education based on the principle of providing places for all qualified and interested candidates. The immense and continuing expansion of higher education since 1963 will ensure the Robbins Report a place of critical significance in the development of education in Britain.

Circular 10/65 on *The Organisation of Secondary Education*

Circular 10/65, issued by the Department of Education and Science on 12 July 1965, requested all local education authorities to prepare and submit plans for reorganising their secondary education along comprehensive lines. Six alternative forms of comprehensive secondary organisation were reviewed but only the *four* presented below were declared acceptable for long-term development.

1 The Orthodox 'All-through' Comprehensive School

This solution, involving the retention of pupils in one eleven to eighteen school throughout their secondary education, was officially considered the best wherever circumstances permitted its adoption.

Advantages = the continuity, familiarity and identification associated with a single 'all-through' school; the greater cost effectiveness, more varied facilities and wider curricula range afforded by the large average size of eleven to eighteen school rolls.

Disadvantages = the unsuitability of most existing secondary schools for conversion into 'all-through' comprehensives requiring a minimum six form entry to support a viable Sixth Form; the resultant choice between highly expensive purpose-built schools and much less satisfactory 'linked' comprehensives using the premises of formerly separate secondary schools; the problems of management, corporate ethos and pastoral care associated with schools housing over a thousand pupils; the danger of uneconomic Sixth Forms arising in 'all-through' comprehensives with less than a six form entry.

2 The Two-Tier Comprehensive System

This pattern, developed from the original Leicestershire plan (1957), involved the transfer of all pupils at eleven plus to a junior comprehensive school and at thirteen or fourteen to a senior comprehensive school.

Advantages = immediate economy and practicality, with most existing secondary schools being suitable for translation into medium sized junior and senior comprehensives; lower average size eases the problems of management, corporate ethos and pastoral care; gives more scope for younger secondary pupils assuming responsibility in their own milieu.

Disadvantages = the potentially disturbing influence of an additional move between schools; transfer at thirteen makes the junior comprehensive into a transit camp whilst transfer at fourteen poses problems for the senior comprehensive in relation to external examinations; the danger of inadequate co-operation between junior comprehensives and recipient senior schools in relation to curricula, syllabuses and teaching methods; the junior comprehensives lack the benefits of Sixth Form stimulus and influence; staff are forcibly restricted to the teaching of younger or older secondary pupils.

3 The Sixth Form College Pattern

This arrangement involves the provision of basic comprehensive schools for the eleven to sixteen group supported by 'tertiary' or Sixth Form colleges; whilst the 'tertiary' college provides for the educational needs of all young people staying on, the Sixth Form college caters primarily for those undertaking A-level studies. A further variation is to combine the basic eleven to sixteen comprehensives with an odd one or two 'all-through' eleven to eighteen comprehensives which monopolise the Sixth Form work.

Advantages = allows utilisation of many existing school buildings without major expense; absence of Sixth Form viability problem permits reasonably sized eleven to sixteen comprehensives in which management and pastoral care problems will not loom large: the more economic use of specialist Sixth Form staff; a more adult and academic context for Sixth Form work; the greater opportunities for leadership and responsibility by younger pupils in eleven to sixteen comprehensives.

Disadvantages = the short duration of attendance at Sixth Form colleges; the creation of a teaching elite, leaving discontented staff in the eleven to sixteen comprehensives; the latter are denied the stimulus and influence of the Sixth Form; the danger of Sixth Form colleges becoming instruments of sixteen plus selection; the problem of co-ordinating this pattern with the wider field of further education.

4 The Middle School Arrangement

This involves the transfer of all pupils from primary school to a comprehensive middle school at eight or nine and later to a senior comprehensive at twelve or thirteen where they would complete their schooling. The two main three-tier patterns would accordingly be 5-8, 8-12, 12-18 *or* 5-9, 9-13, 13-18.

>   *Advantages* = immediate economy and practicality in terms of utilising existing school premises; the problems associated with large size are avoided; all three stages are of satisfactory duration, especially in the case of the nine to thirteen pattern; transfer at thirteen plus occasions no immense difficulties for the senior comprehensives; avoids sudden switch at eleven plus from child-centred to subject-centred approach to learning; provides a change of scene and a new stimulus at thirteen plus when many pupils are normally losing interest.
>
>   *Disadvantages* = the danger of inadequate contact and co-operation between the first, middle and senior schools, with thirteen plus transfer arrangements especially vulnerable; the problem of synthesis and of developing a clear sense of purpose in the new middle school, initially drawing staff from the orthodox primary and secondary sectors; the initial shortage of staff qualified to teach a group of subjects in fair depth and/or on an inter-disciplinary basis.

The Secretary of State made it clear that he favoured only a limited number of experiments incorporating the Sixth Form college idea and that he would approve only a small number of middle school arrangements; however, the official attitude soon became less restrictive and these two alternatives made significant headway later on. The Circular also exhorted the local education authorities to consult with the diocesan authorities and relevant governing bodies to facilitate the inclusion of the voluntary aided, special agreement and direct grant grammar schools in their re-organisation plans. Finally, the plans were to be submitted to the Department within one year.

Arguments For and Against the Comprehensive Organisation of Secondary Education

The arguments advanced in favour of and against the reorganisation of secondary education along comprehensive lines may be summarised under three headings.

1 Economic

(*a*) *For:* the *per capita* cost of providing and maintaining comprehensive schools is lower than that of the tripartite pattern. Thus a comprehensive system provides the same quality of material facilities and staffing at less cost or conversely facilitates a higher quality of provision at the same cost. In the long-term comprehensives are more cost effective in relation to staffing and overheads and allow special facilities housed in a single large school (e.g. elaborate hall, spacious library, modern gymnasium, swimming bath or even a cafeteria) to become economically viable. Of course it is the very large 'all-through' 11–18 comprehensives which can capitalise most fully upon the economies of large-scale educational enterprise. But even in sparsely populated areas the smaller comprehensive school makes much more economic sense than separate selective and non-selective schools with a one or two form entry; indeed the early comprehensives developed in the Isles of Man and Anglesey and in the county areas of rural Wales were economically inspired.

(*b*) *Against:* to be educationally satisfactory comprehensive schools need to be purpose-built. To combine formerly separate schools, often a considerable distance apart, for comprehensive purposes results in a divided and unmanageable institution which does not deserve or receive the corporate loyalty and support of pupils or staff. Two-tier comprehensive arrangements are equally an expedient unless expensive modifications are made to the converted schools. Thus comprehensive reorganisation, if properly undertaken, is a very costly proposition and the limited funds available for educational development could be much better spent in other directions (e.g. on the radical improvement of existing primary and secondary modern schools). To sweep away or absorb the independent and direct grant grammar schools in the cause of a monolithic system of State comprehensive schools would raise the cost of providing secondary education for all by many millions of pounds (i.e.

the sum paid by parents for fee-paying places). Thus the question is whether the country can afford the expense of purpose-built comprehensives or the untoward consequences of cheaper comprehensive expedients.

2 Social

(*a*) *For:* although the 1944 Act introduced formal equality of educational opportunity by the abolition of fee-paying places in State secondary grammar schools, the eleven plus examination and the selective system have proved socially divisive to a degree never anticipated. Because of the social distribution of intelligence and attainment, the eleven plus examination has ensured that the middle class has dominated entry to the grammar schools whilst the secondary modern school has become a second-rate alternative for the great bulk of working class children. This divisive pattern has been reinforced by the practice of local education authorities accepting places in the direct grant grammar schools for the most able children and the continued availability of fee-paying places in independent and direct grant schools for those middle class parents who can afford to pay. Although many working class children obtain selective school places and go on to do very well academically, the usual price is the alienation of these children from their working class families and background. The over-all result of selection at eleven plus is second class educational and occupational opportunities for secondary modern pupils and the perpetuation of outmoded social differences and divisions. The selective system has a strong tendency to encourage a sense of superiority (through the grammar school tradition) in relation to a particular type of education or occupation. Such a situation is inimical to the well-being of a modern democratic society. The solution is the abolition of selection and the education of all children, irrespective of ability or background, in common secondary schools.

(*b*) *Against:* the wide social mix of secondary pupils sought in the comprehensive school is not guaranteed to emerge as a result of such reorganisation. Indeed, the neighbourhood comprehensive school (drawing in all the children from the surrounding primary schools) threatens to be more socially divisive than the tripartite arrangements, for many neighbourhoods in our great cities and towns tend to be dominated by a single socio-economic group. Though banding, zoning and busing may be resorted to as means of providing each comprehensive school with a satisfactory range of ability and family background, parents expect and will even insist upon their children attending the nearest comprehensive school to home. The best hope of blurring social divisions is that afforded by the direct grant and State grammar schools, whose intake of able working class children has been considerable and continuous since 1944. These schools, often drawing on a very large geographical catchment area, have been better social mixers than neighbourhood comprehensives can ever hope to be. And even where the comprehensive school has an intake which encompasses the whole occupational spectrum, there are indications that social mixing takes place to a lesser degree than in the traditional grammar school (see J. Floud, 'Comprehensives as Social Dividers', *New Society*, October 1968). The house or tutor group system employed in many comprehensive schools is rarely an effective means of promoting social integration across the whole ability range. Thus the potentiality of the comprehensive school as a major instrument of progressive social engineering is strongly suspect.

3 Educational

(*a*) *For:* only comprehensive schools can provide real equality of educational opportunity for the younger generation. The eleven plus examination and the selective system stand condemned because of the unacceptable margin of predictive error (as revealed by the N.F.E.R. and other authoritative investigations), the wide variations in the proportion of selective school places offered by the different local education authorities and the psychological damage (adversely affecting future motivation) of eleven plus failure on the majority of modern school pupils. The transfer of less than 2% of modern pupils into selective schools as late developers makes negligible inroads upon the injustices of the eleven plus examination. The result has been the great wastage of potential talent (especially working class) spotlighted by various official reports; this cannot be tolerated in terms of either social justice or national economic needs. The comprehensive school provides a continuing opportunity for the average and less able child to develop, whilst it does not hinder the educational progress of the high-fliers. Because of its considerably larger average size the comprehensive school can provide a wider range of teaching and other resources: it is able to cater for minority interests by mounting viable courses which are tailor-made to suit individual needs and can be supported by specialist teachers (e.g. crafts and remedial work). The range of general facilities and extra-mural activities may similarly benefit from larger size. Finally, the comprehensive system helps to break down the restrictive tradition of early leaving associated with the secondary moderns, encouraging more pupils to prolong their education because they see others staying on in *their* own school.

(b) *Against:* only the selective system with its smaller, differentiated secondary schools can provide a sound basis for educational efficiency. The sheer size and impersonality of large 'all-through' comprehensives render them second-rate educational institutions for young adolescents. The head and other senior members of staff are too remote and in real danger of becoming mere administrators; the opportunity for the development of charismatic influence and a strong corporate spirit with its attendant benefits is lost and the unhappy results of this often include low staff morale and serious disciplinary problems. Whilst a two-tier comprehensive arrangement may avoid the worst of these disadvantages, it suffers from a lack of continuity; pupils are transferred at critical times when they should be continuing to develop working relationships with a familiar staff. On educational grounds the emphasis should be placed on the improvement of selection procedures, the retention of selective schools and the transformation of the secondary moderns. Ability differences cannot be ignored and can be measured with a sufficient degree of accuracy. Educational efficiency depends upon placing secondary pupils in the particular school context which is suited to their abilities and aptitudes. The grammar schools offer the most favourable context for the full development of the really able pupil; the comprehensive can never stretch such pupils to the same extent and in the national interest such talent must be fully capitalised upon. To destroy the grammar schools is to risk losing the services of those specialist graduates who render a considerable service to education but baulk at the prospect of non-academic teaching in a comprehensive school. During the 1950s a minority of secondary modern schools showed their capacity to meet fully the needs of the Newsom pupil; they should become a model, with *all* secondary moderns receiving parity of support and staffing to enable them to do a sound educational job in their own sector.

The foregoing is simply a review of some of the arguments put forward in the controversy surrounding comprehensive secondary organisation. Obviously the immense task of sifting the evidence and weighing the arguments and counter-arguments is not one which can be attempted here. It may be helpful however to refer to the Penguin editions of R. Pedley's *The Comprehensive School* and R. Davis' *The Grammar School* which present the two sides of the issue in considerable depth.

Bibliography

General Texts

BAGLEY, J. J. and A. J. (1969). *The State and Education in England and Wales 1833-1968.* London: Macmillan.

BARNARD, H. C. (1971). *A History of English Education from 1760* (3rd edition). London: University of London Press Ltd.

BERNBAUM, G. (1967). *Social Change and the Schools 1918-1944.* London: Routledge & Kegan Paul.

BOURNE, R. and MACARTHUR, B. (1970). *The Struggle for Education 1870-1970.* London: Schoolmaster Publishing Co.

CURTIS, S. J. (1967). *History of Education in Great Britain* (7th edition). Cambridge: University Tutorial Press.

CURTIS, S. J. and BOULTWOOD, M. E. (1966). *An Introductory History of English Education since 1800* (4th edition). Cambridge: University Tutorial Press.

DENT, H. C. (1970). *1870-1970 Century of Growth in English Education.* Harlow: Longman Group.

EAGLESHAM, E. J. R. (1967). *The Foundations of 20th Century Education in England.* London: Routledge & Kegan Paul.

LOWNDES, G. A. N. (1969). *The Silent Social Revolution* (2nd edition). London: Oxford University Press.

MORRISH, I. (1970). *Education since 1800.* London: Allen & Unwin.

MUSGRAVE, P. W. (1968). *Society and Education in England since 1800.* London: Methuen.

SIMON, B. (1960). *History of Education 1780-1870.* London: Lawrence and Wishart.

SIMON, B. (1965). *Education and the Labour Movement 1870-1920.* London: Lawrence and Wishart.

WARDLE, D. (1970). *English Popular Education 1780-1970.* London: Cambridge University Press.

DEPARTMENT OF EDUCATION AND SCIENCE (1970). *Trends in Education* (1870 Centenary Issue, February). London: H.M.S.O.

Elementary Education

BIRCHENOUGH, C. (1938). *History of Elementary Education in England and Wales from 1800 to the Present Day* (3rd edition). Cambridge: University Tutorial Press.

STURT, M. (1967). *The Education of the People*. London: Routledge & Kegan Paul.

WHITBREAD, M. (1972). *The Evolution of the Nursery-Infant School*. London: Routledge & Kegan Paul.

Secondary Education

ARCHER, R. L. (1966). *Secondary Education in the 19th Century* (2nd edition). London: Frank Cass.

BANKS, O. (1955). *Parity and Prestige in English Secondary Education*. London: Routledge & Kegan Paul.

DAVIS, R. (1967). *The Grammar School*. Harmondsworth: Penguin Books.

GRAVES, J. (1943). *Policy and Progress in Secondary Education 1902-1942*. London: Nelson.

OGILVIE, V. (1957). *The English Public School*. London: Batsford.

PEDLEY, R. (1972). *The Comprehensive School* (revised edition). Harmondsworth: Penguin Books.

RUBINSTEIN, D. and SIMON, B. (1969). *The Evolution of the Comprehensive School 1926-66*. London: Routledge & Kegan Paul.

TAWNEY, R. H. (1922). *Secondary Education for All*. London: Allen & Unwin.

(1972). 'Digest on Comprehensive Schools'. *Education*. Vol. 139, no. 24.

Teacher Training and Employment

TROPP, A. (1957). *The School Teachers*. London: Heinemann.

RICH, R. W. (1933). *The Training of Teachers in England and Wales during the 19th Century*. London: Cambridge University Press.

Technical and Further Education

ARGYLES, M. (1964). *South Kensington to Robbins*. London: Longman Group.

COTGROVE, S. F. (1958). *Technical Education and Social Change*. London: Allen & Unwin.

HARRISON, J. F. C. (1961). *Learning and Living 1790-1900; a study in the history of the English adult education movement*. London: Routledge & Kegan Paul.

VENABLES, Sir P. F. R. (1955). *Technical Education*. London: Bell.

University Education

BERDAHL, R. O. (1959). *British Universities and the State*. London: Cambridge University Press.

CAINE, Sir S. (1969). *British Universities: Purpose and Prospects*. London: The Bodley Head.

GREEN, V. H. H. (1969). *The Universities*. Harmondsworth: Penguin Books.

ROBERTSON, Sir C. G. (1944). *The British Universities* (2nd edition). London: Methuen.

Educational System, Government and Administration

ALEXANDER, Sir W. P. (1964). *Education in England; the National System—How it Works* (2nd edition). London: Ginn.

ARMFELT, R. (1955). *The Structure of English Education*. London: Cohen & West.

BLACKIE, J. (1970). *Inspecting and the Inspectorate*. London: Routledge & Kegan Paul.

BURGESS, T. (1969). *A Guide to English Schools* (2nd edition). Harmondsworth: Penguin Books.

DENT, H. C. (1968). *The Education Act 1944* (12th edition). London: University of London Press Ltd.

DENT, H. C. (1971). *The Educational System of England and Wales* (5th edition). London: University of London Press Ltd.

GOSDEN, P. H. J. H. (1966). *The Development of Educational Administration in England and Wales*. Oxford: Blackwell.

PARRY, J. P. (1971). *The Provision of Education in England and Wales*. London: Allen & Unwin.

DEPARTMENT OF EDUCATION AND SCIENCE (1971). *The Educational System of England and Wales*. London: H.M.S.O.

DEPARTMENT OF EDUCATION AND SCIENCE (1971). *Her Majesty's Inspectorate Today and Tomorrow*. London: H.M.S.O.

Religious Aspects

CRUICKSHANK, M. (1964). *Church and State in English Education*. London: Macmillan.

MURPHY, J. (1971). *Church, State and Schools in Britain, 1800–1970*. London: Routledge & Kegan Paul.

Biographical

ALLEN, B. M. (1934). *Sir Robert Morant*. London: Macmillan.

JUDGES, A. V. (1952). *Pioneers of English Education*. London: Faber & Faber.

LEESE, J. (1950). *Personalities and Power in English Education*. London: Arnold.

SMITH, F. (1923). *The Life and Work of Sir James Kay-Shuttleworth*. London: Murray.

Others

ANDERSON, H. and others (1970). *Education for the Seventies*. London: Heinemann Educational

BANDER, P. (1968). *Looking Forward to the Seventies*. Gerrards Cross: Colin Smythe.

CORBETT, A. (1969). *Much to do about Education* (2nd edition). London: Council for Educational Advance.

LELLO, J. (1964). *The Official View on Education: a summary of the Major Educational Reports since 1944*. Oxford: Pergamon Press.

MONTGOMERY, R. J. (1965). *Examinations: an account of their evolution as administrative devices in England*. London: Longman Group.

NATIONAL ASSOCIATION OF SCHOOLMASTERS (1969). *Thoughts on a New Education Act*. Hemel Hempstead: N.A.S.

NATIONAL UNION OF TEACHERS (1970). *Into the Seventies*. London: N.U.T.

Texts Supplying Documentary and Contemporary Sources

DAWSON, K. and WALL, P. (1969). *Society and Industry in the 19th Century: Education*. London: Oxford University Press.

GOSDEN, P. H. J. H. (1969). *How they were Taught*. Oxford: Blackwell.

MACLURE, J. S. (1968). *Educational Documents: England and Wales 1816-1968* (2nd edition) London: Methuen Educational.

Official Publications

BOARD OF EDUCATION (1926). Report of the Consultative Committee on *The Education of the Adolescent*. London: H.M.S.O.

BOARD OF EDUCATION (1928). Pamphlet on *The New Prospect in Education*. London: H.M.S.O.

BOARD OF EDUCATION (1931). Report of the Consultative Committee on *The Primary School*. London: H.M.S.O.

BOARD OF EDUCATION (1933). Report of the Consultative Committee on *Infant and Nursery Schools*. London: H.M.S.O.

BOARD OF EDUCATION (1938). Report of the Consultative Committee on *Secondary Education with special reference to Grammar Schools and Technical High Schools*. London: H.M.S.O.

BOARD OF EDUCATION (1943). Report of the Committee of the Secondary School Examinations Council on *Curricula and Examinations in Secondary Schools*. London: H.M.S.O.

BOARD OF EDUCATION (1944). Report of the Committee on *Teachers and Youth Leaders*. London: H.M.S.O.

BOARD OF EDUCATION (1944). Report of the Committee on *The Public Schools and the General Educational System*. London: H.M.S.O.

BOARD OF EDUCATION (1943). Government White Paper on *Educational Reconstruction*. London: H.M.S.O.

MINISTRY OF EDUCATION (1945). Report of the Committee on *Higher Technological Education*. London: H.M.S.O.

MINISTRY OF EDUCATION (1959). Report of the Central Advisory Council for Education (England) on *15 to 18*. London: H.M.S.O.

MINISTRY OF EDUCATION (1963). Report of the Central Advisory Council for Education (England) on *Half our Future*. London: H.M.S.O.

DEPARTMENT OF EDUCATION AND SCIENCE (1967). Report of the Central Advisory Council for Education (England) on *Children and their Primary Schools*. London: H.M.S.O.

DEPARTMENT OF EDUCATION AND SCIENCE (1968 & 1970). Reports of the Public Schools Commission on *Independent and Direct-grant Grammar Schools*. London: H.M.S.O.

DEPARTMENT OF EDUCATION AND SCIENCE (1972). Report of the Committee on *Teacher Education and Training*. London: H.M.S.O.

DEPARTMENT OF EDUCATION AND SCIENCE (1972). Government White Paper on *Education: A Framework for Expansion*. London: H.M.S.O.

DEPARTMENT OF EDUCATION AND SCIENCE (1965). Circular 10/65 on *The Organisation of Secondary Education*. London: H.M.S.O.

DEPARTMENT OF EDUCATION AND SCIENCE (1973). Circular 7/73 on the *Development of Higher Education in the Non-University Sector*. London: H.M.S.O.

DEPARTMENT OF EDUCATION AND SCIENCE Reports on Education (1963 +) especially

29 *The Schools Council* (February 1966)
30 *The Council for National Academic Awards* (June 1966)
31 *The Local Education Authorities* (October 1966)
35 *Industrial Training and Education* (April 1967)
37 *H.M. Inspectorate* (June 1967)
47 *The Certificate of Secondary Education* (June 1968)
56 *The Open University* (June 1969)
65 *The Polytechnics* (September 1970)
72 *Raising the School Leaving Age* (September 1971)
74 *The Use of Broadcasts in Schools* (June 1972)

These reports are very short indeed but highly instructive nevertheless.

(1963) Report of the Robbins Committee on *Higher Education*. London: H.M.S.O.

Index